W9-BPT-108

American Bee

 **RODALE**
LIVE YOUR WHOLE LIFE™

Every day our brands connect with and inspire millions of
people to live a life of the mind, body, spirit — a whole life.

American Bee

THE NATIONAL SPELLING BEE

AND THE CULTURE OF WORD NERDS

The lives of five

top spellers as they compete

for glory and fame

James Maguire

RODALE

© 2006 by James Maguire

All rights reserved. No part of this publication may be reproduced or transmitted in any form or by any means, electronic or mechanical, including photocopying, recording, or any other information storage and retrieval system, without the written permission of the publisher.

Printed in the United States of America

Rodale Inc. makes every effort to use acid-free ♾, recycled paper ♺.

Book design by Tara Long

Library of Congress Cataloging-in-Publication Data

Maguire, James.
    American bee : the National Spelling Bee and the culture of word nerds / James Maguire.
        p.   cm.
    Includes bibliographical references.
    ISBN-13 978–1–59486–214–4   hardcover
    ISBN-10 1–59486–214–1   hardcover
    1. Spelling ability—Testing.   2. Spelling bees—United States.   3. National Spelling Bee
(2004)   I. Title.
  LB1574.M27   2006
  372.63'2—dc22
                                                                2005037443

Distributed to the trade by Holtzbrinck Publishers

2   4   6   8   10   9   7   5   3   1   hardcover

We inspire and enable people to improve their lives and the world around them

For more of our products visit **rodalestore.com** or call 800-848-4735

For anyone who grapples with the spelling of the English language—but who loves the language nonetheless

"*In a perfect language, every simple sound would be expressed by a distinct character; and no character would have more than one sound. But languages are not thus perfect; and the English Language, in particular, is, in these respects, extremely irregular.*"

—Noah Webster

Contents

Prologue

As I traveled around the country, talking with the many people I spoke with to report the story of the National Bee, I was often asked: "What made you want to write a book about the spelling bee?" The question was usually asked with great politeness, but with no small wonder, as if to inquire: *That's an odd topic you have there, fellow. What gives?*

It's a reasonable question, and it certainly deserves an answer. I have to confess, though, that I usually gave an abbreviated version of what drew me to the story. To give a full account would have required me to hold forth for several minutes. And at the end of such a lengthy monologue, I feared, some of the questioners might have suggested I sit quietly while they fetch a cool drink of water.

Still, the query calls for a full response, and now is the time. So if you'll grant me just a few minutes—and yes, I have a glass of cool water at hand—I'll tell you why I feel it's important that there be a book about the Bee.

The story of the National Spelling Bee is many stories in one.

It's a sports story of sorts, with all the drama of a high-stakes athletic contest. (In fact, the cable TV channel ESPN broadcasts the Bee alongside sporting events like boxing and basketball.) The contestants win or lose—no second chance—in real time, onstage in front of a live audience. Each year, from a starting pool of ten million kids, spellers compete their way upward in city and regional bees, hoping to become one of the 275 or so who makes it to Washington. The story of how these 275 finalists find one champion has as much narrative drive, as much sweat and tears and joy, as any football or baseball game. (More so, actually—but that's just my personal opinion.)

It's a story of pure Americana, part Norman Rockwell, part Horatio Alger. The Bee is an egalitarian gathering in which kids from every social class compete in a true meritocracy. A window washer's daughter competes with a banker's son; a first-generation Korean goes toe-to-toe with a Mayflower descendant. Give me your tired, your poor, your huddled masses yearning to breathe free: Every year, the audience is sprinkled with immigrant parents, mothers and fathers who speak in a thick accent, watching their children compete in a second language—the event, like the arms of Lady Liberty, is open to all. In the most idealistic American tradition, the Bee offers a level playing field, in which color of skin and your last name mean nothing, but hard work and belief in self mean everything.

It's a language story, in which that cultural sponge known as the English language plays a starring role. The top spellers are obsessive etymologists. They are language detectives, exploring lingual patterns, digging into Latin and Greek and French, looking for clues to help them decipher obscure polysyllabics. Spelling, at this level, is about far more than recitation. It's about understanding how the language is built, and how the history of English created this eccentric patchwork called modern spelling. It's about all the skills that further literacy: voracious reading, a sprawling vocabulary, even knowledge of grammar. The Bee is like a yearly Woodstock for the language arts crowd.

First and foremost—and here we get to the heart of the Bee—it's a story about kids, about how the Bee's challenges transform them. Or, more accurately, how the kids transform themselves. For these top spellers, the Bee is an odyssey that includes the smaller bees they must win, countless hours of study and drill, and a semi-Olympian process of psych-up. The nerves can be fearsome. Finally, they step to the microphone in front of a mass audience (including parents and television cameras) to face an unknown challenge. They're out there all alone, forced to rely upon only their own resources. These moments are like a little pressure cooker. This is necessarily a growth experience, whether or not they spell correctly. And that, really, is what the Bee is all about: young people growing, within the context of a high-profile educational environment. That's a beautiful thing.

As icing on the cake, it's the story of a big party, a yearly gathering of like-minded souls—young souls—who, in between competing with each other, share a subculture with its own idiosyncrasies and status symbols. They are word nerds. They study Latin and play video games. They have fantasies of spelling the perfect eight-syllable word. Many of them stop reading only long enough to drill lunarlike morphemes, carrying their laptops outside to play, lugging their dictionaries on family vacations. They are a strange bunch, which makes them an interesting bunch.

In short, the Bee is an invaluable nugget of American life. Despite the odd niche it occupies, it says a lot about who we are, our oddness, our strengths. And, after enduring for hundreds of years, it's a folk tradition that can safely claim to be a permanent part of the American scene. The Bee is a story that deserves to be told.

One more thing, on a personal note. As I got to know the spellers and their families I profiled in this book, I had a wonderful time. Having dinner with the families, talking with the spellers, learning about their hopes and their worries, being at the Bee in Washington—it was a rich experience. I consider myself lucky for having been able to report this story.

If you enjoy reading this book even a fraction as much as I enjoyed writing it, I'll feel as if I've just spelled *rijsttafel* in the final rounds of the National Bee. In other words, pretty darn good.

And now, let the spelling begin . . .

James Maguire

Part[1]

Life at the Bee: The 2004 National Spelling Bee, Washington, DC

"There are killer words flying around you all the time, the person on your left or your right takes a bullet, and you get an easy one . . ."

—Henry Feldman, 1960 Bee champion

¹ The Pressure

David Tidmarsh is breathing like a runaway pony. And no wonder: The slender fourteen-year-old stands onstage facing six judges and a crowded ballroom, with all eyes on him. In the front row sits an Associated Press reporter, dispatching updates to newspapers across the country. Near the stage huddles an ESPN television crew, beaming David's visage to thousands of viewers. The roving cameraman moves to catch his every grimace; another camera, a crane-operated affair swooping toward the stage, resembles a high-tech dinosaur that might devour David's 110-pound frame as an afternoon snack. A few feet away, also on the red-carpeted stage, sits his mother; the tape later reveals she has a tear suspended at the edge of her right eye, waiting for her son's next word.

David faces *gaminerie*, a French word meaning an impudent or roguish spirit. His face, as wide open as the farmland around his hometown of South Bend, Indiana, jogs quickly through a crowd of emotions: fear, hope, pure anxiety, even a short smile. He's a self-effacing kid, the kind of boy who, when you express amazement at how hard he's studied, replies, "Yeah, I guess so." He steps closer to the microphone and we hear his hyperventilating breath. A few audience members even chuckle lightly—his deep breathing right into the microphone sounds something like Darth Vader's demonic respiration—but the mood in the room is far too close for real laughter.

He asks the official pronouncer, Jacques Bailly, the questions allowed each speller—definition, sample sentence, language of origin—and as he does, his already rapid respiration starts to sprint away from him. By the time he asks about the language of origin, his voice is reduced to a whisper. He's out of breath. He struggles to recover, and uses his knowledge of etymology to dig for clues. "Is it related to the, um, English word *gamin* meaning an impudent child?" Bailly demurs at the query, noting the rule against answering questions about relations between English words. "Okay, that's fine," David says pleasantly, and then the hyperventilating starts galloping again. He bites his lip and pauses. Finally, with effort, he gathers his breath. He's ready to spell.

☉☉☉

So here it is, in the cavernous ballroom of the Grand Hyatt in downtown Washington, DC: the homestretch of the 2004 Scripps National Spelling Bee. Soon, one of the few remaining spellers will be dubbed the champion, the photographers will move in for the glory shot, and a new name will be entered in the record books.

Just offstage gleams the trophy, a florid gold loving cup about two feet high. Along with the cup comes a bounty of spoils: some $20,000 in cash prizes, encyclopedias, and assorted gewgaws. The winner typically meets the president, is interviewed by Diane Sawyer (and myriad others), appears on *David Letterman*, and is lauded by *The New York Times* as one of the nation's bright young minds. Wendy Guey, the 1996 champion and now a Harvard undergrad, will direct a special round of applause to the winner when she speaks at this year's Bee awards banquet.

Now, in the third day of competition, the original 265 spellers have been whittled down to the last hardy survivors. All of the kids came here with dreams, all having battled their way up from a starting pool of some ten million spellers. To earn a spot at Nationals, they all had to win some combination of school, city, and regional bees, competing against ever better spellers at each stage. So all of them are smart and hardworking and lucky—and luck plays a determining role at Nationals, as any Bee veteran will attest. If not for chance, many of the 265 might have survived to these final rounds.

Yet chance favors a prepared mind, and in that regard those who make it to these final rounds go several steps beyond. As a foundation, they have what's possessed by all top orthographers (an orthographer is a speller—the kind who doesn't deign to use spell-check): Each has a working knowledge of the world's major languages, a deep understanding of roots and etymology—which equates to a sprawling vocabulary—and an intuitive grasp of that unpredictable beast known as the English language. Inarguably, they are word geeks, true language nuts. If the word *eccentric* could be used as an honorific, then, truth be told, they are all a dash eccentric. Moreover, each has something extra that sets them apart.

For Katharine "Kerry" Close, for example, making it to the homestretch is a sign of her competitive spirit. All summer long she sails competitively, her blonde hair blowing in the breeze as she mans a one-person sailboat in races off the New Jersey shore. She spells like she sails—to win. She is, improbably, an eleven-year-old who's in the final rounds of a contest dominated by thirteen- and fourteen-year-olds. Even more unlikely given her eleven years, this is her *third year* here. And last year—at age ten—she tied for sixteenth out of 263 spellers.

Early in the competition I asked her how she was doing, and she responded only with a wordless, uneasy grimace. She is, by her parents' description, a tad on the shy side, and also clearly feeling the anxiety of the competition. But you don't see that onstage. While some spellers hem and haw, stalling for time while their brains search for that buried verbal nugget, Kerry is all business. She takes whatever clues the judges provide—definition, origin, sample sentence—and goes to work. No fuss. She has used this focused intensity to fell such monsters as *Bunraku*, *panmyelopathy*, and *warison*.

If Kerry Close is feeling the pressure, then Akshay Buddiga is just barely treading water. A thirteen-year-old whose coach-mother speaks nine languages, Akshay has studied daily for years alongside his brother, the 2002 champion. That his brother won the Bee creates a special incentive, or perhaps a special obstacle: If Akshay wins this year, it will be the first time in the Bee's seventy-seven-year history that siblings have won. And the Colorado boy might do it: In round after round he has spelled like Noah Webster's great-grandson.

The stress, however, is taking its toll. Earlier in the competition, Akshay faced *alopecoid*, a Greek word meaning like a fox, vulpine. It wasn't his toughest challenge, but as he stood at the microphone, a large wave began washing over him, threatening to submerge him. He hadn't slept much the night before and had hardly eaten that day. Too nervous. Adding to the wooziness was that single fact, repeated so often throughout the competition: *He and his brother might be the first sibling winners in the history of the Bee.* That potential honor had loomed large since his brother's 2002 win, and Akshay had trained incessantly. Facing *alopecoid*, he stood just a few words away from this august achievement. But the water was rising ever higher.

A round-faced boy with round glasses and short dark hair, he loves to hike the mountain trails near his house in Colorado Springs. Yet that cool mountain air was far from him now. As he stood facing the expectant audience, he seemed to retreat within himself. His voice had grown quieter in the later rounds. Finally, he began to speak in a slumberous, affectless monotone. Asking the definition and part of speech of *alopecoid*, his already sleepy voice fell to a mumble. He paused, shutting his eyes, as if on the verge of sleep. But just a moment later his soft brown eyes jolted open like he had glimpsed a terrifying sight. He staggered back a step, unsteady, and then . . . he fainted.

The crowd gasped at his fall, a crumpling tumble that landed him flat on the stage. Dozens of adults abruptly stood, ready to rush to help. But before they could take more than a step, he was back on his feet and at the microphone, like a pugilist downed by an unseen punch who rises to fight on gamely. His eyes fluttered open. As numerous adults paused in mid-rescue, a stream of letters ushered forth from his mouth: *a, l, o, p, e,*—he sounded like a sleepwalker, could he spell correctly in his dazed state?—*c, o, i, d.* "That is correct," said head judge Mary Brooks, prompting a deep, sustained round of applause— and considerable amazement—from the crowded ballroom. Such is the mettle of the finalists here at the 2004 National Spelling Bee.

⊙⊙⊙

Two days before, as the competition starts early Tuesday morning, things are not so tense. Throngs of parents and kids, reporters and camera crews, Bee officials and assorted language aficionados pour through the faux elegance of the Grand Hyatt, a massive 880-room affair about four blocks from the White House. Parents with cameras at the ready crowd down escalators, accompanying spellers and their siblings. Many of the kids fit in last-minute cramming with word lists, ignoring the Hyatt's profusion of gaudy aqua blue fountains and the unmanned piano that bangs out show tunes, jauntily if soullessly. The mood is an uneven mix of excitement and tension, as if we're going to a big party, but one that might be attended by the family dentist with drill in hand.

If the idea of a spelling bee comes from Norman Rockwell's America, then the old master would have had to expand his palette considerably to capture these kids. Nicholas Truelson, from Sioux Falls, South Dakota, with blond hair and big owl glasses, shares the stage with Erik Zyman Carrasco from New York, New York, whose parents were born in Mexico. Mehron Price is proud of her Ethiopian heritage, Jamie Ding's mother often speaks to him in her native Chinese, and Samir Patel's Indian-born mother grew up in London before settling in Texas. The Bee is full of parents who still speak with their native accent, accompanying kids who have no trace of it, unless you count the soft drawl of Georgia or the bulldozed nasals of New Jersey.

There's Marshall Winchester, from North Carolina, considered a top contender, who thanked the Lord for his spelling success, and there's Aqsa Ullah, from Florida, also favored to win, who has attended Muslim study sessions on the weekend. Anoopdeep Singh Bal, from Ohio, is a turban-wearing Sikh; in addition to being an ace speller of English he's also fluent in Punjabi, not to mention exceptionally well versed in basketball: He corrected the ESPN television crew about the spelling of a well-known coach's name. Dovie Eisner, from Florida, whose goal is to become an author, has won many awards for his knowledge of the Torah.

The parents of Amber Owens, a star of the 2003 Bee, bought her a horse as a reward for making it to Nationals (she named her pony Alphabet). But many kids couldn't afford to be here if their family's trip wasn't sponsored by a regional newspaper or other sponsor.

Shelby Brianne Smith, from Sacramento, California, wants to be a US

Supreme Court Justice ("It's a cool job, getting people out of jail," she says). If she attains her goal, she'll be the first black female Justice. Mallory Irwinsy, who plays flute in her school band in Piedmont, Oklahoma, wants to be an Air Force pilot. The winner from 2002, Pratyush Buddiga, has a plan for making human life possible on Mars.

The Bee, as a spelling coach from Texas tells me in a thick twang, "is as American as can be." As much as any single event, it gathers together the glorious panoply, first-generation Korean with Mayflower descendant, affluent and working class, Christian and Jew, little burg, big town, and suburb. The kids come from public school (183), parochial (20), private (27), and home-school (35). Bee organizers use the figure ten million when counting how many kids are involved; that figure includes all the school, city, and regional bees across the country. By some mysterious process, when those ten million were winnowed to these final 265 spellers, virtually every American group and class is represented.

Juan Jose Mejia's father is a dairy worker in California. Joe Shepard's father is a cotton merchant in Georgia. Both of Maddy Kloss's parents are attorneys in Arizona. Both of Rajiv Tarigopula's parents are physicians in St. Louis. Chloe Bordewich's mother is a government official in upstate New York, and Adriana Ruf's mother is an accountant in Kentucky. Nektarios Vasilottos's father—the family speaks Greek around the house—manages a restaurant in LaPorte, Indiana.

The father of Elicia Chamberlin (Elicia's so interested in circus arts that she trains on aerial fabric hung in the living room) is a social therapist in New Hampshire. Maithreyi Gopalakrishnan's mother is a technology specialist in Colorado. Morgan McGee's mom, a single mother, works as a cook-waitress. The father of Kay Sackinger, for whom debates and protests are a favorite activity, is a licensed massage therapist in Portland, Oregon. Trevor Leslie's father is a freelance musician in Indiana, Nora Porter's mother is a retail manager in Florida, and Cody Wendt's father drives a transit bus in Idaho. Erik Zyman Carrasco's father is a music professor at Juilliard; his mother is a biomedical scientist. Dakota Koll lives on a farm in Louisiana.

Even the ages are somewhat mixed. To be eligible for the Bee, a speller must not have passed beyond the eighth grade. This means that thirteen- and fourteen-year-olds lead the competition, some returning for their third or fourth time. But plenty of talented eleven- and twelve-year-olds also compete, as do a handful of ten-year-olds. And each year there are a few trembling nine-year-olds, who typically appear quite knock-kneed at having made it to a contest with competitors five years their senior. Then again, in 2003 a nine-year-old took third place. There are few guarantees at the Bee.

Gender, too, is equally matched—well, almost. Of the 79 champions before 2004, 42 are girls and 37 are boys. Of the spellers competing in this year's Bee, 135 are girls and 130 are boys.

There's a great deal of talk at the Bee of how these kids are an elect bunch, an intellectual elite. As one of the fathers confides to me, with an unabashed heap of parental pride, "Well, there's nothing wrong with being average—but these kids aren't." And it's true—these kids are something of a tribe apart. How can a twelve-year-old who wants to study Latin and Greek word roots two hours a day be called typical?

But while the Bee is a kind of yearly party of like-minded kids, with a certain geek chic that runs throughout, this gathering is the most diverse clique any thirteen-year-old is likely to join. The only things this glorious quilt of talented kids have in common are a commitment to scholarship, parents who care, and a facility with the English language. And, of course, the raw chutzpah to confront fearsome words in front of a large audience. Easier said than done.

◯◯◯

As the three-day competition begins early Tuesday morning, Bee officials face a joyless task. The group of 265 bright-eyed spellers is far too large. In every round, each speller spells one word; given that each contestant is allotted a maximum of two minutes (with a thirty-second bonus time period they can use only once during the competition), each round could take hours with a crowd this big. We'd be here for weeks. So Bee officials have devised a method to quickly winnow those who are merely smart, hardworking, and lucky from those who bring a keen dedication to this day. It's a two-part test, made up of a written and then an oral round. The scores from these two rounds are combined to determine who gets to stay in.

The written round is savage. It's twenty-five words picked from anywhere in Webster's *Unabridged*. The spellers sit poised in the Hyatt's grand ballroom with paper and pencil a little after 8:00 a.m., as pronouncer Jacques Bailly prepares to start intoning the words. He greets the spellers with a folksy "howdy," provoking a nervous titter—they know something's coming—and he begins pronouncing the words in his crisp diction. After each word they bend dutifully to their task.

The written test starts as a saunter on level ground, with giveaways like *tenor* and *recede*. Everyone can catch their breath. But then it moves sharply uphill with the likes of *triskaidekaphobia* and *rhinorrhagia*. At about the midway point it enters the high country with obscurities like *acesodyne*, then, finally, makes a sharp, unforgiving descent into the unlit caverns of *boeotian* and *rijsttafel*. Clearly, when Bee officials set out to mow down spellers, they know how to do so. (We later learn that only one of the 265 spellers correctly navigates all twenty-five words. Which means, amazingly, there is one child in America who can spell virtually anything, including *boeotian* and *rijsttafel*.)

Parents are given copies of the test to spell along, just for fun. Most bow out with a chuckle around *netiquette*. The top scoring parent, Bob Deri, a technology specialist from Silicon Valley, spelled twenty-one words correctly.

After the morning's written test, the spellers are sent on a tour of Washington for the day, though some die-hard competitors stay at the hotel and study. For a few of the hypercompetitive kids, these last few hours of drill and review are precious.

The following morning, part two of the written-oral qualifying rounds commences. The oral round is a much gentler challenge, in effect a gift to those who are willing to study for it. Unlike the written test, this round's word list is confined to the *Paideia*, a slender booklet the Bee organizers send out each fall. It contains some 3,800 words, only about 800 of which are advanced. If a speller memorizes all these words (plus an additional 250-word list sent out after the regional bees), she'll know every word in Round Two. In essence, it's the Bee's way of saying: If you want to look good onstage at Nationals for at least one round, here's what you need to know.

The spellers' attitudes toward the *Paideia*'s word list create the first line of demarcation at the Bee. It separates those who got here mainly by smarts from those who got here by smarts and perspiration. For many spellers, brute memorization of the entire list is a given. Asked if they know the *Paideia* list, they give a small nod as if to say, yes, of course, are you kidding? Others claim they've studied it but haven't necessarily memorized it. For other spellers, memorizing the list is seen as superhuman. "Have you seen it?" asks one mother. "It's not possible." On the other hand, some highly dedicated spellers refuse to memorize, preferring to focus on understanding word patterns. For still others, who are naturally bright but whose every minute is filled with activities—from flute lessons to soccer practice—there's simply no time to memorize 4,000 words.

As this first spoken round begins early Wednesday morning, it feels like the true beginning of the Spelling Bee. There's a buzz in the air. The results of the written round along with this first oral round will determine who survives, so the written round was critical. But this spoken round is what we've come for: This is performance spelling. It's the first round in which each speller approaches the microphone and spells—the beginning of the Bee as a spectator event. The Grand Hyatt's main ballroom is decked out for the event. The large red-carpeted stage is equipped with risers to accommodate spellers, with large video screens flanking both sides. The ESPN television crew's production station hums with activity as technicians prepare for the broadcast. The Bee's official photographer, Mark Bowen, snaps at will.

And he's not alone. No moment of this event will escape being recorded, documented, archived, and preserved for posterity. Seemingly all 265 spellers' parents eagerly work cameras or camcorders, in some cases both, and the blur of snapping and videotaping is like a paparazzi sighting of a Hollywood starlet. Two mothers near the stage assemble telephoto lenses while other parents prompt their onstage kids to stand and smile. A big smile is unlikely since it's 7:45 a.m., and many of the kids are still blinker-eyed. Some, like Dovie Eisner, sitting in his wheelchair, merely yawn into the cameras; others, like Sean

Sabino, from Los Angeles (where he's the student council president), look serious and determined.

At 8:00 a.m. sharp—the Bee is always punctual—the spelling begins. Because the source for this round's word list has been publicly available for months, for many spellers it's just a cameo appearance before the going gets tough, no more challenging than fishing in a bathtub. Dovie Eisner, dispatching *sciolism* with aplomb, gives a triumphant thumbs-up as his wheelchair is wheeled away from the microphone. Angela Palomer, working confidently through *luftmensch*, issues a solid "yes!" as the audience applauds her orthographic aptitude. Last year's thirty-first-ranked finisher, Grant Remmen, who confided to me days before the competition that he was nervous, now actually grins while waiting to spell—a rare occurrence at the Bee. And his handling of *corrigendum* justifies his twinkle. Samir Patel, considered a top contender, dismisses *coulisse* so easily he doesn't even wait for confirmation before returning to his seat. He's right and he knows it.

Sachin Raghunathan tackles *Kierkegaardian*, a word that's about a foot longer than he is, as if he's a firm believer in the Danish philosopher's thinking. *Giaour*, a word meaning one outside the Muslim faith, an infidel, is the smallest of leaps for curly-haired Courtney Hartnett, who's won many horseback riding awards in her native Maryland.

Not that missing means a speller must be a slacker. Cindy Yin, a slender thirteen-year-old from Harrison, New Jersey, is an honor student during the week and attends Chinese school on weekends. She fits karate lessons into her spare time. That is, if she has any spare time. An accomplished pianist, she recently performed for the second time at New York's famed Carnegie Hall, rendering a Mozart piece. How did it go? I ask. "It was kind of dull, the second time," she says. "I mean, it was all the same." Wasn't the music different? I ask. "Yes, but everything else, the hall, everything, it was all just the same." Okay, so performing at Carnegie Hall gets boring—it's clear she's not the average thirteen-year-old. But with everything she does she apparently doesn't have time to memorize the *Paideia*. She's stopped by the devilishly hard *rorqual*, which she spells as *wrarqual*.

And some of the spellers have made it here at a remarkably young age, further increasing the odds against them. Tia Thomas, one of the few nine-year-olds, sits onstage looking a little timorous, then stumbles over *senary*. For many spellers, just getting to Nationals has been an achievement, but surviving the preliminary rounds will require a dollop of luck—which doesn't arrive. Like Kentucky's Adriana Ruf, who's mystified by *zetetic*, throwing out the letters in a veritable admission of defeat and walking back to her seat as the judge spells it correctly. Or California's Holly Duitsman, who hasn't a clue about *prolegomenon*, tossing away a failed attempt with a little laugh. Some get lucky with an easy word. Betsy Woodruff gets *chicanery*, a word any self-respecting wordsmith would know (and Betsy, after all, has had a book review published by *The Washington Times*). She spells it like the gift it is.

Erin Clendaniel is dealt a tough hand. A fourteen-year-old with long blonde hair, she plays bass guitar in her own garage band back in Delaware, and she's also a top speller—this is her second year at Nationals. Now she's staring at *virgule*, a diagonal mark used to separate alternatives, as in "and/or." It's not a word you can sound out. Erin is stumped. Making matters worse, her sister—her *identical twin*—tied for thirty-fifth in the 2001 Bee. And here Erin is, having to guess in her first time at the microphone. She gambles with her best guess, only to hear the soft bell that signals a misspell. We might see the hint of a tear.

Snigdha Sur tied with Erin's sister for thirty-fifth place in 2001. But Snigdha, a confident, cheery girl, has faced fierce competition in her regional bee—the New York City contest—for the last two years, and hasn't won a spot at Nationals since then. This year Snigdha made her way back to this hallowed stage, only to be dealt *omphaloskepsis* in her first time at the microphone. The word would be insurmountable to a newbie, but the fourteen-year-old has been at this for four years now. She walks through *omphaloskepsis* as if it's just another trip to Grand Central.

Jacob Trewartha, thirteen, encounters a real struggle as he faces *murrain*, an archaic word meaning an infectious and fast-spreading disease. Offstage the Indiana boy has a klieg-light smile, but as he blanks on the word, a look of real terror crawls across his broad face. Then a light blinks on. Apparently it just took a moment for the memory to surface. After a brief pause he rattles off *murrain*. Terror faced, terror overcome.

⊚⊚⊚

When the morning round ends, with each competitor having one moment in the spotlight, we don't know which spellers will advance to Round Three. The written test is being graded and tabulated along with the score from the oral round; in the early afternoon a Bee official will announce the list of survivors. Of the twenty-six words they've attempted so far—twenty-five on the written test and one in the oral round—they must have correctly spelled seventeen to advance.

As the spellers break for lunch, in the back of each of their minds is one question: *Am I still in?*

² The Field Narrows

At lunch, protesters start marching outside the Grand Hyatt. And yes, oddly, they are protesting the spelling bee. A group of about six middle-aged people, all looking quite earnest and scholarly, carry signs like "Spelling shuud Bee lojical," and "I'm thru with through," and "50,000,000 illiterates can't be wrong." They are members of the Simplified Spelling Society, a British-based group dedicated to reforming English spelling conventions.

They point out, correctly, that English spelling is riddled with inconsistencies—a word's spelling often does not correspond with its sound. The long *e* in *Bee*, for example, is created with a bewildering array of contrasting spellings, as in *bead, chief, police, tedious, weird*. The last syllable of *sister* sounds the same as that of *actor* or *grammar*. And why are similar-sounding words like *wrestle* and *vessel* spelled so differently?

It's this jungle thatch of contradictions, the Society claims, that contributes to the high level of illiteracy in the English-speaking world; some forty-seven million adults are functionally illiterate by the group's count. Among the many benefits of making English spelling consistent, the Society states in its literature, is that "children would have more time to learn many other things— and play." Having more time to play is something most spellers favor, but a glance at the group's proposed reforms suggests that its solutions would simply replace the old mess with a new mess. The Society's mission, which it states using its own spelling, is "werking for plannd chanje in English spelling for the bennefit of lerners and uzers evrywair." In other words, they—gasp—want to *completely rebuild* the millennium-old structural underpinnings of the English language. No one can accuse them of thinking small.

As for the Society's contention that words should be spelled as they sound, Jonathan Swift effectively rebutted it in the early eighteenth century. Swift, author of *Gulliver's Travels* and a passionate essayist on language, wrote the following in a letter to the Earl of Oxford in 1712:

> Another Cause which hath contributed not a little to the maiming of our Language, is a foolish opinion, advanced of late Years, that we ought to spell exactly as we speak; which besides the obvious Inconvenience of utterly destroying our Etymology, would be a thing we should never see an end of. Not only the several towns and counties of England have a different way of pronouncing, but even here in London, they clip their Words after one Manner about the Court, another in the City, and a third in the Suburbs; and in a few years, it is probable, will all differ from themselves, as Fancy of Fashion shall direct.[1]

So the Simplified Spelling Society faces gargantuan obstacles. Still, after I talk with the protesters themselves, it's clear they're thoughtful, well-meaning people, no matter how quixotic their quest. They would be fun to enjoy a stiff afternoon tea with. As seriously as they take their cause, however, their efforts are merely cause for merriment among the Bee crowd. (That is, merriment among the parents—the spellers themselves aren't feeling merry about anything while waiting to see who advances.) "Well," one mother says, looking at the protesters with a laugh, "they have a point." And everyone goes back to ignoring them.

After lunch the spellers gather in the grand ballroom to hear the list of who made it. The spellers and their families sit in anxious silence as a Bee official announces the numbers of the advancing spellers. As the list ends, the crowd emits a big whooshing happy-sad gasp-groan, as hundreds of people get either good or bad news. In one fell swoop, the field of 265 spellers has been narrowed to 94.

Plenty of smart kids must now be content to sit and watch. Adina Laury, who's fluent in Hebrew as well as English, will now have time to finish reading *Sabrina, the Teenage Witch*. The father of Sahiti Surapaneni tells me, with no small pride, that his daughter won a regional competition with 200 spellers to get here. She mastered *monotocous* in the oral round, but her written test score means she's cut.

Ben Brown, an award-winning poet and soccer team captain now in his second trip to Nationals, spelled *rotulet* in the oral round as quickly as if he'd gulped a double espresso. But the written test did him in. So too Rose Marie Van Ryckeghem, who earned a *maxima cum laude* rating in the National Latin Exam and who conquered *springerle* in the oral round. "I studied *so* hard for this," she says. But during the written test, her mother tells me, she may have psyched herself out, as she worried throughout, "Can I survive this?" And she didn't.

Some spellers take the loss with equanimity. For Austin Hoke, a short, slender boy from Greenfield, Indiana, who hopes to be a roller coaster engineer, making it to Nationals at age ten means he'll have plenty of chances. He's out this year but he's sure he'll be back. What makes you want to compete in the Bee? I ask. "I just like to spell, and . . . for the money," he says. I mention the $12,000 cash prize. "Yeah," he sighs, and shakes his head with a quiet awe. Clearly he's been dreaming of more than roller coasters.

While we sit talking in a small conversation nook in the Grand Hyatt lobby, Samir Patel joins us. Samir, who last year at age nine stunned the crowd by placing third, and who has survived the preliminaries this year, will also have plenty of chances. I ask him why he's in the Bee. "A lot of incentives," he says. "Exposure, fame, money." At the mention of money, Austin takes notice. "What did you get for winning regionals?" he asks. "200 bucks," Samir notes. A few minutes later a girl speller joins us and, without much introduction, asks Samir, "How much have you made from spelling?" "$7,500 bucks," Samir says, reporting wins from last year's finish. She seems to appreciate the amount.

As the afternoon round begins with the winnowed field, it's clear these kids are crack spellers. Shortly after Dovie Eisner's wheelchair is wheeled up to the microphone, he voices *pharynx* with hardly a thought. Joe Shepard, a twelve-year-old Georgia boy with a blond buzz cut and a professorial air, takes some time with *macropodous*, but there's never any doubt. Jessy Hwang, with her long dark hair parted in the middle, travels through *archipelago* like a veteran geographer. David Tidmarsh actually giggles at *kiwi*. The Indiana boy has done what few, if any, other spellers have done: He has read the entire dictionary. After that much preparation, getting *kiwi* is pretty funny.

The ease of *kiwi* is fodder for the inevitable quibbling among the spellers. "*Kiwi?*" they ask. "He got *kiwi?*—that's so easy." You hear it between rounds, mainly among spellers who have been eliminated. Many of the early rounds contain words whose difficulty appears to vary considerably. It's unfair, some spellers kvetch. The same round that David Tidmarsh faced the simple *kiwi*, Rachel Karas was dealt the odd *occision* and Amar Mehta faced the lengthy *triglycerides*. The lingual gods smiled on Elicia Chamberlin that round, who received *reggae*—a word most literate tweens can spell without cracking a study guide.

It's a problem there's no clear solution to. It's impossible, or nearly so, to place words on a precise gradation of difficulty. Clearly *rijsttafel* is vastly harder to spell than *tenor*, but when you get into the middle ground of *kiwi* and *triglycerides*, the level of difficulty is deceptive. One of the chief factors determining a word's difficulty is whether it can be sounded out. By that measure, *triglycerides*, despite its length, is fully accessible; a speller who's adept at breaking down words by known roots would have no trouble with *triglycerides*, regardless of its multisyllabic hulk. It's merely a string of roots, all of which follow the rules.

But *kiwi*? Sure, it's short, and any speller who visits the grocery store has likely seen it spelled in the produce section. But the word goes by no rules. The Simplified Spelling Society would spell it *keewee*, but its actual spelling gives no hint of its long *e* sounds. The word, coming to English from the fierce Maori tribes of New Zealand—known for their cannibalism and a language that was strictly oral—is a stumper. You either know it or you don't.

So the quibbling about the word list, the relative difficulty of words in the same round, goes on. The Bee organizers go to great length to step up the words' difficulty round by round, placing roughly equivalent words in the same round. But they would be the first to admit that luck plays a role in the Bee.

And luck's a funny beast, as several spellers learn this afternoon. Ezra-Mel Pasikatan, whose bright orange shirt contrasts with his shock of dark hair, receives no gift with the tricky *vacillant*. Although the thirteen-year-old Oregon boy recently applied for a copyright for twenty-two of his inspirational songs, his inspiration fails him on this word. Faring no better is Charlotte Blacklock, with a brown ponytail and glasses, who's cast into darkness by the uncommon *synovial*. That her older sister Evelyn was a star of the previous year's Bee, barely missing first place after a tense multi-round duel—in which Evelyn stayed ice cool the whole time—might make Charlotte's struggle more freighted. She dives deep into her knowledge of roots, querying the pronouncer repeatedly: "Is it related to . . . ?" But the answer is always no. With zero clues, she rolls the dice and hopes, spelling *synovial* as *scinovial*. Her exit off the stage is a moment of real disappointment.

So, too, goes the departure of Owen Ricker, a redheaded thirteen-year-old with big aviator glasses and dazzling knowledge of *Star Wars* trivia. Owen, who wants to be an actor, stumbles on *turgescent*, which means to act pompously or feel great self-importance. His demoralized trudge off stage, with arms crossed, is far from turgescent.

⊙⊙⊙

As Round Four is about to begin on Wednesday at 3:00 p.m., this Bee is set for a major change. In just moments it will morph from a small educational competition to a national media event. Making all the difference: In this round the ESPN television crew will start its live broadcast.

In the preceding days, as families arrived at the Grand Hyatt and the spellers started socializing, one desire was repeated like a refrain: *I want to survive long enough to get on TV.* That's the ideal. Winning, of course, is all but impossible, but getting on TV is attainable glory. There's something geeky about telling your friends you're serious about spelling, but there's nothing geeky about telling them you'll be on national TV. As the surviving spellers realize they're about to be stars of the small screen, the heat rises.

Aqsa Ullah, a fourteen-year-old from Florida with long black hair and a serious manner, has studied exhaustively for this year's Bee, pushing herself to her limit, and now she's made it to the television broadcast, the first major step toward champion status. Just before she goes on stage, as spellers and their families crowd into the ballroom, she hands off her lollipop to her younger brother. "Tell Mommy I love her," she says.

We're assembled in our seats, ready to begin, but we must sit and wait. Our attention is drawn to the two 15-foot video screens on either side of the stage. Since the broadcast is live, we need to wait until the ESPN feed is ready. It feels odd: A room full of bright young minds must sit and do nothing while waiting for a silent screen. Ironic, too, because many of these kids watch far less TV than average. Many parents tell me they won't allow it in the home at all, and others limit it severely. But that doesn't matter now. We all must bow down in abeyance to the Great Camera.

The ESPN director takes over, telling us to applaud at his signal. A jazzy action montage starts on the screens, with pounding music and a crisp female voice-over. The Bee, she intones, is "a mental challenge like no other . . ." The onscreen image cuts to us in the ballroom, and the ESPN man gives us the sign: *start applauding!*

And we do, with great gusto. What exactly we're applauding is unclear—ourselves, presumably—but it doesn't matter. When it comes to television, we do what we're told. We watch ourselves applaud ourselves for a few moments, until the ESPN director is satisfied and signals that we can stop.

As the excitement has notched up, so too has the skill level required to get this far. Kendra Yoshinaga, a diminutive ten-year-old with a quiet voice, proves she's capable of magic when she gets *ullaged*, the adjectival form of a word meaning the amount by which the contents fall short of filling a container. It's of late Middle English origin, but to Kendra it might as well be from Mars. She struggles with the pronunciation—a speller must pronounce the word correctly before spelling—and she can hardly say it. For the California girl the word is simply too big, or so it appears. Hesitantly she works through it. And there it is—without warning—she's right. She has mastered a word whose pronunciation suggests it could be spelled myriad ways. A little bit of luck, perhaps, but even with luck how many ten-year-olds can spell *ullaged*? (Kendra survives until the next round, when she adds an extra *e* to the impenetrable *Nigerois*.)

Although Hannah Provenza, a tall fourteen-year-old with long red hair who's an obsessive reader, has successfully spelled *salicylate* and *cribral*, she meets her match with *graupel*. She simply doesn't know it. It's a Germanic word meaning precipitation that consists of crisp, white ice particles. In Hannah's hometown of Rockford, Illinois, it would be called "hail." At moments like these confidence comes into play. She's stumped, yes, and sure, there's a ballroom full of people staring at her, along with a bank of TV cameras. So it might be hard to cast around inside, to try to dredge up an educated guess based on everything she has read and studied. But that's a big part of what the Bee is about—daring to think you might be right even though you're in the dark. Hannah goes to work. She issues the letters one by one and . . . she's correct. She walks back to her seat and flashes a big awestruck smile, amazed at her own success, mouthing the words "I guessed" to her parents in the audience.

Kay Sackinger's technique relies on typing the word as she spells, her fingers working a phantom keyboard as the letters tumble from her mouth. This unconscious pantomime provokes some quiet chuckles from the audience, yet it seems to work. It gets her through *supernaculum*, and it also helps her with *laodicean*, meaning someone who lacks religious or political commitment—a word that certainly doesn't describe Kay. When the fourteen-year-old Portland, Oregon, girl isn't working for her regular babysitting clients or developing her creative writing skills, she's often debating the issues of the day with friends. She's particularly fond of protest demonstrations with large crowds. As she faces *silicicolous*, she pauses, then her fingers go to work. She's unfamiliar with the word, and her digits type tentatively in the air in front of her. She adds an *h*, prompting the small ding signaling a misspell. She accepts her stroll off stage as the natural course of events.

Her fate is shared by Dovie Eisner, whose wheelchair trips to the microphone have thus far been a prelude to utterly confident performances. But *syringeal* injects him with doubt. The word appears to be derivative of syringe, but no, it actually means pertaining to the syrinx, the vocal organ of birds. (Or, if it's capitalized, as in Syrinx, it refers to a mountain nymph in classical mythology.) Reasonably, Dovie gambles with *syringial*, after which he's wheeled off stage. He's soon followed by Abhiram Gunturi, a tall, slender twelve-year-old whose brother Sai was the previous year's champion and whose sister Nivedita tied for eighth in 1997. He gets *fanfaronade*, meaning bragging, bravado, and bluster. But in the word's clutches, Abhiram appears to feel only baffled and bewildered. It's rarely good when one's sibling has been a star of the Bee. After the soft ding he disappears off stage like a ghost, as if sudden invisibility would be highly desirable.

◎◎◎

The idea of a spelling bee doesn't denote the pang of defeat and the flesh wounds of psychic combat to most people, but don't tell that to the Bee kids. As one of the kids says to me, "Every year, at the award banquet, they always say 'there are no losers, there are only winners.'" He mimics the sanctity of that with no small disgust, then tells me, "I'm sick of hearing that." Losing is very real to these kids. Gavin King, standing in line for a meal after being eliminated in the 2003 Bee, had red-rimmed eyes and a shell-shocked manner. "What word did you go out on?" I asked him. "I can't remember," he said, turning away.

There are plenty of exceptions, of course, kids for whom being eliminated is a lighthearted affair. "It's a win-win situation," says one speller, proving he's mastered psychobabble as well as spelling. "If you get it right, you get to keep going, but if you miss, you get a great vacation in Washington."

But many spellers are far from that sanguine. It took real work to get here, in some cases all-consuming work. Sacrifices were made, in social activities and in free time. Hearing that bell ding is like a blow, especially if it comes early in the competition. Arjun Modi, a twelve-year-old New Jersey boy, takes it hard after being sent packing by *hygrophilous*. Fortunately his brother Rajan has also traveled here to Washington. The boys' mother tells me that Rajan missed a question in the national geography bee, a defeat that will now help him comfort his brother. "We're leaving the two of them alone," she says.

Even the audience can feel the grief. Losing is not on the mind of Joe Shepard, a serious, blond-haired boy from Waynesboro, Georgia, with glasses and a soft drawl. He's a real contender—at age twelve he's already in his third appearance at Nationals. A homeschooler, Joe brings a deep dedication to his spelling studies. It helps that his family has performed that most subversive of acts: His father tells me that he has removed the television from their home. But Joe, facing *solecism*, experiences an unusual moment of doubt. He labors through it, inflecting the last few letters like a question. *Ding.* The audience, knowing that he had a shot at the final rounds, if not the trophy, lets out an "ohhh . . ." It's as if the entire crowd had to slink offstage.

If Joe Shepard was a contender, then Erik Zyman Carrasco is *the* contender for this year's Bee championship. After placing tenth in 2002, he turned in a dazzling performance to place seventh in 2003, impressing the audience with his comprehensive knowledge of word roots. Since he's from New York City, his third appearance here means he has won that city's ruthlessly competitive bee three years in a row, a remarkable achievement. Increasing his odds this year, only two spellers who placed above him last year have returned, and one of them is just ten years old. So this is Erik's year. It's also his last year; he's now in the eighth grade.

I talk to him a few days beforehand and there's an edge about him. He's worked for this and he's dreamed about this, and here it is. He's mature for his age; at thirteen years old he's a young teen, a clear step past the tween age of many of the spellers. He's personable, but his voice says this isn't a game. A look of tiredness in his eyes suggests he's been working overtime and perhaps worrying overtime. Whatever his stress, though, he brings a lot to the competition. He's fluent in Spanish and advanced in French and Latin; those three tools will allow him to look inside many of the words he'll face. And he's passionate about language; when he grows up, he wants to be a linguist.

As an added coincidence, his picture is one of those that hang above the stage. Each year the Bee organizers post several oversize posters of spellers in various states of competition: thinking, spelling, celebrating. Perhaps because Erik was such a natural photo subject—throwing his hands in the air after each successful spell—his photo from last year now hangs above him as he spells. But his demeanor no longer matches that captured by last year's photo; he's toned down, replacing the triumphant gestures with an earnest, workman-like quality.

Toward the end of the day he gets *Gomorrah*, the ancient city that the Bible says was destroyed, along with Sodom, because of its wickedness. It's an ironic word for a speller from New York City. The metropolis, with its urban mores and ahead-of-the-curve social practices, is sometimes referred to, at least tongue-in-cheek, as a modern-day Sodom and Gomorrah. And indeed, when Erik requests a sample sentence, the pronouncer reads this one: "New York City, during the Jazz Age, was a veritable *Gomorrah*."

The word's sometimes synonymous relationship with his own hometown doesn't jog Erik's thinking, so he's going to have to work for it. Which, fortunately, he's well equipped to do. He's been in many tough spots over his three-year competitive career. With his formidable lingual tools, he can unlock most spelling mysteries: If you know a word's roots, you can usually ferret out its stray vowels and consonants. *Gomorrah*, however, is stubborn. Neither Latin, French, nor Spanish provide any clues. The Old Testament word is, oddly, in the same category as *kiwi*; you either know it or you don't. It's a proper name, not a word that can be broken down by sifting through etymological histories.

He goes to work. Even with the most opaque words, a speller at his level can leverage a storehouse of knowledge, putting together bits and pieces to offer a high-percentage guess. Erik ponders the word, hesitating, focusing on the few letters that are maybes. After some onstage meditation, it's time for his best guess. He takes the plunge, spelling *Gomorrah* as *Gemorrah*. A judge rings the small bell indicating a misspell. The crowd, knowing Erik's record, is dumbstruck. They emit a long, crestfallen "ohh . . ." of surprise, a deep group sympathy from hundreds of people.

It's a bitter disappointment. Erik registers nothing as he walks from the stage, but a sense of loss seems to radiate from him. His errant *e* in *Gomorrah* means that he will tie for forty-seventh place, an ignominious finish for someone who has placed tenth and seventh. Not only will he not make the final rounds, he won't make it into the last day of spelling. Today was supposed to be when the duffers were eliminated, the spellers who were merely smart, hardworking, and lucky, not the ones with three foreign languages and years of competitive experience. To have to sit and watch the kids he would have been competing with is no small heartbreak.

Erik is not seen later in the day, when that afternoon's spelling is done and the kids gather in klatches in the Grand Hyatt lobby. Apparently he prefers not to face everyone. That evening I see him with his parents coming back from a dinner somewhere outside the hotel. A force field surrounds the family unit that even a pesky reporter who can feign casualness dares not try to enter.

The next day I talk with his father, Samuel Zyman, a music professor at the Juilliard School with a thoughtful air about him. "I'm not going to kid you," he says. "It's a blow." But he takes it philosophically, noting that after being eliminated, Erik received an outpouring of support from other spellers; the many pats on the back have, somewhat, made up for it. As we're speaking, the Bee's director, Paige Kimble, stops by to voice concern: "How is Erik?"

By the following day Erik appears to have emerged essentially unscathed. "I have mixed feelings about this year," he says. "On one hand everyone was expecting me to do really well, and I struck out much earlier. But on the other hand, I wasn't the only speller to do that. Everyone knows that it can happen. Even the public knows that those things can happen.

"I guess in the end it's not *that* different," he says, apparently referring to the difference between winning and not winning. He's ready to get back to the rest of life. "I've been using my Palm Pilot to compile a report of everything I've accomplished at the Spelling Bee, to explain to my friends who may not necessarily know that the Bee isn't one of those things where if you tried a little harder you would have won."

He concedes he was really nervous during the competition, though that's not why he missed *Gomorrah*, he explains. The word was simply one he didn't know. He tried to lessen the stress by taking the competition round by round, but his awareness that this was his last year to compete did heighten the pressure, he says.

He's been heartened by the response from other spellers. "Some of them actually said they knew I was the true champion," he says with a laugh, "which is very flattering."

So now one of the leading contenders is out as the Bee heads into its final day. Tomorrow will tell which of the remaining forty-six spellers will hold aloft that large gold trophy.

⚇⚇⚇

That evening the spellers take over the hotel, as they have every night in the few days preceding the Bee. The Grand Hyatt is built so that its 880 rooms surround a voluminous central atrium, which is topped by an open-air skylight ceiling. Its airy and spacious layout offers all manner of sitting areas and nooks and crannies. But as big as the atrium-lobby is, the kids make their presence felt through most of it. To have a group of 265 kids in the same place, all of whom are bright and highly verbal, means the Grand Hyatt is alive with the sound of tweens.

Back home they might be considered odd ducks, the kind of kids who—voluntarily—spend hours studying Latin word roots and French consonant-vowel patterns. But here they're all part of the same clique. They're all word nerds, spelling geeks. There's no one to point a finger and snicker. (Those kids are back home watching reruns.) Friendships are instantaneous in this atmosphere. Some kids know each other from previous years, though most do not. But no matter. The formation of chatty groups of two, three, four, or more is like some kind of inevitable molecular process, a constant combining and recombining.

Early in the week the atrium had been one huge study hall, with several dozen spellers immersed in word lists, huddled over laptops, checking and rechecking themselves, spelling obscure etymons, often out loud. A passerby could improve his spelling immeasurably by strolling through the Grand Hyatt's lobby on those evenings. In the central living room area, a horde of spellers worked as a group, conducting their own mini spelling bees, reviewing any words they missed. Jesse Zymet, a speller from New Jersey who was a star of 2003's competition but who's now too old to be eligible, returned to run study groups. "It's in his blood," his father explained.

26

Some of the real heavyweight spellers, kids who have been here before and are returning with an earnest, dead-eye focus on winning, forgo these groups. They study by themselves in their rooms, usually aided by a parent. When you've come to win, chat time isn't productive.

By this evening, Wednesday, most of the spellers have been eliminated, so the mood has shifted. A party atmosphere is developing. The spelling study has evolved into a talkfest of epic proportions. A sitting area designed for perhaps twenty people has some forty to fifty spellers crammed into it, sitting on the couches at every possible angle, as if sheer physical proximity is a tribal necessity.

Those spellers who are continuing to study don't seem to mind being squeezed shoulder to shoulder with spellers who play games, chat, laugh, horseplay, and otherwise lay the groundwork for fast friendships. Oddly, some of those who are studying are kids who have been eliminated (there's always next year, and some kids—call them atypical—simply enjoy spelling as a fun activity).

Around the atrium, the formerly focused competitors, so serious onstage, have been transformed back into kids. Some just goof off, scampering up the down escalator or, as one boy did, riding the escalator all the way up without touching the steps—an impressive feat. Troops of tweens march around on missions. Some forage for a mid-evening snack. A few go to a nearby restaurant with parents for a karaoke night.

The defining ritual is the signing of each other's Bee book. The Bee organizers print a slender booklet each year with all the spellers' names and photos. Most of the spellers ask as many of their lingual compatriots as possible to sign. "Here, sign my book," is a constant refrain. The signatures of celebrity spellers, those who make it to the final rounds, are particularly sought after.

Along with the book signing is a whirlwind of e-mail exchanging; at no Silicon Valley business development meeting are more e-mail addresses exchanged. Some of the spellers e-mail spelling tips back and forth, and many form real friendships. This year, for example, JJ Goldstein and Naomi Ahsan met again at the Bee after corresponding all year. That JJ's family is Orthodox

Jewish and Naomi's is devoutly Muslim doesn't appear to crimp their friendship as they chat away. If only the world could be more like the Bee.

As JJ and Naomi talk, two remaining top challengers, Snigdha Sur from New York City and Abigail Eustace from Dayton, Ohio, study together intently, paying no mind to the conviviality around them. The two girls know that the time has come. If there was ever an evening to be serious about their studies, it's this one. Tomorrow, to be sure, will be a big day.

3 "Is This as Good as Hollywood Can Make It?"

Early Thursday morning—the Bee's final day—Michelle Bak, a curly-haired thirteen-year-old from Chicago who wants to be a writer, nervously chomps through breakfast as she peruses word lists. She has already survived *fasciculation* and *vaccary*, but it gets tougher from here. Smiling as she admits she has butterflies, she says she's eager to get past the burden of constant studying— she hasn't had time for reading. And she's dying to get back to her guitar. She's in the middle of learning Cream's rock classic "Sunshine of Your Love."

A few tables over, Jack Ausick is the very picture of casualness as he enjoys a sugar doughnut. The red-cheeked Montana boy figures he's been lucky so far and has gotten easy pitches. (True, *phenology* was a softball, but *logodaedaly* was impressive.) As for today, "I'll see what happens," he says, nonchalantly finishing his double glaze.

Spellers, their families, and a now larger crowd noisily bustle into the ballroom, accompanied by a legion of reporters from the many regional newspapers that sponsor contestants. We're ready to get started but, again, we sit in silence while waiting for the television director. Today's competition will be broadcast live in its entirety by ESPN, so we must wait quietly for the director's signal. When he gives us the sign, we applaud obediently, and the contest is under way.

The spellers who make it to this final day receive a special honor: They get to wear the official white Spelling Bee shirt (in fact are required to wear it), so the forty-six spellers onstage present a white-topped phalanx. And as the competition begins, it's clear they deserve it. Aqsa Ullah permits herself a small smile as she commands *Weimaraner*, a German hunting dog. There's nothing small about the beaming grin that Katie Olsen allows herself when she gets *gaucherie*, a lack of grace in social situations. She knows it like an old friend; how sweet to meet an old friend when any kind of lingual monster might emerge from the deep.

Jamie Ding, a sunny, talkative twelve-year-old from suburban Detroit with a round face and glasses, is handed *corticoline*. Jamie's mother, Ning Yan, whose speech is punctuated with a self-effacing little laugh, speaks Mandarin Chinese to Jamie and his sister around the house. She says she'd like to help Jamie with his spelling studies but can't; her English pronunciation is too far from standard. She declined to take the written test along with the spellers, as many parents did just for fun. "I didn't want to be last," she explains with a small chuckle.

Once, when Jamie tried to play volleyball at school, he proved so uncoordinated he didn't touch the ball once during the entire game. Frustrated, he came home and yelled at his mother, "You gave me bad genes!" But his mother counterpointed, "Jamie, you are smart."

And that he is, dispatching words like *anaptyxis* and *Qatari* to make it to this final day in his first year here. Yet when he works on *corticoline*, he adds an errant *h*. Jamie responds to the inevitable misspell bell with an accepting nod—no big deal, he seems to say as he strolls offstage. After the competition he is, as usual, resolutely upbeat. "I think it was really fun," he says, "and I think the champion really deserved it." His mother starts to point out that champions never forget their studies, but Jamie impetuously cuts in and talks over her. And yes, he's definitely coming back next year.

Aaron Ho, who placed thirty-first last year, takes a deeply serious run at *sachem*, a chief of a Native American people. It's one of those apparently tricky words; to get a short word in the later rounds always seems like a trap. How is it that such an innocent-sounding word got in here? But Aaron's hypercareful approach, issuing each letter like a tightrope walker taking a step, allows him to survive. Not so fortunate is Michelle Bak, the Chicago guitarist who's learning "Sunshine of Your Love." She's dealt *solipsistic*, a belief that only the self exists or can be proved to exist. She fishes for clues using her etymological know-how. "Does it contain the Latin root meaning alone or self?" she asks. Yes it does, says the judge who handles etymology queries. She's on the right track, but she's off by one *c*, spelling it as *solipcistic*.

Few of the spellers here have greater knowledge of word roots than Samir Patel, from Colleyville, Texas. Although he's only ten years old, Samir is considered a top contender. Last year he left the audience gasping in amazement with his third-place finish. That a nine-year-old would almost win a contest dominated by thirteen- and fourteen-year-olds was impressive in its own right. But Samir's style made it even more so.

Not much more than four feet tall, with short dark hair and expressive brown eyes, Samir seems like an adult trapped inside a boy's body. He recently skipped the fourth grade and appears ready to skip a few more grades. He speaks in fully formed, articulate sentences when probing a word's origin with the etymology judge or parrying with the main word pronouncer. When last year he was given *boudin*, he retorted, "Is it just my luck, or am I getting all French words?" earning a laugh from the audience. He appears unstoppable, an orthographic freight train who runs over anything in his path.

As the rounds tick by, he doesn't even seem to be working that hard. During the breaks he chats and laughs easily. When given a word, he never seems to be squirming or hoping or chancing a guess. He merely spells it and sits back down. No operatic struggle for him. Sometimes he'll rattle it off and turn away without even checking to see if the judges give him the nod—he knows he's right. His spelling skill earned him a guest appearance on a reality TV show in which celebrities competed; he was the "lifeline" they called when they needed help. Naturally talented at language arts from an early age, Samir at age seven bested a group of thirteen-year-olds in a national spelling contest. (That bee was hosted by the North South Foundation, an Indian-American organization.)

A homeschooler, Samir's primary teacher and spelling coach is his mother, Jyoti. Born in India and raised in London before moving to Texas, Jyoti speaks with a light English accent. Both she and her husband, Sudhir, an engineer, converse amiably about their only child. "He's an extreme child," she says. And that appears true, based on last year's competition; he was either all the way up, competing confidently without a hint of doubt, or, when he was finally stumped, plunging into tears.

His mother tells him "you can quit if you want to," but apparently that's the furthest thought from his mind. Samir usually studies spelling two to three hours a day during the week, more on weekends. "And now, every available minute," he says shortly before this competition began. In the days beforehand, most spellers took part in a board game fest and an essay contest; Samir skipped both, presumably holed up studying with Jyoti.

Jyoti stresses to Samir that the Bee is not about competing with others; it's about competing with yourself. Don't focus on the other spellers, focus on your own performance, she says. Her other guiding principle in coaching Samir: "Don't memorize." Instead, focus on understanding word roots and lingual patterns across many languages. As she points out, short of memorizing the entire dictionary, memorization is always incomplete. Has Samir memorized the word list in the *Paideia*, usually the first step of any serious speller? "Not necessarily," she says.

The elimination of Erik Zyman Carrasco means Samir is that much more favored a contender. All eyes are on him this morning as he steps to the microphone and gets *corposant*, an archaic synonym for St. Elmo's fire. The ten-year-old briskly asks all his queries—definition, language of origin, alternate pronunciation—then he pauses, calmly, to reflect.

Last year, after his dazzling third-place finish, I asked him how he managed to stay so cool onstage. "You can take a deep breath and just concentrate on something," he explained. "Look at something in the back of the ballroom. And just concentrate on it. Pretend you're not at the Spelling Bee, pretend you're at home playing with your friend, to get all the nervousness away, especially right before you go up onstage.

"It's all right if you're nervous when you're sitting in your seat, but especially when you're up spelling, you cannot afford to be nervous." Whether he's using his visualization technique this year is unknown, but he's as steady onstage as far older spellers, if not more so.

Now at the microphone, he digs into the etymology of *corposant*. "Does it come from the Latin root *corpus*, meaning body?" Yes it does, but, uncharacteristically, he needs more information, so he keeps digging. "Does it come from the Latin root *corpusc*, meaning body?" The pronouncer examines his etymology information. He doesn't see that listed. "*Corpisarae*, to become body?" Again, the pronouncer responds that that's not listed. "Could I be on the right track?" Samir asks, prompting an audience chuckle, though his voice reveals that he's momentarily lost.

The pronouncer points out that Samir's first question about the Latin root for body received a yes answer. Samir again pauses reflectively before beginning. The problem, of course, is that middle syllable: What vowel creates that middle syllable's sound? *Corposant* is mysterious because it sounds like it could have either a *u* or an *o* in the middle, or perhaps an *a*. Samir prepares to take his chance. C...o...r...p

Then he pauses again. He has a tough decision to make, and it's time to make it. The letters come out in a rush, as if a faster run is more likely to propel this leap across the canyon: ...u,s,c,a,n,t.

As the bell tells him he's misspelled, his shoulders jerk spasmodically. *Ahh!* After a moment he seems to take it in stride, listening to the correct spelling and accepting the stage assistant's exit handshake with apparent equanimity.

Later in the morning, though, he is all but crushed. Big tears inch down his cheeks as still more well up in his eyes. At this moment he is not fond of the word *corposant*. "I never studied it, I've never even heard of it," he says, with a tone that suggests he was felled only by a surprise blow, not a word that fought fair. As the tears keep coming, I can't help but offer some consolation. "There's next year," I point out. "Three more years," he corrects me. Irrepressible, he plans on taking some time off before beginning to prepare for next year. There's one thing he's sure of: He wants to win. The tears are still falling as his father whisks him away, but he'll be back.

After a lunch break, we go into the final rounds with twenty-six spellers remaining. Any vestige of lightheartedness has evaporated. The Associated Press reporter sits up front, typing away on his laptop, sending updates to news services by the hour. The ESPN roving cameraman moves among the audience and the stage, stopping for close-ups. The temperature in the crowded ballroom seems to have bumped up a few degrees. Camcorders roll, cameras flash, parents whisper nervously. The words have taken a turn toward the impenetrable. There will be no more gifts like *kiwi*.

Irene Park faces *orthostichous*. It's long and twisty, certainly, but a veteran orthographer can sound it out, which the Alaskan resident does without breaking a sweat. So too Maddy Kloss, a fourteen-year-old Arizonan who's already a semi-professional dancer; *shrieval*, for all its apparent impenetrability, gives her no pause.

Emerging as a real contender is Kerry Close, the slender eleven-year-old New Jerseyan who sails competitively off the Atlantic coast. Her style throughout the competition has been one of quiet resolve. "She's shy on the surface but underneath she's very competitive," her father says. (After trying out for the basketball team and failing to make it, she was quite upset; she doesn't like to lose.) She'll ask her spelling questions, take a moment—only a moment—and then spell. No extra back-and-forth with the judges for Kerry. Not that she's antisocial. She has a good friendship with the New York City speller, Erik Zyman Carrasco. After Erik's surprise elimination the day before, he wished Kerry the best for the rest of the competition. She, unlike some of the top spellers, does not come to D.C. and hole up in her room and study. "When you're exercising, you're exercising your brain," says her mother, an occupational therapist.

Now she's looking at *warison*, an obscurity that sounds like it's loaded with trick consonants. It could be spelled *warisun* or *warrison* or *warasan*, among other possibilities. "Warison?" she asks, suggesting she's in the dark. Yet she has no doubts. After a few quick questions she sails through it. She inflects the letters up at the end as if there's some question, but that appears to be simply a polite gesture—like she doesn't want to seem *too* sure. On the way back to her seat, she gives a subtle high five to a fellow speller. (Kerry continues her run until she spells *vitrophyre* as *vitrifier*, which sends her off stage. With two more years to compete, she'll be back.)

Trevor Leslie is also a third-timer at the Bee, but when facing *Balearic*, the athletic fourteen-year-old with ultra-short blond hair appears to see nothing but inky darkness. *Balearic* means of or belonging to the Balearic Islands, a lovely group of Spanish islands boasting 300 days of sunshine a year. According to the islands' tourist literature, "hardly anybody who has spent holidays here didn't wish to return." But Trevor, who basks in the sunshine of Indianapolis, has apparently yet to make his first trip. He ponders the word, considers it this way and that, but—nope—it's just not on the map. He half chuckles, knowing his Bee days are over. He's close, spelling it as *Ballearic*, but close doesn't count.

As Biplab Panda, a Georgia boy who wants to be an astronaut or a physician, finds out. After getting *empennage* he retorts: "Please tell me this is French!" prompting a ripple of laughter through the audience. He's correct about its Gallic ancestry, but the double *n* fools him. *Ding.* So too Katie Brown, a Floridian staring at *intussusception* with the eyes of a veteran—this is her third year here—but she's one *s* short. *Ding.* She takes her loss with a quiet trudge off stage.

Having better luck is Jack Ausick. The sugar doughnut the Montana boy polished off for breakfast must have been followed by a decent lunch; his powers of concentration appear strong as he dispatches a word that sounds like *saxiform* but is actually spelled *sacciform*. He accepts his victory with his usual nonchalance. Iowa speller Jonathan Hahn is issued *almagest*, meaning an important medieval treatise; when capitalized it refers to an astronomy text written by Ptolemy in the second century theorizing that the earth is the center of the universe. When the judge nods yes at his spelling, Jonathan experiences deep shock, which quickly turns into happiness at the center of his own universe. In contrast, when Katie Olsen masters *escharotic*, she experiences no shock, only a joyous 300-watt smile on the way back to her seat. Correct spelling has never seemed like so much fun.

If there's a natural leader among this year's spellers, it's Snigdha Sur, one of two spellers from New York City. Her talent for spelling is accompanied by an advanced set of social skills. The outgoing fourteen-year-old seems mature beyond her years, always at the center of discussions, often leading groups of kids around the Grand Hyatt on some invented mission, usually with a laugh or a smile. She's the pianist in her school's jazz band and an honor student in her studies. This is her second year at Nationals; she first made it here when she was eleven but hasn't won the New York City bee for the last two years.

Her father, who's unusually jovial for a physician, keeps downplaying expectations, setting up his daughter for a win no matter what. "She's hardly studied at all," he explains, more than once, always with a smile—"maybe one month, that's all." He touts her many skills, noting that she knows the Hindu and Bengali languages. Furthermore, "she's not nervous at all," he says. "She's confident."

Snigdha herself confirms that she's been intensely studying not much more than a month. But of course she's been in highly competitive bees for the last three years, and her fifth-grade teacher is now her spelling coach. And, one of her friends pipes up, "I don't think she sleeps, she just studies all night." Snigdha acknowledges that she's been hitting the books hard, "but it's not like I've been a freak about it." In the days preceding the Bee she mostly focused on helping other spellers—in fact, she predicts that Florida speller Aqsa Ullah will win. "But now it's time to do my own studying," she said the evening before this last day.

Now, stepping up to the microphone, Snigdha's word is *carnauba*, a plant native to Brazil that yields a hard wax used in polish and floor wax. When she queries the pronouncer about the word's background, she learns a daunting fact: *Carnauba* has four different pronunciations, all slight variations. This is both good and bad news. The good news: The different pronunciations may offer extra clues about a word's spelling. The bad news: With four different vocalizations, a speller aims at a constantly moving target, and sorting through the pronunciations can eat up most of a speller's two minute time allotment.

Snigdha's brow furrows upon realizing there are four pronunciations, but she gathers the related clues—definition, language of origin (Portuguese)—and works calmly through the thicket of variations, apologizing for making the judge voice all of them three times. Then she pronounces each of the four variations herself. She falls into thought. By this point, however, her allotted time is dwindling and Snigdha's cool is also ticking downward. She starts wringing her hands, her eyes shut in effort, her brow deeply scrunched. She asks again for the language of origin and definition, crossing and clasping her arms. The spelling is not coming to mind. "And the pronunciations again please?" she asks, to which the pronouncer doesn't respond for a moment. "Can I have the pronunciations again?" she repeats, with a slight insistence. She gets them, but her time is almost expired. As she says the word prior to spelling it—her voice slightly quavering—the clock beeps, meaning she's down to her last thirty seconds.

She takes a leap at the word, tapping out the letters in an anxious staccato. But no. She spells *carnauba* as *carnouba*. As the judge spells it correctly, she turns away and mouths, "Shoot!" And with that ends her years in the Bee. Her elimination at this point means she ties for sixteenth with ten other spellers.

She takes it in stride. That evening she's all fun and games, laughing and leading a group off to sing karaoke at a nearby bar, along with parents. The word was "kind of unfair," she says, "but"—she catches herself, she's not going to complain—"no regrets." Then she's off to sing.

⚭⚭⚭

As the final afternoon rolls on, the audience's attentiveness is oddly unwavering, as it has been throughout the competition. Hour after hour they're present, following each speller closely, applauding or groaning or chuckling or some combination thereof. Yes, there are parents here, but only about 500 people in this crowded ballroom are parents, yet the whole group feels attuned as if their own child were onstage.

I feel it, too, some kind of visceral connection between myself, the kids onstage, and the audience as a whole, and I have to ask myself: why? After almost a dozen hours of competitive spelling, why are we still so intensely involved?

[3] "Is This as Good as Hollywood Can Make It?"

And I realize something. The Bee poses as a diversity-fest, and certainly is one, with kids from every group and class. But underneath its rainbow veneer the Bee is something very different. It's an individuality-fest. The task itself is not high drama—the kids are, after all, spelling. No fireworks there. But each speller has his or her own variation on the form. Some worry, some gloat, some accept it stoically, some just breathe hard. This isn't a team sport. Each kid stands at the microphone very much by him- or herself. They are forced to rely upon themselves and their own verbal ability, the number of hours they've studied, their own native intelligence, their own strength under pressure, their own ability to attract the gods of lingual luck—perhaps drawing *libretto* when a competitor draws *arundinaceous*. Win or lose, it's a trial by fire, and that's its value.

It's the irrepressible individuality brought out by this challenge that keeps the competition fresh as the hours wear on. We don't know what's going to happen when the next speller steps up, what little moment of lovable idiosyncrasy, not yet papered over with adult inhibitions, will be revealed. The spellers even amaze themselves with their own ability to transcend their known limits, as when Hannah Provenza flashed a big awestruck smile after mastering *graupel*. Or when Ahmad Rana attempted *gigot* and, realizing he had done it, exclaimed, "No, really, *no*—seriously? Oh my God!"

At a moment like that, it doesn't matter where a kid comes from or what his parents do, it matters that one young person—in the crucible of competition—has reached inside him- or herself and discovered a strength they didn't know they had. And, in fact, a strength that may have been developed in the act of being challenged. At its purest, the Bee is about young people creating themselves, and at moments it's downright inspirational to watch. No wonder the crowd stays attuned.

☉☉☉

Aqsa Ullah has come to win. "I study from the time I wake up until the time I go to bed," she says. "And I worry: Did I study enough?" Based on her results, she certainly has studied enough. This is her third year at Nationals; last year she placed sixteenth. (Aqsa's sister Afra was also a Bee star, competing three times and placing fifth in 1999.) For Aqsa, an eighth-grader, this is her last year. Which means this afternoon is her very last chance to achieve her goal. Today is what those years of study have been for; this is her afternoon to reach for the trophy. The day before the Bee begins, she tells me, "I want this real bad, and my parents want this."

With her long dark curly hair and open smile, she's a bright presence. When she's not studying, she might be drawing or painting—some of her works have been exhibited in a local gallery—or swimming in her native Florida. She's an avid reader and she loves the movies. But that's back home, before the competition began weighing on her. Facing her time onstage, she concedes she's feeling nervous. When she's onstage, she's usually worried about what word she'll get. "You're nervous about your word. You're not thinking about all the people, and ESPN, you're thinking about your word," she says. "When you spell a word right, you're so happy. And then, five minutes after you sit down, you're thinking about your word again."

Aqsa's word this afternoon is *sarwan*. It's one of those short words that seems like a trap: It couldn't be spelled how it sounds, could it? So which vowel is the odd one, and where's the silent double consonant lurking? Aqsa queries the pronouncer for all possible clues: sample sentence, etymology, definition. It is, she realizes with a note of concern, related to a camel—just like the word she missed last year. That might be a clue. She appears stumped, but she uses all the available information to play an educated hunch, issuing each letter confidently as if pure chutzpah will carry her through.

Ding. She seems to crunch inward as she walks off stage. That's disappointment. In the next break, Jesse Zymet, a speller from last year who's coaching this year, asks, "Do you feel like talking?" and she shakes her head wordlessly. Later in the day I see her milling among some spellers and ask how she's doing. Teary eyed, she says nothing.

The next day she seems to have come to terms with being eliminated, though the bruise lingers. "It's not fair," she says. After all her studying, she ranked just as she did last year, tying for sixteenth. "I'm in the same place again," she says with obvious frustration. Adding salt to the wound, she again was dinged out by a camel-related word. What are the odds, two years in a row, of missing a member of the dromedary family?

The Bee, Aqsa says, "is a long journey." The last three years of her life have been "different from normal" because of her dedication to orthographic study. Although she's leaving her spelling studies now, she expects to use the education she received from it, "and nobody can steal that from you."

〰〰〰

By the late afternoon, we're down to the last few hardy survivors. Each of the seven remaining kids in Round Eight has spelled words that few human tongues have ever attempted. Up here in the orthographic high country, nothing is as it seems. *Craquelure. Vibrissae. Zarzuela.* Spelling at this level is far beyond employing quaint classroom rules like "*i* before *e* except after *c*," or memorizing how many *m*'s are in *recommend*. Getting to this chilly altitude requires countless hours of brute memorization, but those who relied on memorization alone are gone. At this level it's about going inside the language, attempting to gain a toehold using every possible tool, from definition and phonetics to knowledge of foreign languages. It requires analysis and understanding, and the ability to make a high-percentage guess based on an intuitive sense of the English language's chaotic construction. It also requires a healthy dollop of luck.

Now that we're down to this last handful of spellers, their parents are invited onstage. They come up with hesitant smiles and ready camcorders and sit in a row off to the left. Whether having one's parents just 20 feet away aids the act of spelling is arguable, but it adds a homey touch. Maddy Kloss's father stops to give his daughter a kiss. She beams. The fourteen-year-old Arizona girl has made it to the final rounds in her first (and last) year here. She's an artsy sort, whiling away her free time playing guitar and creating collages, and she has danced in professional stage productions. Now, her long red hair tied back, she must assemble *mouchoir*. It's clearly French, so she sensibly spells it as *mouchoire*. But no. The crowd lets out a long "oh . . . "

Katie Olsen fares no better with *vinegarroon*, missing the devious double *r*. Upon the bell she shows no expression, though after she gets a big hug from her mother she forces a smile, however briefly. The other spellers prove capable of magic—David Tidmarsh uses his knowledge of Greek to spell *ecdysis*—and the survivors move up yet another round.

Round Nine confounds the statistics: It's all boys. The list of Bee winners is more or less evenly divided between genders, with a tilt toward girls, but regardless of the gender of the winner, the last rounds typically contain representatives of both. Then again, the Bee is known for confounding expectations, as the top-ranked spellers now sitting offstage will attest.

Marshall Winchester walks up to the microphone and takes hold of it, as he always does. He's a tall boy, with glasses that perch slightly down his nose, short dark hair, and, at age twelve, a hint of a mustache. He faces *vimineous*, a Latinate word meaning of or producing long slender shoots. "Vimineous?" he asks, making small music of the word with his soft Southern drawl. Pausing for a moment, he puts his forehead down on the microphone. This one's going to be tough.

But that's the way Marshall likes it. From Waxhaw, North Carolina, he brings a physical exuberance to the event—early this morning he actually galloped across the ballroom, and when spelling he almost yells out his letters. And he's fiercely competitive. "Tomorrow's my favorite day," he said last night. Why? "Because the words are tougher," he explained. Last year, after placing twelfth, he started studying on the way home. In fact, his parents have to discipline him to not study *too* much for the Bee—he has other chores and commitments. He's active in his church, is a student of the Bible, and has won numerous awards for his piano playing. His parents tell him: If you want more Bee study, you have to get up earlier to make time for it. So he's been known to rise at 4:30 a.m. to pore through his word lists. His mother sometimes has to insist he goes out to play, so he does—with his laptop containing word lists. Along with computers and math, his favorite subject is lexicology, the study of the formation and meaning of words. In short, he's a twelve-year-old word fiend. Which translates to great enthusiasm for the Bee; when his orthodontist gives him a new choice for colored braces bands, "Sometimes I get the Bee colors," he says.

Now onstage he's stumped. *Vimineous* gives him no purchase. His mother, to the side of the stage, looks on calmly while aiming her camcorder. Some spellers in this situation would ponder and shift from foot to foot, meditating until the judges tell them they're down to bonus time. But Marshall is not big on hesitation. He again takes hold of the microphone and issues the letters in a strong cadence, like a carpenter confidently tapping in a nail. *Ding.* Marshall,

[3] "Is This as Good as Hollywood Can Make It?"

being Marshall, immediately starts to rush off stage, but he stops to hear the judge spell the word—he's physically exuberant, but he's not impolite.

His mother gives him a hug and Marshall positively beams, his braces reflecting the stage lights. He's happy—and he's ready to come back next year. This is all part of a process for him. "There's no one who was higher ranked than me who can come back next year," he notes later. In the year ahead there will doubtless be plenty of predawn study sessions.

☉☉☉

We're now down to the final three. This remaining trio does something that leaves the audience gasping: They go multiple rounds with each other, all three dispatching their word to survive another round. Given how difficult the words have become, their performance is astonishing. It's possible, or so it appears, that they are robot-trons, each equipped with an orthographic memory chip. Or rather, it might appear that way if each of them did not seem so incredibly human.

Nicholas Truelson, David Tidmarsh, and Akshay Buddiga: the Dreamer, the Ball of Nerves, and the Sleepwalker. Nicholas, the dreamer, appears to lapse into a trancelike state when he spells, conjuring the letters like an ancient blind oracle. David, the ball of nerves, seems to have gulped an espresso and sprinted a fifty-yard dash; between rounds he anxiously keeps his face hidden behind his number placard. Akshay, the sleepwalker, fainted a few rounds ago and still seems closer to asleep than awake, but although he mumbles, the letters spill out flawlessly.

Of the ten million kids who competed, in all those classroom and city and regional bees, then through tough days at Nationals, only these three have survived every hurdle. Now they face the toughest challenge of all—each other. This contest has become the orthographic equivalent of a three-way Super Bowl, and we're in the last few minutes of play.

Akshay steps up and faces a word that sounds like "lan-yap," which is defined as something given gratuitously or as a bonus; in Louisiana it refers to small gifts that storeowners give with a purchase. With little fuss he mumbles out the letters in an affectless monotone: *lagniappe*. His mother-spelling coach speaks nine languages; one of them must be French. In another round he's

42

dealt an esoteric bit of verbiage that's pronounced as "oh-yea." It was a word used by European royal court criers to secure silence before an official proclamation was read. Akshay, as if he lived in seventeenth-century England, spells it correctly as *oyez*. He shows no emotion at his success, neither smiling nor frowning, merely somnambulistically trudging back to his seat.

Nicholas, having mastered such obscurities as *genoise, velleity,* and *ophelimity,* now stares at *parrhesia,* a Greek word meaning boldness or freedom of speech. With his abstracted air, glasses perched far down his nose and a tousled shock of light brown hair, he's central casting's idea of a young college professor. From Sioux Falls, South Dakota, Nicholas is one of the oldest spellers in this year's Bee, at age fifteen. He's a nationally ranked chess player and has won the South Dakota K-8 chess championship three times. This is his third year at the Bee, having placed fifty-ninth in 2002 and sixth in 2003. For the last few days people have predicted that Nick could take the trophy.

Working on *parrhesia,* he stands absolutely still. He stares off into the middle distance, lost in thought, as if peering back through thousands of years to follow the word's journey through various cultures. In the case of *parrhesia,* its known birthplace is Greece. Some form of the word was used in Athens about 2,500 years ago and, we can guess, in the epics of Homer and legends like that of the minotaur.

No one can command the utter silence that Nicholas does. When he falls silent, it's as if the entire ballroom feels compelled to be silent with him. Even the coughing and rustling stop. We are all suspended as Nick imagines the word. His mouth agape, his mien completely inward, he's not spelling, he's channeling. And then, without warning, he sees his vision.

The letters issue forth slowly, as if finally arriving from a long distance, straggling in, exhausted from the trek across the millennia.

P . . . a . . . r . . .

And then he pauses again—apparently the image is indistinct. He waits for the next few arrivals . . .

e . . . s . . . i . . .

It's not a word he knows, and despite his ability to see into the distant twilight, he'll have to rely on instinct alone. So he does what many pros do when they don't know it: He spells it as it sounds. It's not a bad strategy. The alternative is to guess where the errant letters are hidden, and in that way lies madness. *Parrhesia* sounds like *paresia*, and that's how Nick spells it.

After the ding, he listens to the pronouncer spell it, staring off as if trying to imagine that spelling. He walks over to his mother, who gives him a kiss and rubs his back. Then he smiles, virtually the first such smile we've seen in days of competition.

So now we're down to two. In these last rounds, either David or Akshay could misspell a word but still win. If one of the spellers misses, the other speller must spell correctly, plus spell an *additional* word to be declared champion. If he misses that additional word, then the speller who misspelled is back in competition.

These final rounds are legendary for seesawing back and forth. In 2003 it came down to Sai Gunturi and Evelyn Blacklock, both deeply talented orthographers. Sai looked like he had lost after misspelling *gadarene*, but then Evelyn misspelled *gnathonic*, after which Sai went on to win. Considering that the words for the final rounds are chosen from what's called the Championship List—a euphemism for the most tortured bits of lingual madness in Webster's *Unabridged*—even seasoned pros can't feel confident.

In past Bees, the finalists possessed not only remarkable orthographic skills but also one other rare quality: grace under fire. Not this year. David and Akshay are both spelling on borrowed time. Either boy, it appears, might have to be helped off stage if this goes on much longer.

David's previous word was *sophrosyne*, which means restraint over one's impulses—something David is struggling to have right now. Between rounds I'd asked him how he was doing and he gave an anxious shrug: "Pretty nervous," he said, lifting his shoulders in little spasms. I asked him what he had done to prepare. "Read the dictionary," he said. Oh, I asked, how much of it did you get through? "All of it," he said with a little laugh and more shoulder-shrugging spasms. That's hard to believe. You went through the *entire* dictionary? "Yeah, and I made audio tapes of my trouble words so I could test myself." How long did it take? "About three months," he said with another little laugh. The laugh was part nervous reflex, part acknowledgment that reading the entire dictionary—the *Unabridged* is 475,000 words deep—is a colossal feat. I wished him luck and he was off.

Akshay, now at the microphone facing *scheherazadian*, handles the pressure in a completely different way. Having fainted several rounds back, he has been given a chair to sit in as he spells. And he seems to need it. Today he's an odd contradiction: He spells like a lingual freight train, powering through with little hesitation. But his manner is slumberous; his rounded, bespectacled face shows no emotion, his voice barely hovers above a mumble. His sentences, as he asks for definition and part of speech, trail off. Akshay's somnolence and David's espresso-like jitters are perfect opposites. (In fact David, sitting behind Akshay waiting to spell, hides his face behind his number placard in a fit of anxiety.)

Since the families of the finalists are now onstage, Akshay's parents and his brother Pratyush sit just twenty feet to his right. And yes, that's the brother who won the Bee in 2002. Pratyush seems to be feeling all the stress that Akshay is deflecting. As Akshay begins work on *scheherazadian*, Pratyush sits with his eyes shut, then lets his head fall toward his knees, his face buried in his hands. Akshay's father, a technology consultant, sits frozen in place, his arms crossed, his mustachioed face set in a look of concern. His mother, a pleasant-looking woman with shoulder-length hair, a full-time homemaker who has now coached both her sons to the finals, appears to sit in relative calm.

Akshay, in an uncharacteristic gesture, pauses in spelling *scheherazadian*. He masters the first syllable then stares off to his left. The audience holds its breath. Rarely has a full ballroom been so still. He announces that he will start over. (This is allowed, though spellers may not change the letters used in their first attempt—any letter uttered is their official choice and may not be taken back.) When he starts again, he announces each letter with an even cadence, like a drummer at a solemn occasion slowly tapping out a somber beat. He's correct. The crowd breaks into applause, in response to which Akshay slowly blinks and mummy-walks back to his seat.

David, though he's been sitting with his face anxiously buried behind his number placard, seems to have found an oasis of calm as he's dealt *arête*, a

Greek word meaning the sum of good qualities that make character or virtue. He asks for a sample sentence: "Homeric heroes like Odysseus and Achilles are notable for their *arête*," the pronouncer intones. David looks heavenward, curling one leg around the other, and asks if the word passed through French. No, the pronouncer says, it's Greek. "Oh, okay," David says with a little laugh that seems to say, "sorry to have bothered you." And with that he handles *arête* as if it's a commonly used word in his hometown of South Bend, Indiana. As the crowd applauds, he rolls his eyes in amazement at his own success.

When Akshay slouches to the microphone, a judge informs him that he has exhausted regular time twice, so he's now subject to abbreviated time. He'll now have just ninety seconds to spell instead of two minutes. He registers little response to this news, nor to his word, the fiendishly difficult *schwarmerei*. It's a German word meaning excessive and unbridled enthusiasm, of which Akshay himself has not a whit this afternoon.

For a moment, he closes his eyes. He has never fully recovered from fainting, and the waters are again rising higher around him. He asks all the queries, then gets back to the word itself. He has trouble pronouncing it. *Schwarmerei* is something of a three-car collision, with its grouped consonant beginning and a *w* that sounds like a *v*. Worse still, the last syllable is a schwa, an unaccented sound whose spelling is the biggest wild card in the English language.

Akshay makes a couple of awkward attempts to pronounce the word, voicing two mangled versions as a question, even a complaint, as if to say, *Why am I faced with this unspellable word?* Meanwhile, behind Akshay sits David, hunched low, his head totally hidden behind his placard, the only sign of life an occasional jittery placard movement. He's not alone in his anxiety; even the audience is tense at this point.

A beep sound comes from the judges' table; Akshay has exhausted his ninety seconds. He must now spell the word in the next thirty seconds. It's time for his long-shot effort. But something has changed within him. During these many rounds, his inner competitive engine had kept thrumming along, no matter how drowsy his outward countenance. But now even Akshay's inner speller seems to be at low ebb. He spills out the letters as a doubtful guess, the last one inflected upward as a question. In doing do, he spells *schwarmerei* as

46

svermari. The crowd groans in sympathy. He's not eliminated—David must spell two more words; if not, then Akshay is back in. But Akshay has made a surprising mistake. The *sch* spelling is a common German word beginning, and it's unusual that a speller at his level would miss it. It's almost as if he didn't hear it, or he's too tired to muster an educated guess. Akshay trudges back to his seat, his hands in his pockets. (When he gets nervous, he has a habit of balling his hands in his pockets.)

David gets *gaminerie,* a French word meaning impudent or roguish, but that's only one of his challenges. First he has to grab hold of his galloping respiration long enough to utter letters. He has dreamed of this moment for years. His favorite movie is the spelling documentary *Spellbound,* which he has watched ten times. He also has a special fondness for the Charlie Brown video in which Charlie takes part in a spelling bee (and is eliminated, of course). He's been thinking about and studying spelling since his first-grade school bee, in which he misspelled *strengthen.* The slender, modest fourteen-year-old has come a long way since then, tying for sixteenth in last year's Nationals.

Facing *gaminerie,* he works quickly, moving through his queries and pronouncing the word prior to spelling it. A row of photographers sits right beneath him offstage, snapping with flashless snaps. He bites his lip then issues the letters with no hesitation, the look on his face saying, *Well, I can't believe I know this word, but I do.*

"Correct," says head judge Mary Brooks, in her trademark calm intonation. The crowd, momentarily, erupts—he is now just one word away from winning—and David's eyes roll upward in utter marvel that he is standing here at this moment. He puts his placard up to cover his face, holding it there with both hands as the applause goes on. After several seconds he takes it down to dry his tears.

Mary Brooks cuts into the fading applause: "David, since you are the only contestant who spelled the word correctly in Round Fourteen, you will now be given the next word on the pronouncer's list. If you spell it correctly, you will be the champion."

"Okay," he breathes. Akshay sits behind him, expressionless, apparently feeling deep exhaustion. David, upon hearing his word, *autochthonous,* meaning indigenous or aboriginal, looks down, repeating the word. It seems as if he knows it. But if that's true, getting the letters out will still be nearly impossible. He's half crying as he looks skyward, so much so that his voice is down to a whisper as he asks for the definition.

After getting the definition, David asks for a sample sentence, though it's not clear that he hears the pronouncer anymore. He's wiping away his now steady trickle of tears, his breath gone wild, one heave after another. He's climbing near the top of a very high mountain, pulling himself up step by step, even finger by finger, and there's hardly any oxygen up here. He takes hold of the microphone and, with precious little hesitation, starts to spell—taking time to think might be hazardous. He starts to issue the letters, slowly and deliberately, each a small moan, almost a plea, his breath so large and labored that we hear a wind gust on the microphone with every letter. The ESPN roving cameraman adjusts his position. The audience leans forward. The photographers snap wildly. David's mother, the tear in her right eye having paused, sits with a frozen smile. David spells:

A...u...t...o...c...h...t...h...o...n...o...u...s

He's right! David Tidmarsh has won the 2004 Scripps National Spelling Bee! David buries his face in his hands as the ballroom crowd explodes into some kind of deep tribal applause. David's mother, crying and smiling, walks across the stage and gives David, who's also crying and smiling—mostly crying—a huge hug. Akshay walks over to his brother Pratyush, who gives him a deep bear hug as his mother puts her arm around him.

The cheers roll on in a glorious sea of clapping and howling, the cameras snapping like continuous sunlight, the crowd now on its feet. David walks back to the microphone to receive the trophy from the CEO of the E.W. Scripps Company, Kenneth Lowe, a nattily dressed fellow who's clearly at ease onstage. Lowe gives the two-foot-high gold trophy to David, who grasps it in both arms but appears to be unsteady with it. Lowe helps David hold it as the cheers and whistles roll on in wave after wave. David is breathing in spasms, his chest heaving, his face still busy fighting the tears; when once-in-a-lifetime beatitude actually falls on you, you're too overcome to really smile.

An ESPN anchorwoman comes onstage to interview David. She asks a series of questions about how he's feeling, to which he gasps through some short answers that confirm, yes, he was feeling exceptionally nervous.

"Your favorite movie is *Spellbound*," she says. "Is this as good as Hollywood can make it?"

"It's even better," David answers, which sends the audience into a fresh paroxysm of cheering.

⊗⊗⊗

The following evening, the Bee awards dinner banquet is a healthy dose of unadulterated Americana. Flags drape the room, the US Joint Armed Forces Color Guard solemnly parades in decked out in full ceremonial dress, and we stand while the national anthem is played.

We watch excerpts from a collection of interviews that David and Akshay have given in the last twenty-four hours. Matt Lauer on NBC's *Today Show* banters with the two of them. As in all the interviews, Akshay's dramatic faint is replayed, along with a clip from David's final gasping spell. Akshay concedes to Lauer that he had sunk into discouragement at the end. "I didn't care if I was right, I just wanted to get it over with," he says. Lauer imitates Akshay's faint, playing it for humor. In the ABC *Good Morning America* interview, Diane Sawyer addresses the two of them with lighthearted cheer, then imitates David's heavy breathing for chuckles.

At every Bee awards banquet, this one included, speeches are given about how competing in the Bee is its own reward, regardless of the outcome. The theme is "every speller is a winner." Giving a good speech is Wendy Guey, the 1996 champion, who talks about how her high ranking in her first Bee made her a favorite to win, after which the media rained attention on her. Yet the spotlight just as quickly faded when her ranking later slipped, which may have helped her win by taking some pressure off, she says. The best speech is Corrie Loeffler's, who years earlier had been heavily favored to win but did not. She talks about coming to terms with losing, and how it took a number of years to realize that the loss, paradoxically, provided an invaluable education.

When one of the Bee officials speaks, we learn that David Tidmarsh is the sole speller out of 265 who got a perfect score on the 25-word written test that began the Bee, the killer test designed to quickly narrow the field. Which means David can spell even fabulously obscure words like *boeotian* and *rijst-tafel*. It turns out that he wasn't exaggerating when he said he studied the entire *Unabridged* dictionary. Inarguably, he's not a typical kid.

⊙⊙⊙

Several days later, David is a guest on the *Late Show with David Letterman*. Once again, the clip of Akshay fainting is played. Letterman quizzes David, who's clearly nervous, and the host doesn't succeed in getting much in the way of answers. "Are there girl spelling groupies?" "No, there aren't," David responds.

Letterman has created a mock spelling bee. First word: *sumpsimus*. David knocks it out of the park, to Letterman's great shock. Then, *chimichanga*. "Definition?" asks David. "There isn't one," responds Letterman, to audience laughs, after which David easily spells it.

Next word: *Beyoncé*, the pop star. David laughs heartily at the absurdity of a spelling quiz that includes the names of chart-topping singers, and begins to spell. Midway through he pauses and does a dramatic fake fainting, à la Akshay, prompting a huge audience laugh.

To conclude their segment, Letterman's staff has created a special prop for David: It's a custom-built holster for his dictionary. He stands up and puts it on, wearing it like a gunslinger, ready to draw the thick tome at a moment's notice. He stands there beaming, shyly, as the audience chuckles. He's ready for anything now.

Part^2

The Folk Tradition: The American Spelling Bee, from Plymouth Rock to Cable Television

"There was laughing, and talking, and giggling, and simpering, and ogling, and flirting, and courting. What a full-dress party is to Fifth Avenue, a spelling-school is to Hoopole County."

—The Hoosier Schoolmaster, 1871

^{4}A Fine Amusement

Competitive spelling, it might seem, has become ever more tension-filled in recent years. Factors like intense media coverage and a highly organized competition (with a large cash prize) all conspire to increase spellers' anxiety levels. In truth, though, over the long history of competitive spelling, it has never been a sport for sissies. Rigorous toe-to-toe orthography has always required a cast-iron constitution—and the record proves it.

At a 1906 school bee in New York, whose audience was noted for its rowdy spirit—"fully 1,000 persons stormed the school," claimed a reporter— the spellers were so engrossed in the competition that they failed to notice the glee club music intended to cheer them. "Even the Superintendent's long talk about the nobility of failure and other kindred thoughts did not draw them out of their abstraction."

The grueling contest continued apace. One little girl managed *stereopticon*, and a newly arrived immigrant boy navigated through *Mediterranean*—slowly.

"The spelling went on for forty minutes longer before a little girl with black eyes stammered on *accompaniment*. She cried all through the rest of the meeting. She would not let anybody see her face, and when one man asked her name, she only wept harder and would not answer." Still, the hardy survivors hewed bravely to their task. "Sixteen girls and two boys spelled for nearly two hours without making a mistake. They twisted their dresses and blushed, but they spelled."[1]

Indeed, stories of mental stress from competitive orthography are legion. When speller Akshay Budigga fainted onstage at the 2004 Bee, he wasn't the first. In the 1949 national competition, thirteen-year-old James Shea felt dizzy upon realizing he had lost. Then, "Overcome by the strain of almost five hours of competitive spelling, the Brooklyn youth toppled, and would have fallen from the platform if it had not been for a crowd pushing forward to congratulate the finalists."[2]

Perhaps more desperate, at a 1908 spelling match in a New York hotel, which included "brain-crackers" like *eleemosynary* and *martial*, contestants were given malted milk tablets "to recuperate from severe mental strain."[3] Imagine, malted milk tablets. How many hard-battling pugilists in 1908 needed something as stiff as malted milk tablets to buck up under the pressure?

Demonstrating the roughness of the sport still more is an account of an informal contest reported in *The New York Times* in 1877. Two friends, Nellie Wilson and Rosie McGrath, decided to spend a Saturday evening in a spelling match, but emotions soon flared—especially when Rosie threw an "I told you so" at her friend after a misspell. "The expression aroused Nellie's wrath, and the match, which had been solely designed to settle the question of orthographical prowess, became a wrestling match, which ended with both contestants being taken to the station house after a desperate onslaught on each other's fair tresses." The ladies had to appear before a judge, and Nellie, perhaps appropriately, was given five days jail time. "She shook hands with Rosie and departed for a resort where she will have ample leisure to refresh her memory and prepare herself for another spelling bee,"[4] noted the court reporter.

It is, thankfully, the only recorded instance of a jail term resulting from a spelling match.

Congress brought its own brand of rough play to spelling in 1930, when congressmen competed against reporters in a spelling bee broadcast over national radio on a Saturday night. "Twenty-one embarrassed men sat in three rows before an audience of 500 persons and an uncountable radio audience," noted a news account. "The contestants were not uneducated . . . Yet each was eliminated with a comparatively simple word."[5] Simple, indeed: Their misspellings included *abacus* as *abicus*, *achievement* as *achievmemt*, and *optician* as *optitian*.

During the forty minutes of heated congressional-press competition, the group—not surprisingly, given their occupations—played fast and loose with the rules. Scripps Howard reporter Ray Tucker spelled *referable* with two r's but asked to be given another chance because the word had once been spelled that way. His wish was granted, as was Congressman Luce's request for a second try after flubbing *stalactite*. Luce finally sat down after spelling *kimono* with a final *a*. He explained that his fumble on an easy word was due to "such modern conveniences as a secretary and a typist."[6]

The Scripps reporter, Tucker, went on to claim the title of "Champion Speller of the United States," though he conceded that due to the lax rules he should be dubbed "Catch-As-Catch-Can Champ." Representative Luce, garnering second place, noted, "If one must go down to defeat, he can wish no better fate than to be beaten by a member of the press rather than one of his own associates."

Showing far better sportsmanship were the young women of Georgian Court College in New Jersey, who challenged the young men at nearby St. Peter's College to a spelling contest in the winter of 1938. To entice the men into an orthographic match, the women promised to replace their silk stockings with black cotton should they lose. The men took the bait. And the ladies—proving they knew how to snare a man when few were around—even managed to lose the contest, which was broadcast over the radio, by a score of 26 points to 29 points. The college women kept their promise and wore black stockings for a month straight, though it's safe to assume that some of the black-clad spellers soon had gentlemen callers.

۞

The spelling bee, whether fierce or flirtatious, congressional or genteel, is a genuine American folk tradition. The popularity of bees has waxed and waned, but the spelling contest has remained a feature of American life—perhaps to the regret of generations of schoolchildren—since the Puritans landed on Plymouth Rock.

Throughout the 1700s the spelling bee was invariably part of Colonial education. An early American historian named John Howland recorded his technique for winning his class bee in Rhode Island in the late 1700s. In the one-room schoolhouse Howland attended, the teacher allowed each student to pick the word to be spelled by his or her rivals. Having stayed up nights studying the Bible by candlelight, Howland kept a tongue twister in reserve: *Mahershalalhashbaz*. His nine-year-old classmates howled in protest, but Howland himself was able to spell it and, after further protest, find it in the Bible. He was the winner every round.

By the early 1800s the spelling match became a social event. Having no television, apple-cheeked students trooped to the schoolhouse on winter evenings for a high-spirited spelling bee. The emphasis was on fun rather than orthographic rigor, according to one historian: "The small children did not come: it was only for those boys and girls who were in their teens, and were old enough to enjoy and appreciate 'a good time.'"[7]

The fun and frivolity at these evening soirees worried the Puritans, and so these events were dubbed "spelling schools" so the merriment would not be seen as the road to perdition. Dean Dudley, an American writer in the mid-1800s, described one of these "spelling schools" from his youth:

"As soon as the stars began to glisten, boisterous lads and modest misses came from all the neighborhood within two miles. For it is deemed a fine amusement to engage in such spelling matches. A huge pile of fuel lay on the broad hearth; another, torching and crackling, gleamed from the wide fireplace, lighting up a sweet bouquet of faces . . . all became silent and two leaders began choosing their favorite champions. But the prettiest were called first—a pardonable partiality. It was diverting to see the rosy girls flirt bashfully round to their places, holding spelling books up before their sparkling eyes, more to avoid our glances than the fire's bright glare . . . after a hour's sharp contention, the side having a majority of girls, of course, came out victorious . . . As the clock struck nine, our delighted company vanished, the bravest youths offering to escort their favorite lasses home through the bitter air."[8]

As New England society advanced past the Colonial era, the spelling contest fell from fashion, to be remembered with a nostalgic glow. But as countless Conestoga wagons headed west, the new frontier culture once again brought the spelling match to the fore. Those who ventured west were usually the underclass of New England life or recent immigrants. Book learning was a luxury for many frontier families, for whom survival was hoped for but not guaranteed. The ability to spell—correctly, instead of Davy Crockett's famously phonetic tree carving "I killed a bar [bear]"—was a status symbol.

Helping the spelling bee's westward move were several generations of Yankee school teachers who ventured west to take one of the many new jobs. As they had in Rhode Island and Connecticut, these idealistic pedagogues convened "spelling schools" on winter evenings. These western spelling schools were every bit as spirited as their New England predecessors: "It occurs once in a fortnight or so, and has the power to draw out all the young people for miles around, arrayed in their best clothes and their holiday behaviour," wrote one observer. "The excitement of this scene is equal to that afforded by any city spectacle whatever; and toward the close of the evening, when difficult and unusual words are chosen to confound the small number who still hold the floor, it becomes scarcely less than painful."[9]

Not all the spelling contests in the Old West were confined to the rectitude of the schoolhouse. Bret Harte, a writer in the 1800s whose chronicles of the American West were devoured by city dwellers back east, wrote a highly popular poem called "The Spelling Bee at Angels." The verse described a contest in a California gold mining camp between some rough roustabouts:

> There was Poker Dick from Whisky Flat, and Smith of Shooter's Bend,
> And Brown of Calaveras—which I want no better friend

This tough bunch turned out to be surprisingly talented orthographers, spelling *separate*, *rhythm*, and *incinerate*. When Poker Dick misspelled *eiderduck*—uncouthly starting it with an *i*—Bilson from LaGrange thought he might win the bee. However, out flashed Poker Dick's bowie knife:

> And Bilson smiled—then Bilson shrieked! Just how the fight begun
> I never knowed, for Bilson dropped, and Dick, he moved up one.

Harte, claiming the contest's conclusion became too gory to tell, ended his poem thusly:

O little kids, my pretty kids, down on your knees and pray!
You've got your eddication in a peaceful sort of way;
You wants to know the rest, my dears? Thet's all! In me you see
The only gent that lived to tell about the Spellin' Bee![10]

⊚⊚⊚

As the Old West began to be settled, the popularity of spelling contests started to fade. In the same way that spelling schools had fallen from favor in New England, by the end of the Civil War they began to be seen as quaint and old-fashioned west of the Mississippi. But then came a publishing phenomenon that revolutionized the face of American orthography in the 1800s.

A slender novel entitled *The Hoosier Schoolmaster*, published in 1871, became a must-read bestseller, popular from the sod cabins of the Midwest to the perfumed drawing rooms of Philadelphia and New York. It even became a European hit, translated into French, German, and Danish. (In fact, the book is still sold today; a used copy sells for about $8 on Amazon, at last glance.)

Originally published in installments by Edward Eggleston, a newspaper editor, *Hoosier Schoolmaster* transported readers to the rough-hewn days of the Old West, creating a sense of mystique about the primitive lives of frontier settlers. The book's hero, a dashing young teacher named Ralph Hartsook, conquered all challenges by wit and intelligence, overcoming what the book portrays as the simpletons in a small Indiana town.

Readers particularly enjoyed Eggleston's story of a do-or-die spelling contest in Indiana's Hoopole County, with its suggestion of romantic intrigue:

There was laughing, and talking, and giggling, and simpering, and ogling, and flirting, and courting. What a full-dress party is to Fifth Avenue, a spelling-school is to Hoopole County.[11]

The young schoolmaster Ralph finds himself in a toe-to-toe spelling contest with Jim Phillips, the town champion speller and a real lout of a fellow, while everyone looks on. Ralph's spelling skills allow him to win the day, much to the excitement of onlookers:

"Gewhilliky crickets! Thunder and lightning! Licked him all to smash!" said Bud, rubbing his hands on his knees. "That beats my time all holler!"

However, our hero faces one last spelling competitor that evening, the modest and charming servant girl, Hannah. As they spell back and forth, and the words get ever harder, Ralph easily keeps pace with her, until a funny feeling comes over him.

As he saw the fine, timid face of the intelligent brow and the fresh, white complexion, and saw the rich, womanly nature coming to the surface under the influence of applause and sympathy—he did not want to beat. If he had not felt that a victory given would insult her, he would have missed intentionally. The bulldog, the stern, relentless setting of the will, had gone, he knew not whither. And there had come in its place, as he looked in that face, a something which he did not understand. You did not, gentle reader, the first time it came to you.

In other words, Ralph Hartsook is the only character in the history of fiction, possibly in the history of humankind, who *fell in love while spelling*. (Indeed, Ralph and Hannah enjoy a robust courtship, which I won't reveal the end of.)

The wild success of *Hoosier Schoolmaster* propelled spelling bees to great vogue throughout the 1870s. The president of the American Philological Association, J. Hammond Trumbull, addressing the Association in 1875, referred to the "epidemic"[12] of spelling matches.

And a reporter for the London *Times*, traveling in America that same year, noted that spelling contests were "the prevailing infatuation, and every town and village is having its 'bee,' attended by crowds who cheer the successful and laugh at those who are afflicted with a 'bad spell.'"[13] The crowd, noted the reporter, grew quite raucous at these events. At one, a man spelled *receipt* as its homonym, *reseat*, and the judges ruled him out. But, making an emotional appeal to the large audience, the speller refused to leave the stage, and the judges relented after great shouts and jeers. The words that felled those last few spellers that day were *purview, testacious, distension, infinitesimal,* and—when just two spellers remained—*hauser.*

The year 1875, in fact, could hardly get enough spelling bees. In March, 4,000 souls attended a match at the Philadelphia Academy of Music, cheering as eighty contestants competed to the last syllable. The following month New York City held its first public match, at the Cooper Institute, and the large audience became "quite disputatory," according to a newspaper account. "One man insisted on knowing the authority for putting two *L's* in *labeled.* It was found that both ways were correct. The next word created quite a storm. It was spelled *gaconet, gaccanet, jacconette* . . . and no less than ten contestants were retired. The last rendition was given by a gray-haired printer amid peal after peal of laughter. When finally the correct spelling, *jaconet,* was announced, a great clamor arose that the first man had spelled it that way. The Chairman was unable to decide, and the ten were invited back to their seats."[14]

By 9:30 that evening the match had concluded, but "the audience was not satisfied. A hundred suggestions were made looking to a continuance of the sport, but the manager refused to give sanction to anything further, whereat there was great dissatisfaction. Finally the manager withdrew his uncalled for opposition, provided he be released from responsibility, and the crowd, who were filing out of the hall, rushed back." The spectators improvised another match, and "The audience took active part in the fun, making suggestions, demanding authorities, and shouting funny remarks at the contestants."

Two weeks later, across town, an equally spirited "grand spelling match" was held at the Zion Church for the benefit of Zion's Aged Home. "Finally there remained only one bright boy and one bright girl. The pedagogue favored the girl by giving her comparatively easy words, and the little boy hard ones like *cauliflower, rhinoceros, cat-o'-nine tails, dyeing, photograph, rhubarb,* etc., and the audience manifested their disapproval by shouts of 'no partiality.' For a long while the little fellow successfully mastered everything that was given him amid great applause, but finally the relentless pedagogue caught him with *ac-cor-de-on* for *accordion.* The audience hissed vigorously."[15]

After the first prize in the children's category of a $2.50 gold piece went to Miss Georgina Townsend, the adults stood for their match—amidst great giggling. "This match proved very funny, principally on account of the manner of the contestants while engaged in spelling. One fat fellow who slowly digested every word before attempting it, and then slowly brought forth each letter distinct from each other, caused great merriment every time he stood up. Others were overconfident, and when they fell, their discomforture was relished proportionately by the audience . . . at last only the lady and one male contestant was left. Both spelled splendidly for a while and the audience, aroused to a pitch of intense excitement, repeatedly applauded. *Forehead* was given to the man. He looked perplexed, grinned, and scratched his nose. The audience laughed. 'I want to get the word right,' he explained, and there was more laughter. After a few minutes deliberation he spelled it correctly and was roundly applauded. In a minute afterward, however, the word *numbskull* was given him and he went at it without the slightest hesitation, k-n-u-m-b—where he was stopped." The first prize of a $5 gold piece went to Miss Teresa Steward, and the second-prize winner, Mr. T. M. Eato, was awarded a temperance cyclopedia.

〇〇〇

But not everyone was enamored with the fad for public spelling matches. An anonymous social commentator writing in *The New York Times* in 1875 wondered what all the fuss was about. "What could cause the present outbreak of spelling matches . . . is not perhaps easy to determine," he wrote; however, the extent of the "epidemic" was unquestioned. "The Intercollegiate Association may as well disband itself. The spelling matches that have broken out all over the country are far more interesting to the public than intercollegiate contests in speech-making or essay-writing or Greek, or even mathematics," the observer noted. "For, we may be sure that the number of people who could find any intellectual excitement in the bionomial theorem is but a small fraction of the thousands who throng to enjoy these rival endeavors in orthography!"[16]

The spelling bee is particularly American, the observer noted. Orthographic matches "are distinctively ours, not only because they are found nowhere else, but because they are a natural result of certain conditions of life which obtain only in this country."

But these needed conditions—and here's where our observer turns caustic—reveal a flaw in the American character. The popularity of spelling matches is "a natural outgrowth of a widely diffused but very limited education." Moreover, the American fondness for competitive orthography demonstrates "an absence of the copious flow of animal spirits found among the rural population of England, and of that gayety of heart which animates those in corresponding life in France or even in Germany."

In short, he opined, Americans like spelling because they are puritanical sticks in the mud. "People who cannot give themselves up to such spontaneous gayety of heart, and who are possessed of the spirit of Noah Webster, will be likely to seek their recreation in spelling. Could there be a more characteristic and illustrative comment upon the narrow, colorless intellectual and moral tone of the New England life of the rural districts, which is now passing away, than the fact that they were driven to such an arid, barren resource as spelling for amusement!"

Furthermore, the commentator grumbled, the energies of youth could be more profitably spent. If the young lady who had recently won a prize in spelling had won it for cooking, "it would be of better promise for her and for her future husband, who will probably be equally happy whether she spells *khan* with a *c* or a *k*, provided she shows she can and not can't in the management of her household and her children."

Well, goodness, speaking of a narrow intellectual and moral tone . . .

ᘓᘖᘓ

Regardless of any quibbling about the value of competitive orthography, the spelling craze of the 1870s provided a lasting legacy for the contests: In this period the term *spelling bee* was popularized.

During most of the prior 200 years they had been called *spelling schools* (by Puritans uneasy with the idea of amusement) and *spelling matches*. Among Southerners they were sometimes known as *spelling parties*. Edward Eggleston took great delight in the French translation *concourse d'epellation*, noting it in the preface of his *Hoosier Schoolmaster*. Mark Twain used the term *spelling fight* in his classic *Tom Sawyer*, first published in 1876.

The term *bee* in early American life referred to social events in which the entire community came together—like bumblebees in a hive—for a common goal, as in a *quilting bee* or a *barn raising bee* or a *corn husking bee*. As famed journalist H.L. Mencken noted in his discussion of the word, "there was usually some jollification when the work was over."[17] Mencken records that *bee*, by itself, signified a donation party for a pastor, in which neighbors pitched in to repair his house.

Another school of thought suggests that *bee* comes not from the reference to the insect's hive but from English settlers, whose native tongue used *been* or *bean* to mean "voluntary help given by neighbors toward the accomplishment of a particular task."

In any case, the use of the term *spelling bee*, arising during the spelling craze of the 1870s, acknowledged that these contests were as much for amusement as for education. The spelling bee had established itself as a folk tradition built around convivial community life.

◎◎◎

The year 1875 saw one more big event in the history of the spelling bee. The Asylum Hill Congregational Church in Hartford, Connecticut, sponsored a huge spelling bee, and the festivities began with a humorous soliloquy by the town's most famous resident, Mark Twain.

The author had been a masterful speller as a schoolboy, as he wrote in his *Autobiography*. In his class bees he had "slaughtered both divisions and stood alone with the medal around my neck when the campaign was finished."[18] Despite his dazzling orthographic skills, in his remarks that day Twain took characteristic sport with the subject of spelling:

"Some people have an idea that correct spelling can be taught, and taught to anybody. That is a mistake. The spelling faculty is born in man, like poetry, music, and art. It is a gift; it is a talent. People who have this talent in a high degree need only to see a word once in print and it is forever photographed upon their memory. They cannot forget it. People who haven't it must be content to spell more or less like thunder, and expect to splinter the dictionary wherever their orthographic lightning happens to strike.

"I have a relative in New York who is almost sublimely gifted. She can't spell any word right. There is a game called Verbarium. A dozen people are each provided with a sheet of paper, across the top of which is written a long word like kaleidoscopical, or something like that, and the game is to see who can make up the most words out of that in three minutes, always beginning with the initial letter of the word.

"Upon one occasion the word chosen was 'cofferdam.' When time was called, everybody had built from five to twenty words except this young lady. She had only one word—'calf.' We all studied a moment and then said: 'Why, there is no L in cofferdam!' Then we examined her paper. To the eternal honor of that uninspired, unconscious, sublimely independent soul, she had spelled the word 'caff'! If anybody here can spell 'calf' any more sensibly than that, let him step to the front and take his milk.

"The insurrection will now begin."[19]

⊗⊗⊗

With the passing of the 1870s, the spelling bee craze subsided. There continued, however, to be numerous references to competitive orthography as genteel entertainment among people of good breeding.

Typical of these were the Victorian parlor bees of the 1890s hosted by the Orange High School Alumni Association, in Orange, New Jersey. The Association took pleasure in the joys of an orthographic contest, or, as the group put it, "an old-fashioned spelling bee comprised the principle [sic] feature of entertainment."[20] A social reporter from this period noted, "the beauty of this entertainment was that it required no costumes, no scenery, nothing, in fact, but a little advance brushing in of the orthographic art by both sides."[21]

In 1895 the wealthy financier S. V. White, having made a bundle on Wall Street, took part in a bee for charity at the Plymouth Church, proving himself a top speller by besting a gaggle of merchants, lawyers, and high school boys. That is, until he faced *mignonette*. After he spelled it loudly and clearly, "Miss Whitcomb, who gave out the words, looked pained. Like everybody else in

Plymouth Church, Miss Whitcomb is very fond of Mr. White, and she hated to see him humbled . . . a gloomy hush fell on the assemblage."

White, not one to take defeat easily, checked Webster's dictionary himself—which proved him right. However, noted one of the contestants, Mr. White's own wife had decided that the contest's reference volume would be Patterson's Speller, not Webster's.

"'Do you mean to say that if there was an absolute misprint, and it spelled *cat* with a *k*, we would have to be bound by it?' Mr. White demanded to know.

"'I mean to say that I refer you to your wife's rules, and I am glad to do it,' replied Mr. Tupper, with fine diplomacy."[22] At this, general mirth ensued all around, after which the contestants donated their winnings, and the group enjoyed a fine contralto performance by a Mrs. Annie Herling.

⊙⊙⊙

Although the spelling bee's popularity as social entertainment lessened after the craze of the 1870s, the bee as educational method kept gaining momentum. By the turn of the century, the movement toward a national student bee began to coalesce.

In the spring of 1908 a big announcement was made: 31,000 members of the National Education Association would converge in Cleveland in late June for a national meeting. It was going to be quite the shindig. Hosting the event would cost upwards of $60,000, which included the cost of 50 tons of ice to keep the drinking water cool. A 500-boy choir would sing, three bands would perform, and, as one newspaper enthused, "thousands of electric lights would furnish illumination."[23]

"But of all the many interesting features, perhaps none will attract wider popular attention than the old-fashioned 'spelling-bee' which will be held tomorrow morning at 10 o'clock,"[24] the report noted. Touted as the first national bee, the contest gathered eighth-grade students from New Orleans, Pittsburgh, and points in between, all vying to be crowned the country's top orthographer. This first nationwide bee was held on June 29, 1908.

The following day the headline was huge: "Colored Girl Wins Big Spelling Bee,"[25] announced *The New York Times*, which reported: "A little negro [sic] girl, Marie Golden, the 14-year-old daughter of a Cleveland mail carrier, won the international spelling championship . . . The little colored girl had a perfect score."[26] Marie and the finalists were applauded by the audience of 6,000 who had watched the bee, after which she gave a short speech: "I did not enter the spelling contest for personal glory, but to try to help bring honor to my teacher and my school. I studied spelling all I could, and I believe I have learned to spell from reading the newspapers. There are very few words in everyday use that do not appear continually in the papers."[27] And with that, the president of the NEA gave Marie a gold badge signifying that she was the country's champion speller.

Perhaps due to the shock of a black contestant besting all of her white competitors, the next national bee would not be organized until the 1920s. Who would have guessed that competitive orthography would so rattle the status quo?

⊘⊚⊘

Although the idea of a national student bee was on hiatus, Congress in 1913 used a spelling match as a way to play out a traditional battle: legislators vs. the press. In an event at Washington's New Willard Hotel attended by 1,000 spectators, including President Wilson and his daughter Jessie, fourteen members of the Washington press corps went head-to-head against fourteen members of Congress, five Senators, and nine Representatives. The bee's official pronouncer was David F. Houston, the Secretary of Agriculture.

Demonstrating their ability to write the rules in their own favor, the contestants decided that each speller would get *two chances* at their first word. Demonstrating that not everyone in Congress is a mental giant, Representative Foster of Illinois misspelled *Satan*, attempting it as *Saten*. In fairness, the contestants did face some tough challenges. Associated Press reporter Fred Emery missed *reconnaissance*, and Missouri Representative James Lloyd fell to *desiccation*. But Seattle *Post-Intelligencer* reporter Mercer Vernon mangled the straightforward *ecumenical*, and Representative Norris of Nebraska bobbled *cantaloupe*.

The evening was not a fun one for Senator Ashurst, who faced the word *Acacia*.

"The Arizona Senator, tall and erect, stared dreamily at the ceiling a moment, then responded with 'A-c-c-a-k-i-a,'" noted the news account. "Flustered over the laughter his attempt had inspired, he retreated from the stand."[28]

After a vigorous back-and-forth competition, the contest came down to three finalists: *Washington Post* editor Ira Bennett, Ohio Representative Frank Willis, and Washington Senator Miles Poindexter. One might assume a newspaper editor's spelling skills would top those of legislators, but the *Post* editor was dealt *Bdellium*, a tropical tree of Africa, and he missed the silent *b*. Poindexter and Willis kept going word after word, until Poindexter was brought low by *hydrocephalous*, allowing Willis to win. Although the contest had been among only twenty-eight contestants, Willis was proclaimed "Best Speller in the United States"—an example of congressional self-puffery at its finest.

Indeed, Willis's own brother thought the title "Best Speller" was too highfalutin'. So the next day, the representative's brother—expressing classic sibling rivalry—sent Willis a business card on which was printed the name James J. Papptheodorokoummountourgeotopoulous. In a letter the brother sent with the card, he demanded that Willis "justify his reputation"[29] by spelling the name. There is no record as to whether Willis did so.

⁵The Birth of the Modern Bee

As the sunny, optimistic 1920s dawned, the movement to organize a national spelling bee gained cultural currency. Opined one social observer in 1922: "Certainly the indoor sport of spelling bees, so popular in the days when schoolhouses were painted red, is worth reviving—as an antidote to jazz and frivolity."[1] Many states were now bringing together the winners of county championships to compete for statewide titles. These contests were often held at county fairs and were cheered and guffawed at by spectators much like hogtie and apple throw contests.

The big moment came in 1925. That year, the Louisville *Courier-Journal* organized the national spelling bee that is the forerunner of today's Scripps National Bee. (The E.W. Scripps Company assumed Bee sponsorship in 1941.) This same national contest has been held every spring until the present day, except for a three-year hiatus during World War II. Lending the event pomp and circumstance, the *Courier-Journal* held the Bee in Washington, DC, fitting for a contest whose goal was to anoint a national champion.

For that first Bee, more than two million schoolchildren competed at the local and state level, winnowing the field down to nine boys and girls spelling for the championship in Washington. President Calvin Coolidge met with the nine spellers prior to the match.

The winner of that first Bee was Frank Neuhauser, an eleven-year-old from Louisville, Kentucky. His winning word was *gladiolus*. The young champion won a gold medal and $500 for his efforts, then—again—met with the president, this time getting an official handshake of congratulations. Back in Kentucky he was greeted with a hero's welcome. When he grew up, Frank became a patent attorney. At age eighty-eight, he attended the 2002 National Bee, telling CBS News, "The words are, in my judgment, much more difficult."

There's no question that Frank was right about that. Betty Robinson won the 1928 Bee with *knack* (the second-place finalist was unable to spell it—must have been that tricky silent *k*), and in 1937 Waneeta Beckley got away with *promiscuous*—hardly a first-round word in twenty-first-century national competition. In 1940 Laurel Kuykendall gained the self-esteem of the championship for spelling *therapy*.

Certainly there were some brain benders along the way—in 1960 Henry Feldman had to master *eudaemonic* to win, and the following year John Capeheart's final word was *smaragdine*—yet even as late as the late 1960s, some remarkably easy words took the trophy. In 1968 Robert Walker earned gold with *abalone*. The last true giveaway was 1975, when Hugh Tosteson won with *incisor*. In later years, the words became truly tortured. To win in 1999, Nupur Lala had to spell *logorrhea*, and in 2001 Sean Conley's winning word was *succedaneum*.

Indeed, to read coverage of the 1929 Bee is to have doubts about the intellectual capabilities of our predecessors. Words like *planetary* and *monastery* felled spellers early in the day. As one reporter noted, "As the three-hour contest wore on, longer and harder words . . . were brought forth to continue the slaughter."[2] Those harder words? *Adequate, corral, infringement,* and *gamut.* Lest things get too tough, the judges allowed spellers a second chance if they misunderstood. "They were not snared by double meanings. If the judge asked for 'browse' and a speller made it 'brows,' the judge explained: 'I meant cattle grazing, not a part of the head.'" (Oh goodness—was *browse* actually a spelling bee word?) As the competition came down to two finalists, the judges dug out what they thought of as real toughies, like *juniper, mimicked, ingratiate,* and—gasp—*discuss.*

The final word was *luxuriance*, and, after her last competitor missed this softball, Virginia Hogan mastered it to take the trophy. The thirteen-year-old, whose hobbies were basketball and roller-skating, had a grand time after winning. The Omaha, Nebraska, girl pocketed $1,000 as the grand prize and was given a free tour of New York City. "Accompanied by her mother, she is visiting the larger cities of the east," noted a New York reporter, who asked her the secret of her success. "I never forget a word after I see it once," Virginia explained. "No, I don't study words. People tell me spelling is a natural talent of mine. I don't know. I just find words easy to spell."[3]

In Virginia's comment about "not studying words" is the answer to why those early bees were so easy. In that simpler time, it's likely that spellers' study procedures were pretty rudimentary: perhaps a few word lists, maybe some review of basic rules like "*i* before *e* except after *c*." Whatever the case, those spellers' efforts were nowhere near the level of twenty-first-century, Internet-based, year-round, advanced etymological study. In those earlier decades, the champions were essentially just bright kids who showed up to spell.

⊚⊚⊚

The American folk tradition of the spelling bee found its way onto the movie screen in 1930, in the black and white potboiler *Manslaughter*. Starring Claudette Colbert, the movie tells the story of Lydia, a spoiled rich girl who has to learn about life through the school of hard knocks.

Lydia is sent away for a long prison stretch, but when she gets to the Big House, no one likes her—she's too uppity. Yet as the experience humanizes her, she becomes progressively more popular until, finally, the prison spelling bee shows that she's a new person.

Noted one reviewer, "And the climax was when the girls were having a spelling bee in the prison school. Told to choose sides, both at once called 'Lydia.'"[4] With her humanity proven within the context of an orthographic contest, our heroine—whose sentence is miraculously commuted—develops a soft spot for the poor but honest district attorney who sent her away. In the end, she falls hopelessly in love with him, running down the street after him, finally sobbing on his shoulder, "I love you."

While the early national Bees weren't as intellectually challenging as in later years, they were building a tradition. Public interest in the annual spell-off was growing. More newspapers across the country began to accept the Louisville *Courier-Journal*'s invitation to sponsor a speller for the national event. By 1929 there were twenty newspapers sending the winner of a local contest to Washington. After the first few $500 top prizes, the winner was awarded $1,000— big money in the 1920s. In fact, the 1930 winner, whose final word was *albumen*, was given $1,000 in gold.

In the early 1930s emerged a practice that would become a Bee constant: the repeater as winner. In 1931 Dorothy Greenwald did just so-so, placing seventeenth among twenty-three spellers. But the following year she came roaring back to take the trophy, demonstrating that repeating is one of the surest ways to win the top spot. (Dorothy was fortunate to win in 1932, the last year the prize was $1,000. The following year it was reduced to $500 as the cold winds of the Depression caught up with the Bee.)

Throughout the decades of the Bee, the odds have always favored returning spellers, no matter how lackluster their earlier performances. While intelligence and verbal talent were enough to win the Bee back when the winning word was *intelligible* (as it was in 1935), in later decades it helped to have at least a year of national competition under one's belt.

And it helped even in the '30s. The winner in 1934, for example, was the only speller to have returned from the 1933 Bee. That year twelve-year-old Sarah Wilson of Gray, Maine, spelled *brethren* to take the $500 first prize. The contest was broadcast nationwide over the CBS radio network—probably the Bee's first national broadcast. After Sarah won, she was asked to speak to the nation, and she said, "You remember, Daddy, you promised me another $500 if I won first place!"[5] Sarah then announced that she would use the $1,000 for her college education. (The $1,000 would have paid for most of it—tuition even at pricey Harvard was about $800 a year in the mid-1930s.)

The other Bee constant that first appeared in the 1930s was the speller's protest. In the 1931 Bee fourteen-year-old Aaron Butler of Weir, Kansas, spelled *encroachment* as *incroachment*. His errant *i* sent him off stage. But, Aaron protested, *incroachment* is supported by the dictionary. There's no record of what dictionary Aaron pointed to, and no modern dictionary spells it that way; indeed, *encroachment* comes from the Old French *encrocier*—it was likely never spelled with an *i*. Yet the judges put him back in the contest. To help prevent challenges like these, the Bee now lists its official dictionary as the regal Webster's *Unabridged*. If a spelling isn't found in there, the Bee doesn't accept it, no matter what other tome an ousted speller can refer to.

Challenges didn't end with this. Irritated parents have often pointed out—correctly or incorrectly—that their child *did* put the *e* before the *i*. These challenges were greatly reduced once audiotape started capturing the competition; playback settles most disputes. On the other hand, head judge Mary Brooks recalled parents and judges listening to audiotapes after challenges in the 1970s and still struggling to agree. In the modern Bee, successful challenges have fallen to nearly zero, chiefly because the word list is far more carefully assembled, though tape playback is still used.

☉☉☉

The 1938 winner was twelve-year-old Marian Richardson, who mastered words along the lines of *perspicuity, strenuosity,* and *anthropomorphic.* Her winning word was *pronunciation.* News accounts described Marian as "a shy Indiana farm lass with long blond curls," who "can milk a cow as well as spell."[6] Completing the portrait, Marian was educated in a one-room schoolhouse, though she did most of her schoolwork at home with her mother, a former school teacher. "I sort of remember how words look when I read,"[7] said Marian, who told reporters that the prize money would help her attend high school. (In contrast, second-place finisher Jean Pierce, thirteen, from Kenmore, New York, said she would use her $300 prize money to straighten her teeth and have an operation on her nose—possibly the first time a non-Hollywood figure publicly espoused the joys of cosmetic surgery.)

Marian's victory in the national contest, coming as she did from the smallest of small-town America (and a one-room schoolhouse, no less), reflects one of the Bee's most enduring traditions: The list of winners over the decades bears little or no relationship to the size of a speller's hometown. Champions come from tiny villages and from the biggest of big cities. Take a look at recent decades: While 1997's winner was from New York City and 1985's winner hailed from Chicago, the 2004 winner lived in South Bend, Indiana, and the 1995 champion resided in Wynne, Arkansas (population 8,615 in a recent census).

Oddsmakers might assume that a speller from a densely populated area would win almost every year. After all, winning the regional bee in a big city like, say, Atlanta means winning against a much larger talent pool than did the speller from, say, Harrisburg, Pennsylvania. By this line of reasoning, spellers from big burgs like Los Angeles and Chicago would trade the championship year after year, while the hopefuls from Wynne, Arkansas, would just show up to stare longingly at the trophy.

But no. As Marian Richardson and her one-room schoolhouse proved in 1938, the Bee plays no favorites. (Marian, in fact, handily bested that year's speller from Atlanta, who placed third after missing *protocol.*)

The Bee plays no favorites, in fact, in any sense. As early as 1929, a reporter noted that the list of spellers' names sounded like "a League of Nations conference."[8] "Albert Gomo, Vermont State champion, is of French descent. Rose Nelson, selected to represent Maine . . . is of Hebrew descent. Lois Chamberlin and Catherine Green . . . are of English descent. Virginia Hogan . . . suggests the emeralds and shamrock of Ireland. Japan was the fatherland of the ancestors of Teru Hayashi . . . Swedish Americans, especially of Iowa, will expect *The Des Moines Register*'s champion, Irene Olsen, to uphold Scandinavian traditions. The *New Britain Daily Herald* will send the daughter of an Italian immigrant, Teresa Chiarvalleti, into the national finals. Viola Strbac, Wisconsin champion . . . traces her forefathers to Czechoslovakia. Mary Krichov, best speller in the match directed by *The Hartford Times*, is of Polish descent."

As America is a nation of immigrants, the Bee reflects this. The Japanese speller listed above had immigrated to the United States just five years before, with no prior knowledge of English. For recent immigrants, success in this national contest has always been a signifier of acceptance in the New World. Even in the 1920s, a reporter noted that, "in State contests . . . many of the county winners are children of foreign-born parents, so that the spelling contest to some extent plays a part in Americanization work."[9] A word doesn't care if you arrived on the Mayflower or in steerage.

And therein is one of the traits that maintains the Bee's status as a folk tradition. Like America itself, perhaps even more purely, the Bee is a true meritocracy. It is the levelest of level playing fields, paying no regard to whether a speller came from the finest private schools of Philadelphia or a one-room schoolhouse in Floyd County, Indiana, from Japan or from Italy. The old money aristocracy gets no advantage—and neither does anybody else. If you're willing to work hard enough (and you're smart enough), you can do it.

Income is not a key determinant because there is no elaborate uniform or equipment needed. (Though in the twenty-first century, access to a computer is hardly optional.) Some spellers benefit from coaches, which can be an expense, but in truth, virtually all the "coaches" at the Bee are unpaid teachers helping on an ad hoc basis. And as Marian Richardson proved in 1938, a dedicated parent can replace a coach. Furthermore, as National winner David Tidmarsh demonstrated in 2004, an intensely committed speller needs no coach, nor even much spelling help from his parents (in his speech at the awards ceremony, he said, "I want to thank my parents, who helped me occasionally"). So it's clear: Any eligible boy or girl could win in any given year.

❦❦❦

Shortly before World War II there looked to be a movement toward starting an international bee. In January 1938, the NBC radio network, using an elaborate two-way radio hookup, organized a spelling match between Boston and London. On the American side were eight students from Harvard and Radcliffe Colleges; in Europe were eight students from Oxford University. Duplicate word lists were supplied to each team. Each side had a pronouncer, who heaved words across the 3,200 miles to where the other side sat huddled around a microphone and speaker. There, the receiving team's pronouncer repeated the word and its definition. Spellers who missed were not eliminated, but only correct spellings earned their team a point.

As the contest began, the transcontinental orthographers gave no quarter. In the first round the Americans jumped to an early lead as the English misspelled *hemorrhage* and *labyrinthine*. Yet the Londoners pulled even in the next round when an American fumbled *daguerreotype*. The two sides were even at eighteen points each going into the fourth round, when the Americans—who in the previous round had stumbled, characteristically, on *braggadocio*—pulled ahead. The Britons were mowed down by the likes of *isosceles*, *pettifoggery*, and the always treacherous *gamboge*. In the fifth round the carnage came to an end, with the Harvard-Radcliffe students at twenty-eight, the Oxford crew at twenty-four. The English pronouncer noted that his squad, understandably, looked "pale and exhausted"[10] at the match's end.

This match might have been the start of an honorable tradition, but it was never held again. The arrival of war in Europe made that impossible. Yet even without WWII, the event faced a seemingly irresolvable problem: Each team had its own dictionary. The Londoners, of course, used the august Oxford English Dictionary, and the Americans, naturally, clung to the authority of Webster's. The two volumes are so intertwined with their respective cultures that expecting either team to switch would be like asking them to raise a new flag. And the two dictionaries have so many disagreements about spelling that international discord would have been inevitable. It may be best that the event was a one-time affair.

As hopes for a transatlantic bee were interrupted by the war, so too was America's annual Bee. But before it took a three-year break starting in 1943, it saw some notable moments. The 1939 winner, twelve-year-old Elizabeth Rice, spelled *canonical* to win. She had proven her intestinal fortitude the previous year at regionals, where she had to be carried to the competition on a stretcher—there's no record of why—yet she still won the local bee in Worcester, Massachusetts. If there was a trophy for Toughest Speller, she would certainly be a finalist.

In 1941 a thirteen-year-old Detroit boy, Louis Edward Sissman, gave a heart-stopping performance *after* being sent offstage for a misspell. Of twenty-eight spellers who began that Bee, Louis was one of only five remaining kids when he faced *rubicund*. Louis, a tall, bespectacled boy who wore his hair in a neat pompadour, misunderstood the pronunciation, spelling a similarly sounding word that is more commonly known, *Rubicon*. Apparently the definition was not made clear to him: *Rubicund* refers to the rosy skin color that is a sign of good health; *Rubicon* is the point at which any action taken irrevocably commits a person to that course of action, as in "to cross the Rubicon," in reference to the river in Italy that Caesar crossed to march against Pompey in 49 B.C. When the misunderstanding was cleared up, Louis was given another chance and came back onstage to successfully cross the *rubicund*.

Then he, like Caesar before him, kept going. In the last few rounds, Eddie Hall from Richmond missed *paucity*, and Raymundo de la Torre of El Paso stumbled on *beleaguered*. Louis's final word was the tricky *chrysanthemum*, which he mastered to take the $500 first prize.

In the 1942 Bee, Richard Earnhardt achieved a rare feat: He won the contest at age eleven. (Frank Neuhauser, the first winner, had also been eleven years old, so Richard wasn't alone.) To date, no one younger than this has won the national Bee. Richard, by the way, gets credit: Though known for his nervousness, he managed to keep a steady head amidst a field that contained plenty of thirteen-year-olds. As anyone who's ever been eleven years old knows, there's a world of difference between an eleven-year-old and a thirteen-year-old. (Henry Feldman, the 1960 winner, calls the two age groups "different species of humans.")

Because the words in today's Bee are so much more complex, it's likely that the eleven-year-old record will remain—or so one would think. In the 2003 Bee, for a few rounds it looked like nine-year-old Samir Patel might shatter the age record. Yet *boudin* stopped him, and the following year *corposant* felled him. So the eleven-year-old bar remains, though somewhere there's probably a brilliant nine-year-old poring over word lists even as you read this.

ⓥⓞⓥ

Over the years there have been many odd poses from spellers at the microphone, the squirms and skyward looks produced by the anxiety of competition. But few top that of Sylvia Kellum, a speller in the 1948 Bee who came from a one-room schoolhouse in Cazenova, New York. As Sylvia approached the microphone, she invariably crossed the first and second fingers of both hands, and then the third and fourth fingers of both hands—then she hooked her thumbs together. The crowd loved her, and her contortion may have helped: She finished sixth, sent off stage by *desiccate*.

One other speller that year had her own idiosyncrasy. Jean Chappelear, a fourteen-year-old who was the daughter of the town barber in Black Horse, Ohio, placed enormous faith in her lucky penny. She clutched the coin throughout the competition. Whether her talisman played any role is known only by the spelling gods, but certainly luck played a role in that afternoon's match.

In the tense final rounds, it was down to Jean and one other speller, Darrell Flavelle, from Washington, D.C. Darrell faced *variegated*, which he missed, after which Jean nailed it. Just one more word stood between her and the championship. She drew *pharisaical*, relating to or characteristic of the Pharisees, or acting with hypocrisy or self-righteousness. But—her lucky penny wasn't helping much—she missed it, giving Darrell another chance. The next word was *poncho*, which they both missed. Next was *termagant*, which, again, they both missed.

At this point some spellers might have let their lucky penny fall into their pocket, but not Jean. She kept grasping it. It can safely be said that her belief in her penny helped her as much as the coin itself. And when Darrell missed *oligarchy*, Jean made her own good luck by mastering that word and then unlocking *psychiatry*. If further proof were needed, that match demonstrated that chance does play a role in the Bee.

The 1950 Bee will always be remembered as one of the great gladiatorial matches in the history of organized orthography. After twenty-nine rounds, only two survivors stood onstage: Colquitt Dean, a fourteen-year-old from College Park, Georgia, and Diana Reynard, a twelve-year-old from Cleveland. While Colquitt had an age advantage, Diana was a repeater, having earned a spot at Nationals at age eleven. And so the battle began.

They faced some tough words: *heliotaxis, ectogenous, profligacy, alluvial, ossification, rabbinical, psaltery, irradiant, liturgical, resiliency, renege, hackamore*. Both Colquitt and Diana spelled fearlessly, plunging through the letters with cool efficiency. Then Colquitt was given *ferrule*. He issued its letters with his usual aplomb, yet he left out an *r*. No, ruled the judges, that's a misspell— Diana was on the verge of winning.

But then, and there's no record of why, the judges double-checked the word; perhaps Colquitt challenged the ruling. After examining one of their dictionaries—oddly, the Bee had yet to settle on a single volume, as it later did—the judges found that *ferule* was a valid alternate spelling. Clearly, the judges had not done their homework in creating the word list. (In fact, a similar confusion took place earlier in the match. Audrey Matthews, thirteen, had spelled *supersede* as *supercede*. After exiting she went and wept on the shoulder of Benson Alleman, the pronouncer. The judges checked and, yes, it turned out that *supercede* is also correct.)

With Colquitt back in, the match resumed. He and Diana kept up their fearsome pace, pirouetting across word after word as the audience sat on the edge of its seat: *gradient, oblatory, arrogate, prognosis*. Diana faced *tessellated* and knew it had both a double *s* and a double *l*; she dispatched *ichthyology* as if the study of fish was the Ohio girl's favorite pastime. Colquitt was dealt *heterogeneous* and breezed through it as if to say "don't you have any *hard* words?"

And onward they went. Finally, the Bee's director, Charlie Schneider, cried uncle. The dueling spellers had exhausted the third and final supplementary word list. In a first in the twenty-five-year history of the National contest, Diana and Colquitt were declared Co-Champions. The Ohio girl had spelled forty-eight words, the Georgia boy forty-nine. As they sat for photographers, each had a radiant (if exhausted) smile.

There would be two other ties, yet Diana and Colquitt's achievement stands in a category of its own. In 1957 fourteen-year-old Sandra Owens of Navarre, Ohio, (the prior year's runner-up) and thirteen-year-old Dana Bennett of Denver also exhausted the judges' word list; both girls received a trophy that year. But on their final word, *schappe*, which means a silk fabric, both misspelled. So, paradoxically, they were both declared spelling champions after misspelling a word.

Likewise in 1962, when Michael Day of Hardin, Illinois, fourteen, and Nettie Crawford of El Paso, Texas, thirteen, fought a nail-biting match. When that Bee's seventy competitors were whittled down to just the two of them, Michael and Nettie went mano-a-mano for an astonishing fifty-nine words.

Yet at the very end, both misspelled *esquamulose*, meaning without scales, a smooth skin.

So Diana and Colquitt's feat of spelling flawlessly all the way through a heart-pounding duel, then finishing in a tie, sits untouched in the record books.

⊚⊚⊚

The 1951 Bee was most notable for the sartorial panache of its winner, thirteen-year-old Irving Belz from Memphis, Tennessee. Irving was decked out in a plaid shirt, blue shoes, pink shoelaces, chartreuse socks, and a large bow tie—had he been able to sing, he might have been the first Elvis. In the last round, Irving faced Michael Aratingi, thirteen, from New York City. Michael, getting *cuisine*, spelled it with a *q*. Irving easily sautéed *cuisine*, then dashed off *insouciant*—"without anxiety, carefree"—to win. Undoubtedly Irving was an insouciant fellow if he could get away with wearing chartreuse socks in junior high school in 1951. In today's Bee there's a dress code—on the final day spellers must wear the official Bee shirt—so Irving's achievement will likely never be topped.

Beginning in 1953 the Bee winners once again began garnering a huge honor along with their trophy: They got to visit the Oval Office and meet the president. The practice had been standard in the Bee's first few years, in the sunny 1920s, but with the dark days of the Depression, the presidential handshake had been discontinued. In 1953 Elizabeth Hess, thirteen, from Phoenix, took the trophy for spelling *soubrette*. (Soubrette is a dismissive term for a young, flirtatious woman—probably not the type of word today's word panel would choose.) At 9:00 a.m. the next morning, Elizabeth and her mother were ushered into President Eisenhower's office at the White House. Ike, having just been inaugurated six months earlier, apparently felt no rush in his schedule; the leader of the free world and the Spelling Bee champion spent some fifteen minutes discussing the challenges of competitive orthography.

The president, as Elizabeth later recounted to a gaggle of reporters, shared with her a vivid memory of losing a boyhood spelling bee. He had been given the remarkably obscure *syzygy*—the spelling matches in Abilene, Kansas, in the late 1890s must have been fierce affairs. When he was a boy, the word had mowed him down, yet, he told Elizabeth, it's a "perfectly simple word to spell—just like it sounds."[11] Then the president defined the word for her; it's the point of a planet's orbit at which that planet is in conjunction or opposition with another planetary body.

Extending her fifteen minutes of fame, Elizabeth established a tradition that year: She was the first Bee champion to go on television (which had only appeared in American homes about five years earlier). There's no record of what show she went on, though many of the winners in the '50s and '60s appeared on *The Ed Sullivan Show*. The burst of television exposure that all champions now receive has become an important part of the glory of winning. (The 1950s contained one other honor for spellers: They were brought to FBI headquarters to meet J. Edgar Hoover. The FBI director met with all winners up until the early 1960s, and perhaps beyond.)

The 1960s, of course, was a decade of upheaval and change, and its turmoil touched the Bee. In 1962 the Lynchburg, Virginia, branch of the NAACP lodged a protest against what it called the exclusion of black children from the national Bee. But the Bee had no such policy, and national director Jim Wagner told reporters that black students often participated in the national contest. Yet the Lynchburg NAACP said that it had evidence that the rules for the regional spelling bee had been sent to black schools in the area for the first time, apparently by accident, and those schools' officials were later informed that black students would not be allowed to participate. Wagner wrote the NAACP to say that the national Bee did not know about or control the policies of local contests.

After a short period of confusion—during which the threat of litigation hung over the national Bee—the source of the problem became clear. Carter Glass, general manager of the *Lynchburg News*, the paper that sponsored the area's regional bee, issued a statement saying that the newspaper had adopted a whites-only policy, and that the paper "most certainly would not change it under pressure of the NAACP or any other organization."[12] Adding tension to the situation was the recent order by a federal judge to desegregate Lynchburg's E. C. Glass High School, resulting in the enrollment of the school's first two black students within a week of Glass's statement. With time, of course, things changed; over the following decade Glass High School moved toward integration. (By 2004 its racial makeup was 50-50 between white and non-white.) The Bee, for its part, maintained its policy of open admittance to all students, regardless of race.

The Bee, in fact, has been on the forefront of another important social movement, however inadvertently. Since the national Bee began in 1925, the contest has recognized the equality of girls, or rather, the contest organizers set up the Bee by following cultural precedent, which says that spelling bees are gender-blind. No other national contest has for so long offered a level playing field for both genders, acknowledging that boys and girls can compete as intellectual equals.

It is surely one of the great ironies of the Bee: Cloaked in a hallowed aura of schoolmarm appropriateness and educational value, it sponsored a contest whose rules ran so counter to prevailing social norms. In adulthood the boys would go off to run companies and government offices while the girls would be consigned to roles as helpers or supporters, with most of the heavy intellectual work falling to the male side. Yet at age eleven, twelve, and thirteen they competed toe to toe, with brain power and hard work being the determinants of success—and girls more often won. Completing the irony, the Bee's national contest, with its display of girls' intellectual prowess, has always been held in Washington, DC, a town that until recently allowed only boys to hold the big jobs, and of course that's an issue we're still working on.

With the Bee's level playing field, favoring neither gender, the list of winners reveals essential parity, with a tilt toward the girls. As of 2004, the championship had been won forty-two times by girls, thirty-eight times by boys. Up until about the late 1950s, girls trounced boys by almost two to one. In 1959 boys earned a trophy eight years in a row (though one of those years was a tie between a boy and girl). After that it evened out for decades, though in the early twenty-first century, boys have been on a roll. The five winners between 2000 and 2004 are all boys. Then again, the four winners between 1996 and 1999 are all girls. In the eyes of the Bee, they are neither boys nor girls, but spellers. In its gender-blind competition, it rewards only intelligence and effort (with a healthy dose of luck), which, as the contest has proven over the decades, is independent of gender.

☾☉☽

However much the Bee reflects larger social issues, it's really an event about kids, and through the decades it's been the spirit of its preteen spellers that has kept it fresh. In 1964 the last two spellers on stage were William Kerek, a twelve-year-old from Cuyahoga Falls, Ohio, and Robert Matthews, a thirteen-year-old from Gahana, Ohio. The two Ohio boys went an astounding twenty rounds together, each tightrope walking across challenges like *nepenthe* and *peristalsis*. William, though he was the younger of the two, wowed the audience with his steady, cool demeanor. Finally, Robert tripped on *geophagy*, which was mastered by William, who then handled *sycophant* to win the trophy.

Most notable is the news account of Robert's handling of falling to second place: "The loser shook hands and posed for a picture with the winner, then walked to the sidelines and wept briefly on the shoulder of his father."[13] That short reference to weeping sums up what legions of spellers have felt—including many that never got as far as second place. After hours onstage, and months (or years) of study, this is more than a simple spelling match.

In *A Boy Named Charlie Brown*, a film based on the popular comic strip, Charlie faces an ignominious loss in the school spelling bee, shot down without recourse in front of his classmates. Charlie, of course, being Charlie, remains stoic, yet his humiliation is writ large as his mouth, drawn with a single expressive line, turns down. Linus attempts to console him: "The world has not come to an end." Yet that sentient is of little help to the many spellers who have trudged offstage in front of family and friends. Good grief.

The human drama of the Bee must certainly have been clear to the parents of Jennifer Reinke as they watched their daughter triumph in the 1967 national contest. She spelled *Chihuahua* to win and then immediately burst into a torrent of tears. A photo snapped at that moment tells the story: It shows Jennifer hugging second-place finisher Anne Clark; while Anne has a huge smile on her face, Jennifer's face is contorted into what could be called the

82

agony of victory. Her eyes shut, mouth open in a heart-rending gasp, Jennifer is clutching the second-place finisher like a boating disaster victim clinging to a life raft. What the photo doesn't reveal, however, is the fact that made Jennifer's win so improbable: She didn't speak until she was almost four years old. As a little girl, she had worried her parents, but, her mother explained, "all at once she started and there were no more worries."[14] Yet who would have guessed that a child with such a late start to her verbal growth would win the wordfest known as the National Spelling Bee?

(Jennifer, by the way, just missed competing against future Federal Reserve Chairman Ben Bernanke, who participated in the 1965 Bee. Bernanke misspelled *edelweiss*.)

The unpredictability of the Bee was demonstrated again—as it is perennially—in 1971 when Jonathan Knisely, a twelve-year-old from New Jersey, stood just one word away from winning. Sean O'Malley, a thirteen-year-old from Phoenix, had tripped on *gigot*, meaning a leg-of-mutton sleeve, after which Jonathan easily digested the word. Jonathan then faced *shalloon*, a type of fabric, at which point he was a breathless eight letters away from the championship. Yet the word stumped him—he hadn't the foggiest. So he did what spellers have done since the first American bees in the 1600s. "I just made a guess at it," he said. Fortunately for him, he decided to spell it how it sounds and against all odds he was right. If his unlikely gamble hadn't paid off, Jonathan's name might never have been printed in newspapers across the country.

The following year's winner, fourteen-year-old Robin Kral, freely admitted he had never heard the word *macerate* before spelling it to win the championship. And the 1976 victor, Tim Kneale, thirteen, having just spelled *narcolepsy* for the championship, summed it up thusly: "There was no way I thought I could win."[15] The unpredictable winds of fortune blow every which way at the Bee.

And that provides an emotional safety valve for the competition. The element of luck means that no matter how much a speller studies, there's no way to prepare for every single word—there are 475,000 of them in the *Unabridged*. This unpredictability is a source of frustration, but at the end of the day it's a good thing. The knowledge that luck plays a role allows hard workers some comfort: *It wasn't that I didn't study hard enough or that I'm not smart enough, it's that the big wheel didn't spin my way that day.* Many a thirteen-year-old, sipping lemonade in the Comfort Room (where spellers go to gather themselves after a misspell), has relied upon this truth to salve their soul.

☾☾☾

In 1983 Herman Landau, a resident of Louisville, Kentucky, who had been an assistant to the Bee director in the 1930s, wrote a letter to *The New York Times*, which the paper published. Herman complained that the Bee's choice of words was traveling into hitherto forbidden territory. In his day, he noted, the Bee had two unbreakable rules: no proper names and no foreign words. Yet the 1983 Bee, he pointed out, hinged on words like *ratatouille* and *Balmoral*, which, respectively, are a French vegetable dish and a Scottish cap. "I suggest going back to the old rules,"[16] harrumphed Herman.

At one level, Herman's point was a weak one—separating the "foreign" words from the "American" words in English is like separating the thread from the fabric. The American language is a hodgepodge of Old English, French, Greek, Latin, and many other tongues, so who's to say what a "foreign" word is? Yet Herman's complaint contained an element of truth, or at least revealed a trend.

The words used in the Bee from the 1920s to the 1960s generally reflected a hardy Americanism that didn't stray from English's core origins: *Intelligible, sanitarium, knack, dulcimer, meticulosity*—one found no shocks to the American ear. At some point, it's hard to say exactly when—1970 is as good a demarcation point as any—this began to change. The winning word that year was *croissant*; it's inconceivable that this would have been the spotlighted word in the 1930s. In 1983—the year that Herman wrote to complain about—the winning word was *Purim*, a proper name referring to a Jewish festival. Again, not the kind of word that was highlighted in earlier decades. Yet as American culture, always open to new influences, continued to evolve, to digest and embrace its own diversity, the Bee reflected this. And it continues to do so. In early twenty-first-century Bees, words referring to Muslim holy men were part of the word list, unheard of in earlier decades.

A regional bee in 1983 spotlighted these changes. Linn Yann, a twelve-year-old from Chattanooga, Tennessee, won her local bee, enabling her to advance to the Chattanooga-Hamilton County finals. There she did well, finding herself onstage as one of the final ten spellers. But then she faced *enchilada*—very much a "foreign" word, the kind of entry that Herman Landau had complained about. This was going to be tough.

Actually, given her background it was a small miracle that she had gotten so far. A Cambodian refugee, Linn and her family had lived in forced labor camps for three years when she was a young child. To escape, they had to walk one hundred miles, traveling by night and hiding by day. She was eight years old when her family immigrated to the United States, and she knew only ten English words (the numbers one through ten). Nonetheless, four years later here she was, competing as an equal in this most English-intensive contest. Having learned English in Chattanooga, she spoke with a light drawl that was just as musical as that of her competitors'.

Standing onstage pondering *enchilada*, Linn was stumped. Confusion ran across her young face. She gave it a try, but never having eaten in a Mexican restaurant, it proved beyond her. When she misspelled, the crowd of 400 moaned in unison. (But she certainly gained recognition: The story of her life was later made into an ABC made-for-TV movie called *The Girl Who Spelled Freedom*.) It was just the kind of meeting that has become ever more common in recent decades: a girl from Southeast Asia attempting to master the spelling of a Mexican food name; or a boy of Indian descent endeavoring to spell New Zealand sailing jargon; or a Hispanic girl grappling with a Japanese gardening term. The words in the modern Bee (and the spellers themselves) are an eclectic mix, to say the least. If Herman Landau had gotten his wish, many of these odd juxtapositions wouldn't have happened. But the Bee changes with the times.

At the 1983 national contest, one of the spellers revealed a mettle similar to Linn's, though of a far different type. Of the 137 spellers onstage when that Bee began, 84 were eliminated by the end of the first day. To the judges' surprise, Andrew Flosdorf, thirteen, from Fonda, New York, came forward to say that he, too, should have been eliminated. One of his words that day had been *echolalia*, the compulsive repetition of words. Although the judges hadn't noticed, when Andrew spelled he had replaced the *a* in the middle with an *e*—a clear misspell. At the time there had been some confusion; the judges listened to the tape immediately after he spelled yet concluded he was correct.

Later that day, a fellow speller asked how he had spelled it, and after Andrew rattled it off with the errant *e*, he began to wonder—though not for long. He checked the dictionary and, realizing his mistake, went to the judges. Tearfully, he told them he misspelled. As he later recounted, "I didn't want to be a slime."[17] The judges commended him for his integrity, and Andrew, in an odd twist, suddenly found himself to be a minor media celebrity—eliminated by the contest yet mobbed by reporters. Network television producers called to arrange interviews. The young speller admitted to being shocked by the intense interest in his experience—he had, after all, merely done the right thing. "The first rule of scouting is honesty,"[18] he told reporters.

The final round of that year's Bee came down to Eric Rauchway, thirteen, from St. Petersburg, Florida, and Blake Giddens, thirteen, from Alamogordo, New Mexico, whose sister had placed 103rd in 1980 and 43rd in 1981. (The Bee is replete with tales of sibling rivalry, and doubtless they are recounted in therapists' offices across the land.) After Eric spelled *ratatouille* with a final *i*, Blake added the proper *e* then took a guess—a correct one—on his final word, *Purim*, to become champion.

Blake and Eric and a few finalists were invited to meet the president in the White House Rose Garden, though it was the oddest presidential congratulation in Bee history. One of President Reagan's goals (one that he never achieved) was to eliminate the federal department of education. Reporters at the Rose Garden event asked him if he still hoped to do this. It's probable that the reporters were hoping for a journalistic "gotcha"—thinking that a president surrounded by bright students would be hard-pressed to support eliminating the education department. Yet President Reagan never hesitated. "There's too much Federal Government in education,"[19] he replied.

However, lest the afternoon devolve into political infighting, he displayed his characteristically genial persona, offering his compliments to the Bee finalists, adding, "that's compliment with 'i,' not complement with an 'e.'"[20]

6 The Media Age

The Bee grew rapidly throughout the 1980s, both in the amount of news coverage it received and the number of spellers involved. In 1989, 222 spellers competed at Nationals, dwarfing the typically 40 or 50 spellers in earlier decades' Bees, and almost double the amount from just 10 years prior. The 1989 Bee will always be remembered for the performance of Angela Martin, fourteen, from St. Petersburg, Florida, who was a big fan of the TV game show *Wheel of Fortune*. Facing *boulevardier*, she asked, "Can I buy a vowel?"[1] Her request was denied, and though she mastered *boulevardier* she was later eliminated.

The year's winner was Scott Isaacs, a fourteen-year-old from Littleton, Colorado. His background was typical of many modern-day champions: For him, spelling was not just an avocation but almost a career. Beginning in the fourth grade, he had competed in fifteen local, regional, and national bees, winning eight. The 1989 national contest was his third time in Washington, having been eliminated in previous Bees by the words *psittacine*, "pertaining to parrots," and *telencephalon*, "the anterior part of the forebrain."

In January before that June's Bee, Scott began studying in earnest, focusing on 104 challenging words a day. It was an odd number yet it made sense: 104 words was the most he could fit on a sheet of computer paper. (This reference was the first time any speller was quoted mentioning a computer in their preparation.) Yet as well-prepared and experienced as he was, on the Bee's final day he felt a terrible case of jitters. As he told an interviewer for ABC's *Good Morning America*, he suffered a nervous stomach that morning, and "didn't feel like getting up on the stage at all."[2]

He somehow got himself up there and then began to feel better. "I started recognizing a lot more words and I just kept thinking to myself, 'Well, if you can spell a lot of the words that everyone else is getting, you have a pretty good chance of spelling the words you're getting.'"[3] At the end of the day he remained onstage with just one other speller, Ojas Tejani, twelve, from Hixson, Tennessee.

Late in their final spelldown both spellers tripped on *pasigraphy*, a written language created for universal use. Which meant Scott, having competed in fourteen previous bees, stood just a couple of words away from losing to a twelve-year-old who was a relative newcomer. Ojas was given *senescing*, to grow old, which he missed. Scott handled *senescing*, after which his word was *spoliator*. And here his years of competition made all the difference. He had studied the word but he couldn't recall: Did it end with *er* or *or*? He was going to have to roll the dice. Making a successful guess in the final round of the national Bee, in his last possible day (at age fourteen he couldn't come back), required him to be a cool-headed competitor—or really lucky. Scott chose *or*, allowing him to take home the trophy.

He also garnered a cash prize of $1,500—after years of being $1,000, the prize had begun to levitate. And it continued to do so, elevating exponentially in the years ahead. With the help of various sponsors, the cash prize and accompanying goodies totaled close to $30,000 by 2005.

⊚⊚⊚

In 1992 competitive spelling made one of its periodic forays into front-page news. In June, as that year's presidential campaign began ramping up, Vice President Dan Quayle visited an elementary school in Trenton, New Jersey, to direct a classroom spelling bee. What took place that afternoon would focus the eyes of the world on the New Jersey grade school and, perhaps, influence that year's presidential race.

About twenty-five students and a passel of reporters crowded into a classroom as the vice president began the bee. The students, taking no chances, had drilled vigorously on the words ahead of time; they were ready to spell without hesitation. The first word was *president*, which both a student and Mr. Quayle handled with ease; the vice president earned some laughs with his sample sentence: "The president always tells the vice president what to do."[4] The next challenge was *potato*, which Mr. Quayle instructed twelve-year-old William Figueroa to spell on the blackboard. William stepped right up and wrote POTATO.

The vice president commended him on his good start. "That's fine phonetically," he said, "but you're missing just a little bit." William was stumped, but, at Mr. Quayle's directive, he added an *e*. As soon as the chalk left the speller's hand, dozens of reporters in the back of the room dove for a dictionary, which confirmed that, no, *potato* does not end with an *e*. At a news conference later in the day, the vice president said he wasn't aware that he had stumbled on *potato*.

But the rest of the world soon was. In the days following the vice president's spelling gaffe, William Figueroa's family chose to temporarily leave their house to avoid the throng of television and newspaper reporters. The school's principal was deluged with phone calls from as far away as South America and England (including one call from the Potato Museum in Great Falls, Virginia). Apparently hoping to soften the blow to Mr. Quayle's dignity, the principal told reporters, "I'm not an English person, but I've been told that the word used to carry that spelling."

The principal's valiant effort notwithstanding, the vice president's spelling stumble provided fodder for weeks (if not months) of comedians' routines. William Figueroa, however, kept it all in perspective. Interviewed by an Associated Press reporter, the twelve-year-old commented that the vice president was "an okay guy, but he needs to study."

☉☉☉

In 1994 the Bee took a huge step: It began to be broadcast on ESPN, the cable TV sports channel. The contest had always enjoyed major news coverage, sponsored as it was by Scripps, a large media chain. Yet the Bee's annual television broadcast propelled it into the modern media age. The sleepy folk tradition that had begun on snowy nights in Puritan New England was now telecast live to living rooms across the country. (And, several years later, the Bee began posting round-by-round results in real time on the Internet.)

Television affects the contest in myriad ways—the TV camera is rarely a mere observer. Besides the exponential increase in viewership, allowing a mass audience to feel connected to the contest, TV helps attract talented students, upping the level of competition. Amber Owens, for example, happened to come across the Bee on television in the late '90s. When the Memphis girl found out the prize money was $12,000, she thought, "Hey, I could buy my own horse with that!" Her father turned it into an incentive: You make it to Washington, I'll buy you a horse. Amber made it to Nationals in the fifth grade, and in her eighth-grade year was a top finalist. (She named her horse Alphabet.)

Television coverage prompted the Bee to buff up its image. Start times had to be exact; timing and scheduling became much more of an issue. And for the first time, a dress code was instituted. In prior years some of the contestants, with heads buried in word lists and obscure etymologies, had shown up in less than sartorial splendor. No one really noticed until the television camera's merciless eye pointed it out.

Whether the live broadcast increases the kids' anxiety level is debatable—the nerves of contestants at Nationals have always been stretched taut. Yet certainly as a speller realizes an ESPN roving cameraman is focused directly on them—including those numerous close-up shots—he or she can't help but experience a still greater charge of excitement.

To be sure, the spellers feel the presence of television acutely. Every year the kids at the national contest say things like "I want to last at least long enough to get on television" (the preliminary rounds aren't televised). This is understandable: It's the only way to turn spelling into a semi-glamorous activity. Competitive spelling has never carried one whit of social cachet among the junior high crowd; knowing the etymology of *ratatouille* won't get you into the best clique. Yet nothing is as cool as going on national television—and not some nerdy educational channel, but ESPN, which broadcasts sleek, highly paid athletes performing feats of derring-do. Even better, some schools stop classes to allow students to watch their speller on television—after which the speller gets to return to school *having been on TV.* Now that's totally awesome coolness. Owning the latest iPod is nothing compared to being on television.

ᘙᘙᘙ

The 1997 Bee demonstrated a major trend in the competition, one that has become more prevalent in recent years. That year's winner was Rebecca Sealfon, thirteen, from New York City, whose winning word was *euonym.* Rebecca was homeschooled, a population of students that is far greater at the Bee than among the general population. In the 2004 Nationals, for example, 35 of the 265 spellers were homeschooled, or about 13 percent. Compare this to the percentage of homeschoolers among all students, which, depending on whom you ask, is somewhere between 1 to 3 percent, with some sources claiming as high as 6 percent.

Not only do kids who are taught at home make up a proportionally larger percentage at the Bee, but they are also often among the contest's top performers. In addition to Rebecca Sealfon, the winner in 2001, Sean Conley, was largely homeschooled, and the runner-up in 2003, Evelyn Blacklock, took all her classes at home. The reason for their superior performance is clear: Homeschooled students can focus specifically on training for the competition, in contrast to students at most public and private schools, who study spelling only as an adjunct to other disciplines.

The Bee's official regulations state that a student "must not have eschewed normal school activity in preparation for spelling bees," going on to state—perhaps with homeschoolers in mind—that "normal school activity shall be defined as adherence to the full school schedule and varied academic course load maintained by the majority of the speller's age-mates and grade-mates." [5]

But of course this gives homeschoolers a good bit of leeway. Without a classroom of thirty other students to slow down a bright student, a mixed curriculum of history, math, and language arts can be completed in the morning, with the afternoon dedicated to orthography. The flexible schedule of homeschooling allows more hours for extensive study of word origin and patterns, without which it is nearly impossible to compete at the top levels of the Bee.

All factors like verbal ability and native intelligence being equal, a home-schooler has a dramatic advantage at the Bee over a student whose curriculum has no focus on competitive spelling.

Then again, homeschoolers have no lock on the competition. The 2002, 2003, and 2004 winners (two public school kids and a private school student) found time enough to prepare themselves as well as any homeschooler. Despite homeschoolers' apparent competitive advantage, public and private school kids continue to take the trophy in greater numbers. Why this is true may require a phalanx of educational theorists to explain, or perhaps—like much of the Bee's outcome—it's simply a matter of chance. Then again, where a speller goes to school may not be the determinant. Winning the Bee takes some special spark, some odd combination of ambition and abilities, that isn't created by the school a student studies in.

〇〇〇

The 1998 Bee was one for the record books. That year, Prem Trivedi, a twelve-year-old from Howell, New Jersey, attempted to defy the curse of second place. Having won the number two spot the year before, he had his eye on the top spot in the '98 contest. Yet history said that this would be impossible, or close to it. A second-place finish, while it would seem to position its holder to become the champion the following year, instead is almost a voodoo hex. Rarely in the Bee's many decades has a speller gone on from second place to earn the trophy.

A serious boy, a gifted poet, and popular among his classmates, Prem had been good-natured about his 1997 second-place finish. When he returned home that year his school held a rally for him—to his surprise and embarrassment—and his classmates managed to fit his losing word, *cortile*, into numerous classroom discussions. (Which isn't easy to do, since the word means "an open courtyard enclosed by the walls of a building.")

Prem worked hard for the 1998 Bee, studying spelling up to two hours a day during the week and sometimes five hours a day on weekends. And it showed. Tough words bounced off him like bullets off Superman's chest. Finally, he found himself onstage with just one other speller. Of the 249

92

spellers who had begun that year's contest, it was down to him and Jody-Anne Maxwell, a twelve-year-old from Kingston, Jamaica. (As the Bee had grown, spellers from English-speaking regions from outside the United States began to enter.) Prem stood just a tantalizing handful of words away from taking the trophy and banishing the second place curse. He had a big cheering section at home: His classmates and teachers watched on ESPN, chanting his name as he survived round after round.

He was dealt the word *prairllon*, a French word referring to a small prairie. He attempted a characteristically French spelling of *prerillion*, a misspelling that put Jody-Anne in position to win. Getting the word *chiaroscurist*, she carefully worked through the letters—and got it. As the crowd erupted into sustained applause, Prem realized he had achieved something that no one else had, though it was an odd honor—he had come in second *two years in a row*.

For the first few minutes, facing that fact was rough, then he came to terms with it. "After about twenty minutes I was relieved because I was not going to be in another spelling bee again,"[6] he said. As a consolation prize, his school held its second rally for him, and its director, Mrs. Hirschkowitz, promised him a hug and a kiss.

Jody-Anne Maxwell also earned a place in the record books, not only for winning but also for being the first champion from outside the United States. (Actually, the 1975 winner, Hugh Tosteson, is from Puerto Rico; since Puerto Rico is an American protectorate, the issue of "first non-US winner" falls into a gray area.) Jody-Anne became a national hero in Jamaica, hailed throughout the island nation as a model for schoolchildren to emulate. "Jamaica Shone on the World Stage," touted headlines in the *Jamaica Gleaner*. A spokesperson in the Jamaican embassy in Washington, DC, proclaimed, "She's a folk hero. She's like Michael Jordan."

In addition to the honors accorded her in Jamaica, she was royally feted in the large Jamaican community in New York City. The media coverage was filled with stories like that of Troy Armstrong, a thirteen-year-old Jamaican boy living in the Queens borough of New York City. After seeing a television news report of Jody-Anne's victory, Troy received an enormous hug from his mother, who spontaneously broke into the Jamaican national anthem, and told her son, "I hope you grow up to be just like that."[7]

Part³

Champions' Profiles

"[Winning] feels like an electrical current running through you, as if you're an electromagnet being drawn downward to the floor, and it's all you can do just to keep standing up."
—Ned Andrews, 1994 Bee champion

⁷ Champion's Profile: David Tidmarsh, 2004

David Tidmarsh, to the awe of many Bee observers, will always be remembered as the speller who studied the *entire* dictionary. A slender, fair-haired boy from South Bend, Indiana, David had the temerity to work his way, solo, through a vast lingual voyage, traveling across the frozen tundra, deep lakes, and dark forests of Merriam-Webster's *Unabridged*. That's 475,000 words, a journey that no speller has ever taken, or at least none that has lived to tell about it.

But David did it. Deciding he wanted to better his previous year's Bee performance, he set himself to a task whose ambition would leave most mortals gasping. The *complete* dictionary? That's like climbing Mount Everest. Actually, take that back—plenty of people have scaled Mount Everest. But studying the full *Unabridged* is a feat that, at this point, can only be called Tidmarshian.

So, who is David Tidmarsh?

☉☉☉

I know from talking to David at the 2003 and 2004 Bees that he's a sweet, good-natured kid with a modest but upbeat attitude toward life. When I speak with him a few months after his 2004 win, that hasn't changed a bit; all the media exposure, the *David Letterman* appearance, the national news interviews, the speaking requests, and he's still self-effacing David. I congratulate him on his win; it was a remarkable achievement, I note.

"Yeah, I guess so," he replies.

His favorite video is a Charlie Brown special in which Charlie wins his classroom bee, allowing him to advance to a higher bee. Lucy decides she'll be Charlie's spelling coach, which doesn't help much. "He gets to second place and he misspells the word *beagle*," David says. "Snoopy is really angry at him." David has watched the video ten to fifteen times over the last few years.

David's own efforts to win his first local bee were no more glorious. In the third grade he won his class and school bee, making it to the city bee, only to miss the word *strengthen*.

"It motivated me to work a little harder, but I really wasn't serious about it," he says. "It was just something that I liked to do."

David's seriousness about spelling grew over time; "I've always loved words; I learned to read really early, at age two, my mom says." He reads constantly; he loves mysteries, especially Sherlock Holmes and Joan Lowery Nixon, and he's an avid newspaper reader. (Following current events is a passion of his—he often watches the news on television.) Furthermore, "I also like the competitive spirit of spelling bees, because you work hard, and it will hopefully pay off."

He began focusing intently on competitive spelling after winning his city spelling bee in the fifth grade. "I studied the *Paideia*, and I didn't really study anything else"—and here he chuckles at the enormity of the undertaking—"there were just so many words that I didn't think I could get through it all." In regionals that year, he was eliminated after missing *hyperborean*. Like Charlie Brown, he placed second.

Yet he realized he had a dream. Someday, he wanted to make it to the National Spelling Bee.

Determined to do better the following year, he studied hard, but his sixth-grade effort ended abruptly. He ran into some questionable judging in his class bee. "I got out on the word *stationary* with an *-ary*, because the teacher didn't clarify it, and I thought it was *−ery.*" It was a frustrating experience, but it didn't dim his desire to make it to Washington.

By the time of his seventh-grade bee, he was ready. He had memorized the *Paideia* and pored over the Consolidated Word List, as well as studying an array of root words. He won school and city, then spelled *simpatico* to win his regional contest. He recalls going to Washington that year as an awe-inspiring event. "I couldn't really believe that I had made it; I couldn't believe that I would actually be going to the National Bee."

The competition in Washington "was pretty fierce," he says. "There were a lot of kids at the end who really knew what they were doing. I guess it just inspired me to do better."

I spoke with him briefly at the Bee that year and was struck by his enthusiastic attitude. He was enjoying himself, focused on doing well but apparently not anxious about being eliminated. He moved easily through *electroencephalograph, delitescent,* and the obscure *acajou.* "Everyone wants to be a champion, I think it's just human nature," he told me that year. "There's something great about people cheering for you and knowing you're number one." But David wouldn't be number one in 2003, though he did well for a first-time competitor, placing sixteenth. He was eliminated when he spelled *segetal* as *segittal.*

David's parents asked him if he wanted to try to come back the following year. "I was like, *definitely.*"

☙☙☙

He had achieved his dream of making it to Nationals, but as he went into his eighth-grade year, David set himself a higher bar. Not to win—that was never his goal—but to better his sixteenth-place finish.

With that in mind, he began the task that has set him apart. Is it true, I ask him, did you read the entire Webster's *Unabridged?*

"Yeah," he says, drawing out the word and chuckling at the oddness of it. He knows it's an outrageous thing to have done. But that didn't deter him.

He started in September or October of his eighth-grade year, page by page, and made it to the end about eight months later. "I tried to do a little bit every day," he says. "Even if I wasn't up to studying, I tried to do a little bit." He worked seven days a week, more on the weekends than on weekdays. By February 2004, three months before Nationals, the fourteen-year-old was working a couple hours each night and as much as four to five hours on weekend days. That winter he went on a skiing trip, "and I took the dictionary along," he says with a laugh.

The gargantuan job was possible because he knew which of the 475,000 words he could skip. Since he had spent a couple of years studying various editions of the *Paideia* and the Consolidated Word List, he knew what words were likely to be used at the National Bee. He passed over the easy words that he already knew from his reading; he also skipped words with alternate spellings, which are never used in Nationals.

"I studied probably one out of every ten, or one out of every twenty words," in the *Unabridged*, he says.

He used a green highlighter to mark the words to study. He typed these highlighted words into his computer lists, along with the pronunciation, language of origin, and definition. He then spoke the words into a tape recorder, testing himself by listening back to the tape. Any word he misspelled, he wrote down several times, focusing on creating a picture of it in his mind. The list he created this way totaled somewhere between 10,000 and 20,000 words. (This was in addition to the 23,000-word Consolidated Word List and the 3,800-word *Paideia*.) Although he did some work with his parents and with his teacher, Brian Ginzer, most of his work was solo. (At the awards banquet that year, he said, "And I want to thank my parents, who helped me occasionally"— and he meant that affectionately.)

As he labored through his list, he often noticed word patterns, which he then researched using his CD-ROM version of the Webster's *Unabridged* and the *Dictionary of Prefixes, Suffixes, and Combining Forms*. If he found a root he thought he needed to know, he trolled through his Webster's CD-ROM for other words that used this root, making lists to help him learn the variations of this etymological pattern. "I studied how words travel through different languages," he says.

In short, he gave himself an exhaustive education in the English language.

Forget spelling—those months taught David a vast amount of vocabulary and etymological knowledge. By the time of the 2004 Nationals, he was one of the most highly literate eighth-graders in the nation.

⊚⊚⊚

The 2004 Bee began with a twenty-five-word written test, on which David was the only speller to get a perfect score. To do so, he had to spell monsters like *boeotian* and *rijsttafel*. "Probably the words at the end [the hardest ones] were a little easier than the ones before them because I went out of my way to study obscure words," he says.

As the rounds progressed, he found that his study had prepared him for most anything. Until he encountered *balancelle*. "That was the only word that I was totally unsure how to spell," he says. "I was wondering whether it was *bala* or *bali*, and I just couldn't figure it out." Finally, he played his hunch, *bala*, which was correct, but "it was just really an educated guess."

During his time in Washington he kept his nerves steady by taking walks at night around the lobby. Onstage, he had no special technique for performance jitters, but "I tried to take my mind off the words every once in a while," he says. "Just clearing your mind and thinking about something else." Still, as he worked on achieving his goal of besting his prior ranking, "I guess I was just a little worried."

"At the end I still wasn't sure what was going to happen, because Akshay [Buddiga, the runner-up] was a pretty strong speller," he says. David knew all the words at the end, "but I was looking around the corner, wondering if there was a knockout word." In the later rounds he slowed down his spelling style because he wanted to avoid an accidental slip—and because he was so anxious he was almost hyperventilating.

When he was declared the champion, it was "a combination of relief and excitement and happiness; I was just amazed I had gotten through the entire day."

He recalls the moments immediately afterward, as he stood onstage answering questions. "I think I was a little more calmed down then, it had kind of sunk in, and I just had a big smile on my face because I was so happy."

[7] Champion's Profile: David Tidmarsh, 2004

8 Champion's Profile: Nupur Lala, 1999

Spelling was a secret she kept for years, says Nupur Lala. "I never talked about spelling bees at all through middle school. It was something I did—and then I had my other life," she says. She did have a few close friends she confided in, who supported her competitive interest, but as for mentioning it around school—"absolutely not," she says.

Her self-concealment was driven by her fear of being ostracized as a word geek. She had seen it happen to kids her age, the finger pointing, the derisive snickers, the exile from the narrow mainstream of junior high life. "Other kids are distrustful of kids that age who'd rather be sitting inside reading rather than hanging out at the mall," she says. "I think every kid deep down wants to do something different, but to actually have the courage to do something different is something else."

When Nupur first made it to Nationals in the seventh grade, she was thoroughly intimidated. She had studied, but with no set method or strategy. "I hadn't really organized any materials, I didn't delve into words the way I did in eighth grade," she says. She was overwhelmed by the fact that the words could come from anywhere in Merriam-Webster's *Unabridged*. "I didn't know where to start."

She didn't get far. In the third round she faced *commination*. It was a true softball, but that didn't help. "At that time I was used to getting words I knew. So I get up to the microphone and I get a word I don't know, and I just freak out," she says. "It was a very unnerving feeling. You're not used to such a big environment and so much pressure. It was really scary and I just didn't think through the word. Looking back, it was something I probably would have been able to spell. So, not wanting to handle it, and wanting to get off the stage, I just spelled it *comanation* and left."

It was, she recalls, pretty devastating. She went into the Bee's Comfort Room and cried, and that first day she was in too much shock to think about what she'd learned. "But when I came away from Washington, I realized from observing many others who had done better than me that there are certain ways to study that are much better than others."

She began planning for the following year's contest. "I knew I was a better speller than my rank reflected, so that was a huge motivation." Although she loves words, she acknowledges that she was driven by a strong competitive urge. "It wasn't the coolest motivation," she concedes—but she knows she wasn't alone in this. "People forget that there is a real competitive drive amongst those kids there. As much as everybody goes there because they love words, there is that drive to show their stuff."

In the eighth grade she developed a methodical study strategy that she stuck to diligently. Her mother became her spelling coach, and their work traversed many languages. "Not only would we look at patterns from Greek and Latin, we'd look at patterns from Italian, German, French, and Spanish," Nupur recalls. This work on word origin was critical. "All that repeated exposure to words heightens your intuition to a point where sometimes you can take a guess that's purely based on a gut feeling and get it right."

They drilled constantly with three-by-five index cards. "We would take long sheets of paper and write down words that I missed, and write down the definition by them. Usually if I did that a couple of times a word would stick."

While Nupur was at school, her mother spent most of the day looking up words in the dictionary. "At night, we would learn the definition and she would quiz me." At first, it was slow going: "I remember over the course of 500 words

I'd miss up to 300 or so." But they kept exhaustively drilling until her problem words were narrowed to about 70 words from a list of some 50,000. "We became pretty efficient toward the end."

Going into the 1999 Nationals, she certainly was not favored to win—placing eighty-third her first year had seen to that. But her unspectacular prior performance actually "made things a little easier," she says. Less expectations, less pressure.

Still, she ran into a wall, again in the third round. The round was a psychological hurdle because it had been her downfall the year before. Her word was *corollary*. Like her previous year's third-round word, it was easy. Nonetheless, she blanked. "For some reason it just didn't register, and I was fishing around at that point." Then, perhaps due to her extra year of training, or having been on the National stage before, the word came to her. "I think people have these Gestalt moments onstage and everything clears up, and that's how *corollary* came."

The moment she survived *corollary* she felt she had to leave the stage. "I needed to collect myself, so I just went into the bathroom and I walked off for a little bit and then I was fine . . . that was the most racking moment for me in the Bee."

She faced much tougher words in the next few rounds, yet these words, paradoxically, seemed easier for her. "For me, words like *occurrence* and *harassment* were much tougher to remember than, say, those seven-syllable hair diseases."

After conquering *corollary*, Nupur felt a steadiness as she fielded a passel of uncommon words: *palimpsest, balbriggan, akropodion, cabotinage, trianon, bouchon.* "I wasn't even thinking about the end of the competition or placing or anything, I thought 'let's see how far I can go from this point.'" Her goal for the year had been to make it onto the ESPN broadcast, which was simply a matter of surviving to the second day. "Every speller out there knows that there is luck. So spellers will aspire to the top five or maybe the top ten, because I think it's a bit presumptuous to think you could win out there."

She far surpassed her goal, finding herself in Round Ten with just four spellers left. "That's when the competition started to get a little scary," she recalls. "Then one of the people who I thought was one of the best spellers I've ever seen got a very tricky word; she got the root correct but she didn't get the ending correct." Once again, the Bee had done what it so frequently does: confound expectations. "A lot of people think, 'Okay, if this kid's done well, then that's the kid to beat,' but they don't realize that you're basically competing against a dictionary, too."

Toward the very end, "I got a word that I didn't know at all, *poimenics*, the study of pastoral theology." However, her innumerable hours of etymology study enabled her to take an educated guess—and she got it. Then, the speller who had placed fourth the previous year got the word *kirtle*, a long gown worn by women from the Middle Ages to the seventeenth century. When he misspelled, it was down to Nupur and just one other competitor, David Lewandowski, from Schererville, Indiana. And when David misspelled *opsimath*, a slow learner, Nupur's moment had arrived.

Head judge Mary Brooks announced that there was just one speller onstage, and if that speller spelled correctly, she was the champion. It was not until after Brooks's pronouncement that Nupur first thought, "It could happen." She thought she could win. Then she heard the next word: "When he finally said *logorrhea*, I thought, 'Whoa, okay, it's going to happen.'" Nupur knew the word. She knew she could win.

The CEO of Scripps, who usually presents the trophy, was standing just offstage, and someone was handing him the trophy. "He was talking about what he should do with the champion, and I thought, 'Whoa, this could all be mine.'

"So I thought, 'You know, I can't mess up here,' so that's why I asked for the definition, and I asked for the sentence. Because I thought I needed to calm down.

"And then I spelled the word and it was just . . . it was unbelievable, it felt like a dream.

"It's insane really, because there are so many formidable, amazing competitors out there. And when everyone's out there clapping for you, that's when I think the feeling of achievement really sets in. For me it was very surreal. It wasn't even a blur, it was like slow motion.

[8] Champion's Profile: Nupur Lala, 1999

"Now years later, I can look back at it and think 'this is how I felt,' but at the time I hadn't sorted it out. My dad went up to the hotel room to get a camera and there were thirty-six messages fifteen minutes after I'd won."

Immediately after winning she did a short press conference from the Bee stage, then she was whisked off to the Comfort Room. The phone rang; "I got a phone call from Rosie O'Donnell to be on her show—that was very exciting." That night she was interviewed on MSNBC and CNN's Headline News. She was told to go to bed early; she'd hit the interview circuit at 5:00 a.m. the next morning. CNN did her makeup and she appeared on their morning show, then it was one after another: Fox News, CNBC, *Good Morning America, The Today Show.* The Bee champion often meets the president, but Diane Sawyer explained to her that Bill Clinton was out of the country dealing with the Kosovo peace accord.

"It was amazing how gracious everyone was. What also impressed me was how interested they were in what I studied. I thought they'd ask me the typical kiddie questions like 'how do you feel' and 'what are you going to do with the money' but they also asked the human angle, like what I like to do besides spelling. What also surprised me was that nobody asked me to spell."

Nupur extended her fifteen minutes of fame when the spelling documentary *Spellbound* hit theaters. (The film received an Oscar nomination for Best Documentary.) The movie focused on the 1999 Bee, so Nupur was once again in the spotlight, and she did another round of interviews.

Nupur is now a biochemistry major at the University of Michigan and is leaning toward going to medical school. She recalls her Bee experience fondly. Participating in the event "is one of the memories of my life that I hold most sacred," she says. "It teaches you a lot about yourself, surprisingly, and what you're capable of. It teaches you that with enough perseverance and hard work and diligence you can achieve what you put your mind to. Although there are times when luck isn't on your side, all the values that you learn from doing such a competition keep helping you and return tenfold."

9 Champion's Profile: Wendy Guey, 1996

Early in her spelling career, Wendy Guey was unexpectedly bathed in the glow of media attention. She was the Bee's "it" girl, the speller most likely to win. Reporters clamored to interview her—that is, until her career didn't go as they predicted.

In 1993, at the tender age of nine, she breezed through her class bee and regional bee and found herself—to her own amazement—onstage in Washington, DC. "I couldn't have imagined that I would have done that well," she says. "I was too young to actually understand what was going on; you spell your word and you move on to the next round, and you don't really say to yourself, 'Wow, I'm at the National Spelling Bee.'

"I just figured it was another spelling bee," she recalls.

She charmed the audience as she advanced round by round, this cute young girl leaning up to the microphone to spell words that were longer than she was. Shocking everyone, including herself, she placed fourth in a field of 234 spellers, finally missing *meiosis*. She was instantly anointed the media darling. Reporters crowded around this demure nine-year-old who had almost won a contest dominated by thirteen- and fourteen-year-olds. The young finalist smiled sweetly and cameras flashed. Yes, Wendy Guey was a girl to watch.

For the following year, she studied the same amount, about an hour a day. Once again, she moved easily through her local bees and the early and middle rounds in Washington. Toward the very end she was tripped up by *farouche*, earning a ninth-place finish. No, she hadn't won, in fact she had placed lower, but she was only a fifth-grader. Media coverage continued to spotlight her as a likely winner for the next year.

She resumed her studies with the expectations of a soon-to-be winner. For Wendy, studying was a family affair; both her parents and her siblings helped her drill on word lists. She wasn't an obsessive studier by the standards of the Bee, yet she was a voracious reader, and she followed a practice her father instilled in her; he always told her: Whenever you see a word you don't know, write it down and look it up. She bolstered her language skills enormously this way.

Going into the Bee as a sixth-grader, she maintained her daily hour of spelling drill. But the contest in Washington didn't go as expected: She placed thirty-second. That's an impressive performance, but it confounded watchers; the longer she competed, the lower she seemed to fall. Well, the crowd seemed to say, it turned out that she's not a winner after all.

That year's Bee "was kind of big disappointment," Wendy says. "After you place in the top ten two years in a row, and ESPN starts doing these special segments on you, and people are predicting you'll win—it's a huge amount of pressure on you." But now the media watchers started to turn away.

"It was pretty discouraging, because you keep coming back, and it was like, 'Oh, this person's back again.'"

As she showed up for the Bee in her seventh-grade year, in 1996, the spotlight on her had grown cold. "I think at that point ESPN was like, 'Okay, whatever, we're going to move on to our next hot speller.'" Clearly, she had fallen from grace. Wendy who?

〇〇〇

Now that she was in the seventh grade, she felt an extra motivation in her spelling studies: She wanted to improve her SAT test score. She knew that if she took the SAT test early and got a high enough score, she could participate in a college level program, which she was very interested in doing. "Understanding the words' meaning and understanding how you could use these words in everyday life became much more important to me than it was in previous years," she recalls. "The Spelling Bee took on a whole new meaning for me. It wasn't about just knowing your words to spell them for competition; it was 'how can I apply this in my everyday life?'"

Still another motivation for more study was her speller's pride, which prompted her to boost her drill time a bit past the one-hour-a-day mark. "I may have been slightly more motivated because I thought to myself, 'Wow, my performance gets worse and worse every year! I really don't want to bottom out this year.'"

The night before the last day of the Bee in her seventh-grade year, "I had all these strange dreams," she recalls. "I actually dreamt that I won the Spelling Bee, which is very, very weird." And in a break between rounds during the final afternoon, Wendy was traveling up the escalator in the hotel and happened to stand next to a woman who was a psychology professor at Cornell University. The woman asked Wendy how she was feeling, and Wendy said she felt nervous. "And she says, 'I really think you have the potential to win this Bee,'" Wendy recalls. "'Just have confidence in yourself.'" That moment had a great effect on her.

The words seemed to fall her way that year, more than ever before. Wendy survived to the final rounds, and when she was one of only three spellers left onstage, she felt she had a chance of winning. She faced the word *lacertilian*— and missed it. But as she waited for the other two girls to spell, she felt happy about the outcome. She knew she had one more year of eligibility, and it looked like she would place third this year—a ranking to be proud of by anyone's standards. "I felt fine about that," she says.

Yet, in an unusual turn of events, both the other girls also missed their words, which meant all three spellers came back. Wendy stepped up to the microphone and got *kouros*. She gave it her best, but no—she misspelled again. Still, she felt confident that she had done well this year.

However, as the audience leaned forward, expecting a winner any moment, the other two spellers again missed their words. So, again, all three were back in, which meant that Wendy, defying the odds, was given a third chance. This time fortune smiled on her; she got a word she knew. The twelve-year-old spelled *vivisepulture* to take the trophy.

As she points out, "There was a lot of luck involved in the year that I won."

The moment when she realized she had won was "unbelievable," she remembers. "It's something that you dream about, it's almost indescribable—I was crying, and I was so happy. It was probably the first time as a kid that I cried out of happiness.

"It was like your life was transformed overnight, because the next day it's all these interviews . . . It was very cool being able to go on all the morning shows. Being a National Spelling Bee winner is very cool."

◎◎◎

After her spelling days came to an end, Wendy attended an arts-oriented high school and was the editor of the school newspaper.

Now a student at Harvard University, she's considering a career in broadcast journalism, although she also thinks about pursuing finance. She took some economics classes and found them interesting and has done an internship with an investment bank in New York City.

In retrospect, she sees that her spelling career made a difference in her life beyond the thrill of winning. She credits her study with dramatically improving her SAT score, better enabling her to get into a prestigious college. And her increased knowledge of English, both spelling and vocabulary, helps her with her academic papers and any other written communication. "Participating in the Bee, being constantly exposed to words, has definitely contributed," she says.

¹⁰ Champion's Profile: Ned Andrews, 1994

Ned Andrews recalls the day in 1988 when the spelling bug first bit him. He was in the second grade, and his teacher organized a spelling contest. "At first it didn't sound terribly interesting, and I decided to sit out," he says in his precise, careful speech. Now a law student, Ned speaks in measured yet congenial tones, as if he was born to a career before the bar. "But when she started calling out the words, I observed, 'this looks pretty fun,' and I was enjoying figuring things out, and I realized I could do better than the people who were up there at the time."

When the teacher called for more volunteers, Ned took the plunge, winning his class bee. After that victory he also won his school bee, going on to compete in his county bee in Knoxville, Tennessee. There, he placed second to the boy who had gone to Washington the year before—an astonishing finish for a seven-year-old.

After his early success he knew he wanted to continue to compete. "I saw it as an opportunity for me to be good at something," Ned says. Aiding him was his constant reading, especially the hours he spent with encyclopedias. "I didn't have many friends at that time, and I lived in a neighborhood where there weren't that many people my age around, so I think I spent a lot of time reading."

The following year, in third grade, he won county and then placed third at regional. He seemed to be on his way up, until he encountered a bout of hubris in the fourth grade. That year, "I didn't study as hard, I guess I didn't think I needed to study as hard, and I wound up turning in my least successful performance of my career, when I finished middle of the pack in the county," he says. In his fifth-grade year he again made it to regional, though he didn't win.

Yet he stuck with it. By the sixth grade—his fourth year of competitive spelling, though he was only eleven years old—his long career bore fruit, and he earned a trip to Nationals. Some spellers feel awestruck upon arriving in Washington, but not Ned. "I get less nervous as the level advances," he says. "The better you do, the more you've proven already, the less you have to prove." He took it easy that week, socializing when others were studying. "I indulged the opportunity to be around other people like me," he recalls, and he greatly enjoyed the group events, which were "just about the most extravagant parties I'd ever seen—all kinds of ice cream parties and whatnot." He did well onstage, making it to Round Seven, when he attempted to spell *nacelle* with an *s*. He placed fifteenth.

After his high finish he redoubled his efforts. Juggling spelling study with an active school life—including the newspaper club and his school's literary magazine—he studied in the car on the way to school and put in an extra half hour in the evening. His mother coached him (after Ned was done competing in the Bee, his mother, Carolyn Andrews, became the word list manager).

As he began working his way back to Nationals that year, the nerves hit hard. "At the classroom level I was positively quaking in my shoes, because if I mess up then, that doesn't look good . . . the classroom and the school level were the times when I had the hardest time holding it together, psychologically speaking."

Once back in Washington he relaxed, relishing his time there enormously. He enjoyed catching up with friends he had met the prior year, with whom he had corresponded through the year. "Both due to my previous year of competition, and having an extra year of psychological maturing under my belt, from a chronological perspective, I was a bit more poised overall—a bit less excited, in the jumpy sense of the term," he recalls. He improved his prior year's ranking, surviving to the eighth round, when he missed the Greek word *triskelion*, replacing the *k* with a *ch*. His fourteenth-place finish was "encouraging rather than discouraging," he says. He knew he would return.

Going into his third Bee in 1994, he maintained his forty-five-minute-a-day spelling study schedule, though he took fewer days off. Ned's goal that year was to become a top ten finalist, but in Washington he encountered an obstacle. He ran into an unknown word, *fuliginous*, and was forced to make a guess. He thought of a word he knew, *uliginous*, and he added an *f*—and he was right.

As the rounds went by and most of the other 237 spellers exited the stage, he made a point of not focusing on how many other spellers remained. "In a spelling bee, your performance does not depend on what other people do or don't do, it's more like a game of blackjack—you versus the dealer; in the spelling bee it's you versus the dictionary." Yet as much as he focused strictly on his own performance, "when it got down to two, I couldn't not notice." At that point, "I remember thinking, 'I could win this thing.'"

That last speller was Brian Lee, twelve, from North Dakota. (Years later, Brian would graduate from Harvard the same year Ned graduated from Yale.) Brian faced *parvenuism*, the behavior of someone who has risen into a social class by sudden acquisition of wealth or power. He missed it. Ned stepped up to face *antediluvian*, relating to the time before the Biblical flood. He knew the word, not from his spelling study but from his voracious reading.

He maintained a controlled demeanor. Ned was a self-described "moderate" speller in terms of his pace; he never hemmed and hawed, yet he never rushed either. As he issued the letters of *antediluvian*, he used that same even pace, after which head judge Mary Brooks said the words that spellers love to hear: "That is correct." Ned remembers her words clearly. He had won the Bee.

Winning "feels like an electrical current running through you, as if you're an electromagnet being drawn downward to the floor, and it's all you can do just to keep standing up," he says. He began answering questions from reporters, but he has no memory of those moments. (*The New York Times* quoted him as saying, "My mom coaches me, and she ought to get paid.")

[10] Champion's Profile: Ned Andrews, 1994

Hours later he was flown to Disney World by private jet to be feted in a parade, in which he rode on an antique fire truck. He did a round of TV interviews, including one with Charles Gibson for *Good Morning America*. It was all a bit much, he recalls. "I was still rather overwhelmed, I was answering all the questions on autopilot."

⊚⊚⊚

Through his teen years Ned volunteered as a staffer at the Bee. After graduating from Yale with a degree in philosophy, he now attends law school at the University of Virginia.

If he was to give advice to a competitive speller, "The number one piece of advice is 'keep your eyes open'—remember what you see in print, remember the various terms you encounter in your studies and periodicals." His other key recommendation: "Read everything you can get your hands on." And don't devote excessive time to rote memorization, he advises. It's inefficient, and it distracts from learning the etymological patterns that better serve a speller. And, he recommends, understand how to use lingual analogies to decipher unknown spellings. "Use your whole brain."

^{11} Champion's Profile: Paige Kimble, 1981

In 1980 the word *glitch* was all but unknown. Virtually no one owned a personal computer, so virtually no one knew of the various snafus that have well acquainted computer users with *glitch*. Yet as twelve-year-old Paige Pipkin stood onstage in that year's Bee, *glitch* was the word that pronouncer Alex Cameron presented her with. She drew a blank. While she could safely assume most of its letters, she knew she was going to have to guess the word's ending.

Every speller is sometimes forced to take an educated leap into the orthographic darkness, but Paige faced an additional hurdle. She was dealt *glitch* toward the very end of that year's contest. This meant the word was bound by one of the great truths of the Bee: An apparently simple word late in the competition is deeply hazardous. If the word were truly that simple, what's it doing in the final rounds of the National Spelling Bee?

"One of the first things that crops into a speller's mind when offered a short one-syllable word at the very end of the Bee is: 'What trick is there in this word?'" she says.

The contest had begun on Tuesday with 112 spellers. By the end of Wednesday's competition, a series of devilish words—*latkes, mahout, revanche, keeshond*—had narrowed the field to thirty-two spellers. Now, at the end of

Thursday afternoon, just two spellers remained onstage: Jacques Bailly from Denver, Colorado, and Paige Pipkin from El Paso, Texas. This was it. One of these two spellers was walking home with the $1,000 prize and the large gold trophy.

Glitch. She stood onstage, facing the crowd, her own tension, and the inky unknown of this odd word. Then the pronouncer, without a request from her, offered what he thought of as help: He pointed out that the word probably came from German. Hmmm . . . German? The classic German word ending is *sch*; did that mean *glitch* was spelled this way? "Having that thought of 'what trick is there' and the pronouncer telling me that it came from German helped not one bit in my decision to spell it *glitsch*," Paige remembers.

Her misspell didn't mean she was out. Jacques Bailly still had to spell *glitch*, which he did easily—after all, he had just heard Paige attempt the only other reasonable possibility—then he faced one more word, *elucubrate*, which he also spelled without doubt. The trophy would go home with Jacques that year. As for Paige, she was headed back to Texas with a determination to win the following year.

ⓢⓢⓢ

When she returned home, a Dallas-area company named Glitsch wrote her a letter, suggesting that they launch a campaign to reverse the Bee's official results; they wanted Paige declared the co-champion—the company understood the value of a public relations stunt. She graciously declined their offer and dug into her studies.

(However, lest she forget the word *glitch*, she received a reminder in her teenage years. "When I turned sixteen and got my first car, my father as a joke ordered vanity plates that said *glitch*.")

She had always been a good speller and was an early reader. "I grew up in the old times when evening newspapers were a big deal, and I can recall my father coming home and reading the newspaper and playing little games with me, 'can you spell . . .'" And spelling games were invariably part of family car trips. The formative moment came in the mid-1970s when she saw a broadcast of the Bee on PBS. "I spelled along with the words and correctly spelled the word *condominium* before the champion—I remember at that point holding the idea that 'I could do this.'"

Later that year her father bought her the Bee's official study guide, then called *Words of the Champions* (now called the *Paideia*), and she burrowed into it. Entering her local El Paso bee in 1979—the area's contest was considered highly competitive—she placed second. After her near-win she began working with her language arts teacher, Robert Dahl, who had coached a handful of regional champions. "He became the driving force in my success," Paige recalls.

It was her constant work with Dahl that earned her the runner-up spot in the 1980 Nationals, when she ran into *glitch*. Then, knowing she had only one more year of eligibility, she turned to her work with a fresh intensity.

"I look back on it and cringe at my immaturity and optimism," she recalls with a laugh. "I don't think I had a single second thought after placing second." Her mind was made up: "I'm going to get back and do this again." Her parents, she says, were likely suffering from churning stomachs at the thought of once again surmounting the slope of regional-national competition. "I think they probably had more of a grip on reality than I did."

In truth, she enjoyed the process. She liked the competition and she liked studying for it—she looked forward to the prospect of another Bee. Her work was constant. She labored semi-methodically through the dictionary and made trips to the bookstore to bulk up her collection of reference books, poring through them for unknown words.

With guidance from Robert Dahl, she studied old word lists from past Bees. Most helpfully, he ran her through a daily spelling bee, with Dahl playing pronouncer and judge and Paige as the onstage contestant. She had no idea what words she'd be asked to spell on any given day. "It was a tremendous confidence builder," she says.

During the school day she squeezed in practice during her lunch hour, then usually another hour right after school, with one to three more hours later in the day. She worked on spelling seven days a week.

In the 1981 Bee her preparation allowed her to advance through the contest with relative ease, though the stress of the event weighed on her. She spelled slowly and deliberately—she hadn't come this far to let a slip of the tongue send her home. As the rounds went by, she spelled *avocation*, *numen*, *esurient*, *vilipend*, *pergola*, and *patella*, tapping out each word letter by letter.

Then she hit a word she had never seen or heard before, *clavis*, which means a key, or glossary. Phonetically it sounds like *clavus*, or perhaps *clavous*. She knew the word was a Latinate, yet Paige had done only a modest amount of root word study. "I had to make my best guess, a wild stab," she says, "and it was luck that I guessed correctly."

As the rounds flew by, the original 120 spellers were winnowed by the likes of *kulak*, *hibachi*, *athodyd*, and *bourgeoisie*. Traci Dunn, a fourteen-year-old from Kentucky, missed *brevet* and began to weep as she was escorted offstage. In contrast, twelve-year-old Lara Hoth of Mexico City was so relieved to have missed *baize* that she enjoyed a big smile upon learning her ordeal was over. All the while Paige kept going, jumping hurdles like *dolcissimo*, *tarmac*, and *captious*.

She felt the tension inching up, however, and her remaining buoyancy seemed to sink when she found herself onstage with just one other competitor. "I remember welling up with tears and all of a sudden having the reality hit me at the moment when there were only two," she remembers. "Partly it was pride and excitement, but I also remember tremendous trepidation at that point.

"All of a sudden the thought hit me, not that I could perform more poorly, but 'oh my goodness, there's the possibility that I might just do the same'" as last year. A repeat runner-up ranking loomed. "I will forever be second place," she feared.

She and the other speller, Jason Johnston, from Benton Harbor, Michigan, went back and forth for an excruciating six or seven rounds. "It seems like a lifetime once it gets down to two," she recalls. Finally, Jason faced *philippic*. "He misspelled and it was a word that I just flat out knew," she says. Paige worked cautiously through *philippic*, and then, knowing a win was one word away, she was given *sarcophagus*. Again, it was a word she knew, yet she took her time with it, issuing the letters one by one, her voice quivering with the intensity of the moment, and . . . she did it. She nailed shut *sarcophagus*, and the audience applauded mightily as she was pronounced the 1981 National Bee Champion.

She recalls welling up with emotion—much of it relief. "I was a child who had put an extraordinary amount of effort and heart and soul into the remote chance that I might have an opportunity to win, and it was before me—it was great pride and great relief." The moment was colored, too, by her knowledge that her parents had also made sacrifices, as had her spelling coach.

She was soon mobbed by the media. She has a photo of herself surrounded by interviewers, with a plethora of microphones recording her every gasp. Reporters peppered her with questions. How did she feel about the two days of competition? She spelled it out: *"T-e-n-s-i-o-n."* How does she feel about her victory? "Just wonderful," she told the crowd, noting, however "that there were several words I could not spell. It's luck." Her spelling coach chimed in that she was the best prepared of any of the students he had prepped. Reporters asked him the secret of winning the Bee. "Total hard work," he explained.

She was then rushed off to numerous television interviews, which were broadcast on that evening's national news and other outlets. Her favorite interview was by a Chinese reporter, for the Voice of America in China, in which English proved to be very much his second language.

☉☉☉

Her victory, though, was far from the end of her association with the Bee. In high school she was a volunteer staffer for the yearly event. She continued to volunteer throughout her college years, and after earning a degree in English—she planned a career as a teacher—in 1991 she heard of an opening as the assistant director of the Bee. She decided to apply, and was hired.

In 1996 she was promoted as director of the Bee's office of business and public affairs, and in 1998 she became the event's director—in other words, she runs the Bee. Or, as she's been dubbed in press accounts, she's the czarina of the Bee. (And the onetime Paige Pipkin is now Paige Kimble. Not surprisingly, Paige's young daughter Sophie has taken an interest in spelling and seems talented at it. "The apple doesn't fall far from the tree," Paige says, though of course Sophie will be ineligible to compete because her mother is the director.)

Paige works in the Scripps headquarters in Cincinnati, Ohio, supervising the myriad aspects of the contest, from rule changes to parental concerns to the judging panel to television coverage, making the yearly pilgrimage to Washington for the national contest. She is spoken of highly as an administrator; whenever the subject of her tenure comes up, among parents or the event's officials, the superlatives begin to flow. Her administrative style is active; she's constantly reviewing the event with an eye to updating it. "I'm a person who likes change, who likes to look at things often to see what can be improved . . . I can guarantee that as long as I'm in here, I'm a proponent of change."

This erstwhile Bee contestant, who once struggled onstage, now sits in the judge's row, providing a guiding hand to a contest that has grown exponentially since her days as a competitor. "You don't go to college or plan your life around the Spelling Bee," she notes with a chuckle, yet that's where life has taken her.

¹² Champion's Profile: Jacques Bailly, 1980

Life sometimes works out in unforeseen ways, as the spelling career of Jacques Bailly plainly proves. Little did Jacques know, when he was a hard-studying orthographer in the 1970s, that his life would stay so intertwined with the Bee.

He might have thought, reasonably, that his 1980 Bee win would close the curtain on his spelling career. After all, he had no contact with the Bee for the following decade.

But he would, in fact, not only return but go on to become the Bee's official pronouncer. As each hopeful-anxious competitor steps up to the microphone, it's Jacques's voice that delivers their spelling challenge. In the innumerable rebroadcasts of the winner's last spell, it's Jacques's voice that guides the proceedings. And as countless spellers across the land study with the audio *Paideia* every year, it's Jacques's voice they hear. If there is such a thing as The Voice of American Spelling, it's Jacques Bailly's mid-timbered pipes.

And when Hollywood filmmakers produced a film about the Bee, they hired Jacques to play himself—did you think they would cast a mere actor in the role? Jacques played the role of Jacques Bailly in the film *Akeelah and the*

Bee; any moviegoer who trooped to their local multiplex heard Jacques intoning words in his crisp yet warm diction. So he has, over the course of twenty-five years, gone from student speller to Hollywood speller-celeb. Life, indeed, is strange.

⊚⊚⊚

As a boy, Jacques was a good student, working diligently at his studies, but he still hungered for more intellectual challenge. Spelling "was something that took up that intellectual energy," he recalls. He compares competing in spelling matches to taking an advanced placement class, "where I could find smart peers and have fun with them and get that intellectual challenge, while other kids were going off to play basketball or play drums."

He began competing in bees at age eleven, with help from Sister Eileen Kelly, a sixth-grade teacher and spelling coach at his Catholic grade school. After school, all the spellers got together and drilled lists of words, taking turns in a big round-robin. After Jacques won his local bee, he began working one-on-one with Sister Kelly, drilling, drilling, and then drilling some more. "We drilled thousands of words," Jacques recalls. "The whole effort was to get more and more lists—we had lists from national bees going back decades." Yet they did very little conceptual work in terms of word roots and exploring language patterns.

In his early bees he ran into fierce competition. The Rocky Mountain region in that period produced an array of top spellers, possibly because its bee included a rigorous one-hundred-word written test. Various regions of the country take turns putting out top spellers, and this was the Denver Era. (There's no logic to which region is on top, Jacques notes; "There's a sort of stochastic, chaotic rhythm to it." He's one of the few people who use the word *stochastic* in conversation; with all those years at the Bee his vocabulary is considerable.) In his first two attempts to step up from the archdiocesan level to the Colorado-Wyoming regional bee, he was eliminated.

In his third year, as an eighth-grader, he got a helping hand from a special coach: his mother. Florence Bailly would, over time, establish a reputation as one of the Denver area's spelling mainstays. She coached Molly Dieveney, who won the 1982 Bee, as well as several other top spellers. She has also tutored spelling pronouncers, helping them learn how to voice uncommon words.

Although Jacques's mother had always helped him in his spelling studies, supplementing Sister Eileen's drill, "By my third year she was kind of frustrated by the whole memorizing lists approach. Between the two of us, we figured out better, more interesting ways to study." They focused on conceptual work, emphasizing word roots. And Jacques, inspired by a trip to France, was learning French.

Armed with this knowledge, in his third year, 1980, he won the Colorado-Wyoming bee, which earned him his first ticket to Nationals. "I had no expectation of winning, I had never been there before. I just thought, 'All these kids are going to be much better than I am.'"

Yet in Washington he kept advancing, round by round. As he neared the final rounds, his excitement grew. "I kept thinking, 'Oh, I'm going to place highly.'"

Finally, to his amazement—and great nervousness—he found himself onstage with just one other speller, Paige Pipkin from El Paso, Texas (now Paige Kimble, the Bee's director).

After Paige missed *glitch*, Jacques faced *elucubrate*. "Which is not a hard word for a spelling bee at that level," he notes. "It's spelled just how it sounds." Jacques spelled the word easily and then, to his astonishment, realized: *I have won the spelling bee!*

Despite his years of hard drill and dedicated study, he had never considered winning to be a possibility—at all. "I just kind of spelled as best I could and wound up winning," he says.

"I remember mostly relief," he recalls. "I was not an exciting winner. I was exhausted and I was astounded. By nature I'm not someone who's going to jump up and down with glee and skip and shout."

As he stood onstage in a state of near shock, his win felt like an odd serendipity. He had seen plenty of kids spell words he might not have been able to handle. "My main thought was, 'I'm pretty sure I'm not the best speller here.' It wasn't like, 'oh, I don't deserve it,' but . . . I was really impressed with the other kids."

[12] Champion's Profile: Jacques Bailly, 1980

A reporter asked thirteen-year-old Jacques what he would do now that he had won. "Just revel in the glory," he replied.

Amidst the many accolades he received, the one he most enjoyed was a parade given in his honor in Boyd, Minnesota, population 300. His mother had a good friend there, so the whole town turned out. "It was just a lot of fun," Jacques says.

☉☉☉

For ten years after his win, he had no contact with the Bee. In college he majored in Latin and Greek, earning a degree in Classics. He also continued to study French and spent a year in Switzerland on a Fulbright scholarship, which helped him learn German. He became an associate professor of Classics at the University of Vermont.

In 1991 he began working as the Bee's associate pronouncer. He sat alongside pronouncer Dr. Alex Cameron during the yearly contests, providing information for spellers' queries. He saw at least one aspect of the event that needed to be changed.

"Honestly, when I joined the Bee, I kind of had an attitude," he recalls. "I didn't like the [word] list." In his view, the words became too hard too early in the competition. In one of his early years, more than half the spellers missed in the third round. "I nicknamed it the lawnmower round."

As the word list has improved in recent years, these lawnmower rounds are a thing of the past. "It's pretty clear now how many kids are going to miss per round, plus or minus," he says. "It's a lot more gradual than it used to be."

Jacques made the leap from associate pronouncer to pronouncer in 2003, after the death of longtime pronouncer Alex Cameron. (Although tragic, there was something fitting about the way Cameron passed; an English professor, he died while reading a book.)

During the days of the Bee, Jacques must correctly pronounce obscure words for hours on end. Simply maintaining concentration would be difficult for most, but Jacques says that's never been a problem for him. He gets into a rhythm that repeats itself speller by speller, he says. "When I'm pronouncing the word, I'm comfortable and enjoying it and having a little conversation with the speller, and it gets a little tense when they spell the word, then there's kind of a valley—okay, they got it right or they got it wrong—and you feel good or bad, and then the next word comes up. I enjoy it."

In fact, "there are so many ways to enjoy the Bee," he says, noting that he relishes watching the kids. "They do have a game face, in a way, but most of them don't have a very good one—you can read them, and it's real neat."

◉◉◉

Jacques is a thoughtful person, full of musings about the nature of language, of education, and of competition. He has seen some change in the spellers over the years—maybe. "I have the impression these kids are more scheduled, more accomplished, more about building things for future possibilities and less about catching turtles and swimming all summer, but I don't know if it's true," he says.

"I think it's a weird effect that each generation [sees itself as] somehow different in one way or another." After all, "I see them, and I think: The same words that are pretty common, pretty good, pretty hard, will get these kids down as [they] used to get us down." He enjoys a chuckle at the philosophical conundrum; things change, but they also stay the same.

The Bee, as he sees it, has many parallels with democratic ideology. Like a democracy, the Bee is representative, with each speller representing a city or region, and the citizens of that region rooting for their speller.

And, "It's got this element of elitism mixed with enough luck, so that everyone can think 'oh, I can spell that,' or 'I can win,'" he says. "It's a deep-rooted thing in American competition; we really like there to be an element of luck, it makes us more comfortable with it, because we don't like elitism, but we like meritocracy."

In keeping with democratic ideals, the contest is all about education, "and education is the major bootstrapping mechanism for any society that has an ideology that says anyone can make it," he observes.

"I always try to think of competitions that would be more educational about language, but it always comes down to the tradition—the Spelling Bee has this tradition behind it. It would be neat to have some other contest, but I can't think of one that I think would be as dramatic and attract as much positive attention and energy as the Bee."

[12] Champion's Profile: Jacques Bailly, 1980

¹³ Champion's Profile: Katie Kerwin McCrimmon, 1979

For some spellers, those kids who live in regions that aren't competitive, making it to the Bee is comparatively easy. If they're naturally bright and they're avid readers, they need only a minimum of *Paideia* study and a dose of luck at regionals to earn a trip to Washington.

But for Katie Kerwin, growing up in the Denver area meant struggling uphill in take-no-prisoners orthographic contests. No slackers need apply. In the period in which she competed, winning regionals in the Rocky Mountain area required a skill level comparable to that of the finalists in Washington. In four years between the late '70s and the early '80s, three Bee winners came from Denver.

The competition was so tough because there was only one regional bee for all of Wyoming and Colorado, so school districts far and wide sent spellers to the Denver regional. And the Denver-area Catholic schools stressed spelling, offering after-school classes and coaching. Katie recalls that in her Catholic grade school, the teachers often conducted "lightning rounds," in which everyone stood up and spelled one letter of a word, having to sit if they missed a letter. "There was a deep, deep bench of good spellers competing hard to get to Washington," she says.

For Katie, who began competing in the fifth grade, winning the tough Denver regional might have seemed more possible because she came from a spelling family. One of eight kids, she had seen two of her siblings do well in Washington. Her older brother Greg placed ninth in Nationals in 1973, and her sister Mary placed fifth in 1975.

Although she hadn't gone to Washington with her brother or sister, "I had a lot of exposure to what Nationals were like, and"—she laughs at the memory—"there was a lot of drilling going on in the house."

Her mother was the driving force. "My mom was extraordinarily committed to helping, and she would drill my brothers and sister," Katie recalls. "For several years there, it was really common in my home to hear my mom firing off words and one of the kids answering back." The siblings even drilled each other. During family ski trips, Katie's sister rattled off words for her to spell as they were lifted up the slope. "To the point where I'd be spelling in my sleep sometimes."

All of this spelling exposure had a natural consequence: As a young girl, competing in school bees, she had big dreams of besting her older siblings. "I remember in the fourth and fifth grade, imagining myself winning," she says.

⊚⊚⊚

In 1979, in her fourth year of competitive spelling, Katie won the arduous Denver regional for the first time. She was headed to the nation's capitol. Onstage in Washington, she found that her uphill climb had given her the skills of a top contender. To be sure, this stage felt different, she recalls. "To see that bank of news cameras, I felt that I was the president at a news conference—it was a really big media event." This was especially true in the second day of competition, when still more video cameras arrived.

Round by round, as the word list departed from what was then the Bee's official study guide, *Words of the Champions*, the challenges became ever more difficult. "Then you're relying on your training," Katie says. She had studied Latin and Greek word roots as well as many other etymological patterns. She had learned, for example, the difference between the sound-alike suffixes

−*cious* and −*ceous* and −*tious*, and this training allowed her to dispatch the obscure polysyllabics she faced.

Clutching a lucky charm bracelet, she stayed in as the 107 spellers were winnowed to the final few. "I'd be sitting there, holding on to the charm bracelet, literally praying for a word that I'd heard of," she remembers. "With an oral competition, it really is luck of the draw—preparation meets luck."

Amidst the pressure, she maintained the spelling method she had developed over the years: She made sure to ask all the questions (definition, part of speech, language of origin), she voiced the word prior to spelling, and she worked through each challenge syllable by syllable.

Still, it became a trial. At moments the intensity was almost overwhelming. She recalls that as the bright stage lights bore down on her, and she stood concentrating so hard, at times, "it almost felt like the familiarity of the word was slipping away."

Even worse, "toward the end the words turned brutal," Katie says. The competition, too, turned brutal. In the final rounds there were just two spellers onstage, Katie and Julie Won. Julie had placed highly in a prior Bee and was favored by many to win that year.

The duel went back and forth, word by word. "I was just trying to survive round by round, but my mother was there with me and she said she could barely breathe," she says.

Katie missed *cappuccino* and *moussaka*, but, fortunately for her, Julie also missed words those rounds. When Katie spelled correctly, and Julie missed *virescence*, Katie was given *maculature*. If she were to spell it correctly, the trophy was hers.

She had never heard the word before, but with her years of study, "It was common sense." She confirmed with the pronouncer that the word, an engraving term, comes from a Latin root. "When a word is from Latin, the simple way to explain is, 'you keep it simple,'" Katie says. "With Greek, you get really carried away," French is full of complexity, and German "has some fancy tricks." But she knew the word's Latin origin meant it was probably spelled as it sounded. Katie's hunch was correct.

When she was declared champion, "It was absolutely life changing, thrilling; at the end, I can still remember to this day, I burst into tears and pirouetted around the stage. I was shocked and thrilled."

After winning, the attention "was incredible—I had swarms of media people come to me," she says. Among her many interviews and photo sessions, she was flown to Hollywood to be on *The John Davidson Show*. When she arrived back in Denver, billboards proclaiming "Congratulations, Katie" festooned the city. She received letters of congratulations from all over the country, and a news cartoonist included her in his daily panel. She remembers those days fondly. "It was a really, really big deal."

◎◎◎

Her victory at the Bee became an entrée into any number of opportunities. The day she won, as she stood onstage answering reporters' queries, she announced that she planned a career in journalism. And, years later, after earning a degree in English literature from Colorado College (where her Bee win helped her land a full scholarship), she became a reporter for the newspaper that sponsored her, the *Rocky Mountain News*.

As a reporter, her focus is politics, and she was the *News*'s Washington correspondent for a period; she has also covered the environment, the courts, and education. With a team of *News* reporters, she was a finalist for a Pulitzer Prize in 1996. She now works part time, which allows her to take care of her three children. (Katie Kerwin became Katie Kerwin McCrimmon along the way.)

In the early '90s, CNN began broadcasting the Bee and hired Katie as a color commentator. When ESPN took over the broadcast in 1994, she stayed on as a commentator for the annual broadcast and has been on every year since. She was briefly spotlighted in the spelling documentary *Spellbound*, as well as the Hollywood release *Akeelah and the Bee*.

Says Katie: "My sister jokes that I'm squeezing every second out of my fifteen minutes of fame."

[14] Champion's Profile: Barrie Trinkle, 1973

Barrie Trinkle is a gifted conversationalist—warm, good-humored, quick to laugh. As she thinks back to what drew her to competitive spelling, the thought prompts one of her moments of merriment. "I was one of those very linear little children, and spelling is a pretty linear activity," she says, chuckling. "There's not a lot of open-ended thinking." However, she adds, spelling may seem linear to her because of the period in which she competed, the early 1970s. Spellers then didn't have Internet resources and, in her experience, didn't dig deeply into the complexity of word roots. Spelling was more about recitation and less about understanding. "I like to joke, 'You couldn't obsess about things then the way you can now.'"

Making it to Nationals didn't require much obsessing for the Fort Worth, Texas, girl. As a fourth-grader in 1970, she won her class and school bee and came close to winning her regional. The following year was her first in Washington.

At the Bee that year she competed in a field of about eighty spellers. "It was a pretty white-bread group back then," she says, noting how different it was from twenty-first-century Bees. And the media coverage, by comparison to later years, was desultory. "It wasn't as much of a scene then."

But being there was exciting. "I was just a little kid," she recalls. Her biggest thrill was sitting next to Jonathan Knisely, because he ended up winning. She herself did pretty well, landing in the middle of the pack with a twenty-eighth-place finish. She missed *horripilation*.

She decided to try to return the following year, an effort her mother applauded and aided. "My mother always made me study," she says, remembering the maternal push with a laugh. "She was a very old-fashioned, '50s kind of parent. She said, 'If you're going to represent your area, you have to study; otherwise, some other kid who would have studied harder than you missed out on the chance to go.'" That logic was irrefutable, and Barrie dedicated about an hour a day to her spelling study, poring through the *Words of the Champions* and books of commonly misspelled words.

Although her mother was her primary coach, her father also encouraged her. "My parents were both journalists and good spellers," she says.

In her second year at Nationals she advanced all the way to the final rounds, placing fifth after missing *allograph*. If she had found spelling interesting before, she now found it thoroughly thrilling—being a finalist was intoxicating. "I thought, 'Oh, this is fun, I'm going to come back and do this again.'"

To enrich her studying, her mother bought Webster's *Unabridged*. Mrs. Trinkle began quizzing her daughter from the thick tome, choosing only those words that she thought were likely Bee words. (Unlike later years, at that point the Bee didn't use proper nouns, eliminating a major hurdle.) "I think we probably got to the Rs," Barrie recalls.

As she stood onstage at the Bee as a seventh-grader in 1973, she felt well prepared. "I remember thinking that I was getting words that seemed hard but that I had spelled before." The Bee was then held in the ballroom of Washington's Mayflower Hotel, a relic from early decades, decorated with chandeliers and gold leaf. Whatever tension infused the elegant ballroom that year as the final rounds neared, Barrie didn't share it. In fact, she felt not the slightest nerves, nor was she particularly challenged. "I could have come back another year," she explains. "I never really felt that this is my last chance and I can't screw it up."

[14] Champion's Profile: Barrie Trinkle, 1973

Through the rounds she stepped up and spelled without doubt: *fantoccini, denazify, trenchant*; it seemed they were all common words for her. Helping, perhaps, was her lucky dress, which she had worn in all her bees since the fifth grade, including both days of each year of her National contests. "By the seventh grade, it was getting kind of short," she says.

Finally, the Bee came down to Barrie and one other speller, a Washington, DC, boy named Steven Hays. Barrie's word was *worsted*, which she spelled easily. Steven got *onomastics*, which was more than he could handle. Barrie quickly moved through *onomastics*, then spelled *vouchsafe*, and—before she knew it—she had won. "I remember being a little disappointed because the other speller missed right away," she says. "I kind of wanted a little more, I wanted it to go a little longer—this was my last chance to do a little bit of it."

Still, as the audience applauded, she felt pure enjoyment. "It was great, it was wonderful," she recalls. "I enjoyed winning, it wasn't this huge release of tension that kids sometimes have . . . I was delighted, my mother was there and she was thrilled—it was great."

◎◎◎

Barrie earned a college degree in earth and planetary sciences and a master's degree in aerospace. She became an aerospace engineer, working on tracking systems in NASA's Jet Propulsion Laboratory.

"Then a few years down the road I got sick of it and chucked it," she says. In 1996, after spending a year in Poland teaching English, she took a job with Amazon.com, working as a book editor for five years. She left Amazon and now works as a freelance book editor, which allows her to spend time with her young daughter.

In retrospect, "I think the aerospace career was a sort of rebellion, really, against my journalist family. In the end, I came back to words. It's built in," she says, with a laugh. "It's a sickness."

As she points out, "It's really hard to get away from what you imprint on as a child."

Her return to words also brought Barrie back to the Bee in a key role. She is a member of the word panel, the handful of Bee organizers who develop the word list each year. She works on the list for Nationals, for regional bees, and for the *Paideia*.

Like any good word panel member, she refuses to reveal any of the mysterious alchemy by which word lists are formulated. "I'm not sure how much I can say," Barrie says, with a characteristic chuckle. Can you at least say how many people are involved? "Not very many, a handful of people. It varies from meeting to meeting." How do the meetings go? "There's very little politicking, we have a good time, it's a congenial group." Beyond that, she's sworn to secrecy.

Looking back at her Bee experience, she sees that it was her way of finding recognition in a period of life in which it's difficult to get recognized. "It's hard to stand out at age thirteen. It's difficult to find something that distinguishes you from the mass of other uncertain people," she says. "It's a funny time of life, it's really hard to be going through that kind of early adolescence. For me, that [the Bee] was how I distinguished myself."

Yet when she entered the working world, she was ambivalent about touting her Bee victory. "I sort of grudgingly put it on my resume when I was applying to jobs right out of college, and it turned out to be this thing that people were fascinated by," she says.

She laughs at the thought of it—the odd fame that results from winning the Bee. As soon as a job interviewer found out she was a spelling champion, "They would drag out their little list of hard words"—and she would promptly spell them all. "I'm sure I got job offers on the basis of that."

[14] Champion's Profile: Barrie Trinkle, 1973

¹⁵ Champion's Profile: Henry Feldman, 1960

Soon after Henry Feldman won the National Bee in 1960, he was eager to distance himself from his spelling days. Spelling, he recalls, was seen as something "for kids"—it wasn't a suitable teenage interest. "And so, even though I enjoyed it a lot, I kind of wanted to move on and leave it behind me," he says.

He had been feted as the town hero in Oak Ridge, Tennessee, after winning—he was elected "mayor for the day"—but his spelling glory "included a certain amount of teasing," he says. "I'd be in gym class and some rough guy would come up and ask me to spell something unprintable."

Yet as much as Henry wanted to leave his spelling career behind him, the notoriety lingered. In 2005, a full forty-five years after his win, he was back in his hometown giving a speech. By happenstance, he was introduced by the man who, as a young boy, had been runner-up to Henry in the 1960 city bee. As the onetime runner-up introduced Henry, he said, "I can't think back to the spring of 1960 without the word coming to mind, *increscent* ..."

⊘⊘⊘

In 1957 Henry was ten years old, and his hopes of getting to the National Bee seemed far-fetched. He won his class and school bees, but during his city bee in Knoxville, Tennessee, his luck ran out. "My big sister beat me," he says. His older sister Joan went on to win regionals, and in Washington she placed twenty-seventh in a field of about sixty spellers.

Seeing the prestige of his sister's trip to Washington, Henry was resolved to get there himself. The following year he spelled his way to regionals, engaging in a tough toe-to-toe match with a girl named Cynthia Barron. He had spent hours studying the Bee's official study guide, *Words of the Champions*, but so had Cynthia. "We both knew the whole book," Henry remembers. Yet luck smiled on him and he found himself in Washington.

His performance at Nationals "went much better than anyone could have expected," Henry recalls. He finished thirteenth in a field of sixty-eight spellers, being eliminated by *faience*, which is a type of artistic pottery. To this day, if he happens to see the word *faience*, usually in a museum, "It still gives me a twinge," he says.

With a taste of success, he studied far harder for his second National Bee in 1959. (But unlike modern-day leading contenders, who study year-round, Henry began studying about a month before his local bee.) He memorized the entire *Words of the Champions* list as well as the lists used in the 1957 and 1958 Bee (his parents had written them down). In addition, "I had various wire-bound notebooks, and odd scraps of paper, words scattered here and there, words that people would find for me."

In Washington, however, things didn't go according to plan. After all his work Henry placed lower than he had the year before, finishing twentieth. He felt the discouragement, yet as he sat in the audience for the rest of the Bee, he found reason for hope. "After I went down that year, I knew every single word."

Still, in 1960, as he considered resuming his spelling studies, he wasn't sure if he wanted to compete. "I've backslid a little already," he thought, "and I made these two respectable showings—why push it?" His parents were okay either way, telling him it was his decision.

"I don't know what it was that pushed me over the line," he says, but he decided to continue studying. "Maybe it was the thought that I had known every single one of those words" after misspelling at the prior Nationals.

He returned to his word lists with renewed energy. His eighth-grade study hall teacher allowed him and a friend to sit outside the classroom and drill spelling lists. But his preparation, it seemed, might not be enough. At regionals he found himself in a fierce duel with a girl named Lillie Linder, who knew the entire *Words of the Champions* list. Tougher still, the pronouncer lost his concentration and pronounced the word *propinquity* with a *g*. Henry spelled it with a *g* and was sent offstage. Luckily, a family friend figured out what happened and lodged a protest. The judges played back the tape and Henry was reinstated—and went on to win.

"I was happy to be back in Washington, and I was entirely aware that you couldn't count on winning just because you had finished high before," he says. "I wasn't the only one there for the third time."

He was aware, too, of the element of chance. "There's a huge amount of luck involved. There are killer words flying around you all the time, the person on your left or your right takes a bullet, and you get an easy one."

Luck seemed to be with him that year. Some of his words were unknown to him, yet he guessed correctly. As the field of seventy-three spellers (forty-eight girls and twenty-five boys) narrowed, he stayed onstage. Now a seasoned speller, he had developed a careful onstage routine, knowing a slip was likely if he rushed. ("The worst one is *g* for *j*," he observes.) His technique was to back away from the microphone and silently, or very softly, mouth the letters, to rehearse before actually spelling. "The idea was to repeat what you just said."

Finally it was down to him and one other speller, a diminutive twelve-year-old from Norfolk, Virginia, named Betty Jean Altschul. Since Betty Jean was so short and Henry was so tall (he had almost reached his adult height of five feet eleven inches), Bee officials searched for something for her to stand on so the microphone wouldn't need adjusting for every word. Finding no convenient pedestal, they put a Webster's *Unabridged* near the microphone, which she stood on while spelling.

The two were evenly matched. Henry misspelled an astounding three times; however, so did Betty Jean, so they kept going. Finally, Betty Jean missed *velleity*. Due to an odd circumstance, Henry had studied the word. It was one of those his mother had come across and written down for him on a scrap of paper. "I had put it with my stuff to bring to school, but I forgot it several days in a row, so I kept looking at that little scrap," he says. "By the time I finally got it in my school bag, I had seen it about twenty-eight times."

He easily spelled *velleity* and was given one more; if he spelled it, he was the winner. The word was *eudaemonic*, which means producing happiness. "I guess you can call it an easy one," he says, because it was listed in the *Words of the Champions* booklet. As soon as he spelled it, the audience of close to 300 people burst into applause. The pronouncer, Benson Alleman, an English professor from Kentucky, jumped up to congratulate him. "He came over and, like in a boxing match, raised my hand high."

Shortly before Henry walked off stage, a photo was taken. The image: Betty Jean standing on the thick *Unabridged* dictionary, with Henry by her side; one of his arms was around Betty Jean, the other was held high by the pronouncer in a gesture of victory. "It was sweet," he recalls.

☉☉☉

Henry attended Swarthmore College in his undergraduate years and went on to earn a doctorate in mathematics from Harvard. (He didn't mention his Bee victory to his college friends.) He has worked in various medical institutions, including a teaching stint at the Harvard School for Public Health. He now works at Children's Hospital in Boston, in a position involving the design of medical research.

Looking back on his Bee experience, he sees value in it beyond what it taught him about language. In particular, "There's the poise—the poise in a tense situation in front of people." There's a life lesson, too, in "dealing with luck, dealing with circumstances that you really can't control, but being as prepared as best you can." Making it to Washington, whether one wins or not, is a tremendous self-esteem builder, he says. "Everyone who gets to that level has been a winner, and that brings an attitude with it, 'I can do this, I can achieve'—it really does something for you."

Henry went back to Washington to watch the Bee in 2001, having not seen one since his 1960 victory. The dramatic changes struck him, in particular the event's high-tech trappings, its big-screen video projectors and profusion of

¹⁵ Champion's Profile: Henry Feldman, 1960

television cameras (there was no TV coverage in his day). But the kids, he says, haven't changed too much.

"A lot of it is timeless, it's just the same," he says. "There are the fidgeters and the mature young ladies and gentlemen, the writers [who scribble on their placard] and the eye-rollers."

As he sat watching the contest, his own emotions, too, harkened back to 1960. "I was so tense," he says, noting that he felt anxious for the kids. "I was a nervous wreck."

Part[4]

The Strange History of English Spelling (Or, Why It's So Difficult)

"In adjusting the Orthography, which has been to this time unsettled and fortuitous, I found it necessary to distinguish those irregularities that are inherent in our tongue, and perhaps coeval with it, from others which the ignorance or negligence of later writers has produced . . . Such defects are not errours in orthography, but spots of barbarity impressed so deep in the English language, that criticism can never wash them away."

—Samuel Johnson, *from the preface*,
A Dictionary of the English Language, *London, 1755*

16 A Great Darkness

At some point in his or her life, every individual who grapples with the spelling of the English language faces what F. Scott Fitzgerald called "a real dark night of the soul." This troubling moment comes when they realize that, no, the spelling of the word they're in the middle of is not governed by rules; that no, it spells nothing like it sounds; and that no, its spelling does not resemble those of similar words—quite the opposite.

At this point the speller of English must face a basic truth: The spelling system they inhabit is chaotic and untrammeled. The universe, it seems to suggest, is random and uncaring. There is no logic, no order, no sense, just a series of random letter combinations.

Clearly, the biggest obstacle for the English speller is the wildly inconsistent nature of the language. Its spelling system, if it can be called that, contains the longest list of broken rules since Bonnie and Clyde robbed their first bank. It's a crime against the tongue, against common sense, against any hope that we will one day live in a well-organized universe (which we won't). The long *e* sound, for example, can be spelled a baffling number of ways: *seem, he, team, convene, sardine, protein, fiend, people,* and *key*—and some words make the long *e* sound with no *e* at all, like *ski* and *debris.* On the other hand, many syllables that are spelled identically have completely different sounds, like the end of *undermine* and *determine*. *Proceed* needs a double *e* but *procedure* doesn't. *Judge* takes an *e* but *judgment* rules against it. The very thought of *pneumonia* is enough to make you queasy. Oh, and *colonel* is pronounced with an *r* sound.

If English were logical, observed George Bernard Shaw, the word *fish* would be spelled *ghoti*. After all, we know from *enough* that the *f* sound is spelled with the letters *gh*. And the short *i* sound of *fish* must be spelled with an *o*—just listen to *women*. And the *sh* sound of *fish* should be spelled as *ti*; that's the way the *sh* sound is spelled in *ambitious*. So *ghoti* could be pronounced as *fish*. That's a logical system, isn't it?

The English language, says Merriam-Webster senior editor James Lowe in a clear understatement, "is not phonetic." No, indeed it is not.

If you grew up in America, you may not realize how wacky English spelling is because it's your native tongue. But talk to anyone who's learned it as a second language. They'll smile indulgently as you tell them that *their* language seems odd. English spelling, at all hours of the day and night, is causing mass frustration all across the globe (and right here at home).

How did this happen? How, implores the modern speller, did the English language become such a twisted thicket of orthographic inconsistency, a four-alarm fire of verbal conflagration? How did English, the language of a highly civilized culture, become a funhouse mirror of frustrated expectations? More to the point, how did the life of the contemporary speller become so fraught with challenge?

Answering these questions requires a look back at the history of the English language. And thus we will summon up this tangled and checkered tale. But before we do so, I warn you: Please, if you're faint of heart or otherwise infirm, it may be best to skip the forthcoming section. It is the story of war and conquest, of economic subjugation, of ego, of nationalistic pride, and of the intermingling of dissimilar peoples. It is a tale of madness. If you're not already sitting, you may want to do so now.

〇〇〇

The beginning of the English language is an indistinct point, placed at various different times based on which version of history you choose. Linguists most commonly place its birth in the fifth century AD, when several warring Germanic tribes, doing what they do best, invaded what we now call England. They were a rough bunch. Often called barbarians—though not to their face—they pushed the area's not-so-rough Celtic-speaking peoples into Scotland, Cornwall, Wales, and Ireland.

Each Germanic tribe pillaged and plundered a different part of England. The Saxons took the southwest, the Angles (from whose tribal name comes the name *England*) settled in the north and east, the Jutes grabbed the southeast. These various tribes had sharply distinct dialects and lived a few days' horse ride from each other, yet they spoke a mutually intelligible language known as Anglo-Saxon, or Old English. From Old English we get *water, strong,* and, most commonly used, *be.* But few of these words were spelled as they are today. The word *be* could be spelled either *bio* or *beo,* and *strong* was written as either *strang* or *strong.* The barbarians were not sticklers about spelling.

Although Old English is the nucleus of modern-day English, it is just that. It is the small original pond into which many other rivers have flowed. Only a limited portion of Old English words made the journey to contemporary English—most were left behind (after all, we need only so many words for "spear," "conquer," and "horsemeat stew"). Most of the words in today's Merriam-Webster come from sources other than Old English. However, those early Germanic tribes shouldn't feel slighted. While most of our modern-day words originate elsewhere, roughly half of today's most *commonly used* words have Old English roots.

A spelling bee would have been pointless among the Anglo-Saxon tribes. Their spelling, such as it was, was completely phonetic. So a bee would have posed no challenge: If you knew how a word sounded, you knew how it was spelled. (The same is true in modern Germany, where, like most countries, there is no national spelling bee. A German word and its spelling are almost always related. Deutschland's orthographic system is a model of logical organization.)

The Anglo-Saxons took their first tentative step away from purely phonetic spelling as they digested a handful of words from the people they displaced, the Celts. One of these words is *puca,* an evil mischief-maker, on whom

Shakespeare based his character Puck in *A Midsummer Night's Dream*. (By the way, most of the Celtic languages are still alive today in the Gaelic tongues of Scotland, Ireland, and Wales. With one exception. After the mass exodus, Cornish was never the same. The last native Cornish speaker died in 1777 in the colorfully named town of Mousehole, Cornwall. The fact that the Celts named a town Mousehole may provide a clue as to why they lost England.)

The Anglo-Saxon language soon received a fresh foreign influence. In AD 597, an idealistic Christian missionary named Augustine, accompanied by about fifty monks, landed on English soil. Their goal, as they saw it, was to spread religion to the savages. They must have been a brave and hardy band— they were in danger of having their bones turned into small hand tools. Yet Augustine, showing no fear, brought only his beliefs and a small library of Latin, Greek, and Hebrew words. And remarkably, over the next one hundred years his mission succeeded. England became Christian. Old English expanded and merged with Latin as Christian concepts were translated into Anglo-Saxon culture. Augustine's *spiritus sanctus*, Holy Spirit, became the Anglo-Saxon's *Halig Gast*, Holy Ghost. Note the phonetic spelling of *Halig Gast*. The odd silent *h* of *ghost* probably didn't appear until Dutch printers in the fifteenth century started adding it.

Over hundreds of years the dialects of the Anglo-Saxon tribes coalesced into a single language, or at least moved in that direction. (Everything moved slowly in those days; coffee wasn't introduced in Europe until the 1600s.) Helping the process along was the unification of the kingdom and especially one of its first kings, Alfred the Great. Alfred by some accounts was illiterate until the age of thirty-eight, making him an *opsimath*, which is a classic spelling bee word meaning a slow or late learner. But once he got the hang of it he went full bore: In the late 800s Alfred translated Latin writings into English and also promoted the creation of literature. English was moving up in the world.

However, the language and its spelling continued to be irregular. With a literacy rate hovering underneath 5 percent, the concept of standardized spelling was low on the list of hoped-for societal reforms; just getting through the winter was the chief challenge. The spelling of English from this period makes it unreadable by the modern eye. The phrase *Give us this day our daily bread* looked like this: *urne gedæghwamlican hlaf syle us to dæg.* The greatest work of literature in Old English is *Beowulf,* which needs to be translated for modern readers. It's a 3,000-line poem about a brave warrior who sets out to slay a dragon. If you haven't read it, I won't ruin the ending, but suffice it to say the Anglo-Saxons considered themselves pretty swift on the field of battle.

Despite their self-proclaimed battlefield prowess, the Anglo-Saxons faced a series of military threats. As the original Germanic barbarians had once covetously eyed England, so now did other peoples. The Vikings—an even rougher bunch than the Anglo-Saxons—invaded and settled part of English territory, contributing myriad words like *skirt,* which means shirt. They spelled it *skyrta,* give or take a few consonants. The Vikings, like the Anglo-Saxons, weren't sticklers for spelling.

Still more threatening to England—and hence the development of nascent English—was William the Conqueror, the Duke of Normandy. William, who spoke a dialect of French called Norman, cast a desiring eye upon England. Based on his nickname—"the Conqueror"—we know he wasn't a fan of diplomacy. In 1066 William invaded England with an army of fierce Frenchmen. The Anglo-Saxons had been tough hombres against the Celts, but in comparison to William's crew they were, alas, what we now call *girlie-men.* (The term *girlie-man* was popularized by the great linguist Arnold Schwarzenegger, who starred in the 1982 classic *Conan the Barbarian,* a story set in an Anglo-Saxon-style culture. However, there were no victorious French invaders in *Conan.*)

The English language made a radical course change after the Norman Conquest. With William as king, a French-speaking elite ruled an English-speaking citizenry. By some accounts English went into hiatus—few written works, no powerful kings like Alfred to promote it—but that's not quite true. The merging of the two languages on English soil imbued Old English with a fresh character. English was leavened, softened, and made more musical.

The earthbound Anglo-Saxon tongue received an infusion of ornate French words—*omelette, etiquette, finance, potpourri*—as well as many that might never have occurred to the Anglo-Saxons, like *courtesan, mistress, boudoir,* and *romance.* A plethora of new combinations arose: For example, the

French *gentle* and the Anglo-Saxon *man* combined for *gentleman*. English's vocabulary grew as synonyms originating from both languages became established, like the Anglo-Saxon *wish* and the French *desire*. The French-speaking Norman aristocracy called it *beef*; the unwashed Anglo-Saxon commoners who tended the animals used *cow*. The French *uncle* overtook the Old English *eam*, fortunately. And the Norman elite brought a strong Latin influence to Old English (William had received the blessing of the Pope for his conquest). Latin, the lingua franca of scholarship, extended English vocabulary considerably.

But the clash involved in the Norman Conquest would prove to be a lasting source of agony. Not for the brave Anglo-Saxons who were defeated in 1066; they merely died a horrible death on the field of battle. Enduring much greater anguish are those who attempt to spell modern-day English, which is a product of this clash. The French influence (mixed with Latin as used by French speakers) loosened English from its phonetic moorings. Old English had been spelled how it sounded; Old French was not. The countless French words that found their way into English are the bane of the speller's existence: They offer silent consonants, unneeded double consonants, and unpredictable uses of the letter *s*. Whenever a present-day speller of English comes across one of these confounding confections, they can curse William the Conqueror. (The most appropriate epithet would be "maudits Normands!" which is a common French insult meaning "damn the Normans.")

This spelling confusion is seen in the Domesday Book, a survey of land and property commissioned by William in 1086 for taxation purposes. William sent royal commissioners out into the English countryside to, in effect, count the cows and the sod huts. This document was written on sheepskin parchment in Latin—the educated elite would never have considered using the commoner's tongue of English. As these commissioners, whose first language was French, roamed the countryside, their spellings were a comedy of errors. *Calton* was spelled *Colton*, *Malham* as *Malgham*, *Hanlith* as *Hagenlith*. The Normans changed the spelling of *hose* to *house*, and they modified the spelling of *cume* to *come*. They didn't like the Anglo-Saxon *cw* spelling at all, so they changed it to the French *qu*, hence *quest* is not spelled phonetically as *cwest*.

Complicating the book's spellings even further, the Anglo-Saxons themselves had yet to become consistent in spelling, even of household and town names. Spelling was a matter of individual preference.

By the way, the Domesday Book took so long to finish that William died before it was completed. After his death, the entire 413-page book was copied by hand by a single scribe. We can only wonder what liberties he took with his spelling.

⚛️⚛️⚛️

Over the next few hundred years the languages of the noblemen and the commoners merged. The Norman aristocracy began to feel that England, rather than Normandy, was their home, especially when Normandy fell to the King of France in 1204. Over the centuries the elites were forced, much as they tried not to, to mingle with the unwashed masses—someone had to hire the help. The elites' speech evolved into a modified polyglot of French and Old English. Helping mix the languages, the Anglo-Saxons developed a prosperous merchant class, allowing their unvarnished language to play a lead role in commerce. From the confluences of these two lingual streams came what we call Middle English. The watershed year was 1362, when the Statute of Pleading made English the official language of Parliament and the courts. The native tongue once again ruled England—but it was so changed that it could hardly be called the native tongue.

This emerging language had a babble of dialects, resulting in some tortured spellings. The word *one*, for instance, which is spelled nothing like it sounds, is a combination of a Southern England pronunciation with an East Midland spelling. The first syllable of *bury* and *busy* should sound the same; after all, they're spelled the same. But no. That's because they feature a Western England spelling with, respectively, Kent and London pronunciations.

To the modern American reader, Middle English is like a long-lost friend: known, but not quite familiar. The phrase *Give us this day our daily bread* was spelled something like *yeue to us today oure eche dayes bred*. Note the spelling of the word *our* as *oure*. Looks French, doesn't it? In Old English, before the

Norman Conquest, *our* had been spelled *ure*. It's a simpler spelling, following a phonetic pattern; what you see is what you get. But after the French influence spelling would never be simple.

There had been a first failed attempt to reform spelling sometime in the 1200s. A lone monk named Ormin looked at Middle English and saw that its spelling resembled an untended weed field. He proposed reforms to make a word's spelling match its pronunciation. To help readers distinguish between long and short vowels, he doubled the consonants following short vowels; he spelled *fir* as *firr*. He placed a single consonant after long vowels, so *fire* was *fir*. It was a logical system, but few reformers have been as roundly ignored as Ormin—he was just a dreamer with an idea. However, when his manuscript was discovered 600 years later, it provided an invaluable guide to the time period's pronunciation. That Ormin spelled *God* with the current spelling indicates that the word rhymed with *load* in his day.

Ormin saw the need to reform spelling, yet in his day things weren't as bad as they later became. Middle English, whatever its inconsistencies, preserved a relationship between spelling and pronunciation, a kinship that's grown ever more distant. One of the great bedevilments of modern spellers is silent consonants, which Middle English kept to a minimum. In this period the *g* in *gnaw* was pronounced, as was the *k* in *knight* and the *l* in *alms*—why write it if you're not going to voice it? This has changed over hundreds of years, as our tongues, seeking shortcuts, started lazily dropping letters while the spelling stayed true to the original. This combination of original spelling with centuries of pronunciation shortcuts is a leading cause of the confusion in English spelling.

The greatest work of literature written in Middle English is Geoffrey Chaucer's *Canterbury Tales*. It's the only major work in the literary canon that makes extensive reference to farting. (Life was earthy in the late 1300s.) In Chaucer's work is the first bread crumb in a minor spelling mystery. One of the many oddities of English is that when *four* becomes *forty*, we lose the *u*, even though *fourth* keeps the *u*. Odd, isn't it? Chaucer spelled it, sensibly, as *fourty*, and its spelling would remain so until about 1750. After that it begins to show up as *forty*.

It continues to be one of the many unanswered questions about English spelling: Who decided to lose the *u* in *fourty*—and why?

☉☉☉

With the advent of the Renaissance, many scholars and thinkers found the English language to be lacking. Exciting advances were taking place in science, philosophy, and the arts, yet English, with its roots in earthbound Anglo-Saxon culture, was unable to fully describe all this forward movement. So scholars, wanting to turn English into a robust tool for a new age, minted a plethora of new words based on Latin and Greek roots.

Some social critics decried these many additions as "inkhorn" words, a derogatory term referring to language that's excessively scholarly, especially in the use of Latin and Greek terms. Thomas Wilson, who wrote *The Art of Rhetorique*, one of the high points of the English Renaissance, called these additions "outlandish English." Shakespeare had fun with this trend by creating the character Holofernes in *Love's Labor's Lost*. A pedantic schoolmaster, Holofernes goes wildly overboard on Latinates, and when he reads a love letter he can only respond by opining that its writing style needs to be improved. But, quibbling and humor aside, English was getting larger year by year, as a flood of words from antiquity gave the language new depth and versatility.

The advantage of these terms from a speller's viewpoint is that words based on Greek and Latin roots follow rules. If you know *philo*, the Greek root meaning "love of," you know most of the spelling of *philography* (the love of autographs), *philology* (the love of words), and *philogyny* (the love of women). Then again, the spelling of even apparently rule-bound words from Latin and Greek antiquity must be handled with care. A speller at the 2003 National Bee, Michael Martinez, from New Mexico, learned this the hard way. He was given the lovely *borborygmus*, which means, "a rumbling noise produced by the movement of gas through the intestines." He spelled it, reasonably, using the Latinate suffix *ous* meaning "full of," as *borborygmous*—which is precisely how the word sounds. And then, of course, he was sent offstage. Speller beware.

Adding far more woe to the speller's life was the practice, common among

Renaissance scholars, of changing the spellings of existing words to reflect their Latin roots. Many phonetically spelled words now became littered with silent and nonsensical consonants. The word *dette* had been spelled how it sounded, but it came from the Latin *debitum*, so learned thinkers—inkhorn types—decided to spell it as *debt*. An *h* was added to *anchor*, and an *s* was added to *island*. It didn't make any sense, but it allowed scholars to feel they were improving the language.

This infusion of classical word roots in the 1500s and 1600s marked an evolutionary step known as Early Modern English. The biggest change in this period was something called the Great Vowel Shift, a major change in the way people pronounced words. Why this happened is one of the few things linguists admit they don't know, yet whatever the reason, the effect was profound. For the first time, the pronunciation of English approximated what a modern ear would understand. Long vowels began to be voiced higher in the mouth, so a word like *down* came closer to its current pronunciation, rather than "doon"; *five* was no longer "feef."

As Early Modern English emerged, the dialect of London, English's epicenter, became anointed as its standard pronunciation. Mainly, of course, because there was a large group of speakers there who decided that their pronunciations were the "right" pronunciations. Still, this bit of urban chauvinism did have an advantage. The concept of a fixed, "correct" pronunciation was a step toward standardized spelling. While spelling and pronunciation would always have a loose relationship in English, they are not unrelated. Or, put another way, when pronunciation was always in flux, spelling, which tends to lag behind, was that much more random.

Doing far more to push spelling toward standardization—well, sort of— was the printing press. In the late 1400s the printing press was a wildly revolutionary machine. Prior to Gutenberg's invention, only a tiny elite could produce written matter, but now the plebeians could mass-distribute ideas; any wild-eyed theorist could tack up handbills all over the city. Governments would rise and fall with the help of this cumbersome machine.

In theory, the rise of the printing press meant that spelling was no longer determined by individual choice. Wouldn't a pressman set a word with the same letters every time? As it turned out, pressmen have whims of their own. William Caxton, a pioneering fifteenth-century publisher and the first major printer, was English but wrote mostly in Latin and lived much of the time in Belgium. Many of his workers spoke Dutch; for them English was a second language. Adding more chaos, printers were paid by the line and so profited by adding extra letters to words, or wordes, or wourdes. To this day there are English words spelled as they are because Dutch printers felt it right and proper.

For early printers, spelling was like rolling dice—a different combination of letters could come up every time. Caxton, with an eye to the bottom line, published editions of Chaucer's runaway bestseller, *Canterbury Tales*. (Although written in the 1300s, it was still a hit in the late 1400s—with so little competition, a book could enjoy generations on the bestseller list.) Take a look at the first few lines of Chaucer's work, as published by Caxton in two different years:

1476:

Whan that Apprill with his shouris sote
And the droughte of marche hath percid the rote
And badid euery veyne in suche licour

1483:

Whan that Apryll wyth hys shouris sote
The droughte of marche hath percyd the rote
And bathyd euery veyne in suche lycour

Among the many spelling variances is the word *April*—surely a common word, yet printers had yet to decide on a definitive spelling. It's as if the pressmen, like the pen-and-quill scribes before them, spelled willy-nilly based on available letters and individual preference.

Still, as the printing press proliferated over several generations, laying the foundation for mass literacy, it enabled the development that the English language—and its spelling—was waiting for: the first dictionary.

If complex symbolic language is what makes us civilized, then the development of the dictionary, with its codification of the language, was a huge plunge forward for humankind. In codifying the language, the dictionary would provide a spelling reference. A word's spelling would no longer be determined by the mood of a Dutch printer but would be set in type in an authoritative text. Or at least that was one of the possibilities.

The first slender volume, *A Table Alphabeticall of Hard Usual English Words*, was published in 1604 by Robert Cawdrey, a defrocked minister turned entrepreneurial schoolmaster. One of Cawdrey's goals was to protect the language; he felt English was sullied by too many foreign influences and too many inkhorn terms. Lingual purity was his hope.

As he wrote in the volume's preface, "Some men seek so far for outlandish English, that they forget altogether their mothers tongue." In particular, "He that commeth lately out of France, will talk French English, and neuer blush at the matter . . . Another chops in with English Italinated, and applyeth the Italian phrase to our English speaking."

Cawdrey's dictionary was also inspired by the humanist spirit of the Renaissance. He created it in keeping with the era's revolutionary belief that the common people, not just the aristocracy, should receive an education. (One of the Renaissance's defining acts was the translation of the Bible from Latin into English, allowing the masses to read it.) With this in mind, Cawdrey's volume was, in a sense, the first Dummies Guide to the English Language. He decried unneeded complexity so that his dictionary would be accessible to all (which, of course, would also boost sales).

But his hope that English could remain free of complexity and outside influences was a quaint one. And his volume itself belied this hope (as would all subsequent dictionaries). As Cawdrey acknowledged, the 2,543 words he defined were a polyglot of Greek, Latin, French, and Old English. *Mustaches*, "the hayre of the upper lippe," was clearly French, and *parasite*, "a base flatterer, or soothing companion," was almost straight from Greek. Worse—from his point of view—the influences were all jumbled together. *Lunatick*, which he defined as "wanting his wits, at a certaine time of the age of the moone," combined the Latin for *moon* with an Old English ending.

As for standardized spelling, it wasn't something Cawdrey lost sleep over. He was surprisingly sloppy in his orthography (or the printers were when they laid it out). In the introduction, he wrote that his book was a guide to both *words* and *wordes*. Think of it: Two spellings of the same word—just a few paragraphs from each other—in a dictionary. English had a long way to go.

In fairness to Cawdrey, the concept of consistent spelling was still in its infancy. During the lifetime of William Shakespeare, whose most productive years were in the late 1500s and early 1600s, his name was spelled with wild variance. Depending on which scholar you ask, it was spelled anywhere from a handful to several dozen different ways. The Bard himself spelled it perhaps six different ways and apparently signed two contrasting spellings on one document—a creative fellow, indeed.

Cawdrey's first dictionary, despite its limitations, was a major commercial success, one of publishing's first great coups. Other dictionaries soon followed—well, actually not that fast; this was the 1600s. Twelve years later, a scholar named Bullokar hit the shelves with *An English Expositour* (1616), which went further afield than Cawdrey by including archaic terms, or "an olde worde, onely used of some ancient writers and now growne out of use."

Cockeram's *English Dictionarie* (1623) displayed its author's belief in the supremacy of his achievement. Readers, crowed Cockeram, "dare not but acknowledge, that what any before in this kinde have begun, I have not only fully finished but thoroughly perfected." But Thomas Blount disagreed. His *Glossographia* (1656) not only had 11,000 words—more than any before—but his volume also boasted woodcut illustrations. Pictures!

However, Blount's work was soon topped by Edward Phillips's *New World of English Words* (1658), with its jaw-dropping 20,000 entries. But Blount didn't like being one-upped and claimed that Phillips had plagiarized his work; the two men began a years-long squabble. Blount got so upset that he set out to exact literary revenge, publishing *A World of Errors Discovered in the New World of Words* in 1673.

As they bickered, Edward Cocker topped them both with his *English*

Dictionary (1704). The volume was so well respected that the phrase "according to Cocker" came to mean "absolutely correct" (although Cocker himself died a step away from debtor's prison).

Nathan Bailey decided to produce the grandest dictionary of them all, and he clearly succeeded with the *Universal Etymological English Dictionary* (1721). The volume was "not only for the Information of the Ignorant, but the Entertainment of the Curious." The concept of a dictionary had come a long way over the last one hundred years. By the time of Bailey's hefty volume, Cawdrey's quaint sense of a limited and protected language had long since been abandoned. Bailey's work offered etymologies from an extensive list of European and ancient languages, dressed up with more than 500 illustrations.

By the way, the word for someone who conceives of or theorizes about dictionaries is *metalexicographer*. It's an awesome word, truly a 25-center. You might try using it in conversation sometime, perhaps at an informal social gathering. Just begin to speak, casually, and then let slip, "You know, the state of modern metalexicography is far too market driven." Your contemporaries will look at you in bafflement, perhaps even wonderment, and have no choice but to nod in agreement.

◎◎◎

All the early dictionaries, no matter how ambitious, were merely bricks in the foundation upon which was built Samuel Johnson's august *The Dictionary of the English Language*. When people talk about "the first dictionary," they are usually referring to this historic tome. Among its other contributions, *Dictionary* would influence spelling like no volume before it.

Johnson, one of the great *bon vivants* of English culture, led a haphazard career that—through no plan of his own—gave him ideal qualifications to author a dictionary. Forced to leave college for lack of funding, he married an older woman with a large dowry, but he lost the money when the private school he opened shut down due to lack of pupils. Desperately poor, he drifted into journalism, writing articles about everything from politics to religion to business to science, even penning one piece about Chinese architecture. After several years of living so hand to mouth that he sometimes walked the streets at night without a place to live, he applied to law school. His application was denied.

At loose ends, he seized upon a major opportunity. A group of English publishers planned to publish the definitive dictionary, a volume to turn all previous works into historical curiosities. Their motive was profit. By the 1700s the prevalence of the printing press meant all manner of publishers were now selling their own books and pamphlets. Surely there was a huge market for an authoritative dictionary. They asked Samuel Johnson: Would he author the volume? Offered a princely sum, Johnson said yes without hesitation.

The publishers hoped to issue a dictionary like that published in France by the French Academy, which had taken a staggering seventy-some years to create (fifty-five years of writing, eighteen years of revising; presumably quite a few long lunches through the decades). The French Academy was empowered to be the governing authority for the country's language, to create the definitive dictionary and to police public usage. To this day, French and German government agencies oversee their countries' languages and can institute spelling reforms in all official and school documents. (I know what you're thinking: The French language has been reformed? That jungle thatch of mute consonants, from the country that gave us *eaux*, has been reformed? Well, remember, government agencies aren't infallible.)

As Samuel Johnson began his *Dictionary*, the English had spent many years wondering: Should such a central authority for the language be founded in our country?

Many English intellectuals had been in favor of it. Jonathan Swift lobbied hard for it, and Defoe and Dryden had also pushed the plan. The English government briefly flirted with the idea, but by the mid-1700s the proposed central academy had fallen out of favor. Too constricting, said many leading thinkers. Joseph Priestley, known for discovering oxygen, found the idea "unsuitable to the genius of a free nation."

The rejection of an academy by England was a critical turning point in the development of the language—particularly for its spelling.

The absence of a state agency regulating the language meant that English would be formed not by a single body but by a mishmash of factors: common usage, international influences, and market forces. Its spelling would be determined by the vagaries of popular habit.

So when English publishers in the mid-1700s decided to publish the definitive dictionary, they knew the volume would be guided by no governing entity. It would, as would all English dictionaries henceforth, be the work of a small group of people making decisions as they saw fit.

In this case that small group was Samuel Johnson and the group of six Scottish copyists he hired to help him. And Johnson was a man possessed. He closeted himself away on Fleet Street and submerged himself into the task, reading voraciously, examining the usage of tens of thousands of words. He spent nine years on the project. During that time he single-handedly wrote the definitions for more than 40,000 words, some with multiple meanings, accompanying his entries with 114,000 quotations he gathered from myriad sources. When he declared himself done and his *Dictionary* was published in 1755, the new volume was spectacularly well received. It was hailed as a major cultural triumph, and Johnson was feted as a hero. Oxford University gave him an honorary degree.

What most distinguished his *Dictionary*—why it laid the groundwork for all later compendiums—was the joyous, sprawling erudition of Johnson's definitions. Competitors would copy them for decades to come. Some of them were truly profligate, like his 400-word essay for *elephant* that detailed the reproductive activities of the great beast (fortunately with no illustration). Others displayed Johnson's own opinions about cultural differences, as in his *oats*: "A grain, which is generally given to horses, but in Scotland appears to support the people." A portion of them were technical to the point of obscurity, like *network*: "any thing reticulated or decussated, at equal distances, with interstices between the intersections."

But few of his definitions were this idiosyncratic. Instead, his earlier years of eclectic journalism, during which he had written about everything from science to Chinese architecture, meant he brought a well-traveled mind to the art of defining words. His definitions were so rich that *Dictionary* was a sort of condensed encyclopedia.

Johnson's spellings, however, contributed greatly to English's present-day riot of orthographic inconsistency. Oddly, he assigned contrasting spellings to pairs of words that sound almost identical; he spelled *deceit* plainly, yet he added a *p* to *receipt*. He chose *deign* but he also used *disdain*; *slyly* shared the page with *sliness*, and it was *moveable* but *immovable*, as if the word's opposite form had to lose an *e*.

These inconsistencies weren't all his doing; he was following cultural precedent. By the 1700s English spelling was headed toward standardization but it had yet to arrive. Due to the printing press, most English authors now agreed on the spelling of most words, most of the time. However, as Johnson scoured through piles of books and periodicals to gather accepted spellings, he faced a patchwork of possibilities. And his choices were decidedly inconsistent.

He chose the *our* suffix, as in *honour* and *colour*, that is still used in England today. Yet while he followed precedent for *anteriour*, he did not for *posterior*; he went by the plan for *interiour* but broke the rule for *exterior*. Of course, if you wrote 40,000 words using a quill pen, with no electricity and no spell-check, you'd be inconsistent, too.

Despite his inconsistencies, he viewed spelling as an important issue in the development of the language, and saw himself as a reformer, albeit not a revolutionary one. He wanted to drop one *l* from words like *downhill* and *unroll*. But the period's printers didn't like shortened spellings like *catcal* for *catcall*—remember, they were paid more for longer words—so the double *l* convention survives to this day.

And sometimes he was just plain wrong. Being an Englishman, he had a fondness for what he called "Saxon" spellings. So he spelled words like *critik* and *musik* with a final *k*, as if he were in Chaucer's time—although these words came from Latin through French, not from Old English. These idiosyncrasies may have been a result of limited etymological knowledge, though in general Johnson's notations of word origins were considered scholarly.

Whatever its flaws, *Dictionary* stands as one of the capstones of Western civilization. Johnson's volume celebrated the great panorama of English, its depth and specificity, its intellectual robustness. *Dictionary* proclaimed that English is a tool fit for any scholarly task, no matter how advanced. In contrast to Cawdrey, Johnson welcomed foreign words. His attitude was: foreign influences? Absolutely—the more the merrier. So his work at once codified the language yet invited growth from outside sources, suggesting that English's vigor would continuously be in flower. That was good news for the English language, but tragic news for anyone hoping for consistent spelling rules.

☙❧

While Johnson's embrace of foreign influences had a profound effect on the language, another aspect of English culture had a similar and perhaps still greater effect.

No one seemed to love war quite as much as the British. At its pinnacle the relatively small country of England subjugated roughly one quarter of the globe. It was said that the sun never set on the English empire. The effect of this on the planet was questionable—Mahatma Gandhi took umbrage to it— but its benefit to the language is incalculable.

As its army and navy devoured land, its language gorged on foreign terms. Africa, the Far East, Australia, New Zealand, the Caribbean—thanks to English colonial ambitions, the language became a great global sponge. It sopped up new words at every port of call. India contributed *pajamas*, *pundit*, and *juggernaut*, Malay added *amok*, Iceland threw in *berserk* (probably due to all that snow and ice), and Canton handed over *ketchup*.

By the time the language entered what we call its Modern period, beginning in about 1800—these chronological demarcations are the artificial inventions of linguists (they have to do something to feel important)—it clearly sported an international flavor. Some languages resist this; the German and French national academies attempt to keep out corrupting foreign words. But with English the floodgate is wide open.

This plays havoc with spelling. When English borrows words, it does so like no other language. It often simply takes the word, spelling and all, and calls it English—much like those English armies took land. In French, in contrast, a new word is Frenchified; otherwise, a French tongue would prefer not

158

to speak it. *Discotheque*, for example, is a combination of *disc* and the Greek word *theca*. But the French of course changed that last syllable to the classically Gallic *que* suffix. English doesn't do this. When the English language took *buffet* from the French, its spelling wasn't changed to *buffay* to reflect its English pronunciation. Once again, the English tongue does not match the English spelling.

This international infusion gave English the last shove that pushed it off the deep end. Already full of contradictions, with a tangled history, English's profound global inhalation sunk any hope for a logical spelling system, if any vestige remained. Today's modern speller, while cursing William the Conqueror for the French influence, can also curse all those land-hungry British leaders. Curse Fletcher Christian and curse Captain Bligh. Curse them all. Then reach for your spell-check. You'll need it.

17 The New American Vernacular

America. The spirit of the new colonies clearly leaned toward independence, toward freedom, toward self-determination. (Then again, Samuel Johnson, after hearing the colonists' cry of "Give me liberty or give me death!" asked: "How is it that we hear the loudest yelps for liberty among the drivers of Negroes?") This vigorous independent spirit called for its own language, or at least a new suit of clothes on the old language—and there's no faster way to refresh a language than by altering its spelling. With time, a movement would emerge to modify English spelling to reflect the new American tongue, a movement whose leader was uniquely well positioned to accomplish this task.

Whether the American tongue was, or should be, separate from that of the Mother Country was debated by the colonists. It was said that the American language is simply a new dialect of English, but then it was also said that a language is defined as a dialect with an army. And the colonists were assembling one of those.

Various forces helped make the colonists' language a distinct branch of English. Chiefly, the polyglot of tongues spoken in the first thirteen states, including Dutch and—in particular—French. Many core concepts in the US Constitution were based on the writings of French philosophers; the then

160

unthinkable idea that all men are created equal comes from French Enlighten-ment philosophers like Diderot. And without the help of the French military, the ragtag American army might never have defeated their British overlords. From French came *bureau* and *cache*; from Dutch came *scow* and *yankee*.

The pidgin English spoken by Native Americans, slaves, and sailors also flavored the new branch of English. From indigenous peoples came *tomahawk*, *succotash*, and *skunk*. And as fast as the early settlers built shelter, they also minted new words. Some of these new creations were purely functional, like *watershed*, *clearing*, and *sidewalk*. Yet many of these fresh additions were con-ceptual, like *influential*, *lengthy*, and *reliable*.

Benjamin Franklin, understanding that a new nation was being birthed, created a system to reform its spelling. As the colonies neared revolution in 1768, he published *Scheme for a New Alphabet and a Reformed Mode of Spelling*. Typical of Franklin, his plan was iconoclastic. It called for not just spelling changes but a completely revamped alphabet with six new characters. These new letters included a *y* with a curled tail for the *ng* sound and an upside-down *h* for the *u* sound of *unto*. Franklin decided that the letters *c*, *w*, *y*, and *j* were unneeded—he felt they should be jettisoned along with taxation without rep-resentation. He proposed spelling all short vowels with one letter; long vowels got two. He convinced a Philadelphia printer to incorporate the new charac-ters into a printing press.

Ever the ladies' man, Franklin sent a letter using the new alphabet to a Miss Stephenson, in London, known for her literary acumen. Apparently uncharmed, Miss Stephenson replied that it seemed quite inconvenient. The plan passed into obscurity.

Yet the urge for reform was strong. And that called for bold action. Set-ting down the new American language, an independent version of English with a fresh American varnish—and a reformed spelling—required casting off the yoke of the Mother Country. The old authorities had to be overthrown, and in the world of language, that meant debunking the greatest authority to date, Samuel Johnson's revered *Dictionary*. Inarguably, if the new country was to have its own language, it needed its own dictionary. And the man for that was Noah Webster.

As a young man, Noah Webster benefited from a great stroke of luck. Born into a Colonial family of modest means, Webster spent the years of the Revolutionary War safely ensconced in Yale College. While other young men were ducking English minie balls, he was learning his Latin declensions.

Like Samuel Johnson, Webster had a deep love of learning and an ambitious, wide-ranging intellect; over the course of his life he was a legislator, publisher, lawyer, and teacher. He wrote the two-volume *A Brief History of Epidemic and Pestilential Diseases* as well as texts on politics, economics, and physical science. But unlike Johnson, who lived large and was a big tipper in the London alehouses, Webster was humorless and severely puritanical. He wrote a translation of the King James Bible in which he replaced the word *testicles* with "peculiar members" and edited out references to wombs. (You know you're a Puritan when you feel that even the Bible needs to be cleaned up.)

While working as a schoolmaster in the 1780s, Webster became passionate about spelling reform. Yet he scoffed at Benjamin Franklin's plan, feeling it was impractical to create a new alphabet. However, when Webster himself developed a spelling reform plan, he wrote Franklin to tell him of it and to ask: Would Franklin propose the system to Congress for approval? Franklin wrote back saying that perhaps *his* plan should be promoted. Webster demurred. Although they couldn't agree—initially—Webster's desire to reform spelling grew ever more fervent.

George Bernard Shaw famously observed that England and America are two countries divided by a common tongue. But Webster (who lived just before Shaw's time) abhorred the idea that England and America would share a common tongue. "Culture, habits, and language, as well as government should be national. America should have her own, distinct from the rest of the world," Webster wrote. In his view English had been corrupted, prettified, by the English aristocracy. The language was morally tainted. He believed, as did Thomas Jefferson and John Adams, that the new country should have its own tongue, separate from "the old feudal and hierarchical establishments of England." This new language should reflect the more righteous nature of the American character. So he readied himself for the founding act of the new American language: He sat down to write his own dictionary.

He had already single-handedly shaped the teaching of language in the Colonies well before beginning work on his storied dictionary. As a teacher, he had found that classroom materials were poor and, worse, usually from England. To provide a better learning aid for students, in 1783 he published *A Grammatical Institute of the English Language*, a tripartite guide covering spelling, grammar, and reading. It wasn't the snappiest title, and its guides to grammar and reading were less than successful. So when it was republished in 1788, it was chiefly a spelling guide, with a smattering of reading pedagogy. The book earned the nickname *Blue-back Speller* because of its blue-green cover.

This slender volume was a gargantuan success. It became the foundation of American literacy for generations, with tens of millions of copies in print over the next one hundred years. It's one of the best-selling books in American history (in fact it's still in print today, though it's sold as a historical curiosity). Webster's *Blue-back Speller* was the reference book for countless American spelling bees.

In Webster's view, pronunciation and spelling were closely linked—or should be. He dreamed of an American language in which words are spelled as they sound. The greatest offender in this regard, he felt, was the French language. "Our citizens ought not to be perplexed with an orthography to which they are strangers," he wrote. Webster decried the "French dress" that many new American words were taking, in particular the many Indian terms with French spellings. As examples, he pointed to the newly minted words *Ouisconsin* and *Ouabasche*. How, he asked, would an American know that they should be pronounced *Wisconsin* and *Wabash*?

In his *Blue-back Speller*, however, Webster didn't yet reveal his aversion to these foreign influences. His popular spelling primer was not the revolutionary work that his complaints about foreign influences would suggest. Its spellings were essentially English and French in all their inconsistent glory, complete with *diaphragm* and *courtier* and the extra *u* in *honour*. But, as we'll see from the direction that Webster soon took, he must have been chafing even as he wrote these Old World spellings.

Along with spelling and reading lessons, the *Blue-back Speller* dispensed a generous dollop of moral guidance. The primer was very much a reflection of Webster's Puritan upbringing. "Never utter what may offend the chastest ear," the primer advised before covering the pronunciation of three-syllable words. Furthermore, "Spiritous liquors shorten more lives than famine, pestilence and the sword!"

One of his *Blue-back Speller* parables, included as a reading example, began like this: "An old man found a rude boy upon one of his trees stealing Apples, and desired him to come down; but the young Sauce-box told him plainly he would not." While the term "young Sauce-box" may be a quaint insult to the modern eye, the parable's end revealed Webster's strict ethic: "Well, well, said the old Man, if neither words nor grass will do, I must try what virtue there is in Stones; so the old man pelted him heartily with Stones; which soon made the young Chap hasten down from the tree and get the old Man's pardon."

Webster brought this same Puritan ethic to his plans for the first American dictionary. As he began conceiving of his dictionary, he imagined a version of English—called *American*—that lived in an ordered universe, not the sprawling jungle of inconsistent spelling and pronunciation that English had become. He desired to bring his clearly defined sense of right and wrong to the new language.

First, he had to prepare his audience. His reputation made from his *Speller*, Webster toured the major cities of the Northeast in the mid-1780s, giving speeches about the need for language and spelling reform. He published these speeches in a book titled *Dissertations on the English Language*, a volume that became his mission statement. It was in this book that he stepped forward and proclaimed himself a fearless proponent of a new American language.

However, "new" in Webster's view actually meant "old." If he had his way, English would have traveled backward to Anglo-Saxon times. He proposed spelling *word* as *wurd*, *is* as *iz*, and *reason* as *reezon*—a literally phonetic rendering of English that harkened back to before William the Conqueror brought a French influence to the language. Webster supported omitting superfluous letters, so *bread* and *head* would be spelled *bred* and *hed*. As he lectured to generally appreciative audiences, he appealed to their patriotism—this new system would distinguish us from the English, he explained.

Romancing the publishers in his audiences (an important group if you want to reform language), Webster tempted them with rosy visions of a fat bottom line. He explained that adopting his new system would require all books henceforth to be printed in America—so there would be no more English competitors. Most important, he told listeners, adopting his new spelling system would allow America to stand upright as an equal among nations; it would free the young nation of its excessive adoration of England. "Thus a habitual respect for another country, deserved indeed and once laudable, turns their attention from their own interests, and prevents their respecting themselves," Webster opined.

Though the audiences clapped politely, his extensive proposed spelling reforms met with a cool reception, despite the renown of his *Speller*. (*Speller*, after all, had not been so radical.) Many educated Americans at the time did not share Webster's aversion to the mother tongue. Yes, they wanted political independence from England (though some hadn't even been sure of that), but the language itself was revered. English, after all, was the language of Shakespeare and Spenser, the tongue of the grand British Empire. It did not need to be improved by a bunch of scruffy blacksmiths and semiliterate tradesmen.

Webster took these criticisms to heart as he sat down to write his magnum opus, the definitive American dictionary. He retreated from the more radical edge of his hoped-for reforms—but didn't lose his reformer's zeal altogether.

Webster had already published a preliminary volume, *A Compendious Dictionary of the English Language*, in 1806—often referred to as "the first American dictionary"—but he now envisioned a far more ambitious work. He began in his early fifties, after fathering eight children. (Since Webster is so mythologized, accounts of his life differ wildly. While most historians call him strict and humorless, others describe him as a gentle soul who kept candy in his pockets for his many children.) Webster's approach shared something in common with that of Robert Cawdrey, the schoolmaster who created the first dictionary in 1604. As Cawdrey had sought to create a work for the commoner as opposed to the elites, Webster labored to create a volume for the masses. The upper crust was not to be trusted, in Webster's view. "The most difficult task now to be performed by the advocates of pure English is to restrain the influence of men learned in Greek and Latin but ignorant of their own tongue," he wrote.

His dictionary would be descriptive rather than prescriptive. That is, he endeavored to record the language as it was actually used by people, rather than how it should be used in some idealized world. (Given this philosophy, it's likely that the old man would have been happy that the 1961 *Webster's Third* bestowed qualified approval on the word *ain't*. Respectable linguists were horrified, but somewhere Webster was smiling.)

The version of English that Webster codified was simplified and more straightforward, less frilly than its British predecessor. Spelling was a big part of this. He took special care to trim highfalutin English spellings; *colour* was distilled down to *color*, *honour* was brought to heel as *honor*. Those dandified English spellings like *theatre* were Americanized to *theater*. *Travelled* was de-Frenchified to *traveled*. He deplored the silent ending *e*, and so *maize* became *maiz*. Displaying his fondness for phonetic spelling, *acre* was *aker*, *grotesque* was *grotesk*, and tongue was *tung*. One of his most enduring reforms was spelling words sounding like *defense* with an *s* (although, for some reason, *fence* retained its *c*).

Yet for all these reforms, Webster's *American Dictionary of the English Language* hewed fairly closely to its English antecedent. He conceded to the forces of tradition and granted the final *e* to *determine* and *discipline*. In a later revision he even restored *suveran* to *sovereign* and *guillotin* back to *guillotine*—a near embrace of the French influence.

His grand *Dictionary* took him fifteen years to complete. Unlike Johnson, his labor was unpaid. His constant efforts to solicit financial support—always noting that he was creating an *American* dictionary—brought in hardly a penny.

Webster's weakness was in his etymological notations. After finishing the first two letters of the alphabet he realized that his knowledge of word origin was insufficient. So, ambitiously, he put aside his pen and spent several years studying world languages. As a literal interpreter of the Bible, he believed that all languages derived from one original language, which he called Chaldee. He developed his etymologies based on his belief that all languages have several core words in common, a mistake that made his descriptions of word origins more fantasy than fact, despite his many years of study.

Webster completed his sprawling volume—containing 70,000 entries—in 1828. Like Johnson's dictionary, it was hailed as an intellectual achievement of the first order, though of course the people doing the hailing were American rather than English. In 1831 Congress adopted Webster's *Dictionary* as the American standard. The first print of the 1,600-page tome was priced at an astoundingly high $20—and it sold well.

Note the significance of the title: *An American Dictionary of the English Language*. The title seemed to accomplish two goals at once. By calling it a dictionary of the *English Language* (as opposed to the *American Language*), Webster conceded that, no, this wasn't an independent tongue. But in referring to it as an *American Dictionary*, he proclaimed that he had indeed put a new coat of varnish on the tired language of kings and queens.

Webster's dictionary took an important step past Johnson's. Where Johnson's definitions might travel to the ends of the earth—witness his 400-word ramble for *elephant*—Webster's entries were defined with precise lexical frugality. Although Webster's rigid Puritanism sometimes got the better of him, as when he defined *freedom* as "a violation of the rules of decorum," this was the exception. His exacting definitional style would become the model for future dictionaries.

In fact, in Webster's view, his work became *too* close a model for future dictionaries—one competing dictionary in particular. The resultant squabble over plagiarism turned into a marketplace battle that profoundly shaped the emerging American language, including its spelling.

☟☟☟

Webster had hired a young man named Joseph Worcester to help with the massive task of creating his dictionary. Worcester's background was quite similar to Webster's. A strict Calvinist, he came from a working-class family. He didn't attend school until age fourteen, needing to work the family farm with his fourteen brothers and sisters, yet he still graduated from Yale. (The college must have been far easier to get into in those days.) He launched a career as a schoolmaster, then, before working with Webster, he helped produce an abridgment of Samuel Johnson's original dictionary.

After the phenomenal commercial success of Webster's dictionary, Worcester was a man in demand. Eyeing the sales of Webster's debut volume, publishers rushed to offer competing volumes. To Webster's great consternation, Worcester churned out an abridged version of the master's work in 1829, pocketing a cool $2,000 for his efforts. Even more upsetting to Webster, in 1830 Worcester released his own dictionary, *A Comprehensive Pronouncing and Explanatory Dictionary*.

Webster had spent fifteen years on his volume, yet Worcester completed his in only a handful of years. Webster found this to be suspiciously fast— could a truly original dictionary be turned out so quickly? An indignant letter was dashed off to the Massachusetts magazine *Palladium*—anonymously— charging Worcester with gross plagiarism. Clearly, Webster was worried that his hopes for a long-term best seller were about to turn from a solid noun to a wispy adjective.

But the stakes were still higher for the English language—and especially for its spelling. Worcester's volume straddled the worlds of Samuel Johnson and Noah Webster. If Worcester's volume were to become the accepted standard, it would take the new American language in a direction different from that Webster hoped for. And it seemed designed to do just that. Worcester's work offered readers the concise definitions of Webster, eschewing Johnson's rambling definitions. But in many cases Worcester favored the original English spelling of Johnson. Instead of Webster's Americanized *program*, Worcester spelled it *programme*; instead of Webster's *theater*, Worcester stayed true to the mother tongue with *theatre*. He also allowed *mold* to keep its British *u*, spelling it as *mould*. Worcester skipped etymology altogether (which doubtless helped him finish so quickly) and wrote his pronunciation guides based on the opinions of some twenty scholars.

Worcester's dictionary was wildly popular. The same educated professionals who had hailed Webster's work now glanced through Worcester's tome and felt a great kinship with it. Webster's dictionary, now that there was an alternate American volume to compare it to, appeared limited. Surely Webster's *color* was an improvement over *colour*, but some educated Americans, having read Johnson's erudite etymologies, felt Webster's were closer to religious belief than scholarly history. The Puritan schoolmaster's attempt to simplify English spelling looked imperiled.

The battle between the two volumes became known as the Dictionary Wars. It's quaint, from the vantage point of our current MTV-video-game nation, that there was once a heated dispute about dictionaries. Apparently life before television was different. In truth, the Dictionary Wars took on a far larger meaning. The debate became a pitched skirmish between traditionalists and progressives, between the rough-hewn farmers, who liked Webster's emphasis on plain style, and the well-dressed merchants, who appreciated Worcester's nod to British erudition. This lexicographic fisticuffs became a major cultural event in pre-Civil War America. It's only a small exaggeration to say that the very soul of the young nation—and its spelling—was being passionately debated.

⊙⊙⊙

Resolving the battle, money reared its pretty head. Two enterprising brothers who understood bare-knuckle commercial warfare, Charles and George Merriam, bought the rights to Webster's dictionary. (Webster himself died in 1843, deeply unhappy that his great work was being overshadowed by a volume he saw as the work of an Anglophile plagiarist.) The Merriam brothers were determined that their dictionary banish all thought of Worcester's from the market. They hired a linguist to touch up Webster's original, distributing the revised edition at an aggressive price.

Then they got tough. The Merriam brothers threatened to use their market clout to prohibit the books of any publisher who promoted Worcester from being used in Boston schools. They also ran newspaper ads attacking competing publishers. In one episode, the Merriams sent a Webster's *Dictionary* to esteemed author Washington Irving, known for *Rip Van Winkle* and *The Legend of Sleepy Hollow*. Irving wrote back a letter of thanks, offering some faint praise for the dictionary, yet noting that he didn't like Webster's spelling and so wouldn't be using it. The Merriams took his scant praise and included it in a newspaper ad, sparking disputes about whether the ad misrepresented Irving's opinions.

The Merriam brothers' rough tactics prevailed. After decades of market infighting, Worcester's volume was turned into a museum artifact, while the Merriam-Webster *Dictionary* survived to sit on shelves at all modern bookstores.

But the blow that finally vanquished Worcester was not a market tactic but a dictionary revision—most notably a spelling revision. The Merriam brothers hired distinguished German linguist C. F. Mahn to clean up Webster's work, publishing the revised volume in 1864. Mahn greatly improved Webster's wayward etymologies, and he spiffed up the old master's pronunciation guidelines. Most attractive to the public, Mahn eliminated Webster's "nu" spellings, his backward-looking orthography that attempted to closely match pronunciation and spelling. Simplistic spellings like *wurd* for *word* and *reezon* for *reason* were edited out, much to the dismay of future spellers.

In essence, Webster's original sense of the American tongue as a radical redefinition of English, which Webster himself had retreated from, was all but washed out of the Webster-Mahn edition. As Mahn conceived of it, "American" was essentially the same as English, but without the British accent. The public agreed enthusiastically. They adored the new work. Although Mahn's name is but a footnote next to Noah Webster's, he played a definitive role in the making of the American dictionary and hence the language. That a German scholar would "complete" the language is oddly fitting. Remember, it was the marauding Germanic tribes who plundered what is now England and laid the foundation for the language.

If there's an answer to the question, "when was the American language born as we know it today?" it's 1864, the year the Webster-Mahn edition was published. As an interesting historical coincidence, that year is essentially concurrent with the end of the Civil War in 1865, when the American nation was rejoined together in the sense that we live in it today.

☯☯☯

As Noah Webster joined the pantheon of American folk heroes, the controversy over American spelling raged anew. Webster's fervent hope for spelling reform had come to little, yet the American Philological Association refused to let it die. In 1875 the Association formed a committee of learned men, including professors J. Hammond Trumbell of Yale and F. J. Child of Harvard. After a year's consideration the group decided that simplified spelling was a pressing matter and needed to be addressed immediately. They issued eleven new spellings to be put into use as soon as possible: *ar, catalog, definit, gard, giv, hav, infinit, liv, tho, thru,* and *wisht*.

Their proposal quickened the pulse of those who supported spelling reform. Just months later, at the International Convention for the Amendment of English Orthography, in Philadelphia, was born the Spelling Reform Association. The SRA supported the eleven new spellings wholeheartedly. As the reform movement gained steam in America, it attracted compatriots across the Atlantic. In 1879 an English counterpart to the SRA was founded, bolstered by such eminences as Charles Darwin and Alfred Tennyson. Tennyson had authored the poem "Charge of the Light Brigade," with its famous line, "their's not to reason why, their's but to do and die"—a line that summed up the resolve of the spelling reform movement. The American and English groups worked in tandem, each issuing pamphlets endorsing spelling reform and, more important, making the other group feel not so alone in the world.

The decisive moment came in 1886, when the American Philological Association published its manifesto, a slender booklet with 3,500 reformed spellings—not just a major overhaul but a clarion call to orthographic reformers everywhere. Many of these alterations had been proposed by Webster decades earlier, like *tung* for *tongue*; some others represented a new hope for phoneticism, like *trouble* spelled as *troble* and *catch* spelled as *cach*. But as sensible as the changes appeared to reformers, they found few who agreed with them. Editors and publishers looked at the list and guffawed in disbelief. Most of the copies ended up in the trash can.

The spelling reform movement, with the breath momentarily knocked out of it, found itself flat on the canvas. It was down—but it wasn't out.

〇〇〇

Mark Twain, who published his first story in 1865, brought the American language to life like no one before him, and arguably like no one since. In spirit, he agreed with Noah Webster's belief that the American tongue was separate from its English antecedent.

In Twain's 1872 novel *Roughing It*, he trumpeted what he called "the vigorous new vernacular of the occidental plains and mountains." In 1880's *A Tramp Abroad*, he opined that English and American, while once identical, had split asunder: "I could pile up differences until I not only convinced you that English and American are separate languages, but that when I speak my native tongue in its utmost purity an Englishman can't understand me at all." Twain's sentiment was echoed by Walt Whitman, author of *Leaves of Grass*, who wrote in the late 1800s that "ten thousand native idiomatic words are growing, or are today already grown, out of which vast numbers could be used by American writers."

Twain and Whitman and every other scribe writing at this time bore a terrible burden. They had to write in longhand. No word processor, nor even a manual typewriter aided their cramped fingers. To lighten the load, Twain favored an alternate spelling method called the "phonographic alphabet," created by Isaac Pitman. Based on forty characters, this simplified lettering system greatly reduced wear and tear on the hand, Twain claimed.

As he wrote in his essay "A Simplified Alphabet," "Mind, I myself am a Simplified Speller; I belong to that unhappy guild that is patiently and hopefully trying to reform our drunken old alphabet by reducing his whiskey. Well, it [Pitman's system] will improve him. When they get through and have reformed him all they can by their system he will be only HALF drunk. Above that condition their system can never lift him. There is no competent, and lasting, and real reform for him but to take away his whiskey entirely, and fill up his jug with Pitman's wholesome and undiseased alphabet."

To the general public, though, Pitman's phonographic alphabet was no replacement for traditional spelling, however strongly Twain believed in the system. English's spelling would stay as deeply inebriated as ever.

⊙⊙⊙

The American urge to reform spelling, however, ran deep. In 1898 the highly respected National Education Association launched a fresh effort. They proposed a list of improved spellings, a few of which would take hold, like *program* for *programme* and *catalog* for *catalogue*. The fact that these spelling changes were adopted reveals a central truth of spelling reform: The public might accept a polished version of the original, like *catalog* for *catalogue* (then again it might not), but a complete rebuild is always rejected. Spelling *word* as *wurd* won't fly.

Spelling reformers, however, weren't satisfied with a fresh coat of paint; they wanted to clean up the entire basement. As the new century dawned, a surge of energy infused the reform movement. In 1906 the industrialist Andrew Carnegie granted a $15,000 yearly subsidy to a group called the Simplified Spelling Board, a grant he soon increased to $25,000. The Board, feeling the jauntiness that $25,000 can give you, published a list of 300 reformed spellings. No less an authority than President Roosevelt, doubtless swayed by the great Carnegie's belief in moving orthography forward, approved of them. He ordered the Government Printing Office to begin using the new spellings. The American language was on its way toward a more logical foundation.

But the public didn't like the new spellings, no matter who endorsed them. Spellings like *thruout* appeared odd to the American eye. These ungainly inventions became fodder for humorists, who churned out numerous satiric essays lampooning the new versions. Even the Government Printing Office started resisting. Soon the new spellings were used only in the White House, to the great merriment of editorialists.

It would be a delectable irony of American history: The all-powerful Andrew Carnegie, who so ruthlessly dominated American steel, was thrown for a loss when he tangled with the beast known as American spelling. When he died in 1919, the Simplified Spelling Board's funding dried up. The group moved from Madison Avenue to Lake Placid, New York; that is, from the center of American publishing to a lovely but small town in upstate New York, from where they were hardly ever heard from again. In 1921 the National Education Association stopped endorsing the Board's reforms. American spelling seemed doomed to remain unrepentant.

But a highly influential publisher would keep the candle of reform flickering, however slightly. In the 1930s Robert R. McCormick, the crusty and idiosyncratic publisher of the *Chicago Tribune*, began slipping a handful of simplified spellings into his newspaper. If any group has the power to alter spelling, it's newspaper publishers—their publications are married to the daily vernacular. Yet McCormick's readers didn't like his alterations. They found it irritating that he preferred *iland* to *island*, *nite* for *night*, and *cigaret* for *cigarette*.

Over the years he sprinkled a total of 300 alterations into his paper. With the possible exception of *nite*, none of these caught on, and when McCormick died in 1955, the *Tribune's* passion for spelling reform ebbed considerably. In the 1970s the paper gave up the good fight altogether, with a headline that announced "Thru Is Through, and So Is Tho." The readers of the *Trib* would never again have to wonder why *hockey* was spelled as *hokey*.

⊙⊙⊙

It's probably inertia that keeps us from reforming spelling. The garage has been a mess so long that it's easier just to let the heap of stuff sit there.

But a larger force is also at work. Even if we could clean up spelling, flushing the current patchwork to create a logical system, would we want to? It's likely that we resist due not just to inertia but because of an urge we find irresistible: We want to hang on to our past. To reform spelling would be to wipe away part of our cultural memory.

Spelling holds our history. The odd, unlikely collections of letters, four or five or six at a time, each tells a story, often an epic tale that stretches back thousands of years. *Tomahawk. Discotheque. Chutzpah.* In each of these nonphonetic spellings is a narrative yarn, told obliquely by their letters. In fact, some of them contain a virtual four-part TV miniseries, with immigrants, foreign wars, strife, and, toward the end, a shining beam of hope. To spell *buffet* as *buffay* would make it easier to spell, but we'd lose something precious.

When Walt Whitman wrote, "I hear America singing," he was referring to the great cacophony, the wonderful racket made by the many divergent (but somehow unified) voices in American life. That lovely clatter is certainly heard in American spelling. *Connecticut. Georgia. Hawaii. Arkansas.* None of these names is spelled phonetically, thank goodness. To do so would be to wipe away the story behind these words, their narrative. (Of course the story behind many of these state names is about the white man taking land from the Indian—the Connecticut Indians were the first to go—but then again we should never forget that.)

So when a trembling speller steps to the microphone at the National Bee, he or she is getting ready to voice a collection of letters that, however nonsensical, holds a little bit of who we are. Who would want to reform that?

☉☉☉

Against all odds, the spelling reform movement lives on to this day, though it's only a pale shadow of its former self. The members of the Simplified Spelling Society show up at the Bee in Washington, DC, every year to protest. They walk politely in a small circle right in front of the hotel, carrying placards with proclamations like "I'm thru with through." But even the young spellers gathered for the contest, who certainly know the tortured nature of English spelling, view them as merely eccentric.

But the Society members *aren't* eccentric, or at least not very much so. That much was clear from my conversation with the president of the Simplified Spelling Society, John Wells, a professor in the department of phonetics and linguistics in University College, London.

In conversation over a transatlantic telephone line he comes across as a learned, thoughtful scholar who spends a good deal of time thinking about language. The fact that he speaks with a light English accent, in measured, kindly tones, makes his quixotic quest for spelling reform seem almost sensible.

He's an active reformer, working to publicize the Society's views. Shortly before I spoke with him he had been interviewed by Britain's Granada television company as part of a televised English spelling bee.

For Wells, the effort to reform spelling is a matter of common sense. "Schoolchildren learning to read and write have to spend a great deal of unnecessary time and effort learning to spell," he explains. "For adults, it remains for many people a source of embarrassment—it's because our spelling system is very inadequate to represent our language.

"People who are fortunate enough to grow up speaking Finnish, Swedish, Italian, and German don't face this same difficulty, because if you know how to say a word, you know how to spell it. And if you can see it written, you know how to pronounce it—and those things just don't fly with our system."

But, I ask, isn't it difficult to stay committed to simplified spelling, given the long odds the movement faces?

Wells chuckles at the notion. No, he doesn't get discouraged, but he does encounter resistance, especially from his own countrymen. "English people look with horror on America as reformers of spellings. English people are terribly aware that Americans leave out the *-me* at the end of *programme*, the *-ue* at the end of *catalog*, and the *-e* at the end of *axe*. And they've respelled *plough* so that it doesn't have the *-ough* anymore.

"The typical reaction to this is, 'I hope you're not going to recommend we adopt all those American spellings!'"

As someone dedicated to spelling reform, Wells appreciates the American efforts in this arena, however slight the result. "People think of *nite* for *night* and *lite* for *light* as American and therefore nasty. But that's really a silly attitude," he says. "I think Americans can be complimented on showing the right way to set about these things, which is to introduce parallel spellings and reform one thing at a time, rather than having a great big bang and having something quite different."

Wells sees no value in the way that English spelling reflects cultural history, as each idiosyncratic spelling represents a rich etymology. "Oh yes, etymology," he says dryly. "People say how nice it is in the word *receipt* that you've got the *p* there, which reminds you of *reception*. But then what about *deceit*? Where there is exactly the same relationship with *deception*, but we don't write a *p* in *deceit*. It's the inconsistency that's really so unnecessary."

Learning spelling is like memorizing a tangle of illogic, he opines. "It's like learning any arbitrary set of facts. It's fine if you have the kind of mind that loves learning arbitrary facts, but it's not much use in itself."

On the other hand, Wells says, the unpredictability of spelling does serve a useful purpose. What, I ask the president of the Simplified Spelling Society, could be the purpose of our nonlogical spelling system?

Wells laughs: "It's great fun for organizing spelling bees."

⊙⊙⊙

After C. F. Mahn's 1864 revision of Merriam-Webster's *Dictionary*, with its acceptance of most traditional English spellings, the volume held unquestioned market dominance for decades. As competitors entered the market, they used the model created by Merriam-Webster to publish their editions. New American dictionaries were issued on a regular basis, but they would simply be larger. (Or, in some cases, boast of being smaller. Note the so-called college dictionary, which touts itself as being slimmed down, apparently because rushed and mobile college students can't be bothered with a full dictionary; it would be inconvenient. If Noah Webster were alive, he would give these young Sauce-boxes a piece of his mind.)

The tome that capped Merriam-Webster's legacy as the big dog in American dictionaries was the second edition of its sprawling *Unabridged*, published in 1934. The volume would sit heavily upon its throne. After all, that fearsome moniker *Unabridged* means it purports to contain every word in the American language. That's not the kind of archive that can be revised every year, or even every decade. Refreshing the *Unabridged* is like cleaning out the attic—a vast undertaking, to be considered carefully before actually starting. A fully revised *Unabridged* wasn't issued until 1961, and has not been completely overhauled since then, though its Addenda is updated frequently.

This volume is the National Spelling Bee's official dictionary. If a word isn't within its hallowed pages—its 2,816 pages—it cannot be used in the Bee. Its most recent Addenda refresh was in 2002, hence the existence of recently minted words at the Bee.

It's the ever-growing Addenda that adds to the challenges facing spellers. In the 2004 Bee, for example, a speller faced *netiquette* (etiquette on the Internet), a word most certainly not in the 1961 *Unabridged*. Since Americans constantly create new words, the Addenda pours the fresh water of verbal inventions into the language like a swollen stream after a heavy rain.

Accelerating this process is the competitive nature of the modern dictionary business. Every publisher wants to be able to point to their volume as the most all-inclusive compendium. Which means today's dictionaries are giving the serious speller an ever larger ocean to swim. Now that we live on a babbling planet, with a rising torrent of words written and read every day, new words are minted almost as fast as you can spell *blog* (a word that first occurred in Merriam-Webster's dictionary in 2005).

Where Samuel Johnson turned out his first dictionary in 1755 with a team of six copyists, today Merriam-Webster has a team of staffers who read major periodicals to troll for new words. Their goal is to stay current with the language—and with their competitors.

And their competitors are remarkably current. For example, browse the New Words Section of a dictionary that competes with Merriam-Webster's, Random House's *Unabridged*. This list of new arrivals is only slightly less hip than the vocabulary of the trendiest teenager. It contains *bad hair day*, which it defines as "a disagreeable or unpleasant day, esp. one during which one feels unattractive." It also has *yada-yada-yada*—"and so on; and so forth."

It defines *Joe Sixpack* like this: "Slang. The average or typical blue-collar man." And it explains that *inner child* means "the childlike aspects of a person's psyche, esp. when viewed as an independent entity." If Mr. Sixpack is unaware of his inner child, he may be unable to have what the Random House *Unabridged* calls an *LTR*, or "long-term relationship." In this case he may never learn about *stork parking*, "spaces reserved in a car parking lot for cars driven by pregnant women or new mothers."

With competition like this from Random House, is it any wonder that the magisterial Merriam-Webster now contains the word *hottie* ("a physically attractive person")? Yes, a volume originally created by the Puritan schoolmaster Noah Webster now contains *hottie*. What would old Noah think? Then again, Webster did use the term *Sauce-box*, so he himself had a pretty earthy vocabulary.

Long term, the dictionary's expansion influences the Bee. To be sure, the yearly contest won't be using words like *yada-yada-yada* and *hottie*. In fact the Bee has no great preference for new words. Yet it does include the likes of *neti-*

quette, and Bee organizers make it clear that any word in the Addenda is fair game; certainly some of the new words will be appropriate for Bee use. Somewhere, at this very moment, there's a speller leafing through the Addenda, wondering what words she should study. And with every updated Addenda that task gets a little tougher.

So, for the sake of future spellers (both competitive and casual), the question must be asked: How does this process work? Who is it that decides a word is real—and hence adds it to the possible list facing every contestant in the Bee?

And who decides the spelling of these words? Who decided that the new dictionary entry *digerati* ("people skilled with computers") gets an *e* in the middle, instead of being spelled as *digirati*? And who decided that *la-la land*—defined as "1. A state of being out of touch with reality; 2. Los Angeles"—gets a hyphen?

Who, in other words, is the guardian of modern spelling?

☙☙☙

I'm on the phone with the person who's in charge of the English language. Okay, that's a wild exaggeration, but it's not completely wrong either. His name is John Morse, and his job title is president and publisher of Merriam-Webster. In other words, he runs the central clearinghouse, if such a thing exists, for the English language. Clearly, Morse is a kingpin in the world of nouns and verbs, and he has his finger on the pulse of modern orthography. And he seems well suited for this job. For someone who runs a major business, he's surprisingly literary, sort of like a cross between a regular CEO and someone you'd meet at Starbucks with a dog-eared copy of *Anna Karenina*.

He does not, of course, single-handedly decide what words and spellings are admitted into the definitive confines of the Merriam-Webster dictionary. Instead, Morse supervises a team of editors who track the usage of new words in current periodicals of all types. Among the sources they survey, he points to *The New York Times*, *The Wall Street Journal*, *Atlantic Monthly*, *Harper's*, nonfiction books, parts catalogs and repair manuals, company annual reports, menus, cookbooks, and many other printed and online publications.

"If we have evidence that a word has appeared in those kinds of publications and has done so for a period of years and in a variety of publications—we want to see that it's not just in specialized publications but across a variety of publications across a number of years—then that word is established enough to put in the dictionary," he says.

The Merriam-Webster editors categorize each possible new word as a 1, 2, or 3, with the 1's being must-include words, the 2's less so, and the 3's as possibilities that might get cut.

After they compile their list, it's sent to Morse to make the final judgment on which words will be included—hence my wild-eyed claim that he is in charge of the language. But, Morse notes, he's not the sole gatekeeper that every single word must pass on its way to being included in Merriam-Webster; instead, he's often one of a team of three top-level editors who make the final call.

However, for the 2005 update of the *Collegiate* dictionary, Morse *was* the sole arbiter. This is because the total number of potential new words, some twenty to thirty, was small enough for one top-level editor to review.

He made a series of judgment calls. He allowed *blog* in, after holding it off a year, but he decided to wait on *metrosexual*, about which he notes, "We have a lot of citations, but is that a one- or two- or three-year spike, or is that really going to be a word that persists in the language?"

Morse notes that, in the past, many words had to be commonly used for about ten years before being included. But in a nod to modern times, computer words get in fast; within five years, perhaps. And, faster still, a 2004 Merriam-Webster release included the term SARS, the respiratory disease. "Here's a case in which we were saying yes to a word in the summer of 2004 that probably had never even been used before early 2003," he says. "Sometimes, in lexicography, you just have to go by the seat of your pants and say, 'Do we do, or do we don't?' "

And the spelling of the new words? Only occasionally does Morse make spelling decisions, he says. That's because the spellings of new words, by the time they get to his desk, are usually set by the editors who do the word-scouting. And these editors, in turn, get them largely from the popular publications the words appear in.

In other words, the decisions about new American spellings are made by . . . the language itself. They're made by reporters on deadline and by headline writers, by rap singers and textbook scholars and ad agencies, by the masses of Internet users and, well, by all of us. In true American fashion, inventing new spellings is a democratic process. The words and their chosen spellings bubble up from the populace, with no particular regard for what's "correct." The vox populi is the ultimate authority for American spelling, and no higher power, like the language academies of Germany or France, stands above to correct it. Hence, we will always need spell-check.

Morse, naturally, is well aware of the many inconsistencies in English spelling, yet he appreciates the way these odd spellings reflect cultural history. "Spelling takes you back in time," he observes. He notes that Merriam-Webster sponsored a section on its Web site that asked users to list their favorite word, which the site later posted. "A lot of them are kind of tricky to spell," Morse says. "And I think people are drawn to words that have a kind of texture to them, where you can almost feel a history to them.

"I think that's also the attraction of the Spelling Bee. When the Spelling Bee is at its best, it's because there's that love and fascination for words as they evolved over the centuries," he says. "That's what spelling is; spelling is a kind of a palimpsest [a document that has been overwritten] of the word developing over the centuries—I think that's where the real charm is."

This same appreciation that Morse has for the vagaries of English's orthography extends to his feelings for the language as a whole. In particular, he relishes the flexibility and nuance of English. "The wonderful thing about the English language is that it really spans different kinds of uses and different registers," he says. "There are days when we are eloquent and days when we are informal, there are days when we are polysyllabic and days when we are quite abrupt."

As a dictionary maker, he enjoys all of these registers. "You love it when it's belletristic [when language is valued for its elegance alone], and you love it when it's hot and poppin'," he says. "I think if you're a lexicographer, you love it all."

¹⁸ Science Fiction: The Future of Spelling

If we look up from our massive Merriam-Webster's *Unabridged* for a moment and peer off into the future of orthography, what do we see? If we dare gaze into the inky unknown of the future, where is spelling headed in the generations to come?

The English language and the attendant chaos of its spelling has, over the last 1,500 years, seen periods of stability and periods of change—with the emphasis on change. Now in the twenty-first century, the language faces an agent of change even more powerful than marauding Anglo-Saxon tribesmen or William the Conqueror. This revolutionary force is the Internet, that great gaggle of pixel-borne emoticons, and it will surely have a profound impact on written communication between U & me in the yrs a head :)

But how, exactly, will the Internet change language and spelling in the decades (and millennia) ahead? To explore that, I spoke with two leading language theorists, Dennis Baron, professor of linguistics at the University of Illinois at Champaign-Urbana (the day we spoke he was set to give a talk about the Internet's effect on language), and Geoffrey Nunberg, a frequent National Public Radio commentator and a researcher at Stanford University's Center for the Study of Language and Information.

Baron, by the way, often took part in spelling bees as a boy. He was a superb speller but the contests made him terribly anxious. "I couldn't wait to make a mistake so I could sit down," he recalls. Later, for five years he was a judge for a regional bee in central Illinois.

As to how the Internet will affect language, he explains: "I have no idea—but that's one of the questions I put on the final exam."

In truth, Baron does have a vision of a Net-influenced language. He believes that language as we know it will survive; in fact, he postulates that much of its basic structure will remain intact. To back up his hypothesis, he points out that many of the new written forms, like e-mail and text messaging on cell phones, started out with a "frontier mentality"—anything goes, and rules were thrown by the wayside as communication rocketed down the information superhighway. But over time, he observes, a self-organizing ethic has set in. "Now there are all these guides about how to write a correct e-mail, and all our e-mail software has spell-check."

Human tribes, even electronically based ones, have a tendency to self-regulate by establishing norms and then enforcing those norms through peer pressure. "I call it the civilizing of the electronic frontier," Baron says. This is true even in the semiliterate world of instant messaging, he claims—although this statement may strain credulity (and indeed, Baron himself doesn't view instant messaging as semiliterate). With IM, "if you violate the conventions of the community, they jump on you, whether it's for being too formal or too informal."

Baron, demonstrating that he's a truly fearless linguist, has conducted research into IM speech patterns. He finds the subject fascinating, but research was difficult: "It's hard to get IM transcripts—my son won't show me his." After examining extensive records of IM conversations, he concluded that they do not point to the end of traditional language. "A lot of them are fairly formal," he notes. While they're full of acronyms and three-letter words, "there are sentences and punctuation—there's nothing about the medium that says you can't be formal or informal."

Looking ahead to, say, 2050, he sees today's orthographic conventions surviving without major revolution. "I don't see that there will be vast changes in spelling," he says, because "there's enough of a sense of conventionality that underlies how we think about language." (While he's on the subject, he observes that his students' spelling is better than it used to be.)

So to those who feel that the Internet will be the death of English—and he concedes many feel this way—he counters: "Not at all." The Internet is expanding the language in new ways, "but it's an infinitely expandable language—it's always been pretty adaptable."

Geoff Nunberg concurs that contemporary spelling will survive the onslaught of Internet-based communication modes. He dismisses the notion that instant messaging's emoticon-heavy spelling style will alter the language. "They said that about the telegraph, too," he says. (However, he does loathe the word *emoticon*, referring to it as "one of the worst words ever—it deserves to die horribly in a head-on crash with *infotainment*.")

Standardized spelling has attained true cultural saturation, Nunberg notes. "More people spell well now than ever before. That's something that people don't believe," he says. "You read Jefferson, and he didn't know how to spell. With *knowledge* he left out the *w*—and that didn't mean Jefferson didn't know about knowledge, if anybody did.

"Look at eighteenth-century spelling, and they were spelling *publik* with a *k*, but since the time of Dickens [the mid-1800s], spelling has changed very little," points out Nunberg.

In fact, theorizes Nunberg, spelling's evolution has reached a plateau. "Spelling has changed less in the last hundred years than in the last hundred years proceeding, and that was less than the hundred years before. It's changing less and less," he says. "English spelling is pretty much frozen now. I think there'll be very few changes in spelling in the next two hundred years—it's hard to imagine any."

But if spelling will remain stable, the environment it exists in will change markedly, Baron forecasts. Text will be submerged in an increasingly multimedia-saturated visual landscape; language will less often stand on its own. As Renaissance printers felt it was a step forward to include woodcut illustrations in manuscripts, so we will push this practice to its extreme by never allowing words to walk out the door without a video-audio-holograph chaperone.

"People are writing academic papers online with embedded video," Baron notes.

The big break from the past may come when speech recognition software is perfected. At that point we'll be able to write simply by talking: Speak into your computer's recorder, and it'll do all the messy work of punctuation and spelling. This could result in the elimination of the keyboard, Baron speculates. "We'd get back to oral composition—reinventing Homer."

That, it appears, would be a major step backward. Eliminate writing? This painstaking mind-lingual-hand mode of communication is usually far more detailed and evolved than speech. The written word has carried us up from the savanna and given us Shakespeare, Jane Austen, and E.E. Cummings, not to mention *People* magazine.

But Baron, ever the futurist, is unconcerned with the possible extinction of the written word. As to the assertion that writing is typically a more advanced means of communication than speaking, "maybe it is and maybe it isn't," he says. "We have a prejudice in thinking that putting it all down on paper somehow makes it more real than telling it to someone—I wonder if that actually is psychologically the case."

At any rate, Baron opines, whatever changes affect human communication, one thing is certain: "We're not going to give up words—words will never die."

ʘʘʘ

If we're willing to boldly hypothesize about the future of English and its spelling, there's a clue to be had by looking at a formative moment in English's history. After William the Conqueror took control of England, two languages, Old English and the Norman dialect of French, lived side by side; over the course of many years they merged, becoming one language.

The Internet is a global version of this commingling. There are countless Web sites in which Chinese sits next to English, or Spanish mixes with English. And highly trafficked English language sites like Yahoo, with the click of a button, present themselves to Brazilians, Indians, or Italians in their native tongue.

This commingling suggests two possible scenarios for the long-term evolution of language as influenced by global networking.

One possibility is that English's hegemony becomes total. Of the 6 billion people on the planet, some 1.2 to 1.5 billion people speak English, including 400 to 450 million native speakers—more people speak English than any other language (though Chinese has more native speakers). English is currently a dominant, probably *the* dominant, language of the Internet. Because of the commercial and cultural influence of America, that's likely to continue into the foreseeable future.

English's history reveals that it's capable of a great verbal gobbling act. While some languages invent their own words, English happily pilfers from other tongues. ("We vacuum words up," Baron notes.) As English mingles with other languages over the Internet—across centuries—its capacity as a "sponge language" could allow it to absorb enough vocabulary to make it a true one-world global language. Even now the educated classes in many nations speak English, so it's often the case that, say, a Korean and a Spaniard use English to communicate. Since English is already the international language, the Internet could simply cement this process. In this case English spelling would frustrate more people than ever before.

But another scenario is possible. Call it the reverse Tower of Babel phenomenon. As all the languages of the world were cast apart (or so the story goes), they could all merge back together into one. After hundreds or thousands of years of Yugoslavians text messaging Italians, and Chinese creating Web sites read by Mexicans, and Indonesians e-mailing Europeans, one sprawling common tongue begins to coalesce. An intermingling of all languages. Helping this process will be the two forces that have always acted to combine language, commerce and war, both of which will always be with us. Finally, it arrives: a One World language, a single sprawling tongue, spoken everywhere from Austria to Zimbabwe.

For the first few generations, its spelling and grammatical conventions will remain semi-chaotic, until a twenty-fifth-century Noah Webster produces a One World dictionary, hoping to promulgate a simplified spelling like the old Puritan dreamed of. Publishers will release competing holographic online versions as standards for definition (and choice of alphabet) get worked out, and eventually an accepted tome emerges, copyright 2501.

And it will be an elephantine volume. Since the One World dictionary will draw from many tongues, it will dwarf today's dictionaries. The Japanese have dozens of words for raw fish served over rice, the Italians have numerous words for fashion—*stoffe*—and there are all those Russian terms for vodka—*Moskovskaya*! While Merriam-Webster's *Unabridged* has 475,000 words and the Oxford English Dictionary holds 658,000, the One World dictionary will have—let's allow ourselves a guess—some three to five million.

What all this will lead to, of course, is the formation of a World Spelling Bee. The best spellers from not just every state in the United States but every country on the globe will gather to compete in, say, Tokyo, in about the year 2513, give or take a few hundred years. Each speller will be checked to make sure they don't have their built-in retinal scanner-decoder turned on, and the wireless connection to their cerebral implant must be turned off. Word buffs around the world will watch it live on their solar-powered cell phones.

The words will be different from today's Bee but, of course, the kids will be the same. They'll still get nervous while waiting to spell, and they'll still be up late the night before. They'll still be happy if they make it to the late rounds, and they'll still dream of spelling the perfect word before a large audience. And they will still, when they conquer a tough challenge, and the judge says, "That is correct," leap for joy, cry, and breathe hard, and then, trembling, enjoy an uncontrollably joyous smile.

Part⁵

Five Top Spellers Compete for Glory and Fame

"You're just wearing every lucky charm possible, sleeping with lucky charms under your pillow, crossing your fingers, and praying that you're going to get a word that you know."
—Aliya Deri, 13, National Bee contestant

¹⁹ Preface to a Competition

Every winter, the process begins again. Spellers all across the country begin competing to earn a spot at Nationals. It's like a great swim upstream, with some ten million kids at the beginning, getting quickly winnowed at each successive stage, until only the top 275 or so make it to Washington.

Depending on where a speller lives, their qualifying rounds proceed in myriad different ways. In some schools, they must win their classroom bee to compete in their school bee; other schools have an open bee with no preliminary class bees. Then, in some areas of the country, winners of school bees go directly to their regional bees; in other areas, this process is more challenging: A speller must win a district or city bee before advancing to their regional bee.

The regional, held in February or March, is the tough one. A speller must win here to travel to National. At regional, spellers compete against a field of winners. All the kids onstage have studied for this event, and many have studied quite hard. And everyone there knows they're just one win away from a trip to the nation's capital and the attendant prestige. Everyone wants to win.

In theory, spellers who have made it to Nationals in the prior year have an advantage. They know what to study and have an extra year of study behind them. But they are accorded no special privileges. As the competition begins afresh each year, they must start at the bottom and work their way up. And the Bee is replete with stories of competitors who made it to Washington one year but failed to earn a spot the next.

The following chapters profile five spellers who hope to win a spot in the 2005 National Bee. Each of them is a top competitor, based on their performance in the 2004 Nationals. Each of these five spellers, Marshall Winchester in North Carolina, Kerry Close in New Jersey, Samir Patel in Texas, Jamie Ding in Detroit, and Aliya Deri in San Francisco, faces a major challenge. They are proven winners, but, again, they must earn their spot anew. Will they make it to Washington?

With fingers crossed, they step up to the microphone . . .

²⁰ Marshall Winchester

No one spells like Marshall Winchester. Tall, slender, bespectacled, with short-cropped black hair, Marshall takes hold of the microphone before issuing the letters. He stands as if ready to make a firm, declarative statement. He pauses for a moment, perhaps several moments, thinking—but not too long. Others may hem and haw, but not Marshall. When he's ready, he proceeds through a word with no hesitation and no doubt. Speaking in a loud clear voice, made musical by his soft North Carolina drawl, he hammers each letter home—almost shouting them—in an even cadence, much like a master blacksmith taking pleasure in pounding an errant piece of iron into a perfect horseshoe.

"He always has a joy about it," says his father, Eric. "*The Charlotte Observer* described him one year as a 'loud confident speller with a southern accent.'"

And that he is. As when Marshall faced *lignite*, a type of coal. Grasping the microphone firmly, speaking directly into it, he proclaimed his choice of letters as if in a clarion call: L! I! G! N! I! T! E! When he was done with *lignite*, it wasn't just spelled, it was rendered defenseless, dispatched, dispensed. It would never again raise its sulfurous head at a spelling match to challenge him. *Lignite* whimpered offstage. *Lignite* had been spelled by Marshall.

In the days leading up to Marshall's 2005 regional bee in Charlotte, North Carolina, it seemed a given that he would win the contest. Having made it to Nationals the last two years—placing an impressive fourth out of 265 spellers in 2004—winning his regional was expected to be as easy as hanging upside down from a high tree branch, which the thirteen-year-old does regularly. And Marshall, a devoted student of many subjects, including Bible studies and advanced mathematics, focuses like a laser beam on his study of language. He's a word aficionado. He gets the same kind of pleasure from spelling obscure words that other kids get from video games and iPods—neither of which Marshall has any interest in. Moreover, the Winchester family is a tight-knit clan, and spelling, specifically the spelling success of oldest son Marshall, is a central part of that family life.

However, as we sit here on this sunny Thursday morning in February, waiting for the Charlotte bee to begin, winning seems like quite a trick. Up onstage with Marshall are twenty-eight other bright kids, each of whom has won their school bee and county bee. And each of whom would greatly enjoy winning the trip to Washington that results from placing first this morning.

The field is sixteen girls and thirteen boys, and some of the girls, in particular, appear mature beyond their years. They look serious and they look like avid readers. And then there's Janae Jackson, one of three black kids up onstage, whom Marshall went toe-to-toe with in the prior year's regional. She's a tough speller. At the end of last year it was just the two of them, dueling round after round, back and forth, until Janae finally misspelled. With another year of study under her belt, the look on her face this morning says she's been dreaming of Washington this year. No doubt about it: This stage is full of the best young orthographers the Charlotte area has to offer.

Is Marshall really going to outspell all of them?

Approaching Charlotte from the city outskirts, the streets are full of low-lying buildings, some looking squalid and run-down. But upon entering Charlotte proper, a true mini-metropolis emerges, with tall buildings and fashionable euro-bistros, and ads for the Charlotte Symphony. Banking is big business here, and the Bank of America building is sixty stories tall, dwarfing its neighbors. Charlotte's downtown is only about twelve blocks long and perhaps two blocks wide, but within this small area it resembles a large city. Office workers chat into cell phones while frequenting fashionable lunch spots like Dean & Deluca and the faux Italian Coco Osteria. For all its apparent urbanity, however, the twelve-block strip moves with antebellum languor. Even in the middle of a workday there's little traffic, and no one is hurrying.

That same languor is not found inside the Spirit Square building in the middle of downtown Charlotte. It's an ornate performance space, with plush red velvet seats and stained-glass windows—it was once a church—that seats about 500. About half the seats are full, mainly with casually dressed parents who wear concerned looks, in their thirties and early forties. Several parents busily work camcorders.

In fact, the parents, if anything, look more nervous than their verbally gifted offspring. As I walk in, one of the ushers, a prim woman with gray hair, confirms this. The kids are nervous, she notes, "but the parents are even worse. Next year, the Charlotte Chamber of Commerce should hand out Valiums for everyone."

There *is* a buzz of excitement—I feel it distinctly and I'm just observing. Perhaps it's the three TV cameramen getting footage for the local news. Or the fact that winning this morning's contest is a serious resume item: Finalist, Scripps National Spelling Bee, Washington, DC, 2005. Or, more likely to be causing parental jitters, it's that their talented tween has won a school bee and a county bee, has studied for this day, fretted about it, and here, finally, it is. *Our Ashley is up onstage.*

The bee's pronouncer is Don King, a dapper, erudite, fiftyish gentleman who takes a kindly attitude toward his job—he's clearly on the side of the kids. King speaks with the pleasant drawl that identifies him as a native, but his diction is careful and precise.

He starts with true softies: *trinket, protein, cognate.* Unlike at Nationals, where the kids play the game cannily, asking all possible questions—language of origin, part of speech—these kids just get up and spell. No fuss, no muss. That is, until Marshall walks up to the microphone.

He's a beam of energy this morning—like he is all mornings, actually—a tall boy standing straight up in his red shirt and crisp blue jeans, his black hair neatly buzz-cut, his braces and suggestion of a mustache identifying him as very much age thirteen. In conversation, Marshall is polite but outgoing, always willing to make his opinions known. "Mr. Maguire," he'll say, as he always addresses me, pertly and sincerely, after which I know a thoughtful observation is on the way. It could be about most anything: a change in airline schedules, the nature of the German language, his love of tree climbing, the history of the Bee, the budget of the Bee—more than $75,000 in prizes are awarded at Nationals, he explains, a number he takes great relish in. I doubted the number was that large until he took me through the math step-by-step. He wants to be an accountant when he grows up, and if he can sit still that long—which at this point is not clear—he will certainly be a good one.

Unlike the other kids, Marshall knows how to work the bee. He steps up to the microphone, grabs hold of it—in his grasp it's going nowhere—and asks, "Are there any alternate pronunciations?" or "Language of origin?" or "Mr. King, are there any homonyms?" He's like a lawyer who's been in court many times before, while the other spellers are all defendants who have chosen to represent themselves.

In truth he doesn't need any of this extra information. All the words in today's bee are listed in the *Paideia*, the slender book of 3,800 words distributed by Bee organizers several months prior. He's had that memorized for months. If you woke him up in the middle of the night and asked him to spell standing on his head, he could rattle off the 3,800 before dawn.

But he takes no chances this morning. At one point Marshall gets *unobtrusively*, a real softball, and yet still he asks for the language of origin—clearly a clue he has no use for. He queries the judge to give himself a moment to gather his wits. He used to spell fast, sprinting through the letters so rapidly they were almost incomprehensible; in conversation he still does, flying through polysyllabics like a 50-yard dash. But in competition he has learned to slow down. This morning he's here to win, and that calls for a careful approach.

Until he faces *excruciating*. He starts well, proclaiming the word's letters boldly one by one, until—in the middle of the word—he stops. He stands in silence. He announces that he wants to start over. Start over? Is Marshall unsure—on an easy word like *excruciating*? He is surely causing a major lump in the throat of his parents, who sit in the front row looking up expectantly at their oldest child.

Both of Marshall's parents are committed to his spelling success. His father, Eric, who's good-natured and quick to make a joke at his own expense, feels the tension of Marshall's competitions acutely yet is a big believer in his son's abilities. Likewise Marshall's mother, Grindl, a warm, friendly woman who doubles as her son's spelling coach and who firmly believes he can win.

Marshall is allowed to start over on his spelling of *excruciating*, but he can't change the letters from his first attempt. If he made a mistake in his first try, he'll be sitting home in Charlotte this year. Just before the anxiety gets knee deep, Marshall gallops through the word in double time. Relief pervades.

In the first few rounds, Marshall's archrival, Janae Jackson, faces *momentary*. It's an easy word, but something odd happens. Janae spells it with relative ease and sits back down—but the judges inform her that she has misspelled. Apparently she said the letter *e* before beginning, inadvertently voicing it aloud as she mentally considered using an *e* or an *a* at the end of the word. Any letter a speller speaks is counted, and so Janae trudges disconsolately off stage.

(Marshall admits the sight is a welcome one for him; he was quite scared of her as this competition began, and is relieved to see her eliminated.)

After Janae, the boys are the first to fall. Zach Brack, a slender middle-schooler, misses *sluggard*. "Got nervous," he explains to his parents as he sits down in the audience. Rocco Thompson, a big fellow who doubtless will be eyed by high school football coaches, gets tackled by *misinterpret*. Patrick O'Brien, who apparently hasn't yet studied French, takes it in stride when he learns that *ensemble* is not spelled with an *o*. By round five, we're down to three boys and ten girls.

Pronouncer Don King keeps things light with his courtly sense of humor. After a speller masters *crouton*, he jests, "Enjoy your salad," prompting an audience chuckle. He notes that it's a little chilly in the theater, saying, "Wouldn't it be nice to have some chamomile tea? Parents—spell *chamomile*!"

Despite his levity, the spellers bend seriously to their work. Katie Pyler, looking strong, handles the uncommon *tetralemma*, which means a dilemma with four alternatives. Clare Archer, a tall and mature-looking middle-schooler with shoulder-length dark hair, clearly a contender, struggles with *propinquity*. She inserts an *e* where none exists—but as soon as she walks off, she's called back.

Don King tells her he mispronounced the word. So she will, remarkably, get another. Her second word is the obscure *shogunate*, a Japanese dignitary with power greater than the emperor. Clare searches her memory far and wide for the Asian term, yet she misspells for the second time.

In the following round a girl is given an astounding three words due to mispronunciation—surely a record in the history of regional bees. Her first challenge is *erudite*, which a judge informs King that he has added a syllable to. When King tells the speller he'll choose a new one, she thanks him gratefully in a tone that suggests she would've struggled with the first choice. King then voices the tough *cationic*, but again, he tells her he has mispronounced. He moves on to *diverticulum*. The lucky girl masters this third challenge—in effect she was saved by the pronouncer.

When Marshall steps up and faces *chromometer*, he asks for any alternate pronunciations, sending the judges flipping through their dictionaries. It's an almost humorous request—Marshall memorized the word months ago—but he means it sincerely. He's practicing for the big time, when spellers need all the clues they can get because the words aren't handed out ahead of time, as today's are. He gets his answer and spells with ease. His speaking volume has dropped; he's not proclaiming his letters with his typical vigor. He has eased into cruising altitude for the competition—but he's about to face his toughest challenger.

Up steps Tristan Jenkins, who has breezed easily through all his words today. He's a tall, large boy who shambles up to the microphone in sneakers and an oversize sweatshirt. He'd be a tempting target for any football coach, except a quick glance at him reveals that his nose is so often buried in a book he'll never get passionate about sending his big frame hurtling against the opposition. On the other hand, if the field of battle is word-related, he appears ready to block and tackle with the best of them. The eighth-grader has already taken the SAT test and scored in the upper percentile.

Tristan's word is *Hellenic*. After only a short pause, he spells it with just one *l*—the bells rings signaling a misspell. But Don King calls him back. After Tristan spelled, King decided that he hadn't been given the correct pronunciation, so Tristan gets another chance. With the competition narrowed to the final few, this could profoundly alter the outcome. But that's the quirky nature of regional bees; all sorts of odd things happen. Tristan's second word is *rutabaga*, which he devours without hesitation. He's looking good.

The field narrows quickly, as top contenders trudge off stage. Rachel Sams seemed to have the word list down cold, but she misses *tilde*; Sarah Lancaster might have taken the trophy, but she's felled by *crucible*.

After the misspell bell sends a few more spellers off stage, Tristan and Marshall are the only two left. They don't acknowledge one another, but they don't need to. The duel has begun.

Marshall gets *immalleable*; he nails it. Tristan gets *jerkin*; he thinks briefly, asking for language of origin and sample sentence, then dispatches it. Marshall gets *gusset*; he spells without doubt. Tristan gets *redoubt*; he handles it without a second thought.

Facing *cloture*, Marshall pronounces it as "closure"—the words sound close to identical. Don King works him through it, providing plenty of help. Up in the Big Show, in Washington, they don't work you through it. They say the word, and if you don't get it, they'll say it again exactly the same, repeatedly if need be. But here, King emphasizes the *t* in the middle with an extra tap—he all but tells Marshall that he's mistaken if he thinks the word is *closure*. Perhaps Marshall doesn't need the helping hand; at any rate, he finds closure with *cloture*.

Tristan steps up and takes care of *glycerol* without asking a single question. Marshall bangs out *metalloid*, maintaining his method of asking for the definition. The audience leans forward in hushed silence. It's not clear where Tristan's parents are sitting, but Marshall's, in the front row just 15 feet away from this showdown, have their eyes trained on their child. For them, it's almost as if the entire Winchester family were onstage. Marshall's spelling career is an integral part of the family's daily life, and were he to stumble over a letter, no small cloud would settle over the Winchester home.

Tristan gets *topiary* and easily trims it down to size, as the three local TV cameramen keep shooting for tonight's news. *Parquetry* is Marshall's hurdle to leap, and, after asking the language of origin, he hops right over it. Tristan smokes through *carcinogenic* like a pack-a-day man—not a moment of consideration. This kid could go to Nationals.

Marshall faces the lengthy *primogeniture*, a word meaning the state of being the firstborn child, and he spells it like the firstborn he is. Tristan gets the uncommon *ecru*, referring to a shade of pale brown, and, after asking for a sample sentence, spells it confidently.

Tristan has just revealed something. The fact that he spelled *ecru* after asking for only a sample sentence, not definition or language of origin, means that he, like Marshall, is asking questions just to gather his wits. *Ecru* is an odd word that doesn't sound at all like it's spelled; a sample sentence by itself is of little help. It's now clear that Marshall is competing with someone who has spent serious time with the *Paideia*—there's not a thirteen-year-old boy in the country who knows how to spell *ecru* without studying it. Tristan's knowledge of the word suggests that this bee will go beyond the *Paideia*, which means the words could come from anywhere. The anxiety level notches up.

Marshall is dealt *regicide*, spells it, then struggles with the pronunciation as he repeats the word to signal he's finished spelling it—the tension is apparently getting to the thirteen-year-old. Being in a one-on-one match with someone who can rattle off *ecru* makes even a veteran orthographer nervous.

Tristan gets *caldera*. "Repeat?" he drawls nonchalantly—he's a cool customer—then speeds through it as if Spanish were his first language. Marshall gets *domiciliated*. "Domiciliated, please define the word," he asks—Marshall's politeness remains intact even in the heat of battle, though he's now speaking at twice his normal tempo. He spells it handily.

Tristan faces *anemology*, the study of winds. "Anemology?" he inquires, in a tone that indicates complete bafflement. He digs for clues with questions, but his voice reveals that he's psyched out. He's good when he knows the words, and his avid reading and native intelligence (and *Paideia* study) mean he knows most of them. But his sudden confusion shows that if he's forced to guess—an essential skill for any competitive speller—he's a house of cards on a windy day. After his attempt the bell signals a misspell.

Marshall is one word away from winning. His word: *hibernal*. "Hibernal, definition, please," he inquires in a rapid-tempo whisper. The normally full-throated speller is down to sotto voce with the sweet tension of the moment. Not that there's any real doubt here. *Hibernal* isn't a word the average eighth-grader spends a lot of time with, but for someone who's climbed the mountain to Nationals the last two years, it offers not even a foothill. As he spells it, he can hardly slow himself down to his normally even cadence, rushing through the last couple letters in a joyous burst.

"Thank you, you are the champion," announces Don King, prompting the auditorium to leap into sustained cheering.

Marshall lifts his hands in the air in his moment of triumph, smiling a big beaming grin, his orthodontia glinting in the stage spotlights. He has dreamed of this moment, and it has come true: He's going to the 2005 Nationals.

Three minutes later, a reporter from *The Charlotte Observer* is interviewing the new champ. "What's the word you spelled to win?" he asks. Marshall thinks for a moment, lost in thought. "I forget," he says, chuckling.

〇〇〇

Driving back to the Winchester home after the regional bee, we pass through rolling North Carolina countryside—or what used to be countryside. The family lives about forty minutes outside Charlotte, and as we drive, Marshall's father, Eric, points out all the new homes that have sprung up in the last few years. Cropping up among the verdant green are freshly built subdivisions, row upon row of shiny houses—many of them surprisingly large. "There are a lot of Northerners invading North Carolina," Eric notes in a bit of dry humor.

As prosperous as the new McMansions make the area look, all is not well. Eric works as a chemist in a textile plant—"we live paycheck to paycheck," he says—and the textile industry is not so slowly moving overseas. In fact, a month after Marshall's regional, yet another textile mill in South Carolina announced it was relocating to Mexico, at a loss of 700 jobs.

The Winchester home is tucked away in the woods, as much as that's possible with all the new development. Eric himself had the house built some fifteen years ago, back when this location was truly rural. The lot is just five minutes from where he grew up, so he knows every last footpath in these forests. Decorated in earth tones, the three-bedroom house has a comfortable, warm feel, with a living room built around a fireplace. The cozy living room is ideal for the family gatherings that are so central to the Winchesters' daily life.

"The word that best describes us is 'family,'" Eric says. "Most people probably couldn't understand us, because we're very conservative, we're family oriented. We sit around the table each night and eat together, and we talk. They're happy," he says, referring to Marshall and his brother, Tanner, an energetic eight-year-old with a crew cut that's identical to Marshall's, who professes no interest in spelling. "They wake up happy and go to sleep happy."

One item in the Winchester home is all but ignored: the television. The vintage 1985 model is almost never turned on, Grindl says, "because we really don't have time."

"We don't live a traditional life, with a lot of TV and stuff like that, but we love it that way," she says.

Recently, the family bought nine loads of firewood and spent Friday night and Saturday morning splitting and stacking wood for their living room fireplace. "We all do that as a family," Eric says.

At one point during their wood splitting, Marshall commented to the effect that someday he'll pay someone to do this for him. Grindl admonished him: "Hey, you wouldn't appreciate your fire if you had someone to load in your wood. You know what it takes to cut it down, haul it home, split it and stack it, and all that." Marshall understood the value of her point, she says.

"I've tried it both ways," Grindl says of her approach to parenting Marshall and Tanner. "I've tried to cater to them, make them happy. They're rotten when you do that—they're not happy at all.

"So whenever they've mixed it in with a lot of work, they know how to appreciate it," she says. "Being happy all the time, doing what you want to, that becomes boring. But if you work and work and work, and then you enjoy a little time, you enjoy it so much more."

With that in mind, the family day is a busy one. Marshall and Tanner are homeschooled, and Grindl teaches them a full course of study, which Marshall complements each day with about ninety minutes of violin practice and an hour of piano practice, fitting in his chores as he can. He works about two to three hours a day on his spelling, an hour of which Grindl quizzes him, with the remaining time spent on solo spelling study.

In the afternoon Grindl sends her sons out to play, believing in the value of fresh air. Marshall has climbed many of the trees around the house, and he performs like an acrobat on a chin-up bar in the yard. But, hungry for more spelling study, he sometimes brings his laptop outside with him and spends his "playtime" slogging through his word lists.

"He kind of cheats," Eric says with a smile. "He gets outside *and* he works—it's a conspiracy." (Marshall, in fact, wants to get a wireless card for his laptop so he can connect to Internet spelling study tools out in the yard—so much for fresh air.)

Many top spellers are aided by an inability to keep their nose out of a book; reading is like breathing for most finalists. While Marshall has read quite a bit—he's gone through most of the historical fiction of Genevieve Foster—there's nothing he likes to read on a regular basis, he says. "I was trying to read *The Hobbit*, but I could never get through it because I never had time." He greatly prefers nonfiction to fiction. At any rate, his spelling skill "is more from the [word] list" than from voracious reading, he says.

Marshall's room, neat and uncluttered, is clearly the room of a speller. Up on one wall is a large array of framed news articles about his orthographic prowess. After one victory, *The Charlotte Observer* nicknamed him the "Waxhaw Wiz," in honor of the county he lives in.

When he's not immersed in his word lists, "I like going to friends' houses and playing board games—that's my most favorite thing to do." He particularly enjoys chess, Life, and—of course—Scrabble.

His day always begins and ends with Bible study. Grindl reads a Bible devotion to the kids over breakfast, and Eric does a Bible study with the boys each night before they go to bed. Eric describes the church the family belongs to as a "real small, conservative fellowship, probably not more than 150 people." At one point the church hosted a Junior Bible Quiz contest on Sunday nights, in which the kids competed to see who knew the most about various Biblical events; Marshall used to participate but is now too old. As part of his church activities, every other Friday night he volunteers at a food bank.

It's because of his faith that Marshall is one of the few spellers at the Bee who doesn't do anything for luck. "We just do a lot of prayer, don't we, Marshall?" Eric says. "Marshall realizes that God's really blessed him a lot."

☉☉☉

After Marshall competed in the 2003 Nationals, the Winchesters got a call from a television producer in Los Angeles. Would Marshall like to participate in an episode of the game show *Lingo?*

The answer was yes, so Eric, Grindl, Marshall, and Tanner packed their bags and flew to Hollywood. (The Winchesters do everything as a family.) Eric and Grindl asked the TV producers why they chose Marshall. "They said, 'He just stood out to us,'" Grindl recalls. And that's no surprise—Marshall's ebullience at the microphone, with his bold delivery, sets him apart. And his high ranking in Nationals that year undoubtedly helped.

The Winchesters kept a tape of the show, which they play for me. As Grindl turns on the ignored television set, Marshall asks his mother, "You don't think I look too bad on that, do you?"

"No," she says. "You look cute, Marshall."

The show was hosted by the suavely plastic Chuck Woolery, who greeted Marshall with cheery insincerity. "Nice to have you here, buddy, having a good time? Good, I want you to have a good time."

Woolery asked Marshall what word he missed in the previous year's National Bee. "*Quemadero,*" Marshall replied, "it means a place of execution by burning."

Hearing the gruesome definition, another young contestant chimed in, "Nice!" getting a big audience laugh. (In reality the laughter was added later because the show was shot on an empty soundstage.) In response, Woolery gave a wry look that seemed to say, "These young people sure know some strange things."

"You know," Woolery said, "I knew that, Marshall, and I'm disturbed by the fact that I knew that"—big fake audience groan—"because I feel like I'm there, every now and then." The episode ended quickly, in a blizzard of letters and blinking lights, in which Marshall hardly got a chance to say anything.

The most enjoyable moment of the Winchester family's time in Los Angeles was during an evening at the swank hotel at which the show put them up. The family went out to a Subway sandwich shop, bought their dinner, and brought it back to the hotel's pool. They all sat together out at the pool, taking in the night air, relishing their shared dinner in an exotic location. "We were on the side of a mountain, at sunset, the wind was blowing and it was a gorgeous setting," Eric recalls. "It was like something you'd see in a movie."

☾☽☾☽☾☽

Marshall likes most everything about the Bee. He takes pleasure in the words and the competition, and he's a committed historian of the national contest. He can tell you, off the top of his head, what word many top spellers missed, in what round, in many recent Bees.

His enthusiasm for the Bee extends even to his orthodontia. When getting his braces adjusted, his orthodontist offered him a choice of different color bands; in 2003 Marshall chose lime green because the Bee used this distinctive color to decorate the year's official pamphlet. (But, Grindl notes, he doesn't wear colored bands anymore "because he notices his friends at church just have plain.")

Marshall's prize possession also relates to his spelling passion. It's his laptop, on which he stores his copious word lists. It took some extended lobbying and an act of generosity on his part for him to acquire the machine. He had asked for the unit for years, but Eric had always said, "You've got a fine desktop here at the house, you don't need a laptop."

For Marshall's 2003 appearance on the game show *Lingo*, he was paid $1,000. Recalls his father: "We were financially struggling that year, and he said, 'Here, take this.'" Marshall kept just $30 for himself, contributing the rest to the family budget.

Eric, impressed by his son's willingness to help, decided to scrimp and save and find a way to buy Marshall a laptop. "If he's willing to give, then we should be willing to give," he says. As the family got ahead of its monthly bills, the extra money went toward the laptop fund.

When Marshall shows me his laptop, it's clear that the machine is as much a talisman of success as a mere computer. After all, he only has the unit because of his spelling victories. In his hands, the laptop seems to hold an aura of promise; it's a symbol of his abilities, and it's also a high-tech tool that will enable him to go further.

Winning the Bee would mean many more such goodies. As he readies for the 2005 contest, he's well aware that the $28,000 first prize would make a real difference in his and his family's life. "I'm really thinking what I could do with that cash prize if I won," he says.

⚭⚭⚭

Marshall began winning local spelling bees at a very young age, with no special preparation. He entered his first North Carolina regional bee at the tender age of nine. He hadn't known what to study, so he wasn't able to stay in that first contest very long. Yet he found the experience inspiring. "When I was nine, and I got out, I was in awe of people who could spell tough words," he recalls, chuckling at his starstruck younger self. "I just thought the world of them."

In 2003 he again entered the Charlotte regional, though he still hadn't prepared much. "When I won *The Charlotte Observer,* I was shocked," he says. "I hadn't studied any that year."

A few weeks before that year's Nationals, he came to a sobering realization: Many spellers headed for Washington had studied the Consolidated Word List, containing some 23,000 words; plenty of tough words at Nationals come from this list. Since Marshall hadn't even touched it, he knew all he could do was spell and hope—he didn't expect to get far. He did, however, have a goal: The previous winner from Charlotte had topped out at forty-seventh place; Marshall hoped to go higher.

In Washington it soon became apparent that this was a far tougher competition. There was "definitely a noticeable change in the difficulty of the words," he recalls. However, as his parents sat in the audience with dropping jaws, it appeared nothing could stop the Charlotte boy. As veteran spellers exited the stage, Marshall, spelling in his loud, clear voice, grabbing hold of the mike and spitting out letters with the enthusiasm of a high school cheer—A!

C! E!—survived. Grindl recalls: "When he kept going and kept going, each round was like . . . " Eric finishes her sentence: "Nerve wracking."

Against any reasonable prediction, he tied for twelfth place in a field of 251. Suddenly, he had found his passion—his experience in Washington lit a fire under him. He started studying again on the drive home. "I am going back," he announced to his family.

He dove into the Consolidated Word List. Grindl became his coach, drilling him constantly. Realizing it would be more efficient if she recorded the list, she took the summer and recorded a library of cassette tapes, pronouncing more than 20,000 words. She and Marshall made a list of all the words he missed, narrowing the list until he got all of them right. All the while, he dreamed of Washington.

But first he had to win his regional again. Paradoxically, as easily as he had won in 2003 with little studying, it was far harder in 2004 after months of dedicated work. That was the year Janae Jackson went toe-to-toe with him, until they spelled all the words from the *Paideia*-based list. Only when the two competitors went off the list did Marshall take the Charlotte trophy.

The 2004 Nationals began with an arduous written test intended to quickly narrow the field. Marshall's months of study made the difference: He correctly spelled the merciless *boeotian*, as well as the nearly inhuman *rijsttafel*. "We had actually quizzed on that," he recalls of *rijsttafel*. "Because I kept putting two *a*'s in that, but it's two *t*'s. It's"—and here he spells it in one breath—"r-i-j-s-t-t-a-f-e-l."

Even with his months of hard study, in the eighth round he was forced to guess. He encountered *myotonia*, which sounds virtually identical to *myatonia*—and both words refer to muscle, so the definition didn't help. Luck flowed his way. He correctly guessed the *o*.

Late in the competition the tension began to wear on him. So, too, his parents. Knowing that he had placed twelfth the year before, they didn't want him to place lower this year. "We were on pins and needles," Eric recalls. "I was going 'Lord, don't let him get out before twelfth, don't let him get out before twelfth.' Once he got past twelfth I was at perfect ease, I didn't care what he did or what he got. I wasn't so much bent on him winning—you just don't want your child to be disappointed."

In the final rounds, with just a small handful of spellers left and all the finalists' parents called up onstage—and the trophy gleaming right offstage—Marshall faced *vimineous*. In the heat of the moment, he replaced the first *i* with an *e*. Then, "I got so caught up in spelling it, I left out the *e* at the end—I knew there was an *e* at the end, but I guess I was so caught up in spelling it."

When the bell rang signaling a misspell, he felt a rushing wave of disappointment. His personal goal for the year had been to get eighth place, and he had exceeded that. He tied for fourth in a field of 265. Still, unlike the previous year, when he was delighted to get so far, this year felt like a loss.

"When I missed *vimineous*, I was like"—he makes a gesture of disappointment—"because I was so close to the end." Adding a bittersweet touch to his elimination: He knew all the words after he went out.

"I got so high, if I just got a little bit higher, you know . . . I did kind of feel pretty sad that year."

⊙⊙⊙

With another year of laser-beam-like studying, Marshall is ready for the 2005 Nationals. Quite ready. Because he's in the eighth grade, this is his last chance, and he has prepared accordingly. He created a sprawling word list, more than 500 pages long, toiling through it until he knows every word. He picks out random words from Webster's *Unabridged* to include; "I especially like French and German words, so I try to get a lot of those in there." He goes into deep studying drives in which he selects a type of word, say, medical terms, and immerses himself in it.

In the winter of 2005, Eric and Marshall were out walking together, and Eric told his son that, based on his previous year's fourth-place finish, "You'll be looked at as one of the favorites this year." Marshall is acutely aware of that—no speller who placed higher than him will be returning this year. But merely being favored, or even a top finalist, is not what's on his mind. He's dreaming of only one thing. Eric makes it clear: "He wants to win this year."

21 Katharine "Kerry" Close

The first thing you notice when talking with Kerry Close is her intensity of presence. Hidden within her reserve, her native shyness, is a keen awareness, a sharp, sensitive intelligence. She's twelve years old, but she seems far older. There's little that's childish about her. She's watching what's going on around her, her antennas are attuned, and she's taking it all in. She seems to miss nothing.

On the other hand, this sensitive awareness is accompanied by a fierce competitive spirit. As little as she'll talk about herself—and talking about herself is one of her least favorite activities—she'll address this subject. When I asked what she likes about spelling, she answered, "I like the competition, I'm kind of a—" She stopped herself, then finished, "I like the competition." In the middle of that sentence, she almost said, "I'm kind of a competitive person," but that would have been too much self-disclosure. But it is certainly true. As her mother says, "Is she competitive? Very."

Her competitiveness emerges on the soccer field and the basketball court; she's on her school team in both sports. Although tall for her age, last year she failed to make the basketball team, which deeply disappointed her. Now in the seventh grade, she has not just made the team but become a hard-charging player. Not that she's particularly adept at the sport, as she freely admits. "I'm not really good at ballhandling," she says with a little laugh. However, "I score a lot of points, and whenever I'm open I usually take a shot." That's not a brag—Kerry doesn't brag—just a simple statement of fact. She's been known to score more than ten points in a game.

Her competitiveness also comes out every summer when she enters sailing contests. Living right on the Atlantic coast, in Spring Lake, New Jersey, makes boating a natural choice. She started learning how to sail at age eight, when a nearby harbor offered lessons for $50 for the entire summer. She walked down to the harbor five days a week and, despite having parents who are devoted landlubbers, became a skilled sailor. Her long blonde hair blowing in the wind, she mans an Optimist, a one-person sailboat about 7 feet long, designed for sailors weighing from 50 to 120 pounds.

At age nine she began entering boat races off the Jersey shore, contests in which she maneuvers her Optimist through a course of markers, racing in circuits ranging from a few hundred yards to a mile. Some of the races go with the wind—comparatively easy—and some are set up to go against the wind, requiring a sailor to rapidly zigzag to move across the water.

At age eleven, Kerry went to New York to compete in the Atlantic Coast Championships. "It was pretty hard," she says. "Some days it was pretty heavy wind. I came in like 200th [out of 350], I did pretty poorly." However, "It was a good experience."

What Kerry fails to mention—that her mother volunteers—is that she has qualified for the US national sailing team trials. Were she to make the team, she would be part of the crew that competes internationally, in South America and Europe. But she has elected not to try out. Sailing at that level would take too much time away from her real passion.

☉☉☉

If her competitive spirit is evident on the basketball court and in her ocean racing, it's in her spelling matches that she focuses like an athlete in the season's final duel. Seeing her onstage, it's clear she's competing to win. There's nothing casual about her approach, nothing thrown away. (In fact, not even her sailing is a distraction; during the summer she comes home after a day on the water and works on her spelling.)

She made it to her first regional bee at age nine. Helping her get there was an oddity of her New Jersey contest. In many areas of the country, a speller must win her school bee and her area bee (consisting of several schools or a county) before earning a spot at regionals. But in Kerry's northern New Jersey area, winners of school bees go straight to the regional bee. So, simply for spelling *aorta* in her school bee, this nine-year-old found herself about to compete with thirteen- and fourteen-year-olds at regionals.

That morning, she ate her power breakfast: peaches and cream oatmeal, a banana cut into three pieces, and a cup of hot chocolate. She also wore her lucky outfit: a long-sleeve pink shirt and dark pants. Yet as prepared as she was to do battle, she was only partially ready as a speller. She had read through the *Paideia* and was generally familiar with the 3,800-word study guide but hadn't memorized it. Instead, she was relying on her avid reading. She has always been a voracious bookworm, usually devouring a few books at once. (She loves historical fiction; in the spring of 2005 she had just finished *Taking Liberties*, the story of George Washington's runaway slave; then she picked up *The Silver Chair* by C. S. Lewis.)

That evening at the bee, she plowed through far older spellers, staying onstage as they exited, but she found—oddly—that her toughest competitor was another fourth-grader, James Perucho. The bee came down to her and James, with Kerry navigating some polysyllabics that would have felled most nine-year-olds: *quizzically, jerkin, thanatology,* and *Lilliputian.* Finally, James was dealt the Spanish word *jicama* and tried to spell it with an *h.* So Kerry was headed to Nationals—as a fourth-grader. (Only three other nine-year-olds made it to Washington that year.)

Winning her regional at such a young age was "kind of like a luck thing," she says. "Like I won in the fourth grade and just kept going on, and I discovered that I liked it."

As the 2002 Nationals got under way, she realized that Washington offered far more competition than her New Jersey regional. "I was just watching them basically in awe—it was a whole different league," she recalls. She survived the first round, spelling *Watteau,* the French painter, but the second round's written test wiped her out. She tied for ninety-first in the contest, along with dozens of other spellers clumped at the back of the pack.

During the following year, she bulked up her word drill. "I studied a lot more, made sure I knew the *Paideia*, and I studied a lot of other words." But at her regional bee she faced a familiar challenge: James Perucho. Again, the contest came down to the two of them, and again, after many hard-fought rounds, Kerry eventually triumphed.

At the 2003 Nationals she seemed to have the wind in her sails. Surviving round after round, she watched much older competitors leave the stage while she handled ten-pound polysyllabics. It was a year in which many of the spellers were hams—raising their fists in the air after a tough spell, doing little victory dances. In contrast, Kerry was all business. Midway through the contest she confronted a word she had never heard of, *congelifract*. She was going to have to guess. She took her time, sounded it out mentally, then took her best shot—and got it.

Late in the Bee she faced *cubitiere*, which finally sent her to the Comfort Room—"I just had no clue," she says—but not until she tied for sixteenth in a field of 251. Suddenly, at age ten, Kerry Close was one of the top spellers in the country.

怘怘怘

It should have been a snap to return to Nationals in 2004, yet Kerry ran into an obstacle in that year's regional: James Perucho. He was back and he was ready. Really ready.

Again this year—for the third year in a row—her regional bee came down to her and James. Five rounds, ten rounds, fifteen rounds—and neither Kerry nor James missed a word. Twenty rounds, heading past thirty rounds—still, the two went head-to-head. At around the thirty-round point, the judges ran out of the *Paideia* word list and went to one of the special "surprise" lists. Kerry's father, Jim, remembers his feeling of dread upon hearing the first non-*Paideia* word (he had helped her study so much that he knew the *Paideia* thoroughly). "Oh no, we're out of here," he thought.

The words became brutally difficult: *quenelle, dysrhythmia, baignoire, chevesaile*. Minute after agonizing minute, the spellers edged forward on the "surprise" list, knowing that in just moments one of them would earn a trip to Washington and one would stay home in New Jersey. In the third post-*Paideia* round, James got *decile*, which he missed. Kerry was given *apoplexy*, which she spelled correctly. She was headed to Nationals for the third time.

At the 2004 Bee she looked unstoppable. Perhaps it was the benefit of her heart-stopping match against James, or perhaps it was the cumulative effect of her years of study. "It went really well," she recalls. "It was shocking when fifteen were left onstage, and I was like, 'wow.'" Finally, she came up against *vitrophyre*, which she spelled as *vitrofyre*. As the bell rang, she clearly felt disappointed, but she took satisfaction in how far she had come. Her placement "was really good for me, so I was happy." At age 11, she tied for 8th in a field of 265.

◯◯◯

It's early March of 2005 and Kerry's regional bee is nearing. Certainly she feels the pressure, as do her parents, Paula and Jim. "We're just trying to stay calm," Paula says in her light New Jersey accent, a week before the contest.

Both Jim, who's an insurance salesman, and Paula, who's an occupational therapist working with kids in a local school, are veritable bundles of niceness and warmth. You get the feeling that if you were stuck by the roadside, the two of them would stop, fix your tire, then take you to lunch. They share the job of coaching their only child on her word lists. It's a task that calls for precise pronunciation—and Kerry expects that. "I read the words and she corrects my pronunciation," says Jim with a laugh, as Paula chuckles along. "She likes the right pronunciation."

Since their daughter has made it to Nationals three times, winning this year's regional might be considered a given, but that's not how the Closes feel about it. A few factors conspire to boost their anxiety level about the upcoming regional. First, Kerry's past success has raised the stakes; if, after three trips to Nationals, she somehow stumbles at regional—and that's as easy as voicing an *e* when she meant to say *i*—she stays home while her speller friends go to Washington. Serious unhappiness would result.

Also, as Paula notes, the local New Jersey bee has "progressively gotten

21 Katharine "Kerry" Close

more competitive." Specifically, there's James Perucho. Since he's taken second place to Kerry three years in a row, he'll be a tougher competitor than many kids at Nationals. "I know he'll be very well prepared, so that's always something in the back of her mind," Paula says.

Certainly, she points out, Kerry has come a long way as a speller since her first contest at age nine. "On the other hand, as she gets older, she's involved in more things in school. It's harder to put the time in. She's got a very, very tight school schedule and with sports and extracurricular activities, it gets harder." At age twelve, Kerry now very much has a life outside of spelling, "but when she was nine she didn't," Paula says.

The bottom line about regionals is that there are no guarantees: Past performance does not guarantee future results. "You never know," Paula says.

⚬⚬⚬

It's a Friday night in mid-March 2005, at the Monmouth University auditorium in northern New Jersey. This regional bee has a showbiz feel, with a master of ceremonies, Phil Hartman, the *Home News Tribune*'s editorial page editor, introducing each kid as they approach the microphone. The voice of pronouncer Robert Kern, with his neat diction and regular-guy New Jersey accent, bears an uncanny resemblance to that of actor Danny DeVito. A crowd of about 300 parents and friends has gathered, and everyone applauds after each speller's attempt.

Sponsored by the *Asbury Park Press* and the *Home News Tribune*, this bee is a sprawling affair, with ninety-seven kids. It's such a big group that the contest is spread over two nights; tonight is the final night, so it holds a heightened anticipation.

The first night moved at a tortoiselike crawl. With this many spellers, the entire evening progressed through only two rounds. Since these kids had to win only their school bee to get here, with no city or district bee, most have made it here based on native smarts rather than hours of spelling study. So two rounds was enough to eliminate half the field. One of those eliminated was the competition's first deaf contestant, ten-year-old Reena Banerjee, who used an interpreter to sign the word.

The *Asbury Park Press* gives prominent play to Kerry's repeat wins. In an article published right before this bee, the reporter ended the piece: "Stay tuned to see if Kerry can spell C-H-A-M-P-I-O-N again." The kids, too, clearly notice Kerry in their midst. "Oh, so the *champion's* with us," one of them half-sneers.

Apart from the minimal grousing, the first night offered little challenge, as Kerry dispatched *relic* (a giveaway) and *eatage* (surprisingly tough for an early round) with no difficulty. She also received a major bit of relief: James Perucho has not entered this year. Apparently three orthographic thrashings were enough for him.

Still, a freak occurrence pushed the Closes' anxiety level back up: A snowstorm, unusual for New Jersey in March, forced a postponement of this bee's second night. So before this evening, Kerry had to endure ten additional days before finding out if she goes to Washington. She continued her intense spelling study, stopping all other reading; those historical fiction novels were set aside.

Now in the second night, the field is winnowed to fifty-four spellers. Kerry sits in the middle of the group, dressed in jeans and a powder blue top; the top was the same shirt she wore to win her school bee, so she wears it tonight for luck. She's now a full head taller than most kids, unlike when she first showed up here at age nine. That first year, since she hadn't memorized the *Paideia*, she won due to innate intelligence, constant reading, and the luck of the draw—she just happened to avoid a killer word. In contrast, this year she's a grizzled veteran. She is, in effect, playing with marked cards: Bee organizers issued this year's *Paideia* back in September, and she had it memorized by October, or about five months ago. Unless tonight's bee lasts so long that this list is exhausted, all of its words will be as familiar as old friends.

Because these spellers had to win only their school bee to get here, many of them are quite young. Denzel Hercules, a smartly dressed fourth-grader in pressed khakis and a tie, grapples with *synchronization*—a word twice as long as he is—unsuccessfully. Fahd Ahmed, a bespectacled fifth-grader, finds out that *crucible* is not spelled as it sounds when he tries to insert an *s*. One boy, a fourth-grader with a light brown buzz cut and a tiny voice, stands mystified by *laity*. Hands jammed in pockets, he stands completely still, deep in thought as the audience waits. But it's nowhere to be found.

On the other hand, the stage contains some talented orthographers. Rita Esposito, a fourth-grader decked out in a powder blue dress with white stockings and white patent leather shoes, nails *kenning* and flashes a delighted smile. Elliot Chester, an eleven-year-old with longish hair, jeans, and a SpongeBob SquarePants T-shirt, has obviously studied his word list. Facing *capitulation*, he shouts it out, letter by letter, in a huff of certainty, then beams a big grin at his parents.

When Kerry steps to the microphone, her approach bears little similarity to that of the other kids. She's a master navigator, an experienced ship captain who has been asked to navigate across a backyard swimming pool. But instead of performing this task like the fluff it is, she takes every precaution, using a studied, methodical strategy suitable for crossing the Indian Ocean.

Facing *erudite*, she actually asks the definition, though of course she could spell a softie like that in her sleep. She listens, repeats the word carefully, and begins to issue the letters. Her voice is in its lowest register, down where there's control and complete evenness. She spells with her hands jammed into her pockets, hunched over, leaning into the microphone—since she's taller than most of the kids she has to lean over to speak into it.

With her long hair parted in the middle, when she leans over to spell, her hair completely covers her face. She's the champ, sure, but she chooses to remain incognito. If she's going to win, she'll do it while drawing as little attention to herself as possible. Her plan, or so it appears, is to very modestly and methodically wipe out the field. She taps out the letters of *erudite* without inflection, one by one, measuring out the letters with a clocklike cadence. At the moment, she looks unbeatable.

☾☉☽

The kids fall quickly. One girl gets *trefoil* and asks, "Excuse me?" as if someone had just asked her to kiss a frog. Haley Moss, a tall eighth-grader with long hair, garbles the uncommon *doughty*. Seventh-grader James Honsa takes a run at *Hellenic* but leaves out an *l*.

Looking strong, however, is Juliet Taylor, a fourth-grader who wears a jazzy brimmed cap similar to the one favored by pop star Beyoncé for most of 2004. Juliet buzzes through *janiform* with panache.

We take a five-minute break and the kids flee the stage. Many families, in fact, leave for the evening, now that their kid is eliminated—that's unusual in regional bees, where people usually stay to clap until the end. One father with a yellow power tie and a pager on his belt strides purposefully out of the auditorium while his son gallops alongside him in a goofy run-walk. The mother of Elliot Chester, the SpongeBob SquarePants boy who's looking like a contender, realizes he'll have to return to the stage in just a few minutes. "Do you want a snack?" she asks with motherly urgency. The sixth-grader replies by casually dipping his hand in her bag of munchies.

Kerry chats with a couple of girlfriends, then talks with Jesse Zymet, who was a finalist from New Jersey in the 2003 Nationals. Jesse is now a sixteen-year-old tenth-grader and remains passionate about spelling. He cofounded an online spelling community, dispensing advice to kids across the country.

While Kerry's parents help her with word drill, Jesse's Internet-based coaching goes into greater detail: etymology, rules governing foreign languages, obscure words. Jesse is Kerry's biggest fan, so it's no surprise he's here to watch her regional bee and likely give a mid-contest pep talk.

After the break, the field narrows at a rapid clip. One girl attempts to add a second *e* to *pedant*, while another is baffled by *regicide*. A fashionably dressed girl in a shawl misses *etymology*, which, at a spelling bee, is like a baseball player not knowing the word *outfield*.

"Necromancy?" inquires a tall, laid-back middle-school boy with jeans and an untucked shirt, very much the cool contender. "Can I have the definition?" He gets it. "Can you use it in a sentence?" The judge does. "Can you spell it for me?" After just a moment the crowd catches on, breaking into a rolling chuckle. "Nice try," says the judge. Yet for all his kidding, the boy conjures up *necromancy* with no difficulty. (But in the next round he gets—appropriately—*irreverent* and tries to replace the *i* with an *e*.)

A grade-school boy spells *brochette* like the building is on fire, voicing letters as fast as his mouth will allow. "Oh wait!" he says, realizing that in his haste he left out a *t*—and then he spells it again, just as pell-mell, adding the missing *t* in his second attempt. This throws the judges into a quandary. They confer among themselves, quietly talking back and forth, leaving the boy up onstage with an uncertain look on his face. The judges decide they need to play back the tape; they listen, after which they pronounce their ruling: A speller is not allowed to spell a word twice—since he misspelled the first time, he's out. "I know," he says dolefully, as if he realized this basic rule about five minutes before they did. He trudges off stage to rallying applause.

Kerry maintains her strategic steadiness. Spelling *sconce*, *hypochondria*, *unannotated*, and *garderobe*—all, for her, about as challenging as swimming in the shallow end—her method varies not one whit. Hands jammed in her pockets, hunched over to reach the short microphone, hair completely covering her face, she taps out the letters in a steady canter. There's no hint of doubt in her voice, yet neither is there any sense that this is particularly easy.

Ninety minutes into the contest, a rail-thin boy who had appeared to be a top competitor misses *trierarchy* and slumps in disappointment—he had been dreaming of the trophy. And with that the bee is down to the final three, each of whom are sharp spellers: Kerry, Elliot Chester, and Angela Zhou.

Elliot Chester, the SpongeBob boy, is coming on strong. He not only knows his words, he knows them cold. *Infidel*—he shouts out the letters triumphantly. *Sandinista*—he spells the Latin American revolutionaries' name like he's a gun-toting *bandillero*.

Angela Zhou, a grade-schooler with her black hair pulled back, looks almost as confident. Her style is similar to Kerry's; without calling a smidgen of attention to herself she's been quietly felling some big words. Facing *machismo*, she whispers the letters in a soft, feminine whisper, leaning into the microphone so she'll be heard.

Kerry steps up and faces *vrille*, meaning the nose-first descent of an airplane performed as a deliberate maneuver. She makes quick work of it.

SpongeBob Elliot gets *pridian*, a word referring to a previous day or yesterday. He experiences his first moment of doubt. He gives it his all, but . . . it's just not there.

Angela works with *quondam*, which means "of an earlier time." Whoops—she tries to replace the first *o* with an *a*.

Kerry is the last speller onstage, but she's not yet the winner. She must first spell *Catullian*, "of or relating to the Roman poet Catullus, or his lyric poems, which are marked by perfection of form and intensely personal subject matter." She asks for the definition, but the judges realize a problem—the pronouncer has mispronounced it, voicing the middle syllable with an errant long *e* sound.

Kerry waits as the judges confer and rustle through their reference book. She's fully aware that they've mispronounced it but she's ready to spell anyway—she could tell them the correct pronunciation and then spell it—yet she waits patiently. The pronouncer revoices it, at which point Kerry moves through it in the same even cadence she has used for every word in this bee.

She's right! The crowd whoops into hollering cheers, the applause rolling onward. Knowing that she's won, Kerry steps away from the microphone, leans back, and, lifting her hands to about waist level, pumps her clenched fists, just once, her long hair shaking with the move.

It's a powerful gesture. In this one unguarded move, the hidden competitor emerges, for one glorious moment. The clenched fist move is a testament to victory earned through hard, serious effort, the sweetness of an achievement garnered despite worry and obstacle, requiring the bravery to get up onstage and perform when the moment called for it. The gesture says: *Yes, I've won, and I worked for this, and I got it. Yes!*

❧❧❧

The aftermath of the New Jersey bee is surprisingly low-key. Most regional bees make a to-do about the winner, putting on a little ceremony in which she's handed the trophy and someone shakes her hand as flashbulbs pop. But in this case, Kerry is handed her trophy—quite a modest little piece of plastic—as soon as she exits the stage, and most of the crowd disperses quickly.

There's no local TV interview with the champ, though there is a newspaper reporter who attempts, with limited success, to get a pithy quote from her—Kerry is not given to lengthy speechifying.

As the auditorium drains, a small group gathers around the winner: her parents, her friend Jesse Zymet, Jesse's father, and myself. Mr. Zymet, who has followed the Bee for years, heaps praise on Kerry: "Kerry and her parents wouldn't say this, but Kerry is as good as there is going into Nationals this year." To which Jesse chimes in: "It's true—you're going to win." The new champ takes all this in without comment.

How does she feel about Nationals this year? "There's a lot of repeat spellers and of course someone could just come out of the blue," she says. What about her chances for taking the trophy? "It's hard to say," she notes.

What will her strategy be? "I just want to study really hard and go in with the benefit of the doubt, because there are really hard words. Of course, the goal would be to win, but I should be happy with anything, because getting there is an honor."

Her phrase "I should be happy with anything," is, it's safe to assume, Kerry-speak for: "I'm going to give it my all to win." No casual competitors need apply.

Her parents, for their part, are obviously experiencing waves of relief. I ask Paula if she's happy to have this evening over with. "Oh yeah!" she says.

⊙⊙⊙

The Close home, in the sleepy Atlantic coast town of Spring Lake, New Jersey, is about four blocks away from the ocean—step out their front door and you can almost see it. It's also near Kerry's middle school so the seventh-grader can walk to school. The tree-lined neighborhood, once merely middle class, has become quite pricey as housing prices so near the shoreline have escalated. The Closes live not far from where Jim and Paula grew up; both are native to New Jersey.

Their house is an airy glass and polished wood affair, which on a sunny day is flooded with ocean light. Clearly, it's the home of a speller. The kitchen bulletin board is filled with obscure words, a gaggle of foreign terms and deceptive polysyllabics, in no particular order—the orthographic challenges Kerry is grappling with. On the fireplace mantel stands her growing crowd of spelling trophies. The Closes share a chuckle at how modest the New Jersey trophies are.

Their home is just a short trip away from New York City, and in early 2005 the family went up to the city to see a new off-Broadway play, *The 25th Annual Putnam County Spelling Bee* (the show has since gone to Broadway). A comic musical, *Putnam County* depicts a fictional middle-school spelling bee in all its flayed nerves and idiosyncratic personalities. The storyline calls for a few audience members to come up onstage and spell as if they were bee contestants.

When the Closes arrived at the theater, the actors asked for volunteers. The show doesn't normally take kids—it's not funny to see kids eliminated. But after Kerry told them she was an experienced speller they invited her onstage. The actors also brought up three adult volunteers.

As the show progressed, Kerry was called upon to spell as if she were part of the fictional bee. Her real-life spelling skills enabled her to stay onstage while the adult volunteers were sent packing. When she fielded *casserole*, it prompted mock outrage from the other actor-spellers. "Hey, how come the Close kid got an easy word?" one complained. The actors kept ad-libbing jibes at her, making facetious comments based on her last name. Even when the words grew tough, she remained onstage, handling the obscure *epicalyx*. As the script called for her to be eliminated, an increasingly odd slew of words were thrown her way, and finally she missed *vigintillion*. "She knew it but she blanked on it," Paula recalls. After misspelling she was kept onstage and given juice and a cookie, as in the Bee's Comfort Room, and one of the actors sang a song to her.

Afterward in the lobby, she posed for photos with the actors and was feted like a celebrity. Many audience members came up and spoke with her; several complimented her as if she was one of the actors—they didn't realize she was a volunteer. One older gentleman felt compelled to recite to her the short list of words in the English language that are composed of all vowels.

It was, Kerry says, "a really fun experience."

☙☙☙

Both Jim and Paula coach Kerry on her spelling, but, I ask, is there one main coach? "Paula is the head coach," Jim explains. "No, I'm the organizer," Paula says, laughing, "and Jim does all the work." Actually, Jim is right: Paula is very much the head coach, helping Kerry with her word drill on a constant basis. Paula gathers study tips from Carolyn's Corner, the online study guide provided by Bee organizers, and she also videotapes all of Kerry's bees.

Paula's coaching duties have turned her into an expert speller in her own right, a common experience among parent-coaches. As Jim notes, in the 2004 Nationals, on the written test given to parents for fun, "She was competitive."

"No I wasn't," Paula replies in mock irritation. In fact, she spelled twenty out of twenty-five words, just one less than the top parent score. And, Paula concedes with a chuckle, after all the word study, "I could take the SATs and probably do better."

The problem with coaching, she says, is finding time. "If Kerry didn't have to go to school, and I didn't have to go to work, we could sit here all day and work on it. But we have an hour or two now."

It helps that Kerry now does more word study by herself. She works with numerous spelling study guides, makes lists of interesting words from her reading, and labors her way through the dictionary—though not word by word, which would be "a little bit impossible," she says.

Jim explains that Kerry has worked through the entire Consolidated Word List and can spell all but about 1,000 of its words. "We're trying to get that 1,000 down to 500, so the odds get better and better in her favor."

Aiding this process is Kerry's participation in the Readers' Digest Word Power Challenge, a vocabulary contest organized on a national level like the Bee. Contestants get a sample sentence and a list of uncommon vocabulary words like *tintinnabulation* and *pulchritudinous* and are asked, "Which word best completes the sentence?" In 2004 Kerry placed second at the state level.

The Bee and the Word Power contest are highly complementary pursuits. Her Bee study "kind of kills two birds with one stone," she says. "When I'm studying the Bee, if I look at the definition, that'll help me for Word Power, too."

She qualified for the state Word Power contest again in 2005, but the contest will be on the same day as the Bee, so she's skipping Word Power this year. Both her vocabulary and spelling study relate to her career goal: She wants to be a writer, perhaps a newspaper columnist.

Most helpful in her spelling study is the online community of young orthographers she's part of, a group that calls itself "Speller Nation." Administering the Internet study group are three former Bee participants who are now teens: Jesse Zymet, Erik Zyman Carrasco, and Josh Dawsey. (Erik was a top contender in 2004, and after he misspelled he went to Kerry and wished her the best in the rest of the competition.)

Using an Internet-based phone line, this group of eight to ten spellers conduct practice bees, with participants in various locations across the country all competing as if they were in the same room. "They make it like a real bee, with round one, round two," Kerry notes. When she's in peak study mode, she competes in these online practice bees twice a week in addition to her two-hour daily sessions. Her study mates in this group are a talented bunch. Many of the kids in Speller Nation competed in the 2004 Nationals and are returning to Washington in 2005, including Anurag Kashyap from San Diego, Rachel Karas from Michigan, Saryn Hooks from North Carolina, George Hornedo from Indiana, and Elicia Chamberlin from New Hampshire.

More than simply a study aid, the online get-togethers are morale boosters, providing the support of a shared pursuit, a shared age group, and shared challenges. Kerry's membership in such a focused group of spellers is an advantage of her long run at Nationals: She's had time to find a community that nurtures competitors.

"She has a great support system of kids, some wonderful friends who she's met through the Bee that she stays in contact with," Paula says. "I love how they keep in touch, no matter where they live—that's a good thing to learn." Kerry "has learned more in other ways" than improved spelling, her mother says.

"I think somewhere along the way some of them will see each other again, like in college—they seem to be on the same track. I have a feeling they'll keep these friendships."

〰〰〰

Going into her fourth year at the Bee, Kerry has seen some changes in the contest. Chiefly, the fact that the words are tougher than ever. "When I was first there, they used all the Consolidated Word List, and now they're just using abstract words to get people out, words you can't figure out or have studied," she says. "It just seems to have gotten more competitive since 2002."

Her father, pointing out that the family has been to Nationals three times, notes, "We're kind of professional Bee people by now." From his experience he has his own theory about the changes. "It seems to me they put the mystery words in the earlier rounds. It's like they're trying to make an orderly progression, so they get some kids out in the third round, some out in the fourth round—they don't want them all out in the fifth and sixth round." At any rate, he clearly agrees that the contest has grown more competitive. "Going down to Washington, there are at least twenty kids that are *very* good spellers."

Still, despite the hurdles, Kerry is well positioned to win this year. Having placed sixteenth two years ago and eighth last year, she appears headed for at least a finalist's spot. With her cumulative knowledge only a very small handful of this year's 270 spellers will be able to keep up with her.

As to whether a first-place finish for Kerry is the overriding goal, that's something the Closes are divided about, at least in terms of how they speak about it. Jim is a believer in well-balanced, big-picture thinking, understanding that the Bee is a great addition to a full life. But win or lose, "life is going to go on, and even if you win, it's fifteen minutes of fame," he says. "I don't think you can put your whole life into it. So you're the best and you don't win anyway— you've got to be well rounded."

Paula will say similar things. "It's almost a relief that you're going to Washington, that's the big thing, and whatever happens there happens," she says. "What can you do? There are no guarantees." But within Paula there seems to be more of a direct focus on winning, a desire to see her daughter not just compete but add the champion's trophy to the living room mantel. She points to the example of Sai Gunturi, a speller from Texas. Over the course of years he steadily improved his ranking, and in 2003 he won the Bee. "We watched him go higher," Paula notes. "He's a good person to model yourself after."

As for Kerry herself, as she sits in her kitchen some seven weeks before Nationals, her approach is properly politic. She forecasts, "I'll probably get by Round One since I know all those words. The written test, there's a good chance I'll get by that, too. After that, I'm just glad I'm there."

And as for winning: "I guess everyone would like to win, I would too. Sometimes, kind of banking on it is unrealistic."

It's certainly true that banking on the top spot is unrealistic—luck is a big factor—but it's also true she has her eyes on the prize. There's a photo of her competing in a sailboat race off the coast of Miami. In the photo, taken when she was ten years old, the sun is bright and the water is a brilliant blue. In the center of the shot is Kerry on her Optimist, racing full bore into the wind, pushing herself and her boat for all they're worth. On her face is a determined look. She's headed, fiercely and directly, right toward the finish line.

²² Samir Patel

Life isn't pretty here at the Fort Worth regional spelling bee. That is, not if you've won the last two years and you're now competing for your third trip to Washington, as Samir Patel is. If that's the case, few of your fellow spellers think warm thoughts about you.

Between rounds, some of the kids make remarks. Samir, eleven, has developed a new, methodical spelling style. He asks the pronouncer for a word's clues—definition, language of origin—even if he clearly knows the word's spelling; he wants to ensure he's focused before his first letter. His deliberate approach irritates some of his competitors, who, in truth, are resentful that he shows up every year to claim the trophy. They chime in: "Stop, you're annoying us—if you know the word just spell it." He shoots back, "No, I want to be methodical, I do not want to make a mistake. It's my choice."

One of his older competitors goes a step further. By Samir's account, the boy tells him, "I hope someone's going to take you down this year." Samir, slender and standing less than four and a half feet tall, retorts that no one's going to take him down, and sets out to try and prove it.

Which will be no small feat. Every one of these forty-six kids has won their area bee, so this group represents the best spellers from more than 600 schools in Forth Worth and its surrounding counties. This city's bee is one of the country's toughest. To take the trophy on this stage, you've got to be ready to compete.

☉☉☉

As I ride over to the Fort Worth regional bee this early March morning with Samir and his parents, Sudhir and Jyoti—they pick me up at my hotel—the Patels' sense of anxiety is palpable.

The night before, Sudhir had graciously given me a tour of Dallas, with its imposing glass-covered skyscrapers and wide open spaces. As we munched through some of the best barbecue ever made, he was his normally talkative, humorous self—Sudhir finds something to chuckle about on a regular basis. This morning, however, he's hunched in the driver's seat in a tense scowl, his eyes hidden by sunglasses. Jyoti, too, though she's affable as always, has a look of concern clouding her face. Samir is the only relaxed member of the Patel family. After a burst of nervousness earlier this morning, he now chats easily.

The good luck charms are in place. Jyoti, at her son's request, wears her purple pantsuit that Samir feels brings good luck—she wore it during 2003 Nationals, when he placed third. To further court good fortune, Samir carries in his pocket a small red envelope decorated with a Chinese design, given to him by a family friend, with $20 tucked inside.

Jyoti, who is Samir's coach, had remained a bundle of busy energy until today, wanting her son to study until the last minute. But Samir didn't want to—he works hard until the day of competition, then lets go. To ready himself for a bee, he spends time with his father; Samir finds Sudhir's presence calming.

Samir, in fact, seems to have a calm of his own. The verbally gifted eleven-year-old is the model of intellectual confidence. He's smart, he knows he's smart, and he ventures out into the world with the knowledge that he'll probably win contests involving intelligence. His sharp brown eyes sparkle with curiosity and awareness—when he's at a museum, he insists on reading every display. He's a nice kid, but no one would ever describe him as fawning; he has a sense of himself and he's not afraid to speak his mind. In conversation, he voices opinions with an articulateness that most people don't attain until their adult years. Yes, he's a boy, but as he talks with a sense of easy sureness, there might be a twenty-five-year-old trapped in there. He skipped the fourth grade, jumping from third to fifth, and at moments he appears ready to skip childhood altogether.

He has won the Fort Worth regional bee twice before, so this morning's bee is his to lose. Then again, there are no guarantees. One mistakenly uttered letter, or one memory lapse on an obscure Latinate, and he sits at home for this year's Nationals.

☺☺☺

Today's bee is held in the Texas Room, a meeting hall in Will Rogers Auditorium. Like everything in the Lone Star State, the nondescript Texas Room is big—it's about five times larger than needed for the 200-member audience, a collection of parents (both fathers and mothers on this Monday morning), friends, and teachers. As we settle into our seats to wait for the start, Samir spots something he wants no contact with: It's the collection bin where contestants who have misspelled place their placards when exiting the stage. "There's the dreaded bin," he says.

Onstage, the spellers face a row of four judges, all veteran schoolmarms, who between them have more than fifty years of experience at bees. Even more experienced is the pronouncer, David Keith, who's been at this some twenty years. A genial gray-haired language aficionado, in conversation Keith chats with enthusiasm about the pitfalls of the schwa and the remarkably mad chaos of English spelling. Although he's a longtime Texan, he has no discernable accent, and his diction is precise.

Keith starts the bee off with some softballs, slow pitches like *infancy*, *protein*, and *trinket*. Nathan Hyde, who looks like he might be a natural athlete, manages to miss *defer*, spelling it as *difer*, walking off in a stunned state, but for most spellers this round is just a chance to catch their breath.

One boy faces *unobtrusively* and tries in vain to pronounce it himself, consistently mangling it, adding an errant *p* or *dt* as he voices it. Keith pronounces it for him several times until a man in the audience—presumably a father or teacher —interrupts to shout out the word, syllable by syllable, with hyperclarity. Helped by this extra clue, the boy spells correctly without doubt. Keith gently informs the audience that this won't be allowed, and the contest goes on.

This type of low blow is typical of regional contests. If that happened at Nationals, the father would likely have been asked to leave, and the speller given a new word. But one never knows what one might encounter at regionals. Indeed, over the course of this morning there are numerous challenges to the judges, one of which reinstates a boy who had misspelled.

Samir gets *scrim* but doesn't hear it correctly. "Scram?" he asks. The pronouncer doesn't say no—that would be too much help—all he's allowed to do is pronounce it again, which Keith does. Fortunately for Samir, his new methodical method means he asks the definition. Upon realizing it's *scrim*, he easily dispatches it. In between rounds he says that in earlier years he may have simply spat out s-c-r-a-m, and that would have been the end of him.

In the break, Samir gets a parental hug, and Sudhir gives him an urgent reminder: "Don't spell other people's words." That is, when waiting his turn to spell, he shouldn't work on silently spelling other contestants' words—the Patels feel this is too distracting. "But," replies Samir, "they just pop into my mind."

〇〇〇

Over several rounds the words creep toward difficulty. Joseph Martinez, whose black hair is tinted with blond highlights, hesitates on *labyrinth*, scribbling with his finger on his placard, and gets it. Ronnie Castillo, who wears a long gown and whispers all her letters, attempts *synapse* but misses the silent *e* at the end. By the fifth round, with just seventeen of forty-six kids left, any sense of casualness is long gone. The eliminated spellers made it here on innate verbal ability and constant reading; these remaining competitors have worked and sweated for this day.

Sivaram Namburu steps up and masters *augean* with ease. Angela Lutz offers a fretful frown at *arbutus*, then nails it. Tony Montgomery, a tall boy who wears a windbreaker, breezes through *stellated* like it's an everyday word. Samir gets *Catullian* and, after checking the definition, tackles it with ease. The most confident of these kids—mostly thirteen-year-olds who are a full head taller than Samir—look like they could easily keep up at Nationals.

In the break, Sudhir hustles Samir off for a bathroom visit and a mid-bee conference. When they return, Jyoti asks her son in a worried tone, "Are you okay?" He is, but as the competition enters its third hour, he's facing avid studiers. Hannah Chi spells *charcuterie* without the slightest pause, and Angela Lutz spells *rapprochement* after pondering it only briefly.

Then, as the clock strikes noon, a judge announces: "The following words will no longer be from the 2005 *Paideia*." It's a fearsome proclamation. Until now, the word list came from the 3,800 words in the *Paideia*, the booklet Bee organizers sent out the previous September. But the judge's announcement means we're leaving the predictability of the *Paideia* to journey into the wilds of Webster's *Unabridged*. Suddenly, anything's possible. As many hours as Samir has drilled, there's no telling if he'll get a word he knows. If luck is against him, he'll face an odd French-British confection while another finalist enjoys a sampling of traditional Americana.

Soon after the announcement, up steps Sivaram Namburu to face *opprobrium*. "Opprobrium?" he asks, mystified, as if wondering how a word from outside the planet Earth has landed in Fort Worth. After some floundering he soon exits. Sooji Kim, who could pass for a diminutive professor, gets *rejuvenescent*. It's her last word.

Samir walks up to the microphone to face *anorak*. "Language of origin?" he asks. He learns it's an Eskimo word meaning heavy coat. His parents hold their breath. Jyoti's eyes are shut. *Anorak?* Where's that from? He confirms the definition, takes a breath, and spells it—without hesitation, correctly. Jyoti opens her eyes and continues making her list of the bee's words.

Hannah Chi tries to spell *wunderkind* with a *c*, and Angela Lutz attempts to render *picayune* with an *o*. Ammon Lutz—Angela's brother, they high-five each other after correct spellings—is issued *querimonious*. "Could you say it again?" he asks. But the judge's repetition doesn't help. Suddenly, there are only two kids on stage, Samir and the very tall Tony Montgomery. Tony gets *internecine*. He considers it thoughtfully before muffing it.

But Samir hasn't won. He must spell one more word; otherwise, all the kids from this round will be back in the competition. With all eyes on him, he steps up to face *fritillary*. Instead of his usual request for the definition, he interrupts the judge with a question: "Is it a butterfly?" Yes, it is, and Samir floats through the spelling as if he's a lifelong lepidopterist.

"We have a champion," announces one of the judges in a sweet Texas drawl, and Samir, after accepting his applause, runs into his mother's arms for a big hug. Then he gets a loving arm wrap from his father, followed by a ceremony that awards him a big gaudy trophy that's about half as tall as he is.

He's done it. He has won the Fort Worth regional. He's going to Washington, DC, for the 2005 Nationals.

⚉⚉⚉

After the bee, Sudhir is back to his normally sunny nature. The Patels and I go out to a nice Mexican restaurant, where in Dallas it's warm enough to sit outside even in March. Sudhir knocks back a couple of margaritas and kids around with the waitress.

As we eat, he makes some deliberately silly observations, then jokes: "You see, I don't have a brain, so I have an excuse." Jyoti attempts to explain her husband's levity with a smile of her own, in case a visitor might conclude she's married to a goofball. "He has a very dry sense of humor," she notes archly. "Not everyone gets it."

When the bill comes, Sudhir pretends to be too broke to pay it. "Can I wash dishes?" he inquires of the waitress. She laughs, telling him it would take too long to work off his bill. In response, he points to me: "Perhaps *he* can wash dishes?" She chuckles and walks away.

The Patels are happy. Very happy.

⚉⚉⚉

Sudhir and Jyoti had never seen each other face-to-face before they decided to get married. He lived in the United States, she lived in India, and although she traveled to America to marry him, "I never met him until I came here," she says.

Sudhir came to Dallas from India in 1969 as a twenty-year-old engineering student (he now works as a quality control supervisor-engineer for Motorola). His English was so rudimentary that he could hardly make himself understood, but he was committed to learning about American culture. He searched the city for a family he could both rent a room from and get to know; he turned down straight rental offers until he found a family who he felt was willing to take him in as something of a family member. His plan worked. Sudhir truly bonded with his adopted family, he learned about America from natives, and they eventually toured India with his help.

Jyoti, ten years Sudhir's junior, was born in London and lived there until age thirteen, when her family moved to India; consequently, she speaks with a light British accent. Her and Sudhir's cross-continent romance was a traditional Indian fix-up. Sudhir's mother's cousin was Jyoti's next-door neighbor— a distant connection, indeed, so Sudhir's sisters in India went to visit Jyoti, after which they called Sudhir in the United States and pronounced her a good choice.

The two of them corresponded and talked on the phone and, after a period of long-distance courtship, decided to take the plunge. Jyoti entered the United States with a fiancée visa to meet her future husband. "He could have been a con man for all I knew," she says with a laugh.

When she arrived in the Fort Worth area, much of its present-day development hadn't taken place. "I felt like I was out in the middle of nowhere," she recalls.

Samir, the couple's only child, sums it up: "This was worse than a blind date—it was a blind marriage."

But they share some important things. Both Sudhir and Jyoti have a warm, easygoing nature, and they both laugh easily—especially Sudhir, who often indulges in a long, rolling chuckle. Both have a deep reverence for learning and education. And both are passionately committed to the advancement of their son.

When Samir was ready to enter school, the Patels were told that he was too young, he'd have to wait a year. Jyoti decided to homeschool him for the year, and after that year she and Sudhir decided to continue homeschooling him. So Jyoti is his primary teacher as well as his spelling coach. Monday through Friday they follow a full school curriculum, with Samir taking swimming and judo lessons at a neighborhood community center.

Samir entered his first spelling bee at age seven, "just for fun," he says, "to see how far I would get." That first bee was hosted by an Indian-American group called the North South Foundation, which organized it through Hindu temples across the country. Similar to the Scripps Bee, North South holds regional bees all over the nation, culminating in a national bee in Washington, DC. In the Dallas area North South regional, Samir placed fourth. He shouldn't have been eligible to go to the organization's national bee; only the top three finishers from each region get to go to the North South national. But since he was so young, they invited him to compete in Washington.

There, astoundingly, he won first place—spelling against thirteen- and fourteen-year-olds. So, explains Sudhir with one of his long, happy laughs, "He goes up there and comes home with a big trophy." For the Patels, it was the beginning of a new era. They had become a spelling family.

⊙⊙⊙

In 2002, having won North South the year before, Samir competed in the Scripps regional bee in Fort Worth, but was eliminated. Part of his loss was due to spelling too fast; his word was *conscientious* and he, without stopping to verify, spelled *consciousness* (or vice versa, he can't remember). He concedes he wasn't ready that year: He had studied the 3,800 words in the *Paideia* but not beyond.

He went into the 2003 Fort Worth regional far better prepared. He had memorized the *Paideia*, learned a plethora of roots, and worked through the sprawling Consolidated Word List, with its 23,000 words from past bees. Yet even with all this studying, it took an odd bit of serendipity to win the Fort Worth contest.

As Samir tells it, one of the other spellers was given the word *whodunit*. "The boy spelled it 'nnit.' For some reason the judges kept him in. I'm not sure whether they heard him wrong . . . . if he had been out, I would have been one place up in order, and I would have gotten the word *shamateurism*, which I did not know. So that one boy really earned me my trip to Washington."

However it happened, winning was joyous: "I jumped off the stage!" he recalls.

At the 2003 Nationals, Samir was the star of the show. That he was a nine-year-old in a field dominated by thirteen-year-olds lent a certain David-and-Goliath dimension to his performance. But more than that, he wowed the audience with his dazzling wunderkind persona. Other kids hemmed and hawed, twisted their hands, and beseeched the lingual gods for some miracle of luck. Samir stood up, dispatched polysyllabics without a sliver of a doubt, then trotted back to his seat without waiting to see if he was right—he knew he was right.

Round after round he left far older kids by the side of the road. If he paused, which was rare, it was only to confirm a word's etymology before sailing through it, this diminutive speller, with big dark eyes and dark bangs, confidently confirming in an adult tone of voice, "Does it contain the prefix 'a,' meaning without?"

His hyperconfident performance—he even joked around at the microphone, mock complaining that he was getting all the French words—had the crowd bubbling with admiration. Between rounds, other spellers' parents were heard to exclaim, "That boy . . . " as if they had just heard Mozart spiel off his latest rondo. They would have been jealous, but his sheer proficiency seemed to relieve even that. It was as if to say, "Well, if he's *that* good, it's okay if he bests my child." For several rounds it seemed as if he might even win; from the original 251 spellers he made it to the final three. When he finally tripped on *boudin*, the tears came, revealing that, indeed, he was a young boy, not a machine. But after a big hug from his mother and several moments of loud applause, he flashed a wide smile to the crowd. Third place in Nationals at age nine—that was nothing to cry about.

In fact, "*Boudin* was one of the words we had done, but I was just so tired I didn't remember anything," he says. It had been a long Bee, and he missed in the late afternoon on the final day.

His outsized performance turned him into a celebrity, as replays of his confident spellings were broadcast on ESPN and TV news programs.

"People recognized me on the [Washington] subway, people stopped me in the street, a crowd of teenagers came up to me in the Smithsonian," he recalls, "girls asked me to sign their arms and their purses, the girls started kissing me, the boys were shaking my hand."

234

When the Patels went to the passport office to get passports for their vacation to India, a man in the passport room "jumped up, shook my hand, and he asked for an autograph. He said his family was talking about me over dinner last night."

Television producers had noticed Samir's bravura stage presence; his parents started fielding offers. There was something about the kid. Sure, he was a great speller, but he also had something else, a sense of himself onstage, a naturalness, an unaffected chutzpah. While all the other competitors grew heavier amidst the anxiety, he seemed to stay as light as air.

The Fox Network hired him to play a "lifeline" for three episodes of a celebrity spelling show in which minor luminaries competed head-to-head; they could appeal to Samir for help only once. During the taping he got to meet 1970s rock star Alice Cooper, whom he found to be really nice. "He's the only one who agrees with me. My mom always wants me to cut my hair really, really short. He says that it looks good long. He gave me a free CD and an autograph." Additionally, the producer of the variety-talk show *Jimmy Kimmel Live* invited Samir to appear, but the short notice caused Jyoti and Sudhir to decline.

◎◎◎

After his third-place finish, Samir took a couple of months off from spelling. Facing the prospect of gearing up for another National contest, he felt ambivalent—but not for long. "It was kind of a half and half thing, because I had worked really hard that year, and I was like, I don't want to have to do this again," he says. Upon reflection, however, "I was like, I want that prize, and I want that fame and I want that money—I want to win. It's something that, once you get into, you can't stop it until either you can't do it anymore or you've won."

And so the preparations began again, this time with a deepening intensity. "In 2004 we were really serious," he says. "For at least a month before the Bee, I would just, literally, get up, do my studies, do spelling for the whole rest of the day, then sleep." Every day he drilled word lists, studied lingual patterns, and worked on memorization. "Before the Bee, my mom would try to get me to do some [spelling] rules while I was eating; she would have me take my snack into the front room so we could be doing spelling while I was eating."

Going into the 2004 Bee, plenty of observers saw Samir as a potential winner. The only spellers from 2003 who had placed above him were not returning, and with another year of study he would be that much more fearsome. If he were to win, at age ten, he would go into the record books as the youngest champion ever.

As the contest began, he was his usual assured self, breezing through Latinates and French derivatives with equal insouciance. In the final day, he faced *corposant*. It was far from the hardest word he had faced, but it had somehow never come up in his studying.

It forced him to guess, something that Samir, or so it appeared, had never had to do. As the time clock beeped, he attempted it as *corpuscant*. His stumble meant that he placed twenty-seventh—an exceptional performance for the average ten-year-old, but a dramatic upset for Samir.

There was some chattering in the crowd—"nobody's perfect," pronounced one young onlooker with obvious relief—and a clear uptick among the remaining competitors. For the handful of spellers seriously eyeing the trophy, a big obstacle had just been removed.

As Samir paced the auditorium after his misspell, big tears rolled down his face. It was a terrible defeat. But the contest, despite its frustration, had been a learning experience. Samir would be back.

❦❦❦

The Patels live in a homey ranch-style house on a wooded lot in Colleyville, Texas, a suburb of Fort Worth. As we sit in the living room in the afternoon after Samir's 2005 regional win, Jyoti works the phone; one of the calls is a local reporter wanting details about the bee—he knows the Patels are a good source. As she handles press relations, Samir holds forth volubly about life and spelling, and Sudhir inserts comments, often with a laugh. After the phone calls subside, we take a tour of the house.

In the middle of Samir's bedroom, right next to the large bay window and his double-size bed, is the result of one of his great enthusiasms. It's a fanciful structure he built with Harry Potter–themed Legos (he loves Legos, and he's a major Potter fan). The elaborate castle-fort is constructed with bursts of turrets and ornate outcroppings sprouting every which way. A free imagination went into its design.

On his desk sits a computer, one of four the family owns, surrounded by toys, dinosaur models, and books—he has a walk-in closet chock full of books, and that's just part of his reading collection. He's partial to the adventure books of Enid Blyton, a British author whom Jyoti read as a girl, and he also peruses the *Smithsonian* and his father's *U.S. News and World Report*.

Right next to the door is a memento from the 2003 Bee. It's a picture of JJ Goldstein, one of that year's stars, holding Samir upside down. The goofy shot was possible because JJ, at age thirteen, was a couple of heads taller than Samir at age nine. It was a moment of supreme good spirit on JJ's part. Then in her last year, she had been a contender until *betony* tripped her up. That she was clowning around with Samir demonstrates an oddity of the Bee: Even top competitors can be friends.

On the living room mantel is a small forest of Samir's spelling trophies and plaques. There's his trophy from his first-place finish at North South at age seven, and there's the certificate from the Governor of Texas after his third-place finish at the 2003 Nationals (the Governor sent no certificate after Samir's twenty-seventh-place finish in 2004).

Also gracing the living room is a framed newspaper article by the Fort Worth *Star-Telegram*. The paper did an overview of the city's most noteworthy celebrities, including Dallas Cowboys football coach Bill Parcells and the surgeon who separated the conjoined twins. In this hallowed list was a full-page spread about Samir, complete with a photo of him looking out inquisitively from inside a tree trunk.

☺☺☺

Samir's spelling success is, of course, not about his efforts alone. His achievement is very much a team effort. Jyoti is his full-time spelling coach, and Sudhir handles chores like grocery shopping so his wife can dedicate herself to Samir's training. As Samir explains the division of labor, "She's the coach, I'm the speller, and my dad is doing all the legwork." Sudhir also helps with researching words and maintaining word lists.

Sudhir, however, is not allowed to help with spelling drill. With his accented English his pronunciation is not precisely standard. He describes his son's objections by scrunching up his face to mimic Samir: "'No, Dad!'" In contrast, Jyoti, with her lightly accented British English, is the perfect drillmaster. (Sudhir's first language is Gujarati, one of several languages spoken in India; Jyoti also speaks Gujarati but her first language is English.)

When Samir isn't spelling, he might watch a little TV, though very little. He's a huge fan of *Walker, Texas Ranger*, featuring the leather-skinned Chuck Norris walloping the tar out of a new bad guy every episode. And he's a fanatic fan of the Dallas Cowboys football team, which he watches every Sunday. When the Cowboys lose, he's been known to exclaim, "They must have changed uniforms with the other team," because he can't countenance a Dallas defeat.

His love of football played a role in one of his bees. To stay relaxed during competition, "sometimes what I'll do is take one person or thing that's in the room and I'll focus on that, and it keeps me from being nervous, because my whole mind is devoted to that." Before one of his earliest bees his mother told him that if he won he could use the prize, a gift certificate, to buy a video game, "so I was focusing on what game I wanted to buy and how fun it would be. It was a Madden game, a football game." Several rounds in, Jyoti looked up onstage and saw Samir, lost in his thoughts while waiting to spell, clutching his chest and swaying side to side, "And I thought, what was he doing?" Samir explains: "I was pretending to be [football running back] Emmitt Smith in my mind." While waiting to spell, he was mentally sprinting downfield across a grassy expanse, evading tacklers as he flashed toward the end zone.

In fact, a few years ago he briefly considered being a football player when he grows up, then realized he's too small for the job. So what's his alternate career choice? "I don't exactly know, but I know I want to be rich," he says. "I'm probably going to be a doctor, but I want to make some sort of invention or something that will change everybody's life and make it easier."

Samir's one trip to India, a vacation with his parents, left him less than impressed. However attached his parents may be to their Indian roots, he himself is rooted strictly in America. He enjoyed meeting his grandparents and cousins there, yet that's as far as his enjoyment went. "I had fun there, but I wouldn't want to live there—I don't like the country itself." He finds the quality of life unattractive. "It's a Third World country," he notes. "A lot of pollution . . . It was very crowded . . . No seat belts, it scared the heck out of me how they drove on the wrong side of the road." He refused to go into the bathrooms while traveling on the road; his father had to take him to the trees.

And besides, Samir says, India lacks the social freedom of America. "Here in America, you have freedom of choice. There, you're kind of restricted by social customs. You're pressurized," he explains.

⊙⊙⊙

As Sudhir sees it, all the exposure Samir gained after his bravura third-place finish at the 2003 Nationals created a problem. "He had lost some of the focus," Sudhir says. This loss of focus contributed to his son's tumble to a twenty-seventh-place finish in 2004, Sudhir opines. "And I have discussed that with him—sometimes he doesn't want to discuss it, but I talk about it. I think all the TV exposure, becoming a celebrity and whatnot, went to his head."

If lack of focus was an issue, then it certainly is no more. Now in the spring of 2005, as Samir readies for this year's Nationals in June, his mind is set on winning. His studying has not yet ramped up to full intensity, but it's heading that way. When he's working at full bore, "it's kind of intense," Samir says. "We do our studies, and we're going to take a few breaks, of course, but the rest of the day we are mostly doing spelling."

To increase his study effectiveness, his word lists are entered in the software program Excel. This allows him to randomize a word list with a mouse click; so if he starts spelling by rote, he can quickly scramble his lists, forcing fresh mental effort. All of his lists are stored on his laptop so he can easily transport his study system to Washington in June.

He knows his years of studying add up to real expertise. He can confidently spell the entire 23,000-word Consolidated Word List. "The regional seemed a little easier this year," he says. "For the last few years, there have been a few words that other people got that I did not know how to spell. But this year, if you would have changed my number around to any other number, I still would have won."

For Jyoti's part, her focus continues to be on word roots, stressing Latin and Greek etymology and numerous foreign languages. "I would love for him to win this bee—obviously that is our ultimate goal—but in the process I also want him to learn word roots from a point of view that you can associate with the meaning of the word." She notes that this will help when he studies a foreign language in school.

Sudhir has his own strategy to urge Samir to victory. He doesn't directly tell his son to win; he feels that would be counterproductive. Instead, Sudhir tells him, "Let's get it over with this year, so we don't have to go back." As an added bonus, if Samir wins this year at age eleven, he'll tie with the youngest winner ever.

The event will be hard for him either way. The pressure of the contest in Washington is very real, Samir notes. "At Nationals, you have to be really prepared because there are 251 kids, there are TV cameras, you can see the TV cameras in the back, a whole string of them. You can see the people up there commentating, there's an audience that has to contain at least a few thousand people."

But he's ready. At this point, with his competitive experience and his deep spelling study, Samir clearly has the skills to be a top contender in Washington. "If he wants to do it, he can do it," notes Jyoti.

²³ Jamie Ding

On the surface, it looked as if Yuchuan Ding had achieved the good life. By his mid-thirties he was a highly successful cosmetic surgeon in China. His superb reputation meant he had a thriving practice. He and his wife, Ning Yan, who taught physics, lived a privileged lifestyle in a nice neighborhood in Beijing. Yuchuan, in fact, had known privilege all his life. Since both his parents were Communist party members who held government posts, his family was affluent. As a boy, his family's chauffeur had driven them wherever they wanted to go.

But being a surgeon caused Yuchuan great anxiety. He worried constantly—he could hardly sleep nights, wondering, "What if I don't provide perfect treatment?" The thought that he might possibly provide less than ideal care made him feel "very bad and guilty," he recalls. He had no reason to worry—he had never had a problem with a patient—but still, "I was too nervous." The specter of a failure with a patient led to years of angst. Finally, toward the late 1980s, he could no longer stand it. He decided to change careers. He was, in effect, simply too anxious to go on.

But that nervous self-doubt was nowhere to be found in the spring of 1989, as Yuchuan saw the Chinese student uprising begin. That year, crowds of students gathered in Beijing's Tiananmen Square to protest government repression. The square was close to Yuchuan's house, and in a gesture of solidarity—he hated the government as much as they did, despite his upbringing—he stood shoulder to shoulder with them. The government, attempting to quash the rebellion, sent a mass of soldiers to take control of the square.

The students refused to give way. It was push and pull as the two sides stared eyeball to eyeball and the soldiers manhandled the students. Over the course of days the conflict escalated. Yuchuan, risking his career as well as his safety, stayed with the students. The same man who wanted to give up a medical practice out of worry for cosmetic surgery patients was, when his very life looked imperiled, apparently fearless.

After about a week, with emotions frayed on both sides—and with the government dangerously embarrassed by its loss of control—the standoff became a tinderbox, heading rapidly toward combustion. Yuchuan remembers that last day. His wife, Ning Yan, in a moment of panic, all but dragged him away from the student gathering. Not a moment too soon. "Ten minutes later, the soldiers opened fire," he recalls. Approximately 700 people died, perhaps far more.

After that, Yuchuan and Ning Yan knew it was time to leave China. They moved to Australia, where Yuchuan began working on a doctorate in neuroscience; he left his career as a surgeon to become a researcher, so he'd have no more worries about patients. When Yuchuan visited the United States for a research conference, he was deeply impressed by the quality of American scientific research. So in 1994, two years after the birth of their son Jamie, they moved to Tennessee, where Yuchuan completed his doctorate at Vanderbilt University and Ning Yan worked in day care. Their son Jamie was soon joined by a sister, Jessie. (Both children's names are English versions of Chinese names.)

In 1998 the family moved to suburban Grosse Pointe, right outside Detroit. Yuchuan now works as a researcher in stroke therapy at Wayne State University, and Ning Yan works as a high school math teacher in Detroit's inner city.

Yuchuan and Ning Yan agree wholeheartedly: They miss China—deeply.

But there's no going back. They want to raise their children in America. This is their new home.

⊚⊚⊚

It's early Tuesday evening, shortly before dinner in the Ding home, and the house is abuzz with activity.

Ten-year-old Jessie is fitting in some last-minute piano practice, her fingers gliding over the keyboard as she renders light classics. She's slender with long dark hair, and within the Ding clan she's considered to be the family princess. Her room is painted pink, she's performing in the school play, and, in a family that views hard work as a primary virtue, she's thought to be less interested in constant industry—though her excellent grades and piano skills prove she's no slacker.

Ning Yan is at the wok; it sizzles as she stir-fries a mixture of shrimp and cauliflower and greens. She's talking about the difficulties of teaching math in an inner-city classroom; Detroit's urban area is truly distressed. "It's hard," she says. "The students don't know how to study." She manages to smile even when talking about this uphill battle. That's not surprising, because Ning Yan is the family's official beam of light. If her husband, Yuchuan, however sweet and kind, is a brooder, with his worries that drove him from medical practice, Ning Yan is sunshine and warmth, gifted in the art of praising and encouraging. The laughter in the Ding home tends to originate with Ning Yan.

Yuchuan is busy setting the table for dinner, opening the jumbo bottle of red wine that the family serves from during dinner. He is, as always, on the quiet side—but unfailingly considerate. It's important, for example, that guests be well taken care of. "Red wine is good for you," he explains, filling my glass to the very brim.

Twelve-year-old Jamie—the family's star speller, who placed 27th out of 265 in the 2004 Nationals—shows me his prize possession, a handheld Sony PlayStation Portable. He's a round-faced boy with round glasses, about average height, usually talkative, confident, seemingly always relaxed—life is nonchalant for Jamie—with a sense of humor that tends toward the goofy. He plays a clip from the *Spiderman 2* movie (his small unit holds the whole movie) and shows me some fiendishly complex video games. When the Portable was first released, Jamie wanted one so badly that Yuchuan got up early to stand in line at the store to make sure he snagged one. However, claims his mother, Jamie places a limit on his video game playing. "He has good self-control," Ning Yan says. "He knows to not play too much."

Dinner with the Ding family is a mixture of Mandarin Chinese and English. Around the house, the family speaks only Chinese, but they politely use English when a guest is present, lapsing into Chinese only occasionally. Yuchuan and Ning Yan's speech is heavily accented, but Jamie and Jessie sound like every other American kid on the block. So Jamie is an odd mix, linguistically speaking: At home he's immersed in a language that bears no relation to English, yet his proficiency with English enables him to be a top speller.

He can spell monstrously difficult words like *boeotian* and *rijsttafel* off the top of his head, yet he also explains to me the intricacies of Mandarin. The Chinese word pronounced as "ma," for example, can mean either mother, horse, or be an insult, depending on the speaker's intonation; he demonstrates the subtle tonal differences that indicate the various meanings. And, says Jamie with a hint of mischief, "I actually know every language." You do? I ask. Yes, "because I know the word 'ugh,' and that's used in every language." He proceeds to do an imitation of Spanish, Chinese, English, and other language speakers all using the syllable 'ugh' in speech—in some examples it's just a speech stutter. Okay, I get it. It's that rare beast known as a language joke.

As Jamie sits at the dinner table in his red baseball cap, slurping down his stir-fry, he talks about working his way up to the National Bee. For him, spelling at that level is one of many advanced academic pursuits. During the spring of 2005 he will compete in a raft of national contests: Mathcounts, the Geography Bee, the Social Studies Olympiad, and the Science Olympiad. He's the first chair cello player in his middle school orchestra and will travel with the ensemble to Toronto for a concert, and he's also entered in a piano contest. Although he's in the eighth grade, he's taking a twelfth-grade math class. A math teacher requested that Jamie tutor some high school students, but he's uncomfortable with the idea—he's afraid the upperclassmen would feel humiliated to be tutored by someone so young—so he has declined.

Amidst it all, he can't dedicate much time to his spelling study, yet he still won the Detroit 2005 regional bee, so he's headed for Washington again this year. At age twelve, he's young to be in the eighth grade; he skipped a grade early in elementary school. His teachers wanted to advance him more grades, but his parents were afraid to put him too far ahead of his age group.

Still, for all his prodigious talents, his first bee was a minor ego bruise. As he describes it, "I tried out and I lost." In the sixth grade he heard about his school bee and on a whim decided to participate. He stumbled on the word *bolero*. Actually it wasn't much of a loss—he came in second, and the winner represented Detroit at Nationals that year.

The following year he started his spelling study much earlier, going into his seventh-grade school bee with the *Paideia* fully memorized. "It really wasn't a struggle," he remembers, "but I almost missed lunch." His winning word was *vigil*. In Detroit there's no intermediate bee, so school winners go straight to regionals. There he found a much tougher field, with a group of skilled orthographers all vying to get to Washington.

"Most everyone in the regionals did really well, but they just got a little nervous," Jamie says charitably. Late in the match the tension got to him, too—a little. "At the end, my hands turned all clammy." But after a long contest Jamie prevailed. He was headed to the 2004 Nationals.

☉☉☉

Going into Nationals he had no idea what to expect. "I didn't really know anything about it. In the beginning of the year we thought the entire competition would be decided by the *Paideia*." Ning Yan laughs at the memory. After Jamie's English teacher, Dan Bens, started coaching him, Ning Yan asked Bens, "Jamie knows the *Paideia*, how can the other kids not know that?"

They soon found out how mistaken they were. Ning Yan gets another good chuckle recalling when Bens showed her the Consolidated Word List, with its 23,000 words. "My goodness, I couldn't find any word I know," she says, laughing. "Mr. Bens was very nice, he said, 'Don't feel bad, I don't know them all either.'"

A coach was essential, Ning Yan felt, because she and her husband couldn't help Jamie; their accent is too heavy. "We worry we cannot pronounce, so we ask Mr. Bens to test." (Even when Jamie learned to read, which he did long before kindergarten, she bought him a book with an accompanying audiocassette so he would learn standard English.)

Even with a coach, Jamie found the sprawling CWL daunting. "It was a pretty rude shock," he recalls. He began working with Dan Bens once a week, for intense three-hour coaching sessions. Bens helped Jamie to better study by himself by teaching him the dictionary's diacritical marks, enabling him to pronounce unknown words. Bens also drilled Jamie on word lists and taught him fundamental etymology. And when Jamie went to Washington, Bens accompanied him and Ning Yan for last-minute prep sessions.

As the 2004 Bee got under way, one thing about Jamie stood out—or so it seemed. The pressure of standing onstage in front of thousands of viewers turns many spellers into a simmering pot of anxiety. Yet Jamie seemed the picture of cool. He shambled up to the microphone, took his best shot, and sat back down casually, spelling words like *jaundice* and *Qatari*. But all was not as it appeared. "I was quite nervous," he confides, but "I don't really show it much." It helped him that "the stage lights are always so bright that the audience is invisible." He brought a big wad of chewing gum to help work off the nerves. He also carried his good luck charm, a plastic California raisin, a gift from one of his English teachers.

Everyone back home was watching Jamie on ESPN, including his classmates at Parcells Middle School and his sister Jessie's classmates at her grade school. Before he had left for Washington, his eighth-grade class presented him with a huge handmade greeting card, signed by 200 students. A girl named Ginger wrote: "You are my IDOL You work it in Washington!" And Nancy enthused: "Way to electrify us!"

But, recalls Jamie, thinking of all those home viewers hanging on his every letter, "Then I managed to get spectacularly eliminated." Despite his downbeat assessment, he placed highly, tying for 27th in a field of 265—impressive for a first-timer.

"Most people think it's horrible," Jamie says. "Because five rounds does sound pretty . . . "—his sister suggests a word, "bad," and Jamie agrees.

"I thought he could do better," chimes in Ning Yan, turning what might be seen as criticism into motherly encouragement: "Because Mr. Bens says he has a very good memory." Yuchuan takes a similar tack, saying that Jamie is "not happy" with his twenty-seventh-place finish, then adding: "He did pretty good, I'm very proud of him, and wish he could do better."

The word that tripped him up was *corticoline*; he tried to put an *h* in front of the second *o*. Jessie, sitting next to him at the dinner table, points out her big brother's misspell and quickly rattles off the letters with machinelike surety. In response, Jamie makes the sound of the misspell bell—he's not going to let his sister one-up him. However, he then admits she spelled correctly. "That's right," he concedes quietly.

All things considered, he looks back at the 2004 Bee as "really fun." As for the following year's spelling fortunes, he had no doubt. He felt utterly certain he would return to Washington in 2005.

⊙⊙⊙

But first he had to work his way back, and that included one very brutal school bee. Most of the spellers in his junior high contest fell away quickly, but after a dozen or so rounds two spellers remained, both determined not to exit: Jamie and Matthew Vengalil, a tall, dark-haired, serious-looking boy in glasses and a turtleneck.

Standing onstage in the school auditorium, facing a small row of judges and a pronouncer, they took turns approaching the microphone. Matthew drummed his hands on his legs, somberly issuing the letters. Jamie walked casually to the microphone, his glasses sliding down his nose like those of an abstracted professor.

Both spelled as if they had an internal dictionary to refer to. Round after round they kept going; the sheer length of the event became a school record. Back and forth they went:

> Jamie: *dissymmetry*
> Matthew: *Machiavellian*
> Jamie: *scythe*
> Matthew: *aphasia*

Jamie: *hermetically*
Matthew: *stratocracy*

As the two-person contest extended toward the one-hour mark, the next period's English classes were brought in to watch. As the contest, incredibly, neared the two-hour mark, those classes had to leave, to be replaced by the following classes. Jamie felt as if it would go on . . . forever.

Jamie: *myriads*
Matthew: *genuflect*
Jamie: *palooka*
Matthew: *cinephile*
Jamie: *scabbard*
Matthew: *espionage*

Neither boy revealed much emotion, but both spelled with ultimate care—no simple slip of the tongue would send either offstage. Jamie, in most cases, took the precaution of asking for definitions, while Matthew attacked each word with a minimum of hesitation, sometimes spelling the moment he heard it. Both, clearly, had memorized the complete 3,800-word *Paideia*, so this was as much an endurance test as a spelling match. The rounds went on and on . . .

Finally, somewhere after the two-hour mark, Matthew tripped on *miscible*. Jamie could win with one more correct spelling. He stepped up and, for the first time, took hold of the microphone stand, as if needing to hang on to steady himself.

His word was *selenic*. He announced the letters carefully, in a steady walking pace—and he was correct. The judge pronounced him the winner and the auditorium burst into applause.

Jamie, however, gave hardly any smile and made no gesture of victory. Instead, he immediately turned around and shook Matthew's hand. The brief gesture had a quality of apology, a kind of sheepishness, as if he was sorry that he had gone ahead and won.

As Yuchuan recalls, "Jamie felt bad for the loser."

Jamie's spelling coach, Dan Bens, is a member of that all-important tribe: idealistic English teachers who love language and work vigorously to communicate that passion to their students. With his thoughtful, articulate manner, the bespectacled Bens carries on in the tradition of reading and writing crusaders—where would we be without them?—explaining the joys of literacy to antsy adolescents.

In his classroom at Parcells Middle School sit about forty chairs, over which hovers a portrait of James Joyce. Lest anyone in those forty chairs suggests that spelling is insignificant, Bens will quickly correct them. A few of the boys in his class suggested that a spelling bee was pretty wimpy compared with the rigors of ice hockey. Au contraire, proclaimed Bens. He pointed out that in the 2004 Nationals, Akshay Buddiga actually fainted from the exertion. When was the last time you saw a hockey player work so hard he fainted? Moreover, he noted, Buddiga got right back up and carried on—if that's not tough, what is? The boys gained a new respect, the English teacher says.

Despite his friendly demeanor, Bens has a fierce reputation as a spelling coach; of the last five kids from the Detroit area to make it to Nationals, he has tutored four of them, and he has gone to Washington each of those years. At the 2001 Nationals the spelling coach added a feather to his cap: His student was eliminated, but Bens successfully challenged the word she was given and got her reinstated. He knew upon hearing it that it contained an ambiguous spelling; after quickly consulting Webster's *Unabridged* he proved his case. A successful challenge is rare in modern Nationals; such a feat requires an expert.

Jamie, says Bens, is a student of remarkable ability, even among the bright kids he has coached. With a nearly photographic memory, he can encounter an obscure polysyllabic just once and instantly store it to his mental hard drive.

Once a week, Bens and Jamie meet for an intense three-hour tutoring session. They've worked out a routine, at Jamie's insistence, that moves their sessions faster. When they drill through word lists, with Bens pronouncing and Jamie rapidly spelling, Jamie often nods his head to indicate he wants to skip a word. If Jamie is sure he knows it, he doesn't want to waste time spelling it.

"I've learned to trust him, even if I'd sort of like to hear him spell it," Bens says. There are plenty of uncommon words Jamie gives his little headshake to, but if he thinks he knows it, Bens feels confident he does, too. The two also work on word patterns, exploring and dissecting the etymological currents that run through English.

"Jamie could win the spelling bee," Bens asserts without any doubt. The obstacle, he notes, and his parents second the notion, is that Jamie's plate is too full to make the Bee a single-minded pursuit. Between his geography bee, Mathcounts, his science and social studies contests, and his regular school-work—topped by twelfth-grade math and his cello and piano practice—his approach lacks the single-minded focus required to win in Washington. Jamie's parents want him to work with Bens twice a week, but the eighth-grader's schedule is too chock-full to do so. That, of course, is not a bad thing—he may be too well rounded to win. Then again, with a touch of lingual luck, and his all-consuming memory, anything's possible.

⊚⊚⊚

As we finish dinner at the Ding home, Ning Yan serves a dessert that's simple and delicious: a plate of fresh-cut pineapple. Jamie instantly appropriates a couple large slices and quickly begins devouring them. Yuchuan notices I haven't touched the oversize glass of wine he poured me, and he offers to take it off my hands, making fast work of it.

Although the dinner conversation is light and convivial, it turns otherwise when I broach the subject of sports. Are there any that Jamie likes? It's a question of no import, but every kid usually enjoys one of them, so it's a stock query.

An awkward silence ensues. Jamie mentions that he likes swimming. "But I don't like to swim fast," he adds, looking uncomfortable.

"He doesn't like to swim fast," agrees Ning Yan, with one of her sweet chuckles. But, as she points out to her son in her gentle motherly way, equal parts encouragement and guidance, "for the competition you have to." The exchange between mother and son reveals the one pursuit at which Jamie is—there's no way around it—truly abysmal. He is not an athlete, not even sort of.

The oblique reference to not swimming fast, it turns out, refers to his summer swim team experience. His parents cajole him into joining the team at the local pool, where he ends up dead last in every contest.

As the dinner table discussion of sports extends past thirty seconds, Jamie leaves the table for the evening. He hasn't, ostensibly, fled from the topic—he may need to begin his studies. But if the subject had been how he feels about reading the encyclopedia—one of his passions—he might be still munching pineapple.

His swimming, Yuchuan says, is an embarrassment for him. But, Yuchuan tells his son, "You don't have to win at everything." Despite the parental understanding, Jamie's lack of athletic ability is frustrating for him. In school volleyball matches he'll go entire games without touching the ball once. He also plays tennis, with more energy than grace. "He's not good," Yuchuan notes.

"We want him to do more sports because he studies too much, we think," Ning Yan says. "He just likes to study. He started reading at three years old and just never stopped."

Jamie's greatest athletic grace is revealed as he plays his full-body video game. Down in the Dings' basement—their four-bedroom home has a finished lower level—is a deluxe video-game setup. It's a video-game module connected to a 48-inch widescreen TV and a small video camera. When Jamie turns on the video game, the widescreen TV is full of onrushing monsters and demons. As he stands in front of the widescreen, the video camera picks up his movements, allowing him to wave his arms to squash whatever evil creatures the video game throws at him.

It's a fully interactive system; instead of squinting at a monitor and working a joystick, the game involves his entire body. Given the speed and dexterity with which he destroys the flying whirligigs—Smash! Bam! Splat!— there's no reason he couldn't be some kind of athlete; he certainly has the reflexes and hand-eye coordination.

In a brisk predinner match, he and Jessie take turns, each waving their arms frantically to obliterate a sprawling legion of electronic villains (she's just as adept as he is). Video games, by Yuchuan's account, are just one of many play activities that brother and sister share. The ten-year-old and twelve-year-old are the best of friends—so much so that one misses the other if he or she stays over at a friend's house for a night.

When they're goofing around together, Jamie will get laughs from his sister by imitating a dim-witted boy. She, in turn, orders him around, sending him hither and yon to perform tasks for her. Their parents make a regular practice of rewarding Jessie whenever Jamie makes it into yet another national academic contest, like Mathcounts or the Geography Bee. "We give her a gift every time he wins," Yuchuan explains, "because she must leave him alone to study."

Perhaps because her brother has seen renown as a speller, Jessie, too, has dreams of making it to the National Bee. But brother and sister don't agree on her chances for success as a competitive speller. After Jessie announces her intention to go to the Bee, Jamie counters:

Jamie: But she doesn't like it.

Jessie: Yeah, I do.

Jamie: You like competing but you don't like to practice.

And with that, Ning Yan breaks in with one of her loving motherly encouragements. "But Jessie says she will [practice]." That seems to settle the matter, though Ning Yan adds a postscript. "But with her big brother it's hard to catch up. He is a hard worker."

〇〇〇

Jamie's work ethic, and the resultant intellectual achievement, is something the Ding family puts the highest premium on.

Yuchuan, normally the most congenial of people, gets declamatory about the subject of hard work. "In America people think education should be fun. In China we think it should be work, hard work." He and his wife have imbued this spirit in Jamie.

As Ning Yan notes, "The life is so hard for him, compared to other children. You know, they play. Of course, he enjoys [his studies], that's the good thing. But he has to schedule."

And that schedule is something they remind him of, gently but firmly, if he starts to tarry. Jamie loves the stories behind words; as he studies his spelling lists, he often comes across words whose history he finds fascinating. He'll spend time digging into a word's past, leaving his desk to share his discovery with his parents, telling them the neat little tale behind a word.

But his mother wakes him from his reverie, nudging him to stay goal oriented: "He finds a story that he will share with us. And we say 'Jamie, go back!' He has so much to do, each evening we have to remind him, 'Jamie! How much do you want to do today?'" Yuchuan adds: "I can't imagine how he can amuse himself with words so much."

For all his intense work ethic, Jamie doesn't seem like a driven kid. He meanders around at times, he pauses after dinner to peruse *Time* magazine before beginning his studies (he looks forward to *Time* every week), he interrupts his studies to play games, he's got friends; he's been friends with two boys, William Colding and Keith Porter, for more than six years. (But his friends have no interest in spelling, he notes.) He's an open-faced kid who seems to move forward at an ambling pace.

He apparently dives into his full feast of intellectual pursuits because, left to his own devices, that's what he enjoys doing—though certainly parental prodding keeps him on track. It's as if intellectual exploration, all the facts and concepts he's absorbing, is a type of play for him.

His parents have even wondered: Does Jamie really want to engage in his long and demanding list of extracurricular contests, the Bee, MathCounts, Social Studies Olympiad, etc.? Is it all too much weight to put on a twelve-year-old's shoulders? "I've asked him a million times," Yuchuan says. "He said yes."

☽☉☾

Jamie will gladly share his uncensored opinion on most any topic. His sister's school play was "horrible," he opines, and his own school play, called *Reading, Writing and Rocking*, was equally bad, he says. He describes one of the spellers at last year's Bee as "a braggart, whom nobody seemed to like." There are, however, topics about which Jamie will remain mum, absolutely so. If such a subject comes up, he can lapse into a monosyllabic shell. It's all but impenetrable.

Ask him about his study method and he'll say, "I'm not sure"—his strategy is under wraps. Ask him how he's feeling about going to Nationals this year, and he makes it clear: "Nothing"—that set of feelings needs to be guarded. But there is one surefire way to extract an answer from him, in any case. As polite as he is—and he's a sweet kid—he can hardly resist an opportunity to correct his parents.

Ask Yuchuan or Ning Yan a question about Jamie, let them get perhaps one sentence out, and he will interrupt to correct them. He will run over his parents verbally as reliably as a fast galloping horse runs over something left carelessly in his path.

Ning Yan starts to tout her son's reading level: "His reading skill is very fast—"

Jamie cuts her off. "Books that I read for fun, I read once just to get the whole story. Then I read them again and again and again, until I get the details."

Jamie's 2004 regional bee was a long match. Did it come down to Jamie and just one speller, or a number?

"One kid," Yuchuan recalls.

"Actually a number," Jamie corrects him.

Ning Yan: "He has passed Geography Bee—"

Jamie (cutting in to correct): "National Geographic Bee."

Ning Yan (again later touting her son's reading): "And he has *Readers' Digest*—"

Jamie (correcting): "That was yours."

Later I ask Yuchuan about this. Yes, he says, with a knowing chuckle, Jamie does tend to be verbally assertive. Yuchuan allows himself a long smile. He appreciates his son's spirit. The approach seems to be, as long as Jamie is doing his work, he's allowed to be free. Their headstrong son can speak whenever he wants to.

⚬⚬⚬

It's mid-evening in the Ding household, and Jamie and I are in the den, a book-lined room with a wraparound desk and a computer with an oversize monitor.

He's done with his homework—keeping up with middle school doesn't take much time—and he's on to his spelling study. It's four weeks before Nationals. Time to bear down.

To study, he uses software from Merriam-Webster that includes the complete *Unabridged*, all 475,000 words. The program's built-in audio enables him to hear the pronunciation of any word he types, and it also offers all manner of list-building and advanced search options. In short, it's an all-purpose tool for studying the English language.

He sits at his computer, going through word after word, typing it in—which of course requires spelling it—and listening to it. "I wonder why they have so many words," he says. It's less a question than an expression of enjoyment at the unending variety.

As his spelling work progresses, he takes one of his favorite detours: word games. He likes the games posted on the Merriam-Webster Web site, and tonight he plays a brisk game of Citation, a test of vocabulary—never let it be said that he doesn't look up from the grind.

He returns to his word drill, soon to discover a term he finds interesting. "Have you heard of dihydrogen monoxide?" he asks.

"Never," I say.

"It's a very horrible poison," he explains. "It's one of the main components of acid rain. If ingested it can damage you. The solid form of it can cause permanent damage. And worst of all, the government knows all about it, but they still decide to use it."

He has me going. "You mean in fertilizer?" I ask naively.

"No," he says. "And you know what else about it? It can be found inside tumors."

"Oh, really," I say, wondering where he's going with this.

Then he reveals his ruse with a flourish of minor triumph: "It's water," he says, as if he's a magician pulling back the curtain. "That explains everything, doesn't it?"

Of course—dihydrogen monoxide—it's H_2O. And yes, it's a component of acid rain, the government certainly knows about it, and the solid form (ice) can harm you. As I'm digesting that one, he moves on:

"Wouldn't it be funny if the winning word one year was the same the next year, like if *autochthonous* [from 2004] was this year's word?" His amusement over this theory leads to a discussion of the Bee's winning words; he can hardly believe how easy the winning words were in earlier Nationals. From a list of the winning words he keeps handy, he points out that the word *initials* was the winner in 1941. He takes particular delight in 1983's winner, *luge*.

"The easiest word was 'No Bee' and they had to repeat it," he says. He's referring to the entry in place of a winning word for the World War II years, when there was no Bee. He takes a minor delight in pretending that the term was an actual winning word. "That was a really easy one," he says. "They should have 'No Bee' every year."

His kidding aside, he's well aware that the Bee is traveling ever further from the simple days when *initials* was the winning word. "This year the *Paideia* got harder," Jamie says. "They deleted the categories with only two or three advanced words, and they replaced them with really hard ones, and long ones."

But that, as he sits studying this evening, doesn't faze him. Or at least it doesn't diminish his ability to enjoy words for their own sake. As he studies, he comes across the word *julep*. "I love this word," he says with very real excitement. He launches into a full narrative related to the word's history. "The guy who invented the artificial straw loved mint juleps," Jamie says, explaining that before the invention of artificial straws, "they put grass straws in it. It tasted like grass, so you'd think it's a grass julep. And they were often kind of dirty, because it's hard to wash grass. So then a guy who loved mint juleps, he owned a cigarette company, and instead of cigarettes he started making straws."

The anecdote goes on—the inventor's name was Marvin Stone, and the story is true. It's an elaborate and unlikely tale: how the invention of a ubiquitous item was driven by one man's affection for mint juleps. The story's stranger-than-fiction quality enchants Jamie. He ignores the mundane work of spelling drill as he relishes the odd elements of this fantastic anecdote.

It's as if his mind is too far ranging, too free in its intellectual curiosity, to sit and drill spelling lists. His natural intelligence will allow him to do well at the Bee, but his lively curiosity might prevent him from taking home the trophy. Winning requires plenty of conceptual understanding, like his little stories, but it also requires putting the shoulder down and plowing through the rote work of drill (and more drill). By the time he fully explores one of his word histories, he has spent time that another speller has used to pore through pages of obscure words.

The concept of winning is, for him, beside the point. For Jamie the Bee is largely an educational exercise—as it is for the majority of kids involved. I ask what feels like an irrelevant question: Do you ever think about winning? His answer is nonchalant. "Winning would be nice," he says.

Indeed it would be, and after all, he tied for twenty-seventh the year before with only basic preparation. Anything's possible, and he's now only a stone's throw away from being a top finalist. Yet whether he places highly or not, one thing is clear: In the process of competing he's going to learn an enormous amount.

²⁴ Aliya Deri

If the group of spellers that gathers every year for the National Bee is distinguished by a certain geek chic—the attractive nerdiness of the intellectually inclined—by comparison to many in this group, Aliya Deri falls closer to the chic end of the continuum.

Personable, mature beyond her years, with an easy laugh, Aliya has a touch of the Bay Area's sophistication. She's a longtime devotee of tai chi, a pretty fair jazz pianist, and an avid, adventurous reader who raids her father's paperback collection. "I think my parents will agree that I read *way* too much," she says with a chuckle.

In fact, she's an intellectual omnivore. In addition to being a top speller, she also competes in Mathcounts, performs in two orchestras—playing both violin and viola—and is a creative writer. In her rare free time, she's a competitive swimmer and diver and an accomplished dancer. Aliya (pronounced "Olly–ah"), in short, is something of a supergirl.

But, like many superheroes, something separates her from absolute perfection, at least in the realm of competitive orthography.

It's her nerves. The fluttering butterflies can bother her terribly. That everyone is staring at her, waiting for her to issue letters, weighs on her. Certainly she pays homage to the gods of lingual fortune: "You're just wearing every lucky charm possible, sleeping with lucky charms under your pillow, crossing your fingers, and praying that you're going to get a word that you know." Still, stage nerves can play havoc with her spelling, as they did in the 2004 Nationals.

At the microphone, Aliya, then in the seventh grade, spelled with a deep seriousness. She stood nearly still, her arms at her sides, with her long dark hair pulled back and parted in the middle. Despite her focus, toward the later rounds her nerves seemed to be creeping up.

Impressively, she conquered a word she had never seen before, *peritonitis*, by sounding it out at the microphone. But when she faced *toxophily*—which she knew—she started to struggle. She had trouble getting the pronunciation, going back and forth with the judges, voicing it numerous times, the anxiety in her voice escalating as she went. Finally, she closed her eyes (an essential part of her ritual), shutting out the crowded ballroom. The letters came evenly, almost floating out. She was correct. Unsmiling, she walked quietly back to her seat.

She had survived, yet the next round, facing *belonoid*, things got tougher still. She didn't know the word, and as she ruminated on the possibilities, a cloud cover of semi-fear moved in.

She had prepared for this moment, but when it arrived, the waves were cresting higher than expected. "I definitely practice a lot. I try to envision myself spelling in front of an audience. I close my eyes a lot because the glare, and people staring at you, and people taking pictures, can be really distracting.

"And breathing is good. Just making sure that you're keeping on breathing. Because a lot of people I've seen just stop for a moment. And it's not something you want to do."

She kept breathing, but it wasn't enough. Having thousands of eyeballs directed at her was not, for her, the ideal space for peace of mind. "I think part of the reason I got *belonoid* wrong is because I panicked," she recalls. "Which is not something you ever want to do in a bee, because all the letters count."

Panic. That's a tough thing to overcome.

As the bell rang, sending her offstage, a minor storm moved in. "Well, of course you have a certain feeling that the sky is about to fall, and the world's about to end. Once you hear the fateful bell ring, you kind of feel the world is collapsing around you. You really feel that every eye is on you. It's an experience that, I think, everyone feels a certain number of times."

However, she recalls months later, "It wasn't the biggest thing in the world. I usually take it pretty well." Overall, the experience was "definitely a lot more good than bad."

She had tied for 27th in a field of 265. If she could return in 2005—and master her stage nerves—she had a realistic shot at the trophy. Could she do it?

The Deri family lives in a four-bedroom house in Pleasanton, California, a suburb forty miles southeast of San Francisco where the median house price is $829,000. With its proximity to the city, the suburb is more diverse than most. As Aliya's father, Bob, notes, "You meet a lot of different types of people from a lot of different parts of the world, which is always kind of fun."

The Deri family itself is an example of people from different parts of the world. Bob's parents emigrated from Germany, and when he was a boy growing up in the New York City area, his family spoke German around the house. His father had been a student of Einstein's, and his grandmother's name was Hertz, as in Heinrich Hertz, the famed German physicist. Bob is a project manager at a Silicon Valley technology company. He's a hip dad who wears 1960s-retro high-top sneakers in his off hours, but whose belief in close-knit family life is distinctly traditional.

Aliya's mother, Chandan, grew up in Bangladesh. As a young girl she dreamed of a career in music, but her father vetoed that notion, telling her that physics was a better choice—she had always been talented in math. In 1976 she came to the United States for two years—"just to check it out," she says—and to earn her master's degree in physics from Tufts University. She and Bob met when they both happened to rent rooms at the same house in Boston.

Chandan is now a full-time homemaker who supplements Aliya's classes at the Harvest Park Middle School and Amador High School with extensive tutoring, in between chauffeuring her two daughters to their myriad activities. Although she has come to accept the United States as her home, she still holds dear her Bengali roots.

Over dinner with the Deri family, one aspect of Chandan's nostalgia for her native land gives her two daughters something to chuckle about. Chandan has taken to listening to Bengali CDs around the house. Her enthusiasm for this traditional folk music is not shared by Aliya, thirteen, and her sister Joya, sixteen, an eleventh-grader.

"The Bengali music is very . . . *unique*," opines Aliya. "She likes to listen to it a lot while we're home. And we beg her to stop putting it on, and she says, 'I listen to your rock 'n' roll, you can listen to my music.'"

Chandan tries to stick up for her musical preference, noting that its composer is "the guy who wrote the Bengali national anthem."

But the Deri girls don't buy this rationale. "It's all done by one guy—which is bad," Aliya says. "It's very . . ."

Chandan appears to have lost this round, but she takes it all with a grain of salt. She's the Deri most likely to laugh, and she's also the family's fountain of warmth.

The conversation moves on to Chandan's newfound love of Bengali movies from the 1950s; she rents them on DVD and they bring her back to her youth.

"Bengali movies . . . " Aliya begins dryly, expressing something less than enthusiasm. Then, catching herself, she plays the diplomat. "Some of them are very good," she says. And when Chandan talks about why she enjoys them so—"Most of the old movies are so nice," she says—Aliya steps in to explain their attraction. The movies "make you think about what you would have done in that person's life," she says. "It's people doing what society tells them to do in a situation where you're thinking, should they really have done that, in humane terms?"

That affectionate give-and-take between family members, the free sharing of opinions, is typical of the Deri family. The family is a cohesive unit in which laughter, conversation, and contradictory views are shared without reservation. They relish their togetherness. They are extraordinarily busy people—"We're really challenged in time management," Bob says—but they eat dinner together every night, and most days breakfast, too.

Every Wednesday and Saturday, the family goes to tai chi class together. Taking a tai chi movement class together as a family "is a California thing more than anything," Aliya explains with a smile. She and her sister are accomplished at the ancient Asian discipline, advancing to the point where they gracefully handle safety-blade swords as they move.

However, in the family tai chi classes, "Mom cheats," Aliya says, claiming her mother cuts a few corners as they practice.

But, her mother replies, the swords are "a bit heavy—it's not easy."

"They're not that heavy," Aliya clarifies.

Bob, playing the diplomatic father, says, "Certainly when you begin, they *feel* heavy."

Like their tai chi classes, spelling study has been a family affair. The Deris' first spelling star was Joya, who did well in the California state bees, and Aliya was her coach. The two sisters share a room at home and call each other their best friends—even sharing clothes—yet when Aliya coached her big sister, she was a tough taskmaster. "If she just slipped on a syllable, I wasn't lenient at all," Aliya says. "I made her learn everything."

"She wouldn't cut me any slack," Joya concurs.

"She was a mean coach," their mother agrees. "I think she liked the pleasure of bossing her."

This coaching, of course, helped Aliya herself when she began spelling competitively. "I definitely learned a lot of words from coaching her," she says. Even more, "seeing her do it and seeing her learn something, and be very good in a competition, really inspired me to work hard." And now, whenever Aliya shows up for a bee, she wears her older sister's red hooded sweatshirt for luck.

◎◎◎

Now that Aliya is competing in bees, Joya is too busy to return the favor and be a dedicated coach. Joya takes six advanced placement courses and also teaches piano and swimming. Aliya's schedule is just as crowded. There's schoolwork, rehearsals for two orchestras (plus the practice required for violin and viola), daily piano practice, and, somewhere in there, dance class. Although she's an eighth-grader, she takes high school algebra and French classes, and she's a teaching assistant for a middle school math class. She also participates in regular swimming and diving activities, which in California are year-round.

Where, amidst the bustle, does she fit in spelling sessions with her father-coach?

Typically twice a day, early morning and late evening. The morning sessions are the less tough of the two. "I'm more zoned out then," she says. "They're easy and they go by so quickly because I know when I have to leave." Not that early morning spelling is all sweetness and sunshine. Promptly at 7:00 a.m. each morning, "Dad comes in and turns on the lights and says, 'Aliya, get up.' It's not very fun—I like to sleep in."

Bob agrees that's an early schedule. "I wake her up on my way before I go into the shower. So then we'll typically do spelling over breakfast, for about an hour, maybe a little bit longer." If Aliya gets her homework done early, she fits in extra spelling study in the late afternoon.

The late evening sessions, typically lasting a couple hours, are more taxing because both father and daughter are battling fatigue. "When you're going a couple hours after dinner, still doing spelling, it's pretty tough," Bob says.

"He would call it a really big fight, because I tend to fall asleep a lot," Aliya says, laughing and getting a knowing laugh from her family. Fueled by the laughter, she dramatizes her plight to comic effect, in that special way of thirteen-year-olds who love the attention: "And he's addicted to caffeine. So after his twentieth cup of coffee, he tends to start yelling at me [doing her father voice], 'Why are you falling asleep? I am awake. You're thirteen years old, you stay awake.' I'm thinking, 'Dad, you won't let me drink anything. It's not my fault!'" The evening sessions continue, she says, "until I'm dead on my feet." What she leaves unsaid as she portrays her father as a stern taskmaster is that she plainly loves the work; to talk with her is to know she enjoys her spelling study.

The father-daughter sessions include extensive drill, using a wide-ranging word list. "We try to expand beyond the Consolidated Word List, like words used in the definition of a word," Bob says. Their sessions also focus on under-standing root patterns. "Basically we're trying to simplify what needs to be memorized as compared to what can be figured out on the spot," he says. "Because it's not very practical to memorize the whole dictionary, and so you've just got to be able to take the words apart." Aiding Aliya is her knowledge of French and her father's knowledge of French and German; the two of them travel across many other languages, including African languages, Japanese, and of course Latin and Greek.

"Dutch is nasty," Aliya notes, referring to its spelling contradictions. "They'll take anything and pronounce it the wrong way." She points out *muis-hond*, which sounds like "mice hont." "The Dutch refuse to follow any logic—every time I meet a Dutch person, I think"—here she pretends great disgust and her family laughs—"it's all your fault."

She knows that Dutch printers in the fifteenth century added chaos to English by taking liberties with spelling as they printed early books. Momen-tarily adopting the voice of a Dutch printer, she proclaims, "Oh, I can't find an *o*, I'll just put an *e* in there—they make the same sound anyway."

"Probably the worst part of the English language is the ubiquitous schwa," she says, bemoaning the vowel sound that's spelled myriad ways, which is quicksand for orthographers. "Nationals seem to really focus on the schwas—I've noticed that."

Despite her exhaustive study, she's aware she can't deny the element of luck in competitive spelling, and it's her least favorite element. Luck can make a bee "really unfair," she says. "I may know how to spell the word the kid in front of me gets but not know how to spell my word. So if I just switch places with that kid, I could have gotten the word right and still be in."

For this reason she would prefer a written bee, which would test her broader knowledge rather than make each word a win-or-lose proposition.

"I like written spelling bees because [in oral bees] I'll never really feel that I hold up to my best potential," she says. In an oral bee, "you always feel that if you make just one small mistake, you're out. But when you have to miss four words and you're out, you don't feel so bad about that one little mistake.

"I feel better and more comfortable in a written bee because I know that

I'm probably in one of the top levels of spellers who are going to be there. But in an oral bee, it's just whatever—whatever they throw at you."

Ultimately, she accepts that luck will continue to play a role, regardless of her hopes otherwise. In fact, dealing with the vagaries of fortune in a spelling match "is a good life lesson," she says.

⚬⚬⚬

In her social life, her life with friends, Aliya is a free agent, she explains.

"I don't like being part of a set group of people. Like there's an Indian girls' clique there [at school], and they go to the Asian club, and do this and that together. I don't want to be associated with any group, whatsoever. I just sort of jump in and out of groups, and she [her sister Joya] does the same thing."

Her social life "is not a 'I hang out with these people' kind of thing," she says. "I'll hang out with five or six groups, so I don't specifically walk between classes with any one person. I just sort of hang out with whoever."

Her best friend is her sister Joya, she says. The two sisters, who talk and laugh together easily, share a room at home. They've never gotten around to redecorating it since their younger years, so in terms of wall hangings, Aliya explains, "You might expect Led Zeppelin or something like that—no, it's zoo animals and various Pocahontas posters here and there."

"She's the clean one and I'm the messy one in our room," Aliya admits. As for any minor tension this might create, well, "we deal with it," she says. Over time their bedroom has grown too crowded to study in, so the living room has been turned into a study area, with two big tables in the center. (There's little distraction there, because the family chooses not to have cable TV. "Only broadcast," says Bob proudly.)

Looking ahead, toward what she might want to do when she gets older, Aliya is pondering a few possibilities.

She knows, surely, she does not want to be an astronaut. Some of her classmates are interested in a career in aerospace, "but the first time I went to the Air and Space Museum, I went into that G-Force exhibit and I thought 'boy, do I *not* want to be an astronaut,' because I don't want to be going down through the atmosphere . . . I just don't want to do it."

"She doesn't have my permission," says her mother with a laugh.

"Yeah, I would be under like ten times more stress with Mom . . . " she concurs.

She's also considering a career in medicine—maybe. Her father likes the idea, her mother not at all, Aliya says. A career in medicine, explains her mother, "is not a happy life."

But, counters Aliya, "You can be miserable for ten years, and then you can become really rich and not be miserable."

Closer to her own interest is a career in journalism. But, whatever the case, she knows her options are numerous. "I could be anything," she says. "I'm pretty sure that whatever I do, I'll do well."

⊚⊚⊚

It's a Saturday morning in mid-March, the day of Aliya's 2005 regional bee, sponsored by the *San Francisco Chronicle*, and all eyes are on her. The fact that she made it to Nationals last year—placing twenty-seventh, no less—means this contest is hers to lose. She approaches this day with a sense of worry. Many of her classmates expect her to win, yet she herself feels far from sure.

In fact, her gut instinct is that she won't win. Her anxieties mount as she wonders, "How am I going to feel if I went one year, and this year I'm sitting here on Memorial Weekend and thinking I could have been in Washington right now, and watching other people get coverage?"

Ready to compete with Aliya this morning is a crew of ace orthographers. Close to 200 school champions from the Bay Area competed in a preliminary round in February. Now, standing onstage in a ritzy hotel in downtown San Francisco are the fifty-two survivors from that qualifying round.

Apart from their verbal skills, these kids are clearly some of the best dressed and best looking of any regional bee in the country. There are no SpongeBob SquarePants T-shirts, and the haircuts and hairdos, in most cases, look pretty pricey. If a fashion photographer showed up to shoot a spread for a Gap Kids catalog, he'd have all the models he needed.

Today's pronouncer is Stan Bunger, a spare, precise man in wire frame glasses and an elegant coat and tie. He's a morning news anchor on San Francisco's CBS radio affiliate. With his well-modulated baritone he crisply enunciates each syllable, and he's flawlessly accurate in his pronunciations—he knows his diacritical symbols. Accompanied by a row of four judges, one of whom is armed with a large bell to signal misspells, Bunger bends seriously to his work.

His first few words are warmups. Grade-schooler Jacob Howard easily handles *designer*—that silent *g* in the middle isn't fooling him—and Kyle Vanderberg gets the seriously easy *stomach*, tapping out the letters with clear confidence. Almost all the kids step up and hit the slow pitch out of the park, except for one boy who apparently never creates elaborate table settings and yet must spell *doily*. He's a goner.

When Aliya walks to the microphone, she's wearing her potent good luck charm: her older sister Joya's red hooded sweatshirt. As a fashion statement, the sweatshirt might be slightly downscale in this crowd, but its comforting quality is more important. And Aliya needs that support today.

The thirteen-year-old is battling a buzzing case of nerves. Perhaps it's her status as a returning winner, or, more likely, it's just a simple case of stage jitters. Her word is *mobilize*, and as she pronounces it, her voice cracks. For her it's not a hard word, of course, but, as is her custom, she shuts her eyes to spell, entering her own world to slowly call out the letters, working hard until the final, relief-filled *e*. She accepts news of her success with a sober, downcast look. *Mobilize* required a careful focus.

Parents are here with cameras at the ready, and their flashes accompany the contest throughout. Talented speller Robert Lipman, in an elegant lime green button-down shirt, eagerly spells *anarchy*. Flash. The confident Saachi Gupta, in a classic white knit sweater over a red-striped top, sails through *ream*. Flash.

These spellers have studied. A few go down, like Hannah Joy Wirshing, who adds an *i* to *lathe*, but most keep going. Gregory Zilboorg, in a floral-patterned black and white shirt, does the Mendocino Middle School proud, flying through *rubella*. Molly Montgomery, with a big happy smile, recites *quesadilla* as if she's a Mexican food critic about to devour one.

There are, amidst what is an intense proceeding, tiny moments of levity.

The diminutive Serena Smiley, with her long brown hair tied back, asks the language of origin for *sapphire*. "You're going to love this," pronouncer Stan Bunger tells her. "Sanskrit, through Hebrew, through Greek, through Latin, through French, through English—I think that covers them all." At the list's conclusion the audience chortles and Serena flashes a big smile. The etymology is longer than she is—she has to tilt the microphone down to spell—but she masters it with ease.

When Aliya steps up to face *mahogany*, her voice again rasps with her nerves. She may be the most visibly anxious speller here this morning. "Can I please have the language of origin?" she asks. Bunger stumps her with his response: "Unknown." It's rare when the list includes a word with an unknown etymology, though it happens. It's always a curveball. Worse, Aliya misunderstands him, thinking he has said "no," as if the pronouncer has for some reason refused to give her basic information. She stares at him in baffled incomprehension, until Bunger explains with a kindly air that it's not that he himself doesn't know, it's that the origin itself is unknown. This prompts an audience laugh and extracts a relief-anxiety chuckle from Aliya. She shuts her eyes and walks through the letters, pausing before the *a*—is it an *o* or an *a?*—and she gets it. Nothing about today is going to be easy.

⊙⊙⊙

As the rounds progress, a few complex words begin to creep in. Jeremy Geist, from the Gideon Hausner Jewish Day School, is dealt *eatage*. He's momentarily unsure but gathers his wits and plows through it. Kyle Vanderberg, who's been the picture of confidence, now haltingly start-stops through *dactylion*, but the bell ring sends him offstage.

When Aliya is given *propinquity*, it looks as if she's beginning to leave her jitters behind. With eyes closed she steps through it with ease; her certainty is total. Yet when she pronounces it again after spelling, in her moment of small triumph, the word comes out mangled. Perhaps the nerves aren't totally gone.

Robert Lipman, in his lime green shirt, attempts *erudite* as *eriadate*. Saachi Gupta's eyes widen in concern upon hearing her word is *cationic*. She digs for clues, seemingly unsure, yet jogs through it without doubt. All these words come from the *Paideia*, and Saachi has evidently spent hours with the 3,800-word list.

Benjamin Kelly looks like he knows it in his sleep. About medium height, with short spiky brown hair, freckles, and glasses that fall down his nose, he goes methodically through his paces on each word. He makes every possible query, after which his supremely confident spelling reveals he could have skipped the preliminaries. He has, it seems, been coached to take full advantage of his time at the microphone. He dispenses with *Hellenic* with total surety.

In contrast, Caroline Graham appears as if she's made it here today based on natural smarts rather than *Paideia* study. She wears a chic urban-style black T-shirt with a logo that says "Random & Weird," along with matching black earrings. She had buzzed through *brocade* with ease, but when she hears her word is *gibbet*, she gives a little laugh, as if to say, "I have no idea." Indeed she doesn't, starting it with a *j*.

Aliya is relaxing. With her new confidence—she's warming up—she dispatches *protean* with ease. Was this the same girl who was close to petrified a few rounds ago?

Nicolas Robinette, with his easy smile and light brown mop top, gets *interstice* but doesn't know it. He lets go of each letter begrudgingly, knowing he's headed for doom. At the end, he realizes, to his utter amazement . . . he's correct! Surprise! He screws up his face into a silent whoop of joy—he's amazed at his own ability. In the next round he shocks himself yet again with *parquetry*. With each letter, his tone of voice says, "This couldn't possibly be it, could it?" and then he enjoys a small smile when he learns he's correct.

Not everyone is so fortunate. Gregory Zilboorg, with his hair cut short on the sides and left long on top, buzzes through *tilde* with unthinking confidence, but—whoops—he replaces the *e* with an *a*. Morgan Gautho, a grade-schooler in a jean jacket, rushes out the last few letters of *redoubt* as if to escape the bell's ring by sheer speed, but no. She leaves out the word's silent, lurking *b*. Franchesca Finnigan has been a bubbling font of life throughout, with her long dark hair and freely expressive features, yet when she spells *primogeniture* with an *a*, the resulting bell brings a rare frown to her face.

This bee is a particularly businesslike proceeding. No flubs by pronouncer Stan Bunger—he's a complete pro—no outbursts from parents, no delays, not even that much hemming and hawing by spellers. As the words continue their uphill climb toward obscurity, the kids exit the stage in a regular rhythm. The contest moves efficiently toward its conclusion.

⚛⚛⚛

Aliya has reached her inner calm. Gone are the voice quivers. Having made it this far, and finding out that, yes, her brain works well under pressure, she has found a new strength. She gets the uncommon *chiral*, meaning "of, relating to, or being a molecule that is non-superimposable upon its mirror image." Shutting her eyes, she thinks for just a moment, then swings with no fear. She's right.

She is now one of just five remaining spellers. Judging by the aplomb with which these last five step up and spell, it's safe to assume that all their families have kept an open week on their schedule in early June to attend Nationals in Washington.

Benjamin Kelly, with his glasses sliding down his nose and his spiky hair, has surely been dreaming of the trophy. The eighth-grader makes all possible queries about *perimysium*, then dispatches it like it's a simple monosyllable.

Besides Benjamin and Aliya, the three remaining spellers are, incredibly, all fifth-graders, an unlikely outcome given that this contest is open to any student up to the eighth grade.

Serena Smiley, with shoulder-length light brown hair, appears as if she will someday be CEO of a Fortune 500 company, or a lawyer for one. She has an easy smile, accompanied by a verbal sharpness that makes her sound like a young adult. She spells *chayote* as if it's a mere formality.

John Doner, a compact boy in glasses and short dark hair who seems to be having fun, makes his queries and then dispenses *blepharal*, "of or relating to the eyelids," in his small, professorial voice. You don't get as sure as he is without a lot of study.

Gunjan Baid's navy blue sweater is frosted with a sparkling material that glints in the stage light. With her light-reflecting outfit and shiny dark hair pulled back, she might be an ambitious ingénue attending a Hollywood opening. She spells *trochanter* as a question, inflecting the letters upward, and she's right.

When Aliya steps up to face *charcuterie*, the French delicatessen specializing in meat dishes, the butterflies have reappeared en masse. Her voice rasps with the pressure as she pronounces the word, and she stammers when asking for the definition. But no, after a couple breaths, Nervous Girl is not going to make a comeback. She's been banished. Aliya pronounces it again, clearly this time. She then closes her eyes and slices through *charcuterie* like a Parisian master chef.

Serena Smiley, the young lawyer-to-be, crisply requests the definition and language of origin of *rapprochement* as cameras flash. She spells with no hesitation, and as a final touch she pronounces the word with an authentic French accent, with a nasal attack and a silent *t* on the accented last syllable.

Benjamin Kelly is beginning to resemble an automaton, asking for all the information he doesn't seem to need in a knee-jerk style, peppering the pronouncer with queries. Still, he's flawless, mastering the obscure *ormolu* as easily as another middle-schooler might spell *video game*.

John Doner doesn't bother to ask any questions about *alstroemeria*. He spells it without clues. For the fifth-grader this uncommon polysyllabic never makes his anxiety meter rise above the midway point.

Gunjan Baid takes even less time spelling *pentateuchal*. None of these kids have any plans to leave the stage.

Aliya is in the zone, as athletes say when they've reached their optimum performance level. She makes fast work of the esoteric *ikat*.

Serena Smiley conquers *putsch*, Benjamin Kelly handles *myxomatosis*—the pronouncer knows Benjamin's fusillade of queries are coming and so interrupts mid-query to field them—John Doner walks through *chatelaine*, and Gunjan Baid spells *pierrotage* without a hint of doubt. Cameras keep flashing. Everyone stays in for the next round.

Aliya is now veritably bursting with confidence, running through *chenet*, pronouncing the word after spelling it with a definitive cadence.

Serena Smiley steps up to face *kraken*, a mythic Scandinavian sea monster. She spells it phonetically, as *crockin*, and exits.

Benjamin Kelly almost breaks out laughing upon hearing *ayuntamiento*, but bites his lip to keep a straight face. It's not clear why he's laughing—the word is devilishly difficult, with a first syllable that confounds a phonetic approach. After his requisite queries he tosses it off without thinking. He's looking tough.

So is John Doner, who dispatches *mandir* without much thought, and Gunjan Baid, who tosses off the tricky *skirret* with ease.

The words are now from the world of the obscure, but we're about to travel to a still further planet: *Skirret* was the last word from the *Paideia*. From this point on we move into the "surprise" list. The upcoming words can come from anywhere in Webster's *Unabridged*. The spellers now have no idea what challenges they'll face.

First up is Aliya, who attacks *antemortem*. She's relaxed and strong. Part of the way through she even opens her eyes—she's in such a groove she no longer needs to shut out the world to spell.

Benjamin Kelly faces *coercion*. He asks all the questions and then issues the letters without a shadow of a doubt—but in the middle he inserts an *s*. Apparently his secret is that he's a hard worker; no matter how complex the word, as long as it was listed in the *Paideia* he could memorize it. The bell rings and he accepts his fate with no sign of emotion.

John Doner gets *opprobrium*. It's a weighty word but it can be sounded out, and that's what he starts to do. But John, formerly a buoyant, no-hesitation speller, now works to stay afloat, voicing the last few letters as a gaping question. Nope. He, too, has lost his *Paideia* life raft.

We're now down to two spellers. For the final two, the San Francisco regional uses a rule the National Bee has long since dispensed with. That is, if one speller misses, his or her competitor must spell the word they missed, plus one additional word, to win. (At Nationals and many regionals, the second speller must spell a fresh word, plus an additional word, to win.)

Gunjan Baid, clad in her spangle-covered navy blue top, steps up to get her first non-*Paideia* word, *rejuvenescent*. With a little Latin training it's a giveaway. "Rejuvenescent?" Gunjan asks in a tone that reveals that Latin is not one of her languages. She throws the dice and, except for replacing the *j* with a *g*, gets all the letters. She walks off with a worried look—but she's not out yet. Aliya must spell *rejuvenescent* and one more to win.

As Aliya walks up and begins to work through *rejuvenescent*, her assurance is so complete that she's almost that conversational, at-ease girl that one chats with offstage. She takes her time, but her letters come out as absolute statements, not attempts. Her voice is even and firm. After the first three letters her eyes open—even her eyes-shut ritual can now be dispensed with. Oddly, unlike most spellers, the further she goes in competition, the calmer she gets.

"That's correct," the pronouncer says. "Now if you spell this word correctly, we're done." Everyone knows that, but it still serves to notch up the pressure.

"The word is . . . *anorak*." It's the same word that Samir Patel faced near the end of his regional bee in Texas. (Scripps has a total of five "surprise" lists, so various regionals will get the same one.)

As the word is pronounced, cameras flash, and Aliya can't avoid a smile. She's beyond relaxed. With victory in her grasp, she's actually enjoying herself. The very last moment of a tough test is, for her, fun. She asks the definition and language of origin, though the questions appear unnecessary. As she begins to spell, she shuts her eyes and states the letters in a big, sure voice, crossing the finish line with the breeze at her back.

"That's it," proclaims Bunger as the crowd politely applauds and myriad cameras begin flashing.

Aliya, in her moment of glory, simply grins quietly. No gestures, no celebratory move, just a joyous smile. The camera flashes become an almost solid wall of light, which she turns to look into.

Her smile gets bigger still, widening in the camera's sunshine. Happiness reigns. She's going to Washington this year.

²⁵ The Annual Ritual: Word List Creation

As spellers all across the country work toward the Bee, the Bee organizers are also preparing for the national gathering. Over the course of the year, during multiple meetings, they are creating the thing that will strike deep anxiety into hundreds of talented orthographers. They are developing what is referred to as, in Scripps' official parlance, the word list.

This compendium of spelling challenges, the 850 or so words to be used in the National Bee, holds the dragons and monsters that will devour many spellers. It's a dicey thing, this list. Each year it's created based on the same mold—or pretty similar—yet each year it's as unknowable to spellers as the laws of unpredictable fortune, which is to say, not at all.

Oh, there is one thing that spellers know about the list. All of its words come from Merriam-Webster's *Unabridged*—so that narrows it down to 475,000 possibilities.

But, you ask, does that mean that I can just open up the *Unabridged* and put my finger on some odd geographical term, like an obscure German city, and it might be used? Yes, it might be. But, you're thinking, with growing unease, certainly the Bee doesn't allow proper names, like the name of some obscure seventeenth-century English author, known chiefly by his direct descendents? Yes, those obscure authors can rise from the dead at the Bee.

But, you ask, as the enormity of it sets in, are the Bee organizers cruel people? Why are they asking thirteen-year-olds to spell words that have been spelled by no humans, except for a lone linguist at Merriam-Webster, and perhaps about 250 English graduate students?

Well, you have to understand, as Bee organizers create the word list, they're faced with a challenge of their own. They have to stump some brilliant thirteen-year-olds. You don't outwit these kids with *separate* and *recommend*. These are kids who can spell *eudaemonic* and *objicient* and *Lysenkoism*. (Actually, *Lysenkoism* is one of those words based on a proper name, that of Trofim Lysenko, who was wildly famous in Soviet agriculture in the 1930s. And the kid who was given *Lysenkoism* at the Bee spelled it correctly.)

So if Bee organizers are going to bewilder these spellers—and they have to, otherwise they'd never find a winner—they have to get obscure. Really obscure.

☙❦❧

To be sure, the word list is shrouded in secrecy. Only a small handful of insiders view the list before it is read aloud, speller by speller, at the Bee. The list is like the ending of *The Da Vinci Code*. We know it's there, and we can surmise a few things about it, but its truth won't be revealed until the appropriate moment. And not only are the list's contents guarded—of course they're kept from young eyes—but even the way in which the list is created is guarded. We cannot know its words and we cannot know the way these words are chosen.

For those scrounging for clues, Bee organizers offer opaque statements like, "It is not standard practice for word panelists to consult old Bee word lists when composing new word lists." Hmmm . . . does that mean they *might* use old word lists? Yes, definitely—maybe. It's been common practice over the years for audience members at the Bee to write down all the words as they are given. This doubtless improves the spelling of these spectators, but it provides no real clues. The list is made afresh every year, and words aren't necessarily repeated—although they might be.

Any effort to uncover the secrets of the list is fruitless. Even an intrepid reporter, looking under all possible rocks and knocking on all possible doors, was unable to uncover the alchemy. The word list is, and will remain, a mystery . . .

☉☉☉

The word list as it is tended and managed in the twenty-first century is a far cry from its earlier humble self. Up until 1960, there's no record of who put together the list or what their rationale was in assembling it. "We just don't know," says Bee director Paige Kimble.

In 1961 Scripps Howard asked its editorial promotions director, Jim Wagner, to add "Bee director" to his list of duties. Wagner, a longtime newspaperman and WWII veteran, assembled the list on an impromptu basis. He created some of the list himself, and he also took suggestions from others. Wherever he went, he brought a small spiral notebook with him; if he happened to read *Life* magazine and come across an interesting word, he'd jot it down, and it would pop up in Nationals that year. When *Life* ran one of its pictorials on the fierce New Zealand Maoris, one could assume that native terms for outrigger and seafaring would be included.

But Wagner was far from exacting in his list management. As head judge Mary Brooks, who began working with the Bee in the early 1970s, recalled, "When I started, selecting words was sort of a happenstance that was not researched and studied and justified the way that we do now. Truly, when you came to Washington, you didn't know where the words came from or how they were going to progress. You were clueless."

Challenges to judges' rulings were not uncommon. A judge would ring the bell signaling a misspell only to be confronted by irate parents. The parents would claim that their child's version was the correct spelling. "Or there is an alternate spelling, or the pronouncer didn't pronounce it correctly, or it could just be a multitude of things," Brooks remembers.

Wagner knew that he needed help, and in the mid-1970s that help arrived. Harvey Elentuck was a brilliant young MIT student who had organized a student bee at MIT in 1975. He approached Wagner, offering to lend a hand with the word list, which Wagner gladly accepted. Elentuck's improvements were numerous: In addition to adding his erudition to the list's creation and overseeing various list contributors, at the conclusion of each Bee he would retire to a private room and furiously type immaculate press-ready round-by-round descriptions of the event. (And, as a Jew, he enjoyed adding Jewish/Hebrew words to the contest; it was likely due to his additions that *Purim* was the winning word in 1983.) When Wagner retired in 1984, the Bee took the process of assembling the word list to a still higher level. Among the event's organizers there was a firm decision about the list, which Brooks sums up: "There has to be somewhat of a science to this process."

For the first time, the Bee formed a word panel, recruiting experts from Encyclopedia Britannica and Merriam-Webster to contribute words. However, the initial work of this panel, whose word list was first used in the 1985 Bee, suffered from a major drawback: The group wasn't given much direction. As a result, the list became increasingly more difficult, year after year, between 1985 and 1991. The word list in 1991 remains notorious. Due to the words' complexity, that year was known "by all accounts, hands down, for being the most difficult Bee in history," Kimble says.

"Since the 1992 Bee, things were brought back under what I would call control," Kimble says. The list's level of difficulty has remained fairly predictable since then, she says. Beginning with the early '90s, then, the word list entered what could be called its Modern Period.

༄༅༅

The word list's present-day manager, its chief lingual sorceress, is Carolyn Andrews. Equipped with an easy laugh and a light Tennessee drawl, she could be your twelfth-grade English teacher, except for the fact that she's a serious biker, known to roar across the Tennessee hills on her Honda while decked out in an all-leather outfit. Andrews is a constant traveler in the world of words, and there are few places she hasn't visited. She knows new words like *bling*, invented recently by hip-hop musicians, and she knows that *portmanteau* was coined by Lewis Carroll in *Through the Looking-Glass*. She follows words as they make their way into Webster's *Unabridged*, and she tracks the relation of certain words to current events to determine whether they're in vogue. She has a special fondness for—and this might be a clue, so pay attention—blended words, new creations created by combining two existing terms. For example, *netiquette*, which combines *Net* and *etiquette* and refers to the laws governing interaction over the Internet.

When a word is a blend, she says, it "gives that word a little extra kick." She's the kind of person who talks about words having a little extra kick, as if they're mild intoxicants, perhaps a rum toddy with an extra shot of spirits. Yes, she's a word nut.

Andrews worked as a technical editor until her son Ned won the Bee in 1994. Immediately afterward, aboard a private jet that was whisking her and her family down to Disney World so Ned could be on *Good Morning America*, she met Bee director Paige Kimble. As a result of this chance meeting (and her credentials), she was hired to be a member of the panel that develops the word list every year. "I'm one of the few people whose child has gotten them a job," she quips. When the panel's manager retired in 1998, Carolyn became the word list manager.

Under Andrews's tutelage, successful challenges to judges' rulings have fallen to near zero. Notes Paige Kimble: "Historically, many of the protests would relate to an individual finding in the dictionary an alternate spelling or some variant, and that just doesn't happen much nowadays." Given how thoroughly the modern-day list is pummeled and polished, that's not surprising.

⊚⊚⊚

The creation of each year's word list—this most secretive process—starts almost a year in advance of the Bee. Soon after the prior year's competition in June, word panelists begin to gather lists of possibilities. These words might come from anywhere: the panelists' daily lives, a news item, a restaurant menu, or their reading habits, both serious and casual.

(Their reading habits? Hmmm . . . could this be a clue? So Carolyn, what magazines do you read? "We don't take many magazines," she says, "but we do get *National Geographic*." However, she adds, she does get catalogs at her home. She recounts the experience of a girl who missed *Limoges*, a type of porcelain.

Shortly thereafter, "all these knockoffs of limoge boxes were flooding the catalogs. If she had picked up a bunch of catalogs, she might have run into that word." Hmmm, picked up catalogs . . . .)

After a rough list of words is compiled in the summer, with suggestions from several Bee officials, the pruning and reshaping begins. To aid this process, each word is assigned its necessary chaperones: definition, part of speech, sample sentence, and a pronunciation guide. Jacques Bailly, the Bee's official pronouncer, uses Webster's *Unabridged* and his extensive knowledge of etymology to add each word's language of origin.

The words must be accompanied by their dressings so that in the fall, when word panelists and Bee officials get together for a two-day review of the list, they'll have full portraits of each possibility. Over the course of these two days the list is hammered and sculpted. Words are dropped. Entries are changed. The air is thick with discussion of linguistics and trends in language. Occasionally there is disagreement, although Andrews, in response to my question, makes it clear that it has never yet resulted in fisticuffs.

Also at this meeting, the process that Andrews confirms is the hardest part of list creation takes place: The words are rated by level of difficulty. In theory, during competition the words become ever more difficult round by round. Surviving Round Eight simply means you'll meet a bigger challenge in Round Nine. The problem is that there are about seventeen or so rounds in a typical Bee, but there are not seventeen precise gradations of spelling difficulty. Making the process harder still, there are no well-codified guidelines about how to rank words based on spelling difficulty. It's an imprecise science, more of an art, really, close to guesswork in some cases.

What's harder to spell, *ruminate* or *excelsior*? They're about the same, based on the Bee's judgment—they were in the same round. One round later in the 2004 Bee was *banausic*. Still another round hence, we saw *pudibund*. Is *banausic* easier to spell than *pudibund*? That's hard to say—and the answer may vary speller by speller. But somebody's got to make the decision, and that's the goal of this fall meeting.

To make their decisions, the word panelists use factors like whether a word could be spelled phonetically, whether a speller with knowledge of word roots could figure it out, the length of a word, number of syllables, and overall familiarity.

One of the factors determining familiarity is how fashionable a word is, and this waxes and wanes with time. "Words will change in 'difficulty' over the years depending on how familiar they are at the time because of what's going on in the world," Andrews notes.

For example, the word *cortege*, a procession of mourners in a funeral. The word was on the potential Bee list a long time and was considered to be fairly difficult. "But then Princess Diana died. You could not pick up a newspaper or magazine without seeing the word *cortege*," she says. "That word got bumped down in difficulty for the next couple of years because everybody was so familiar with it. But now since there hasn't been a lot of exposure to it, the word has risen again in difficulty."

Another word that fell in perceived difficulty is *millennium*, due of course to the blizzard of usage. And the most recent victim of overuse, Andrews says, is *carbohydrate*. One would need to be in a cave to not be exposed to the word all too often. Although presumably, as the low-carb craze fades from memory, this word's perceived difficulty will rise again.

⊚⊚⊚

After the two-day fall meeting, Carolyn gathers all the input and creates a list, though it remains open to discussion. She prunes and waters the list and may do some other things that are not disclosed. In February there is another two-day word panel meeting. Again, the list is taken apart, examined and reexamined. Discussion ensues. Numerous marks are made on paper. The ranking of several words' difficulty might change. Possible problems are avoided. The list, in essence, is polished to a high sheen.

From this winter review, something referred to as a "final list" emerges, yet it might still be changed before the spring competition.

The list is then given to pronouncer Jacques Bailly, who begins working on the pronunciations. That he gets the list months ahead of time—and that he has the training to correctly pronounce all its words—is a chief factor distinguishing Nationals from local bees. In lower-level contests, this task is sometimes handled by a volunteer who shows up on a lark. An individual with a regional dialect, voicing uncommon words with an uneven knowledge of diacritical symbols, adds a wild set of curveballs to the contest. Bailly's skills and his months spent with the list (and his region-neutral diction) allow the Bee to be a level playing field. Nobody is going to get a bum pronunciation. They still might not be able to spell *triskaidekaphobia* or *chresard*, but at least they'll hear them voiced correctly. (Indeed, some of these words will be correctly spoken only at the Bee, if they're spoken at all.)

In May, after Bailly has worked through the list, it is sent to the judges for their final perusal. They read it through, ruminate on it, and one day before the Bee there's a final meeting of all who will run the competition: the judges, the word panelists, Jacques Bailly, and the assistant pronouncer, Dr. Brian Sietsema. Some minor changes might be made—perhaps a word that a judge still feels uneasy about is deleted. After this last huddle, the list is, finally, pronounced done.

And so the list is ready. Its hundreds of words, the softies and the monsters, the giveaways and the all-but-unspellables, sit quietly and secretly, waiting for their appointment with destiny. The Bee can now begin . . .

Part[6]

The Showdown: The 2005 National Spelling Bee, Washington, DC

" . . . You will be given the next word on the pronouncer's list, and if you spell this word correctly, you will be the champion."

—Mary Brooks, head judge, Scripps National Spelling Bee

²⁶ The Tribe Gathers

It's nine in the morning, and I'm standing onstage at the National Spelling Bee. At this hour the cavernous ballroom in the Grand Hyatt is almost empty, except for Jim Close, father of Kerry Close, who got here early to stake out the best seat. In one hour the great conflagration will begin, the final day of competition, with its massive media coverage, its anxious parents, and its more-than-anxious spellers. But at this hour the ballroom is calm, almost ghostly.

I stand where the spellers will stand, at the microphone, looking out into the hall. Focused on this stage is a set of six spotlights, suspended from the ceiling; they are so klieg-light bright they obscure the top half of my field of vision. With the lights in my eyes the hall appears to recede into inky dimness, and it seems I'm suspended, even floating, over a sea of seats. As my eyes adjust, I see a daunting sight: At the back of the hall, on a raised platform, is a row of sixteen video cameras, all pointed directly at me.

As my eyes further adjust, I notice something still more unsettling. Down in front of the stage is a wall, a kind of barricade, behind which will sit a cadre of judges and officials. In the middle, on a raised platform, are seats for a pronouncer and his assistant. On either side will sit all manner of timekeepers, record keepers, and word judges, all focused intently on whoever stands at this microphone. With that thought in mind, I'm relieved to be a reporter who can step off stage, rather than a speller who will be inspected and detected by this squad of watchers.

As I step off stage, a teenage staffer walks in with the Bee trophy, the two-foot-tall gold loving cup that today's winner will hoist high as countless cameras flash. He's carrying it casually, like it's just a thing, but as he places it on its onstage pedestal, it assumes magic powers. It gleams, and most powerfully, it offers its winner a place in the record books. Those who compete today will remember who placed number two, but no one else will. Long after today's $28,000 first prize is spent, the champion's name will sit quietly in the record book, and will be referred to with the laurel wreath, *Winner, 2005, Scripps National Spelling Bee.*

That individual will be able to rightfully boast of having taken an expansive lingual journey; he or she must be conversant in Latin, Greek, French, and a host of other languages, must have a breathtaking vocabulary, and must possess upper-level conceptual skills. They must be willing to work long hours in single-minded dedication to a goal. They must believe in themselves enough to think they can win. And, most challenging of all, they must put all these abilities together in the pressure of the moment, under great stress, as thousands of viewers watch. Today's contest is about maturity and presence of mind as well as spelling skills. The winner, in short, must be a true intellectual athlete.

All across the country, as the hour nears, people are switching on their televisions, turning to ESPN, and wondering: Who will become the champion today?

⚬⚬⚬

The annual gathering known as the National Spelling Bee is much more than a spelling contest. This weeklong get-together is actually a bee in the traditional sense, like the barn-building bees of yesteryear. It's a gathering of neighbors, in this case from all over the country, with a full palette of socializing: a pizza party, a barbecue, tours of Washington, DC, and days and nights of nearly continuous chatting.

And it's a big group. This year's Bee hosts 273 spellers. Most are accompanied by two parents, siblings, and sometimes a grandparent or uncle; some bring their coach. Filling out the gathering is a full complement of staffers and Bee officials along with their spouses and kids. Altogether, the group numbers about a thousand people.

When this gathering takes up residence at the Grand Hyatt, an 880-room affair four blocks from the White House, it essentially takes over the hotel. The Hyatt features a voluminous open-air atrium and numerous conversation nooks, and the Bee group occupies much of this space, forming a community whose members originate everywhere from Martha's Vineyard, where the wealthy go to enjoy the Atlantic breeze, to Teec Nos Pos, a Navajo Indian reservation in Arizona.

Over the course of Bee Week, the group feels a range of emotions in tandem, almost like one collective organism. On Sunday it's the lightness of registration and a pizza party; Monday is the neighborliness of a Memorial Day barbecue, with games and assorted festivities; Tuesday, as families tour Washington, DC, presents a growing sense of anticipation; on Wednesday, when competition begins, lightness gives way to intensity; and Thursday, as the crowd leans forward in its seats, offers the nail-biting culmination of the Bee's final rounds. After the group takes a collective breath, Friday provides the feel-good congratulations of an awards banquet, and on Saturday comes a long round of bleary-eyed and heartfelt good-byes. It's a complete emotional life cycle.

ooo

Hosting a pizza party for a thousand people requires a large space, so this Sunday night we're in the Hyatt's grand ballroom, where the Bee will begin on Wednesday. A room that will soon be filled with tense spellers is filled this evening with chattering twelve- and thirteen-year-olds and their equally social parents, busily grabbing slices of pepperoni and cheese pizza off long tables.

There *is* a competition tonight, of sorts. All manner of game boards are placed on the tables in the ballroom: Scrabble, Monopoly, chess, Risk. Bee director Paige Kimble stands onstage and says hello to everyone, and at her signal, we all move to the game of our choice; about a thousand people adjust position, settling in for a focused, take-no-prisoners board game. Dice are rolled and pieces are moved, pizza is munched and e-mail addresses are exchanged. Spelling, for the moment, is all but forgotten.

The five spellers profiled in this book are all present and armed with pizza. Each of them, Samir Patel, Kerry Close, Marshall Winchester, Aliya Deri, and Jamie Ding, is a returning speller who placed high last year. So each faces an expectation that he or she will make it into the torturous later rounds. But tonight is just for fun.

Samir Patel gives me a chipper "Hi, James!" and a good-natured palm-slap greeting. I saw him just a few months ago, but at age eleven it's amazing how fast a human can grow. Samir has always seemed mature for his age, and in the last ninety days he appears to have taken a few more steps.

The Texas boy's sense of being older than his years is probably helped by having spent last week in London, filming a TV pilot for a British show called *Celebrity Spelling Bee*. He played the show's "lifeline," the expert that celebrities turned to when they were stumped. By his father Sudhir's account, he was his normally hammy self, issuing commands and directives and making his opinion known at all times.

Marshall Winchester from North Carolina also enjoys a certain celebrity. Now in his third year at Nationals, the thirteen-year-old is surprised that everyone here seems to know him; in elevators and in the lobby, people he hasn't even met greet him with a respectful "Hello, Marshall." The reason for his notoriety is clear: Since he placed fourth last year and no one who placed higher has returned, he's the default top contender.

Marshall is engrossed in a game of Scrabble with Kerry Close from New Jersey and two teenage Bee staffers. Kerry notes with minor exasperation that the letters she has drawn have allowed her only limited options. "Three-letter words," the twelve-year-old says with dismay. (Actually, she has put down plenty of four- and five-letter words, but Kerry is anything but a braggart.) Almost out of options, she puts down "IQ"—an acronym, and so a no-no in Scrabble. "Well," Marshall says, in a generous spirit, "if we're playing by 'stretch' rules, I guess that's okay."

Despite her questionable Scrabble fortune, Kerry, too, has enjoyed a burst of limelight. The day before coming here, a CBS-TV crew spent three hours in her living room, interviewing her and her parents for a piece about the Bee. Now in her fourth year here, having placed eighth last year, many see her as a possible winner.

Jamie Ding, from Detroit, focuses intently on a game of Monopoly, a Lord of the Rings edition, yet he and two other players are taking a shellacking at the hands of his younger sister, Jessie. She smiles angelically as everyone notes how badly she's beating them.

Jamie has had a too-full schedule of academic competitions this spring; just last week he competed in the National Geographic Bee, placing eleventh out of fifty-five. To catch up on his spelling studies, he has immersed himself in his word lists over the last several days. His coach Dan Bens, his middle school English teacher, will fly in Monday for last-minute prep sessions. Perhaps the load is getting to Jamie; the twelve-year-old is not his usual sunny self this evening.

Aliya Deri sits with her family, taking delight in a family Scrabble game. The Deris had to get up at 3:00 a.m. for their flight and are still on San Francisco time, so getting over jet lag will take a few days. But Aliya seems perky nonetheless, flashing a bright smile. Her mother, Chandan, chuckles merrily at how overwhelmingly her daughters are vanquishing her at Scrabble. Her father, Bob, also smiles, though he's bent seriously to his letter rack. He'll have some intense work in the days ahead. Having coached his daughter over breakfast and late evening sessions these many months, he'll continue working with her in the next couple days.

This evening's pizza party is full of kids who've been spotlighted in the media for their spelling prowess—at the very least they've been featured in local newspaper articles. But no one in this room has garnered as much media buzz as George Hornedo. The fourteen-year-old did just so-so in last year's Bee, but his naturally ebullient stage presence caught the eye of Hollywood producers. The casting agent for the film *Akeelah and the Bee*, about a disadvantaged African-American girl who competes in the National Bee, was looking for a Hispanic boy to play a supporting role. George was invited to audition, got the part, and spent a month in Los Angeles with his mother, Cecelia, during filming.

This was the big time. Starring Laurence Fishburne and Angela Bassett, the movie is scheduled for national release in 2006. During filming, George and his mother mingled with the in-crowd while staying in Los Angeles's ultra-trendy Mondrian Hotel. Cecelia found herself in an elevator with pop star John Mayer, and she spotted filmmaker Spike Lee in the lobby. George, who at age fourteen already understands the art of Hollywood schmoozing, always made a point of shaking Laurence Fishburne's hand in cast get-togethers.

On the set, George suggested alternate lines for his character, which the director filmed takes of, though it's unknown if they'll make the final cut. During one scene, George's character leaves to go to the restroom, and he improvised the dialogue line, "I need to go lose some weight, if you know what I mean."

When the director realized during filming that George's regional bee in Indiana was about to happen, he dispatched a crew to film it—causing the Hornedo family a major dose of stress. What if he lost—and it was recorded in full-fledged 35-millimeter glory? When George won, allowing him to come to Washington this year, his parents breathed a double sigh of relief.

The media noticed this orthographically talented ingénue. As this year's Bee approached, media outlets kept his parents' phone ringing with interview requests. By his father Dagoberto's count, the list includes VH1 Radio, ESPN's *Cold Pizza*, and CBS's *Sunday Morning*.

The experience has given George at least the patina of a movie star persona. While at the 2004 Bee he exuded a natural assurance, this year he has blossomed, projecting a good-natured cockiness. He's a wholesome-looking boy—some casting agent has probably dubbed him the All-American Hispanic—and he wears a small white necklace that accentuates his new glow. He wants an agent, and two Los Angeles talent reps have expressed interest.

His father is happy to see George pursue acting; his mother is less comfortable with the idea. As for George, he sees both options. "My first priority is education, get into an Ivy League college, be a lawyer-sports agent-politician," he says. "But I'm open. I do impressions."

With all eyes on him, George has worked doubly hard for this year's Bee. A high-ranking finish would not only earn him academic kudos but also boost his show business career. He has studied constantly with the online "Speller Nation" group. This is the same group that Kerry Close works with; it's eight to ten spellers who use an Internet phone line to conduct real-time bees at all hours of the day and night. As part of Speller Nation, George, in his bedroom in Indiana, participates in bees with kids in New Hampshire, California, and elsewhere. They all wear headphones and spell into a tiny microphone attached to their home computer. According to general scuttlebutt, the winner has often been Anurag Kashyap, a San Diego boy who placed forty-seventh in 2004. George, ever confident, predicts that this year's Bee will come down to himself, Anurag, and just a few others.

Over the last few months, George's mother has often found him absorbed in online bees, headphones on, hunched over his computer at odd hours. At one point she attempted to shoo him off—enough, she said. But something compelling had mesmerized George. Apparently, the online bees included a make-believe speller named Winchester, as in Marshall Winchester, the top returning finalist (though Marshall himself doesn't take part in the online bees). One evening when George's mother tried to get her son to take a break, he protested, "Not now, Mom, I'm almost beating the Virtual Winchester!"

⊚⊚⊚

Monday, Memorial Day, is bright and sunny, and spirits are blithe as the entire group, all one thousand or so, piles into buses and heads out to the picnic grounds. On the way out, right behind me sits Anurag Kashyap, an eighth-grader from San Diego, sharing a seat with Akshat Skekhar, a fifth-grader from Massachusetts. However hard the two have studied to get here, at the moment they are giggly, goofy boys, finding reason to fall into fits of silly laughter with every passing street. Akshat, in a momentary pause in the fun, makes a grand proclamation: "I'm going to go to Harvard!" A girl sitting behind them, joining in their frivolities, can't resist raining on his parade. "You're not going to make it," she announces. "You might as well start crying now."

At the barbecue we help ourselves from huge tubs of ribs, beans, corn, and other classic Memorial Day fare. As we're munching off paper plates, the karaoke starts, causing general wincing and laughter throughout the crowd. A brave father gets up and massacres a moldy 1980s ballad. Another father, undaunted by the reaction to the first, labors through an almost passable version of James Brown's classic "I Feel Good," complete with vocal groans and screeches. "He's in pain," observes Katelynn Inman, a fourteen-year-old Idaho girl. Most impressive is David Nabhan, a fourteen-year-old who belts out the Rolling Stones' "(I Can't Get No) Satisfaction" with a convincing rock feel.

"I *love* being onstage," David tells me after his performance. He had once hoped for an acting career but decided against it. It might be fun, but he feels it wouldn't be profitable. "I might as well do something that will help me for the rest of my life." So the Texas boy, whose mother is Mexican and father is Lebanese, now plans a business career. He has worked long to get to Nationals. For the last four years he competed in the El Paso regional, winning this year for the first time. (One year he lost to his brother; "He did bad," at Nationals, David notes.) Now the fourteen-year-old is ready. He studies ninety minutes a day and knows the entire 23,000-word Consolidated Word List. After his lengthy struggle to get here, his air is confident and relaxed.

That same relaxed feel is true for most of the group today, as the kids, fueled by tubs of barbecue, jump about and play all sorts of games. Some compete in sack races, hopping madly across a field with their feet in burlap sacks; others run up and down a wide field in an impromptu soccer game; one bunch has put together a kickball game, whose teams change with every inning as kids run off to get sodas or a second helping of chocolate cake. In a moment of serendipity, the sister of speller Christian Perez—she's the Bee's first blind speller, and she used Braille to study her word lists—finds a four-leaf clover. Will it bring luck on Wednesday?

Marshall Winchester is tossing a Frisbee with his father, Eric, and his eight-year-old brother, Tanner. Bob and Chandan Deri, getting over the jet lag of their flight from San Francisco, sit and watch their daughter Aliya run around a soccer field while they chat with another couple. Jamie Ding is not a big fan of athletics, but the Detroit boy hurries after a ball as his mother Ning Yan looks on.

Jyoti Patel, mother of eleven-year-old Samir, sits enjoying the sun. She has, she notes, been sleepless the last couple of nights and is suffering from a headache—she has coached her son long and hard for this event, and here it is. Jyoti is surely not the only anxious parent here. It's commonly accepted Bee wisdom that parents get as nervous as their young spellers, perhaps more so.

As I sit talking with her and a few other parents, Samir comes up, takes a chair, and pulls it several feet away from the group. "I want some peace and quiet," he says. What he means, it appears, is that he's been working virtually nonstop as the Bee has neared, and he's ready to be left alone. When his mother mentions going back to the hotel, he says he doesn't want to—he knows that means still more studying. However, after a few moments of self-imposed exile, he joins the group.

He's actually in good spirits, despite the heavy workload; there's something irrepressible about Samir. Is he ready for this year? "I hope so," he says quietly.

Paula and Jim Close are chatting in the bright sun, with Kerry nowhere in sight. She's off playing with friends. "She doesn't want to be with us," Paula says with a smile and a touch of motherly lament. "We're just loser parents."

In Paula's comment is one of the great truths about the National Spelling Bee. There's some spelling that goes on, to be sure, but for many of the kids it's a weeklong party, a tween gabfest of epic proportions. E-mail addresses are exchanged, friendships are formed, confidences are shared. Like-minded kids revel in being in an atmosphere where immersive studying is hip and cool. A kinship of verbal talent connects these kids.

But, while like-minded, their backgrounds aren't all of a type, or even that similar. As parties go, these 273 spellers are likely the most divergent group of people gathered in the nation's capital this week. Once again this year, the Bee is the definition of diversity.

Nektarios Vasilottos's parents are from Greece, and the family speaks Greek around the house; Amanda Redhouse is a Navajo Indian who lives on a reservation in Arizona, and her family speaks Navajo around the house. Mehron Price values her Ethiopian heritage, and Dominic Errazo—a huge

Monty Python fan who quotes from the movies at odd moments—hails from the Philippines. The names of the spellers read like a trip around the world: Rachel Hernandez, Alyssa Tomaskovic, Truc Viet Ho, Harvest Zhang.

Indeed, this event is America in all its multiethnic glory—if you're not careful, you can almost hear a distant horn section playing, with a stentorian voice talking about the immigrant experience, its sacrifice, its hope for a better life, and its heartfelt pride in having found a home in a place called America. Jamie Ding's parents left China after the horror of the Tiananmen Square massacre; they had to buy him an audiocassette as an infant to teach him standard English. Anurag Kashyap's father competed with thousands of applicants in his native India for an academic post that would enable him to land a job in the United States.

On the other hand, Ben Reinig is a farmer's son who lives in Harlan, Iowa, and his father—who drove a tractor at age ten—speaks with an earthy twang as he talks about managing the family farm; the Reinigs are as connected to domestic soil as one can be. But the Reinigs' farm life is far different from that of Seth Martin, who lives in New York City, or Phillip Acevedo, who hails from Chicago, or Christian Medina, who lives in Los Angeles. Some big towns, yes, and some not so big towns: Katie Brown—now in her fourth year at the Bee—lives in Stuart, Florida, and Carlie Gakstatter goes to school in Iron Mountain, Michigan.

But whether the towns are big or small, the dreams tend toward the larger. Marlee Labroo, a twelve-year-old from Quincy, Illinois, wants to go into politics, and Austin Hoke, an eleven-year-old from Anderson, Indiana, wants to design roller coasters. Kasey Leger, fourteen, from Lafayette, Louisiana, helps with the family farm and dreams of being a psychiatrist. Manasa Reddy, twelve, from Steubenville, Ohio—she loves watching professional basketball—wants to be the CEO of a large corporation.

The parents of these young dreamers come from all walks of life. The father of Hong De Sa, from Stroudsburg, Pennsylvania, is a truck driver and her mother is a hair stylist. The father of Megan Courtney, from Sedalia, Missouri, is a full-time National Guardsman and her mother is a licensed practical nurse. Emelia Armstead's father is a hedge fund manager, Arlene Hasbrouck's mother is a speech pathologist (Arlene has three blue goldfish as pets), and Reed Lawson's mother is a detective. The father of Sean Hadley—Sean helped create an experiment that will be conducted in the Space Station—is an environmental engineer.

Many of the kids are strivers in several areas, involved in the Geography Bee and Mathcounts as well as spelling. Most take private music lessons and have a crowded schedule of extracurricular activities. Still, they're actual kids, not achievement machines. Liane Libranda, twelve, from Albany, New York, never misses an episode of *CSI: Crime Scene Investigation*. Allison Frankfother, twelve, from Sterling, Illinois, loves to stay up late and listen to music, and really likes to shop with her friends.

The kids go to public schools (173), private schools (38), home schools (34), parochial schools (25), and charter schools (3). Of the 273 spellers, 143 are eighth-graders, 65 are seventh-graders, 37 are sixth-graders, 23 are fifth-graders, and there are 5 trembling fourth-graders—it takes real courage to compete as a fourth-grader. In recent years, the crowd has been about evenly divided between girls and boys, with typically just a few more girls. This year is an anomaly— perhaps there's something in the water—with 127 girls and 146 boys.

The Bee group, both the kids and their parents, is a pretty well-scrubbed bunch. There are no Harley Davidson T-shirts, virtually no smokers, the barbecue is alcohol free and no one seems to miss it, and the kids are very light on the piercings—if there was a single boy who wore an earring, I missed him.

There is, let's face it, a certain nerdiness about being so involved with spelling. These are families who get their kids to bed on time, tend to eat family dinner together, and often choose vacations for their educational value. These are families where one of the parents packs nutritious snacks so that their kids won't be eating junk food. There are no statistics to prove this, but almost all the parents appear to be on their first marriage.

Not that everyone is Ward and June Cleaver. Ginny Butler, a fourteen-year-old from Mount Vernon, Washington, with her black eye shadow, studded leather belt, punk rock T-shirts, and her fondness for professional bull riding contests, is one of those who adds spice to the crowd. One morning her mother is having a quick smoke outside the hotel, and she sums it up: "My daughter's not like these other kids—and I like that."

But whatever the variations in lifestyles, these are parents who take an active role in their kids' education. Making it to the National Bee is no small achievement, and none of the 273 kids got here by themselves. In the language of contemporary psychology, these are child-centered families.

In some cases, the kids have been nudged—or pushed—to get here. As one mother told me about her son, "He just won the statewide math competition—spelling is a side hobby I make him do." It's unlikely, though, that a kid would do all the drill and study required, then stand up and perform under pressure, if he or she didn't have some kind of enthusiasm for competitive spelling. In fact there's a rumor this year of a boy whose older brother was a top speller from a prior year, and whose parents were grooming him to repeat his older brother's success. But the boy himself wasn't interested and so purposely misspelled at the school level to put himself out of competition. It's an unusual truth: Most of these kids are here because—oddly—they find spelling truly interesting.

That interest alone, however, is not enough. They've needed copious support and cheering from parents to arrive here; in many instances a mother or father is the speller's coach. To be sure, behind every speller's performance onstage is the story of a family who cares deeply about that speller. For all the recognition that finalists receive, their trophies could as well go to the family members who were quiet during a car trip so Ted could study or who made sacrifices in their daily schedule so Jenny could fit in some extra word drill.

And now, those sacrifices having been made, the Bee is almost here. The camcorders are ready, the cameras are loaded. Many of these spellers will be on the ESPN broadcast—the Tivo is set to record. Today is sunshine and Frisbees and kickball, but the anticipation, underneath the spirit of fun, is growing . . .

☉☉☉

On Monday evening, with the barbecue digested, the ritual begins. It happens every year, and it's an essential part of Bee Week: the speller talkfest in the lobby of the Grand Hyatt. In the hotel's largest conversation nook is a living room setting with two couches and a few oversize armchairs. At all hours of the evening, a few dozen kids gather here for a concentrated session of power socializing.

As a tribe, the speller-tween has one very distinct characteristic. All the tribe members must sit or stand very, very close to one another. So the forty-five kids gathered tonight all cluster into one confined area, perhaps no more than sixty square feet. The socializing of this compacted clan resembles molecular cell activity as seen through a microscope; it's active motion in a very small space. No one is as much as an arm's length from his or her seatmate. This tight clustering creates a social force field—they are so interconnected that no adult, or no one of any age who's not a tribe member, can enter.

It also facilitates the intense socializing, the buzzing, cross-conversation sharing, where everyone appears to be talking to everyone else. These kids have come from across the country to find like-minded souls, not their usual classmates but speller-types, who memorize word lists and understand Latin and French etymology. No moment of this precious social opportunity should be wasted, and so they sit in a tight group and relish their immersive social-izing. This gathering in the lobby is truly a bee—a buzzing hive of twelve-, thirteen-, and fourteen-year-old anthropological action.

In past years this gathering has been a mixed bag: power socializing with power studying, casual chatting with joking around. While a few kids plowed through word lists, quizzing others in mock bees, their seatmates power-chatted over and around them, and a few blithe souls managed Scrabble or Risk games amidst the hubbub.

This year the tenor has changed. The group is one big mock spelling bee. Although there's some socializing mixed in at the edges, the Scrabble games and informal word drill have been forgone in favor of an earnest competition. That may have been inevitable. The Bee grows ever more competitive every year; like the speed of the top pitcher's fast ball, the orthographic level required of its participants keeps inching upward. Just making it to Nationals is tougher, and getting to be a finalist or—gulp—having a chance at winning is *really* getting tougher. So the tween-tribe has put aside its playtime to dedicate itself to the pressing business at hand.

Organizing the lobby bee are the three founders of the Internet study group that calls itself Speller Nation, each of whom is now too old to compete: Jesse Zymet, a finalist in 2003, Erik Zyman Carrasco, a top speller whose last year was 2004, and Josh Dawsey, who participated in the 2004 Bee. For this evening, the group's usual clique of eight to ten spellers is expanded to include about forty participants.

As the kids conduct their mock bee, Cecelia Hornedo, the mother of George (the speller who landed a film role), sits chatting amiably nearby. But one of the parents, pointing to the kids at work, shushes her. "These kids are having a bee!" the offended parent reprimands Cecelia.

As a measure of the practice bee's seriousness, Jesse Zymet gives a written test, a twenty-five-word multiple-choice exam, just as the actual Bee will on Wednesday morning. The spellers focus seriously with pencils poised, the tests are graded, then handed back by one of the teen organizers. He calls out each speller's name and announces their score to the group—this is all about social standing, apparently. Out of a perfect twenty-five, most of the kids get somewhere between seventeen and twenty-three, until Kerry Close's test is given back, and the organizer yells out that she scored twenty-four. "Give her a hand," he bellows, and the forty spellers applaud heartily.

As the oral rounds commence, the spellers form a semicircle. Jesse or Erik is the pronouncer, giving only the clues given in the real Bee, as each speller steps up for their turn. The lobby bee goes on for hours, boisterous but focused, as the other hotel occupants walk by and largely ignore the proceedings. A few spellers fit in some power socializing along the periphery—no matter how intense the competition, power chatting can't be given up entirely.

There is a chat of another kind running through the lobby's conversation nooks tonight. In fact it started running the moment families arrived on Sunday. It's an informal question, passed around from person to person: Who's going to win this year? It is not, in truth, a pressing question for many spellers or their parents. Most spellers are well aware they have no realistic hope of winning. Still, the question is noshed on with a certain relish. Names are bandied about.

Besides the obvious favored choices—Marshall Winchester, Kerry Close, Samir Patel—one of those mentioned is Jack Ausick, a fourteen-year-old from rural Park County, Montana. Having tied for eighth place in 2004, he has worked hard this year. The apple-cheeked boy is easygoing and unassuming, and he's a confirmed culture buff. He runs an online movie forum—his favorite films include Hitchcock's *The Man Who Knew Too Much* and De Sica's *The Bicycle Thief*—and he's a playwright, having submitted a play to a children's theater festival. In the mock written test in the lobby bee, he scored a perfect twenty-five.

Another speller who's whispered about as a potential winner is Anurag Kashyap. The thirteen-year-old San Diego boy is not an obvious choice: He placed forty-seventh in 2004, his first year here. In 2003 he failed to make it to Nationals, placing second in the San Diego regional. Yet he has labored doggedly on his spelling this year, up to four hours a day. He's talked about as a winner due to his performance with the Internet study group Speller Nation. Over the course of the year he often won the virtual bees conducted by these ten or so hyperdedicated spellers. During his many hours online he struck up a cross-country friendship with Kerry Close, with whom he often chats and laughs. And that's Anurag: For all his hard work, he seems to be having fun. Being here is exciting for him. In truth, he admits to me, over the course of his spelling career he feels the pressure has grown, from his second-place finish in San Diego, to his first year at Nationals last year, then going into this year— his nerves have ratcheted up. But more often than not he's seen smiling, his glasses sliding down his nose, his prominent orthodontia flashing.

Both Jack and Anurag are in the lobby tonight, taking part in mock bees that will continue on into the late evening. For these forty or so lobby dwellers, this communal spell-in is what the Bee is all about.

There are plenty of top spellers who steer clear of these lobby bees. For them, the group spell is inefficient use of study time; all those minutes spent waiting for a word are better spent reviewing etymology or drilling word lists. Aliya Deri is up in her room, with her coach-father, Bob; the San Francisco girl is getting in some last-minute study. Samir Patel is far too focused on winning to spend time chatting in the lobby—he's flown here from Texas to bring home the trophy, not exchange e-mail addresses. He and his mother, Jyoti, are working tonight. Marshall Winchester has brought his laptop from North Carolina for just this moment.

Jamie Ding's coach-English teacher, Dan Bens, has flown in from Detroit for final prep sessions. Tonight, Bens works with Jamie until late in the evening, until finally, Jamie, exhausted, spells the same word twice. At that point Bens tells him it's time to get to sleep. There are big days ahead.

◎◎◎

Tuesday morning dawns sunny—a good day for happy denial. Today is an off-day for the spellers, a day to tour Washington, DC. A day, in other words, to pretend that there are no high-pressure moments pending. Many spellers say that they manage to remain calm through the end of Tuesday—with all the activities, it's possible to think about something else. Tomorrow is for spelling. Today is for sunshine.

The Bee's mission is primarily an educational one, despite the contestants' emphasis on competition, and today is a part of that. Bee organizers put together tours of Washington, and the kids spend the day visiting the city's cultural and civic institutions. Some families who have been here before choose to go on their own tours. The Winchester family visits the Holocaust museum. The Deri family takes in the Botanical Garden and the Museum of the American Indian. The Closes enjoy a family bike ride.

On the other hand, the Patel family stays in, Samir and Jyoti using the time for final Bee review. If you've come to win, why use your last day of study time wandering around the Lincoln Memorial?

The Grand Hyatt, without the 273 bright minds running about, feels like a balloon with the air let out. Its spacious lobby is reduced to the usual groups of cell phone–clutching professionals, invariably well groomed, quickly and efficiently toting luggage rollers. It's . . . quiet.

Down in the lower level, however, the hotel is abuzz with activity. The grand ballroom is being turned into a spelling arena. Crews are assembling the

300

stage, setting up rows of chairs, and building the huge riser for video cameras. An information desk run by Bee staffers, equipped with computers and telephones, begins fielding requests as media types start filing in—most of the 273 kids are sponsored by a newspaper, so the place will soon be lousy with reporters. A press room is set up with Internet terminals and phone connections. Outside the hotel, an eighteen-wheel truck full of audio and video equipment has parked, and technicians are laying yards of cable and hauling a mass of equipment. Near the truck is a van with a satellite dish that extends some fifty feet high, so images from the contest can be broadcast in real time.

The only place where it's absolutely silent and still—overwhelmingly so— is the Comfort Room. This is where spellers go after they misspell. When the dreaded bell rings, letting him or her know they must exit the stage, a speller begins the long walk to the Comfort Room. At the stage's edge, a young Bee staffer shakes their hand and takes them by the arm, gently, and walks them down a 15-foot incline on the side of the stage. The speller is then walked down a 130-foot hallway that's not open to the public, a forlorn passageway crowded with unused folding chairs and lit by cold fluorescent light, until they reach the Comfort Room.

The room's actual name is the Cherry Blossom Boardroom—it's called the Comfort Room only by Bee organizers. Designed for corporate meetings, it's about twenty-five feet square, with an imposing dark red meeting table in the middle. With its somber green carpet, heavy wood paneling, and crystal chandelier, it's not a place for idle chitchat. Some corporate guys and gals have made important decisions in this room. The air is heavy in here.

Tomorrow the room will be equipped with a Kleenex box, a punch bowl, a Webster's *Unabridged*, and a big plate of cookies (normally peanut butter and chocolate chip). Offering assistance in the room will be two or three teenage Bee staffers, kindly souls who are well aware of the disappointment the speller might be feeling. The spellers will be greeted by Angela Rose, the stage manager and a veteran Bee crewmember.

The Comfort Room is not open to the public. So the swarm of reporters is, thankfully, barred from entering. A Bee staffer keeps watch over the door, allowing only parents to come and talk with their kids.

The reactions among spellers to landing in the Comfort Room are as varied as the spellers themselves. Some kids are completely nonchalant, plopping down in a chair, grabbing a cookie, then sauntering off with a parent to be interviewed by reporters ("What word did you go out on? Could you spell that for me?—and what do you want to do when you grow up?").

Other kids have worked too hard to be casual about their trip to the Comfort Room. Most spellers are well aware they're not going to win—only about 20 of the 273 have a realistic chance, and everybody knows it—so a seat in the Comfort Room is inevitable for most all. Still, plenty of spellers have individual goals, apart from taking the trophy, and missing those goals can be a real bump in the road. There are kids who were middle-of-the-pack last year who desperately hope for a finalist's spot this year. There are kids who have always been at the top of the class, and being sent offstage so publicly for lack of academic knowledge is a new and unpleasant experience. The contest is a two-day event yet only the second day is televised, so all the kids crave making it to the second day; walking to the Comfort Room on the first day is no fun.

Perhaps the toughest Comfort Room experience is endured by those high-ranking finishers from the prior year who expected to be a finalist this year and have failed to do so. Having earned, say, sixteenth the year before, they have pushed themselves all year long, feeling they have a chance to win or place gloriously high. They study when others are playing, they study when they're tired, they study during most of their available minutes. And then, onstage in front of everyone, some odd word comes up in an early round, and they miss by a single vowel. In most cases they even make an intelligent guess, which, if English were logical, would be correct. But no. The bell rings and a staffer walks them to the Comfort Room.

That is indeed a bitter pill, and it flies in the face of everything they've been taught. If you work hard, aren't you rewarded with honors? All those hours and hours—and hours—of word drill, and now . . . you actually place *lower?* It is absolute proof, in case proof were needed, that life is unfair. Luck plays a role and sometimes things don't turn out, no matter how hard you try. Sitting next to a plate of peanut butter cookies in the Comfort Room, you can't help feeling the abject failure of it. *Am I not a smart person?* Worse, now you have to tell your friends back home that you tied for seventy-sixth, even though you spent all spring telling them you couldn't go out because you had to study.

Under the circumstances, a tear is well earned. The disappointment is very real, and it's not just the overreaction of a thirteen-year-old. Many fifty-year-olds have become a little unbalanced for less. The Comfort Room, undoubtedly, will be the site of considerable discomfort over the next two days.

²⁷ The Spellers Step Up

Wednesday morning dawns with a real gravitas. Today is when the spelling starts. This event has thus far been a lighthearted get-together, but that now comes to an abrupt end.

The Bee begins with a written round and an oral round, the combined results of which will determine who gets to stay in. It's impractical to conduct a bee with hundreds of spellers—each round could take hours—so Bee officials must quickly lop off the bottom two-thirds of the field. By lunchtime, about 180 kids will have to sit and watch for the next day and a half.

The score from each speller's twenty-five-word written test will be added to their score from the oral round. Spellers need a combined score of twenty-two points to remain in the competition. Each written word counts for one point; the oral round word counts for three points. In other words, they must spell at least nineteen of the twenty-five written words, plus their oral round word, to survive. (Or they could get twenty-two written words correct and miss their oral, but that's tough to do—the written test gets brutal in its last few words.)

Although the written test won't begin until 8:00 a.m., by 7:30 many spellers and their parents gather outside the doors to the grand ballroom, quietly, with a moody buzz to the crowd.

Aliya Deri and her family are here and ready. For good luck, the San Francisco girl wears her big sister Joya's red hooded sweatshirt, just as she has in past bees; it's a precious talisman. "Last night I had a dream about the Bee," she says brightly, apparently in good spirits. (Later, she notes, "I was talking in my sleep as I tend to do under moments of great stress. I was spelling all these words that Dad had called a friend in California to look up for us. And I was repeating all of them in my sleep.")

Jamie Ding, here with his mother Ning Yan, appears less chipper. The Detroit boy was up last night working with his coach, and this morning his outlook seems fair to partly cloudy.

The 273 spellers file in quietly and take their seats at long tables. The mood is heavy. Clustered in the back, looking on in concern, are hundreds of parents and siblings. Florida speller Dovie Eisner's grandmother Yaffa Eisner, who speaks in a heavy Hungarian accent as she touts Dovie's abilities, looks toward her grandson; Tom Reinig, who grows soybeans in Iowa, cranes his head to see his son.

At precisely 8:00 a.m., the event begins. The punctual start time is true to form: The competition at the National Bee is run efficiently and professionally. The ad hoc spirit of many of the regionals around the country, where the rules are fudged any number of ways, is nowhere to be seen. This is the big time.

Bee director Paige Kimble greets everyone from the stage; behind her sits a row of nine Bee officials and judges who will watch over the test takers. After a warm hello, she points out that the time has come. "The most anticipated moment on your calendar in months has arrived," she says. "In thirty-two hours, the Champion will be declared." As she speaks, three roving video cameramen walk among the spellers, getting close-up shots—though the kids are doing nothing but sitting motionlessly at long tables.

In front of each speller is an envelope and two freshly sharpened No. 2 pencils. At 8:10 a.m. the order is given for two minutes of silence, after which the test begins. There are no questions allowed during the test period. This morning's test is multiple choice; in past years it has been fill-in-the-blank. The multiple choice format will enable Bee officials to grade it electronically, allowing the contest to move along faster—there will be no handwriting to decipher.

Several of the parents have voiced anxiety about the multiple choice format over the past few days; they point out that even a kid who knows the right spelling might be confused by seeing several choices. The consensus, among nervous parents, is that a speller should spell a word mentally before examining the choices. But the spellers themselves have appeared perfectly happy about the switch to the multiple choice format.

The Bee's official pronouncer, Dr. Jacques Bailly, reads each word aloud in diction that is precise but comfortable. As the spellers focus on their test papers, he provides the definition, sample sentence, part of speech, and language of origin—all the clues spellers can request when the oral rounds begin. The parents click cameras and work camcorders; a cameraman leans in for an action close-up of a test taker.

The test begins as a stroll in the sunshine, with softies like *souvenir* and *censor*, moves into cloud cover with challenges like *syncope* and *thelytokous*, encounters stormy weather with obscurities like *chaetophorous* and *scilicet*, and is then swallowed by the swirling flood waters of *Kneippism* and *glacis*. At the very end, word No. 25, it's washed out to sea with *scherenschnitte*. And the multiple-choice format, which in theory had offered a life raft, instead added to the navigational hazards. Question No. 12—still in the easy section—asks: Is the correct spelling *repelled, rapelled, rhapelled, rappeled,* or *rappelled*? Note that these choices contain more than one correct spelling; this test is about listening and understanding as much as regurgitating memorized facts.

At 8:45, just some thirty minutes after the twenty-five-question test began, time is called—there wasn't much time for pondering. And some spellers didn't need much time. Later this morning we learn that seven kids scored a perfect twenty-five, an unusually high number of perfect scores. In 2004 only one speller earned a perfect twenty-five, and he went on to win. The fact that seven spellers earned a perfect score suggests that this Bee will be hard fought at the end.

☯☯☯

After just a brief break, half of the 273 spellers assemble onstage to begin the first oral round. Their walk onstage is greeted with a flurry of excitement. A phalanx of some forty parents approaches the stage and operates a blizzard of cameras and camcorders, while parents in the audience set up video cameras on tripods. This might be the Academy Awards, though the Academy wouldn't allow such an enthusiastic horde of paparazzi so close to its stars. The kids themselves look pert and ready. This, finally, is when the public spelling begins. This is what we've come for.

Head judge Mary Brooks asks the various crewmembers if they are ready to begin. Brooks, a middle school drama teacher in Des Moines, Iowa, could be considered the heart and soul of the judging squad. She has been involved with the Bee for thirty-four years (including five years as codirector and twenty years as judge) and oversees the event with the benefit of that experience, as well as an empathetic, if firm, approach. She's the referee of the Bee, making sure that each speller gets what they need at the microphone. She listens to ensure that they've pronounced the word correctly, and if she feels they haven't, she requests that they repeat it. She tends to make eye contact with the spellers, so they're not up there by themselves. As a judge, she's on the side of the kids, though she allows no rule to be bent.

As we prepare to start this morning, her steady, clear Midwestern voice rings out in the ballroom in a cadence that announces something profound is about to begin. She asks:

Are we ready on the record desk?

Yes.

Are the tapes rolling?

Yes.

Dr. Bailly, are you ready?

Yes.

And so we begin. This first oral round is slow-pitch softball. All of its words come from the *Paideia* (and a list of 250 extra words issued after regionals), and hence many spellers have them memorized. Since the *Paideia* was sent out the previous September, some spellers have had it down cold for eight months now. This round, in essence, is the Bee's way of saying: Everyone can look good in Washington for at least one round.

But that's not as simple as it sounds. In three quarters of regionals around the country, a winner is declared before the *Paideia* list is exhausted. So some of these spellers are only marginally familiar with its word list. They've earned a trip here for being bright, verbally talented kids who read a lot and study spelling a modest amount. For these kids, this first round is roulette; if luck is with them, they'll get words they know.

The kids spell quickly. Since each speller is allotted a maximum of two minutes, plus a thirty-second bonus time period, it could take several hours for 273 spellers to complete a round. But this first round is an assembly line. Most spellers step up and spell with no fuss. The pros, the ones who've had this list memorized for months, don't need much time. And the duffers, the kids who are here due to natural smarts, don't know how to ask all the questions and use the clues for an educated guess. So, on average, each speller steps up to the microphone, spells, and steps away in about forty seconds. And every kid, whether they spell correctly or not, gets a round of polite applause from the full ballroom.

Laura Ann Brown from Birmingham, Alabama, walks to the microphone as gracefully as a ballerina—and the thirteen-year-old really is a student ballet dancer—and dispatches *tergiversation* with ease. The winner of the Los Angeles bee, thirteen-year-old Christian Medina, handles *aition* without a care. The diminutive Kendra Yoshinaga from Ventura, California, is just eleven years old, but she masters *brummagem* like an old pro (and indeed she placed twenty-seventh in the 2004 Bee).

It takes considerable courage for Morgan Gillian to be on this stage. A few months ago the South Carolina girl won her regional bee, and now, at age nine, she stands at a microphone in Washington with a full ballroom and a long row of judges all looking at her. Morgan is one of just two nine-year-olds who made it here—she's definitely playing with the big kids today. Dressed in black pants and a white top, with glasses and short blond hair, she speaks in a small, hesitant voice; she's clearly battling stage fright. Her word is *podilegous*. With her hands folded in front of her, she takes a run at it. She states a few letters, then pauses . . . the audience seems to lean forward as she spells, as if willing the letters . . . and then she finishes it as *podillogous*. Nope. But her spelling career has just begun.

Vastly more self-assured is Marlee Labroo, a twelve-year-old from Quincy, Illinois, who plans on a career in politics. She's a big fan of debate, of foreign languages and world religions, and she has three chickens as pets. Her word is *hartebeest*. She doesn't have the *Paideia* memorized—she's going to have to guess. Her process of guessing is a series of halts and backtracks. She says a few letters, stops, goes back and repeats herself, then re-pronounces the word in her pause. For most spellers, all this twisting in the wind would be unnerving, but she seems perfectly relaxed throughout, as if struggling in front of a large audience was as comfortable as going to the refrigerator for a snack. In the end she misses the word, but she proves herself capable of the confident self-possession necessary to be a public speaker and politician.

In contrast, Rajdeep Chahal grapples with *feuilleton* in a quiet voice filled with doubt, finally attempting it as *fuolyurtone*. That wouldn't be noteworthy, except for the fact that Rajdeep is the winner of the New York City bee. His misspell once again demonstrates a great contradiction of the National Bee. At first glance it's reasonable to assume that the winner of the regional bee in a big burg like New York—a densely populated area full of brainy professionals— would be a shoo-in to make it to the final rounds at Nationals. But no. The Bee is all about individual effort, about the elbow grease that one kid puts in by him or herself sitting quietly at a desk, regardless of where that desk is. So in the same round that a New York City speller fumbles *feuilleton,* Jack Ausick from Park County, Montana, knocks out *isagoge,* and Sydney Matlock from Wichita Falls, Texas—she's an aspiring astrophysicist whose favorite book is *2001: A Space Odyssey*—handles *boiserie*.

As the kids spell, a roving crew of ESPN cameramen with handheld cameras gets reaction shots from the spellers and the crowd. Outside in the lobby, network television crews have set up interview stations—just a camera, a chair, and an interviewer—and they'll flag spellers throughout the day. These mini-chats will be beamed to affiliate stations across the country. The media coverage is headed toward the saturation point, but it's not yet at full bore.

Amidst it all, the quiet Amanda Redhouse appears all that more reserved. The thirteen-year-old Navajo girl lives on a reservation in Arizona, and her family speaks Navajo around the house. Her town, Teec Nos Pos, has a population of

800 and consists largely of a general store. Amanda is a sports enthusiast who's captain of her volleyball and basketball teams, and she likes to play games with her twelve-year-old sister Veronica; the sisters are avid hacky sack players. In conversation she's clearly shy—her father, Jonathan, gently motions for her to speak louder as I talk with her and her family. But even at age thirteen, her ambition is clear: She wants to be a lawyer, and at least early in her career she wants to live off the reservation.

A dedicated student, she has long dreamed of getting to the National Bee. For the last four years she has competed in local bees, winning the Navajo Nation regional for the first time this year. To win, her final word was *futurity*, "of or relating to the future." There's some kind of connection there: a Navajo girl who dreams of a big future and who makes it to Washington by spelling *futurity*.

This morning she walks to the microphone in an Indian beaded belt, her long black hair falling toward her waist. Her word is *capuan*. It's not a *Paideia* word; it's from the 250-word list sent out after regionals, and she doesn't have it memorized. With a slightly quizzical look she tries it as *capuin*. Not quite. As she walks away from the microphone she turns toward her father, who sits near the front, and she flashes a shy smile as he snaps a photo. That's a valuable photo.

In every Bee there is a smattering of kids from outside the United States; for instance, there's always an American student who lives in Europe whose trip is sponsored by the US military newspaper, *Stars and Stripes*. This year the *Stars & Stripes* sent Calvin Lau, a thirteen-year-old who attends Schweinfurt Middle School in Germany and whose father is in the military. Calvin, whose favorite novel is *Moby Dick* and who loves hip-hop music, is dealt *upaithric*. Logically, but unfortunately, he attempts it as *eupythric*.

Making the international crew much larger is, for the first time, a group of Canadian spellers. A couple of the Canadians do quite well, and one, Finola Hackett, a plucky seventh-grader from Alberta, will eventually tie for eleventh. Having less luck is the Bee's first speller from New Zealand, Charlotte Roose. The twelve-year-old Auckland girl is small but fiercely athletic; her favorite sport is karate, and her idols are the three New Zealand gold medalists in the 2004 Olympics. A two-man video crew traveled with her from New Zealand, and they trail her throughout the week, giving Charlotte the appearance of an adoring entourage. Her word this morning is *erythrophobia*, which, in her broad down-under accent, she takes a leap at as *arithrophobia*. This misspell and her written test score keep her from advancing, which means she flew for twenty-seven hours (and another twenty-seven hours home) to spell a total of one word onstage. Then again, she'll be the star of a documentary in her home country, so she won't lack exposure.

Erin Jones from Martinsburg, West Virginia, approaches the microphone with great seriousness. Dressed in a pink top with a pink bow in her hair, the eleven-year-old is young to be here, but she seems determined to do her best. She's an avid reader who loves to ride her bike, and she plans on a career in interior decoration or clothing design. Her word is *monomeniscous*, and when she tries to say it she trips over its umpteen syllables, which sends her into a fit of laughter, which works its way into a giggling spell. Recovering, she simplifies it as *monomuniscus*, and that's the last we hear from her.

It's the audience who laughs when Megan Courtney from Sedalia, Missouri, gets *trichotillomania*. Pronouncer Jacques Bailly states the definition as "an abnormal desire to pull one's hair out," which the audience realizes is all too appropriate for today's proceedings and so chortles heartily. Megan, a thirteen-year-old school cheerleader who plans on a teaching career, is the only one not laughing—she has to spell this extensive assortment of letters. She misses by a single *l*, which hopefully doesn't send her into a bout of trichotillomania.

The pros in this round, the contenders, all sail through like veteran actors making a cameo in a high school play. Aliya Deri shuts her eyes and lets the letters of *acetarious* ring out loud and strong; there's no doubt there. Marshall Winchester's word, *puissant*, means powerful, and that's how he handles it, hammering out each letter, pronouncing the final consonant with a definitive cadence.

For Samir Patel, the crisp professionalism with which he rattles off *maquiladora* suggests that he'll be a powerhouse in the later rounds. Kerry Close spells *otiosity* like she knows it cold—which she does—but she still asks the definition; seasoned competitors have rules, and they go by them in the heat of competition. Jamie Ding absentmindedly fingers the microphone, then devours *vichyssoise* as if the creamy French soup is served daily at his Detroit middle school.

These spellers are, in fact, simply waiting for the real Bee to begin, that part of the contest where the word list isn't limited to the narrow confines of the *Paideia*. Which is due to start any moment, as soon as we hear the list of spellers who will advance past the first two rounds.

◉◉◉

The first line of demarcation has arrived. At 12:30 p.m., after Bee officials have tabulated the results of the written and oral rounds, it's time to announce who has survived. Bee director Paige Kimble stands onstage holding the list of spellers who have passed. The audience waits with an ambient anxiety, a feeling that Kimble shares. "My hands are shaking—I'm nervous," she says. Since she herself was a competitor some twenty-five years ago, she knows the tension in this contest. Kimble requests that the audience remain quiet while she reads the list of spellers who will advance—she doesn't want a series of explosive "yeahs!" to punctuate her list. So the crowd's emotions must remain bottled up during the reading of a lengthy list. Most important, she says, "let's comfort those spellers whose moment of disappointment has arrived."

As she reads aloud the numbers of the kids who will advance, her voice resounds in the silent ballroom. The crowd listening to her is now swelled with reporters, associated media types, and invited guests (although the Bee is broadcast, it's not open to the public). During the list, roving cameramen get in position for reaction shots; a big group of them, along with a bevy of photographers, all cluster around George Hornedo, the boy who will be in *Akeelah and the Bee*. Apparently they think he's good for a dramatic facial shot, and they're right—George is a naturally expressive kid (and fortunately he makes it).

When Kimble's list ends, two sounds compete with each other, one washing over the other. The first sound is a low "awww"—those who didn't make it—and the second is a big burst of relieved and happy applause—those who did make it. Only 97 of the 273 will advance, so the Bee is now down to manageable size. Based on the expressions of each speller, it's not necessary to ask if they'll advance. Those who will advance have a great lightness of being, a buoyant smile, like they've just been told that today's lunch menu is all chocolate cake. Those who have been eliminated have, at best, a kind of neutral blankness, and some have a very real distressed look.

Although the survivors are a smaller bunch, their mood is happy enough to give the entire hall a jubilant air, so the crowd bustles out to lunch with a pronounced ebullience. Dominic Errazo, a wisecracking South Carolina boy who's here to enjoy himself without getting too concerned with the results, notes that again this year his number was the *very last* one called. Still, it was called, so he's joyfully rattling off impressions from his favorite Monty Python movies.

I see Ning Yan, Jamie Ding's mother, and walk over to congratulate her, but as I approach I see there are clouds over the Ding family. Jamie, remarkably, will not advance. He handled his oral round with ease but his written score was too low. Given that last year he tied for twenty-seventh, and that this year he worked with a coach—who flew to Washington to help—the news is a real shocker. And, to the Dings, it's a deep disappointment. Ning Yan is teary-eyed, and Jamie's younger sister, Jessie, is crying. Jamie himself is quiet, expressionless, kind of shell-shocked; he approaches us and walks away a couple of times, apparently walking aimlessly through the crowd.

Jamie's coach, Dan Bens, is with Ning Yan, and he notes that Jamie felt nervous going into the competition. The problem has been the sheer number of competitions the thirteen-year-old participated in this spring: Mathcounts, the Science Olympiad, the Social Studies Olympiad, and the Geography Bee; and all this on top of a course load that includes a twelfth-grade math class. The eighth-grader was spread too thin to fully prepare for today.

Jamie takes it hard. For someone who has known only academic success, it's not just dispiriting, it's novel. He's always been the student that teachers point to as hardworking and successful, a model student. It completely disrupts his self-image to be eliminated when a stage full of bright kids gets to keep going. He's been tossed into a cold ocean; he'll still be able to tread water, but it's a shock to the system. As his coach notes, "Jamie is going to need some time to process this."

In the immediate aftermath, Jamie doesn't want to go back in the ball-room; in fact, he doesn't want anything to do with the Bee. Ning Yan takes him up to their hotel room, where he keeps repeating, "I'm a loser, I'm a loser." He sees a balcony in the hotel and asks—presumably not with full serious-ness—should I jump off? Ning Yan talks him through it, and they spend the rest of the day at Washington's zoological park.

Late in the day, he says, "Tomorrow, Mom, I'm going to feel better." And indeed he does. After his deep plunge, he rises to the surface without, all told, too much effort, though he has faced some uncomfortable feelings. The very fact that he has so many academic pursuits, from the Science Olympiad to Mathcounts, helps him put his loss in perspective. After all, it's not like he's been working solely on spelling for months—far from it. The Dings spend Thursday morning in their hotel room, and then, after lunch, Jamie announces he'd like to watch the Bee in the ballroom.

⊚⊚⊚

In the hotel's café at lunch the mood is festive, or at least those who feel festive broadcast their feelings enough to give the overall crowd a lighthearted ambi-ance. The glow of accomplishment is everywhere. The Clark family from Atlanta raise their sodas in a toast to the fact that their son James has made it: "To one of the top one hundred spellers in North America," the toast maker proclaims, and about ten people, from three generations, all tip their sodas in honor of the fourteen-year-old.

As the spellers and their parents file back into the ballroom, thirteen-year-old Jasmine Kaneshiro sits leaning against her mother, shoulder to shoulder, as if maternal contact will give her the sustenance to continue this afternoon. A quiet girl with long black hair and glasses, the Hawaiian speller did well on the written test and made quick work of her morning word, *puerile*. It's not surprising that she's a good student; both of her parents are grade-school teachers. Her passion is following current events, and she's committed to issues involving women's rights, the environment, and homelessness. How, I ask, does she stay involved with these issues? "I read the newspaper, and I always try to make sure that women get equal treatment, and I recycle," Jasmine says. As she speaks, her father smiles with great pride. "Yesterday on the Washington Mall, she wanted to give all her money away" to the homeless people there, he says. "Other people were giving quarters, and she wanted to give $5 and $10. She brought extra change with her so she could give it away."

Jasmine is soon called onstage with the other kids. The spellers seem in a perkier, elevated mood now. Having dispensed with the written test and successfully spelled onstage, they can take a breath. Kerry Close chats animatedly with Anurag Kashyap; although the New Jersey girl lives a country away from the San Diego boy, they've communicated online so constantly that they're friends.

Adding to the spellers' light mood is their knowledge that this round will be a softie. At one level it poses a fresh challenge: It's the first oral round whose word list will not be confined to the *Paideia*; from now on the words can come from anywhere in the Merriam-Webster *Unabridged*, that bottomless reservoir of 475,000 words. However, this first oral round will lean toward easier words. As the rounds progress, the words will get progressively harder, but this first post-*Paideia* round, the first step in a climb toward obscurity, offers a gentle incline.

Kerry Close, standing with her hands jammed in her pockets, buzzes through *unregenerate* without taking a breath; for someone in her fourth time at Nationals, the word is almost embarrassingly easy. Marshall Winchester steamrolls *transilience* without doubt. The North Carolina boy is a cooler customer than in years past, not proclaiming the letters loudly as is his custom, nor taking hold of the microphone. He simply spells at an even pace and sits back down—for him, this round is just a formality.

Samir Patel, too, is businesslike. The eleven-year-old Texas boy seems to have left his former self behind. In his first year here, at age nine, he was the wunderkind, spelling his way to a third-place finish with a this-is-all-*so*-easy style, waiting impatiently for the pronouncer to finish so he could slam-dunk the word. Now, he's evenhanded as he puts away *deleteriously*.

Aliya Deri, still wearing her sister Joya's red hooded sweatshirt for luck, shouldn't have much difficulty with *reticulated*. But it seems the San Francisco girl's nerves have returned. She struggles with the pronunciation, oddly, having a hard time repeating the word, finally asking Jacques Bailly to say it away from the microphone. As she struggles, the two-minute time clock beeps; she'll have to use precious bonus time to keep working on a giveaway like *reticulated*. She gathers herself together and takes a run at it—yes, that's it, she gets it. She rolls her eyes dramatically, as if to say, "Wow, I really made that difficult." When Aliya sits back down, her seatmate Anurag Kashyap gives her a high five to congratulate her. Anurag himself, having studied up to four hours a day, breezes through *priscilla* as if he's waiting for the real Bee to begin.

Still, nothing about standing onstage in front of a huge crowd and spelling an unknown word is easy. Sarah Wang, a diminutive eleven-year-old from Dover, Delaware, who back home is never seen without a book, faces *perjury*. In her moment in the spotlight, alas, she spells it as *perjure*. It's proof that an orthographic trap can linger in the safest of words. Here's Sarah, who won her regional bee (competing against older kids), passed a twenty-five-word written test that included the likes of *chaetophorous* and *scilicet*, and in this morning's oral round conquered the fearsome *nephrolithiasis*. Now she is sent offstage by the simple *perjury*. If her place onstage had been one back or one forward, she likely would have gotten a word she knew. But the wheel of spelling fortune didn't land on the right word for her this afternoon.

The wheel of spelling fortune, of course, tends to spin better for those who've spent innumerable hours studying, and there are many of those here today. Amanda Foy, a fourteen-year-old from Louisiana, gets a word that sounds like *plecture*. She gathers all the clues, takes an educated guess, and comes up with the correct spelling of *plexure*, earning extra applause for her detective work. Claire Nieman, a thirteen-year-old from Seattle who takes martial arts classes, sends *sabbatical* flying to the mat.

George Hornedo is the picture of confidence as he steps up to face *proprietorial*. With his time in front of the camera for his role in Hollywood's *Akeelah and the Bee*, George is comfortable in the spotlight. And since the fourteen-year-old Indiana boy was here last year and has studied hard with the Internet study group, he's well prepared for today. "May I have the definition, please?" he asks in a cool voice, his hands in his pockets in a gesture of nonchalance.

Armed with some clues, he lifts up his number placard and scribbles on it with his finger; no writing implements are allowed but many spellers mock spell on their placards to visualize the word. For all his apparent relaxation, he scribbles furiously. After just a moment, he begins to state the letters of *proprietorial*. P, R, I—whoops! He meant to say P, R, O, but he was thinking of the middle syllable as he voiced the beginning syllable.

He knows instantly that he's blown it, and of course changing a letter once it's voiced isn't allowed. What a frustration. Due to his film role he's getting more media attention, so his stumble is all that more public. Moreover, a high-ranking finish in this year's Bee would have been a sweet complement to the publicity from his movie role. Tougher still, ESPN doesn't begin televising this contest until tomorrow, so any hopes that George had of looking good on TV—and he's angling to get signed by a Los Angeles talent agent—have now been dashed.

Even worse, from a public relations standpoint, is how he handles it. When he realizes his tongue pronounced an *i* when he meant to say *o*, he stops spelling, takes off his placard, and walks offstage in a fit of pique—so quickly that the misspell bell doesn't even ring until he's a dozen steps toward the Comfort Room. There is nothing gracious or starlike about his fleeing off the stage. He has, in the space of about thirty seconds, gone from Hollywood cool guy to thoroughly normal fourteen-year-old boy.

His experience points out a key thing that this competition is about. George's slip, of course, is a common one, and one that's especially hard to avoid in the spotlight's glare. When nerves get jittery, everything is harder to control. That's where presence of mind and coolness under fire come in. Surviving to the final rounds requires serious spelling skills, as well as something far more precious. Maturity. The Bee's finalists will have spelled about fifteen (or more) difficult words in trying circumstances. Mentally, that calls for some very real mojo.

༺༼༽༻

As Round Four begins, the field of ninety-seven spellers is now winnowed to seventy-one. This is the last round for the day, and it won't be an easy one. The words begin their descent into the dark caverns of obscurity. Martin

Alexander, one of two spellers from New York City, hears the dreaded ding after attempting *dissilient*, which means bursting apart, as some seeds do. Phillip Acevedo, one of two spellers from Chicago, hears the same unfortunate bell after grappling with *acarophobia*, an abnormal fear of mites or other small insects.

Dovie Eisner is here to do battle. The fourteen-year-old Miami Beach boy, wheelchair-bound, placed forty-seventh last year, and he's back this year determined to go as far as he can. An expert in Judaic studies, having won several awards for his knowledge of the Torah, he's also a budding novelist. He's writing his first book, which he calls *Jonathan of the Red Corps*. As he explained it to me, it's about a deaf-mute boy fighting in a war against a gang who attacked his community. Since the protagonist can't speak, he develops a way of communicating with his brother by pulling on his collarbone. Overall, the story is "very macabre," Dovie says. In the end, I ask, is it tragic or is there redemption? "That depends on how you see it," he explains. His grandmother Yaffa has accompanied him to the Bee, and she's looking forward to Dovie's book. "I'm *sure* people will read it," she says in a thick Hungarian accent. We all need a grandmother like Yaffa.

Dovie, facing *diphthongize*, goes to work. As he questions the judge, asking for definition and part of speech, his right arm begins to palpitate, slowly but rhythmically. His breathing grows deep, becoming a light wheeze as he breathes into the microphone. When he's ready, he gathers himself and begins to spell the word as if it might be his last: *D* . . . *I* . . . *P* . . . *H* . . . Each letter is a hammer blow that appears aimed at some overwhelming obstacle before him. And when he's finished, and he learns that he got it, the victory is writ large upon his face. All of him seems to light up. He raises his clenched fists in triumph as he's wheeled back to his seat. He lives to fight another day.

Not so fortunate is Kyle Rogaicon, a sixth-grader from Salinas, California, who loves the music of Scott Joplin, has created his own cartoon character, and often reads classic novels; Kyle hears the dreaded ding after attempting *pruritus* as *pruritis*. Having no better luck is Jennifer Black, a fourteen-year-old from Casper, Wyoming, who loves art history and classical mythology, as well as *Star Trek: Enterprise* (in fact she supervises science fiction message boards).

Getting *arcology*, she sensibly spells it as *archology*, but alas, common sense doesn't go far in English spelling.

John Tamplin steps up to face a word that sounds like *flamborra*. In his fourth year here, John marches to his own drummer in his approach to the Bee. Most spellers, by the time they get to be four-timers, are casting a very covetous eye on the trophy; these grizzled veterans let life fall away as they stay glued to their word lists. But not John.

The tall Louisville, Kentucky, boy wins his regional every year, does his best in Washington without sacrificing the rest of his life, and takes it all with a grain of salt. In 2003 he placed forty-seventh; in 2004 he moved up to thirty-first. There are those who talk about him as a contender this year, but John's not sweating it. (And, because he's in the seventh grade, he can return for a fifth time next year.) Being at Nationals this year "is the least scary point, because I don't feel I have anything to live up to," he says. He certainly works on his spelling, but he doesn't obsess about it. "Weird words are fun, and being able to add on to your vocabulary is fun, but just sitting down and repeating words and spelling, that's not what I consider fun." When he grows up, he wants to be an actor, and in conversation he has a naturalness of expression that suggests he'll be a good one. The twelve-year-old is mature beyond his years and clearly intelligent.

But facing what sounds like *flamborra*, he's facing the unknown. He shuts his eyes and falls into silence. The audience falls correspondingly silent. The first syllable is obviously *flam*, but that second syllable is a puzzle. As he stands pondering, John makes some connections. He considers the spelling of the last name of the author Stephen McCullough; also coming to mind is the *borough* of Manhattan. With the time clock ticking, he opens his eyes and prepares to throw the dice. He spells it as *flamborough*.

And he's right! His mouth forms a silent O of amazement, and the audience applauds with extra enthusiasm. Over the next few days his spelling of *flamborough* will be remarked upon as one of this year's most noteworthy performances. In a crowd full of crack spellers, few had imagined the word as he saw it.

A few other kids attempt to pull a similar rabbit out of the hat—making it this far requires the capacity to make a high-percentage guess. Hannah Rae

Smith, a fourteen-year-old Minneapolis girl who unicycles after school and who wins over the crowd with her ready smile, is full of doubt when she's dealt *cyclolysis*. But after some deep thought she amazes herself with her ability to work out a puzzle in a tight spot. Rajiv Tarigopula is widely seen as a contender after his sixteenth-place finish last year, but the twelve-year-old St. Louis boy peers into the gloom when facing *graveolent*. His eyes blink rapidly, as if responding to his mental gymnastics. When he spells, he rushes through the last few letters and inflects them up as a question—his fate is up in the air— and he's astounded that he gets to stay onstage.

Claire Nieman seems to believe that *esurient* is beyond her. When the thirteen-year-old from Seattle hears the definition, "having a huge appetite," she laughs at the sheer oddness of it. There's no way. She thinks, she ponders, she sighs. She simply doesn't know it. Well, here goes nothing . . . and . . . she gets it! The audience cheers in appreciation. Having never heard the word prior to facing it in front of a full ballroom, she managed to conquer it. Forget spelling, this is what we've come for: one small human against one large challenge, and the human wins. It's enough to give you hope for the future.

Among the hypercompetitive group, the small crew who has worked unstintingly for this event (and who knows it will soon be narrowed to them alone), this round is still just a formality. Marshall Winchester spells with his hands behind his back, which for a physical speller like him—known to grab hold of the microphone—is like tightrope walking without a balancing pole. He takes his time with *cancellous*, but only out of professional caution, not doubt. Of all the words that all the contestants have spelled today, Marhsall has known all except one (*sherpa*).

Aliya Deri's mother, Chandan, went up to the family's hotel room after Round Three—she can't bear the tension of watching her daughter onstage. But Aliya herself has found her rhythm, stuffing her hands in her pockets, not bothering to shut her eyes as she sometimes does to help her focus. The San Francisco girl dispenses with *tonitruous* without much pause.

Samir Patel, facing the cream puff *syllogize*—which he could have spelled when he was on this stage two years ago—takes the word apart. The eleven-year-old Texas boy defines the word's two roots, asking for confirmation of the roots' meaning from the judges; yes, he's correct. By the time he's done he has all but given a lecture about the word's etymological history, much less spelled it.

Kerry Close won't reveal that *abeyance* offers not even a suggestion of a challenge. Instead, the twelve-year-old New Jersey girl asks for language of origin, as if an extra clue might be needed. She then shakes her long blonde hair away from her face and puts the word out of its misery before it can so much as whimper.

Apple-cheeked Jack Ausick nails *fretum* like the word is used constantly in his hometown back in Montana. Anurag Kashyap's glasses are beginning to slide down his nose, giving him the air of a distracted professor, an effect that's heightened as the San Diego boy moves easily through *oligopsony*.

Dominic Errazo might be uptight today—his sixteenth-place finish last year places some expectations on him. Instead the South Carolina speller has a wisecrack for every occasion. That might be an act, his way of dealing with anxiety, but if so, he turns in an Oscar-winning portrayal of a fully relaxed thirteen-year-old boy. (And over lunch he shows me how to balance a half-full can of soda at a perfect 45-degree angle—his talents are numerous.) His word is *emetic*, and pronouncer Jacques Bailly gives the definition: "an agent that induces vomiting." For Dominic that's a setup he can't resist. "Sounds like the nervousness before I get up here," he cracks, prompting an audience laugh. Bailly chuckles along, replying, "Let's hope not." Dominic easily handles *emetic*.

Nektarios Vasilottos, too, could admit to feeling queasy, but he's in no mood to joke about it. He's profoundly nervous today. Nektarios has a key advantage as a speller: He speaks Greek fluently. His parents emigrated from Greece, and his family speaks their native language around the house. With so much of English's spelling grounded in Greek, this background helps.

In his first year here in 2003, he surprised himself and his family with his success, placing sixteenth; his mother says that he felt "no stress" that year—with no expectations, why worry? But the following year, after a year of hard study, the lanky Indiana boy was a bundle of jittery butterflies. He ran into the word *wastrel* in an early round and was eliminated. "It was an easy word," his father notes, "but he was nervous." Looking for advice, just prior to this Bee he called the 2004 champion, David Tidmarsh, who also lives in Indiana. David gave Nektarios a simple recommendation: relax. (Then again, David himself practically collapsed onstage from hyperventilating, so he knows his advice is hard to follow.)

Now in his third Bee, and having studied up to four hours per day, Nektarios knows he's well prepared; he's one of only seven spellers who scored a perfect twenty-five on the written test. But his battle with anxiety is epic.

In the third round, Nektarios quickly genuflected before approaching the microphone. He was given a gift, the simple *leprosy*, and he rushed through it, even interrupting the pronouncer to spell, then sprint-walking back to his seat. Now in the fourth round his word is *putrilage*, and he attacks it like the ballroom is on fire. He hurriedly asks the language of origin and then races through the letters, not even stopping to think, misspelling it as *putrelage*—even before the bell rings his whole body jolts at his own mistake. Ouch. The audience groans at his frustration. Had he been at home, relaxed over his computer, he would have gotten it. His walk to the Comfort Room will be a long one.

As hard as Nektarios labored to get here, Elizabeth Pisaniello stands on this stage having hardly studied at all. She's here due to sheer verbal ability. Remarkably, the fourteen-year-old from Watertown, New York, didn't even know about the *Paideia* until *after* she won her regional bee. While the other kids knew what words to memorize, she simply showed up and took the prize by being ready to spell anything. Her winning word was *bourgeoisie*.

Her secret, she notes, is that "I love language." A tall girl with shoulder-length light brown hair, glasses, braces, and a cheery outlook on life, Elizabeth is an insatiable reader. She'll even read while walking. She likes anything with dragons and princesses and kings. She's currently writing her own story about a conflict between two countries, in which the king is captured, then he escapes, yet the two countries are plunged into war.

She's also creating her own language, which she calls Islorien. At this point she's invented about 900 words for it. In Islorien, the word for "hello" is *aspi*, and "spelling" translates to *kummeckluj* (in her language, the *luj* suffix is the equivalent to English's *ing*). The language's use is spreading throughout the Watertown area, or at least in her immediate circle. Her friends, mother, and her three sisters all know some Islorien. "Dad speaks the least of it," she notes.

She loves being at the Bee. The pizza party on Sunday was "so awesome," she says. To combat her stage nerves, she focuses on one hard word, keeping it in the front of her mind to avoid thinking about the pressure. In Round Three she got lucky: Her word was *sclerosis*. Since both her parents are physicians she's steeped in medical terminology.

Now, in Round Four, she encounters one of the fundamental truths of the Bee: At a certain point, intelligence is no longer enough. Too many uncommon words are thrown at you; to stay onstage you need to have studied long and hard. Facing *flammulated*, she omits an *m*. She leaves the stage happily—coming to Washington has been loads of fun for her.

As Round Four ends at 5:00 p.m., and with it this long day of spelling, the kids walk offstage to get hearty congratulations from their families. Heather van Stolk, a thirteen-year-old Memphis girl who's in her second Bee, gets a loving greeting from her mother. Mrs. van Stolk shuts her eyes and puts her arms around her daughter in a deep hug, holding her tightly. Of the 273 spellers who began this day, only fifty-five remain for tomorrow—including Heather. That definitely calls for a big hug.

◎◎◎

The mood Wednesday night in the lobby of the Grand Hyatt is far lighter than during the last two evenings. In contrast to the it's-almost-here anticipation of Monday and Tuesday nights, with competitors anxiously cramming, this evening feels like a party. With most of the spellers eliminated, this event magically turns into a vacation. Groups of tweens troop around the lobby, scrounging up snacks, playing games, and, as always, power socializing—the chat sessions are more numerous. And since only a few dozen kids are still focused on spelling, the socializing is more often punctuated by laughter.

The parents of Laura Brown, the speller from Alabama, are parked on a couch, taking it all in. They're chatty and convivial and profoundly impressed by their daughter's success. Laura is still in the competition, having fielded some toughies like *tergiversation* and *pharisaical*. "In regionals, she went round after round with one other speller for forty-five minutes," her mother says. "I needed an ambulance but she had her game face on."

John Tamplin, the Kentucky boy who's in his fourth year here, talks about how he figured out *jiggety*. "I thought about the French word *gigot*, but then I thought the word sounded too American for that," and so he opted to try the fully down-home spelling of *jiggety*. He, too, is still in the Bee.

George Hornedo, having flamed out while spelling *proprietorial*, practically running offstage after his miss, is back to his sunny, upbeat self. George's world returns to normal with great ease. His misspell was just a slip of the tongue, he explains. If not for that one letter, he would be one of the finalists, he's sure. "It would have come down to Anurag and me and a few others." That's possible, of course, but it's a lot like hearing a fisherman talk about the one that got away.

George isn't the only one who mentions Anurag Kashyap tonight. As I talk to people in the lobby, the San Diego boy's name comes up again as a potential winner—as it did last night. The kid's got some buzz going. His mother, Archana, is in the lobby tonight, and I let her know that her son's being talked about as a winner. Archana is a quiet, sweet woman, dressed in traditional Indian garb, and in response she merely chuckles and says nothing. Unlike some parents, she would never be so bold as to suggest that her son might win. But she's happy to hear it.

Of course, the buzz doesn't mean much. The Bee is famous at upsetting expectations; a highly favored speller drops out early and a dark horse comes out of nowhere to lead the pack. Yet clearly, Anurag, based on official gossip and seat-of-the-pants oddsmakers, has joined the short list that includes Marshall Winchester, Kerry Close, Aliya Deri, and Samir Patel.

So, given that he's considered a top contender, who is Anurag Kashyap?

Although he was born in India and his parents immigrated here in the mid '90s when he was three years old, he bears no trace of an Indian accent. He's a classic first generation immigrant child: fully at home with his parents' culture, yet appearing just as Americanized as every other kid on the baseball diamond. Or, in Anurag's case, the tennis court—that's his only sport, though his mother says he's not very good at it. His father, Chandra, an effusive, warm man with a big smile, is a chemist for a biotech company in San Diego. His mother is a full-time homemaker. Anurag is their only child.

At first glance, Anurag appears to be an absolutely average eighth-grade boy: about average height and weight, about typical style for a well-dressed eighth-grader, minus the piercings and the iPod, but with the glasses and braces. He even seems average—perhaps above average—in his social skills: By all accounts he's pretty popular in his middle school in San Diego, which is easy to believe; around the Hyatt he's often seen talking and laughing with friends.

But he has, inarguably, a very unaverage dedication to his studies. He's a top student in his classes—he calls his homework load "not hard, but excessive"—and he also competes in Mathcounts, the Science Olympiad, and the Geography Bee. He juggles it all yet always saves a big time block for his spelling study. Usually an avid bookworm—he likes Harry Potter—in the weeks before the Bee, "I didn't have any time for any pleasure reading," he says.

An early reader, he also grew interested in spelling early. At age eleven, he memorized the *Paideia* and competed in the San Diego regional; he survived until the later rounds, but when the contest went beyond the *Paideia* he was eliminated, missing *adjuvant*. Undaunted, he studied all the harder for the following year, and he won the 2004 San Diego regional by spelling *Sikhism*.

In Washington that year, he found the competition to be "tougher than I expected," yet he had a pretty good run, tying for forty-seventh—not exceptional for a first-timer but still impressive. "I was disappointed but I wasn't that distraught," he recalls. Most important for his further advancement, in Washington that year he met Jesse Zymet and Erik Zyman Carrasco, organizers of the online study group Speller Nation. "We started the online group the day after 2004 nationals," Anurag says. Jesse supervised the drilling, as spellers used Internet-based phone lines to conduct real-time bees, and Erik tutored spellers on word rules. "Erik's *really* good at etymology," Anurag says. In the months before this year's Bee, he participated in the online bees every day as part of his four hours of daily spelling study.

On this Wednesday night, he's still competing in mock bees with his study group, which now inhabits the lobby of the Hyatt. With the Bee winnowed to its last few dozen spellers, the lobby study group is down to its core denizens and has an earnest, focused air. Late into the evening they work, each hopeful speller getting his or her chance, preparing for a day that for some of them will be the last day of their spelling careers.

^{28} The Heart Pounds

Thursday dawns seriously. Today is the day. By mid-afternoon, one of the spellers will hoist the gleaming trophy that sits on an onstage pedestal, not to mention pocketing nearly $30,000 in prize money. That individual's name and photo will be beamed all over the country, and the interview requests will rush in.

The media army is in full encampment. The ESPN crew is finishing its prep work to televise the event, as technicians move between the ballroom and their sixteen-wheeler audio-video truck parked outside the hotel. Katie Kerwin McCrimmon, the 1979 Bee champion and now an anchor for ESPN's Bee coverage, works with producers and camera people as they run through a video check prior to broadcast.

In the ballroom the forest of video cameras set up near the back of the room has swelled to fill the forty-foot-long riser. Roving cameramen stand ready to get reaction shots from spellers or parents, and a large crane-operated camera swoops toward the stage, able to zoom in if need be. Joining the ESPN crew is a bevy of network television crews and a legion of newspaper reporters from around the country—a media chain sponsors this event. A contingent of photographers gathers in a roped-off area near the stage. No millisecond of today's proceedings will go undocumented.

Samir Patel woke up nervous this morning; he got sick to his stomach and refused breakfast, except for some chocolate milk. His mother, Jyoti, has learned that her son knows his own system, and so she doesn't press her request that he have breakfast. Despite the jitters, he's ready to spell.

Kerry Close's father, Jim, got to the ballroom early to grab the best seat, and now he sets up a little video tripod to record the event. Kerry joins him for a while, sitting next to him with a study guide, *Ultimate Spelling Book*, open on her lap. She doesn't really look at it, but apparently it makes her feel good to have it open. When she goes to chat with some speller friends, mainly listening as they speak, her mother snaps photos of her from afar.

Aliya Deri's father, Bob, sits with her big sister, Joya, though Aliya's mother is notably absent. Chandan still can't bear to watch her daughter compete—the tension's just too great for her. Aliya herself seems comparatively relaxed.

Marshall Winchester, just moments before the Bee starts, comes over to say hello to me. It's impressive that just prior to the biggest day of his life so far—one in which his family has very high hopes for a new trophy—he can chat comfortably. He says he got a good night's sleep, talks about word rules (he notes that missing the *x* beginning of words like *xeno* is a common mistake), and lists the Bee staffers he's spoken with. He mentions that a boy sitting behind him yesterday had red eyes. "I guess he was nervous," Marshall observes casually.

At 9:45 a.m. the spellers gather onstage. Today all the contestants wear the official white Bee T-shirt with the little bee insignia. The T-shirt also carries—this year for the first time—the logo of an educational toy maker that cosponsors the Bee's television broadcast. If there was any doubt that the Bee is a fully modern event, this additional marketing logo dispenses with it. Once, bees were held on snowy New England nights among Puritan children who trooped through the cold to have spelling parties. This morning's Bee, with its two-minute time limit, its blanket media coverage, and its product logo on every T-shirt, is very much a twenty-first-century event.

At two minutes after 10:00 a.m., ESPN begins broadcasting images from the stage. Speller No. 1, Laura Brown from Alabama, a graceful amateur ballerina, steps up to face *daguerreotypes*. Laura's mother sits in the audience wearing a T-shirt that says, in huge letters, "We're rooting for #1, Laura Brown." Laura dispatches *daguerreotypes* as easily as if she were a nineteenth-century photographer.

Foster Levi is dealt *brigantine*. The wholesome-looking Arkansas eighth-grader has battled up through some tough local bees; the Little Rock bee is always competitive and usually goes beyond the *Paideia*. He made it to regionals the last two years but won this year for the first time. During his etymological study he developed a predilection that amazes his mother; she doesn't understand why, but Foster has become fascinated with the Welsh language. He is now determined to study in Wales when he gets older. In the meantime, he easily spells *brigantine*.

Katherine Seymour, a cheery fourteen-year-old from Prince Frederick, Maryland, in a short black skirt, is stumped by *incunabula*. Upon realizing she's going to have to make a guess, she flashes a big smile that says, "Heck, I have *no* idea." She digs for clues, asking for definition and language of origin, and then, slyly, asks for one more: "How do you spell that?" The audience laughs, and Bailly responds: "I wish I could tell you." She makes her best attempt, missing by one letter, and walks offstage with a laugh and a huge grin.

She is soon joined by Harvest Zhang of Rochester, New York, who tries to spell *dioscuric* as *diascuric*, and Matthew Betley, of Lowell, Massachusetts, who attempts *termagancy* as *termigancy*. The word list is beginning to travel toward the nether regions of the English language, as oddities like *jabot* and *naumachia* fly hither and yon.

Meg Mathis's word is the uncommon *thurible*. The fourteen-year-old Mississippi girl, whose long dark hair is parted in the middle and whose attitude is distinctly perky, plans on being a science teacher and loves reading science encyclopedias; she's also a dedicated coin collector. The stage is a natural element for her. "I love cameras," she says. Even as a child, her parents could get her to stop crying by photographing her. As for spelling, her father made her a deal: She can study spelling as much as she wants as long as she keeps her grades up. Since she was her school's valedictorian, her grades are no problem, so she's been poring over word lists several hours per day, always with music on. She usually listens to hip-hop—she likes the R&B star Ja Rule—but she'll switch to rock "when I get bored." Yet all her hours of studying haven't prepared her for *thurible*; apart from memorizing the dictionary, it's hard to be ready for such a word. Attempting it as *thurable*, she hears the gentle bell and exits the stage with no visible emotion.

Facing *salaam*, Ava Lintz is going to have to take a guess. Based on its sound, the originally Arabic word could be spelled *salam*, *salom*, or several other ways. She states the first few letters, *s,a,l,a*; then pauses. She ruminates. Hmmm . . .

A first-timer at the Bee, Ava has been on a good run over the last two days, getting some tough words and handling them with her signature cool. The fourteen-year-old Morgantown, West Virginia, girl appears more worldly than her spelling colleagues. It may be because she has four parents (due to divorce; and in fact three of them are here today—getting along splendidly, it appears). It may be because all four parents are professional musicians, gigging around the United States and the world, and that Ava herself has lived several years in Switzerland. Either way, when Ava steps up to spell, with her black plastic glasses and her shoulder-length brown hair, she presents a dash more poise and urbanity than those before and after her.

Adding to her sense of confidence, she has worked constantly on her spelling studies, coached by her mother, Jenny. She learned the dictionary's diacritical marks and spent myriad hours listening to audio spelling guides. "Dr. Bailly has been at our house for months," says her mother, referring to the audio study guide narrated by Bailly that Scripps distributes. Moreover, her mother notes that Ava keeps a dictionary in the bathroom for extra study, and in her spare time she's an avid Scrabble and Boggle player.

Now, pondering *salaam*, it's time for her to make a decision. Paused in mid-word, she again asks for the pronunciation and, digging deeper, asks for any alternate pronunciations; perhaps that will confirm her suspicion that a double *a* lurks in there. Bailly voices the alternate version, which elongates the second syllable, after which Ava briskly spells *salaam* correctly. She looks to be headed for the final rounds.

The top spellers are still cruising along, not yet having been dealt anything that prompts hemming and hawing. Marshall Winchester belies not a hint of doubt as he assuredly taps each letter of *fulgurant* in his musical North Carolina drawl, returning to his seat with a joyous grin that shows off his orthodontia. Samir Patel asks for origin and definition, then spells the devilish *objicient* in a confident cadence without a moment's pause.

Kerry Close asks all the basic questions and then moves through *irrefragable* easily, her voice projecting authoritatively in the ballroom. Aliya Deri gets the odd *pasqueflower* yet shuts her eyes and spells it surely. Anurag Kashyap, after some furious scribbling on his placard with his finger, steps definitively through the sesquipedalian *sphygmomanometer*.

Saryn Hooks's mother gasps with amazement as the North Carolina girl steps up, asks a single question—"Is it French?"—and spells *jabot* with a crisp coolness. At that, Mrs. Hook almost collapses in her seat, her hand to her chest as if in shock at having glimpsed an apparition, while Saryn steps quickly back to her seat.

The apple-cheeked Jack Ausick is dealt *renascent* and, querying to confirm what he already knows—"Does this come from the Latin root *nasare*, meaning to be born?"—he spells it like the gift it is. The following round the Montana boy faces the odd *jamrosade*, "the fruit of the rose apple," and asks Dr. Bailly for the etymology. "It's a long one," Bailly notes. "It's Sanskrit to Hindi, then possibly Iranian to Greek to Latin to English, then a Latin to English combining form." The audience chortles appreciatively—it's as if Jack is some kind of verbal Harry Houdini, about to try to extricate himself from a dozen locks. Indefatigably, he again uses his knowledge of roots—"Does this contain the Latin root *rosa*, meaning rose?"—and works his way through *jamrosade*, raising his fists in triumph at having escaped from a tough spot.

Dominic Errazo gets a softball, *Chinook*, and, being Dominic, takes the opportunity to crack a joke. After hearing the word, he quotes a line from the tongue-in-cheek indie film *Napoleon Dynamite*: "Do the chickens have large talons?" The quote has no connection to his word, so Dominic is entertaining only himself. The audience chuckles unsurely, more from the strangeness of it than anything else, and Dominic blows out *Chinook* with ease.

As the morning wears on, the little stash of luck that many spellers brought to this Bee begins to run low. Bonny Jain, a sweet eleven-year-old from

Moline, Illinois, whose eyes begin fluttering rapidly when he gets nervous, jerks his head back when the bell rings after he attempts *periegesis*. He'll have a warm welcome offstage; his entire family wears buttons made from Bonny's photo, and his father smiles hugely while videotaping his son's exit. (Bonny, who earned an almost perfect score on the high school-level SAT, tells me later, "I'll be coming back next year.")

Foster Levi, the Arkansas boy who's obsessed with the Welsh language, gets the impenetrable *nuchal* and starts his detective work uncertainly. When he asks for alternate definitions, associate pronouncer Dr. Brian Sietsema informs him, "It can also mean 'situated on the back of the prothorax of an insect immediately behind the head.'" Foster, pondering this esoterica, replies dryly, "That's helpful." The crowd chuckles, but Foster's goose is cooked and he soon exits.

He'll have company in the Comfort Room. Kimberly Olson tries to spell the first syllable of *drepaniform* as *dry*, Andrew Peters adds a second *e* to the end of *moiré*, and Ava Lintz, finally stumbling, spells *sciosophy* as *cyosophy*. The graceful Laura Brown sighs deeply in between syllables while working on *tropholytic*, after which the bell's ding confirms her doubt.

The bell continues to ring, the field narrows, the words edge upward in complexity. As we break for lunch, we're down to twenty-nine spellers.

⚬⚬⚬

Luck. As the Bee nears the final rounds, the role of luck looms ever larger.

Luck plays a role for even the most virtuosic speller. David Tidmarsh, the 2004 champion, was forced to guess on a word. He studied the entire dictionary yet still the moment came when he had to roll the dice; lucky for him, he guessed correctly. Sai Gunturi, the 2003 winner, misspelled a word in his final showdown with Evelyn Blacklock, but Evelyn also missed one, allowing Sai to win. Luck definitely weighed in: If the two spellers had gotten different words, Evelyn might have won.

Chance is not a factor for top spellers through most of the early and middle rounds. The words aren't challenging enough; for a superior speller they require no luck. (Then again, there are always some tough words sprin-

332

kled in the early rounds, so there are no guarantees.) But as we move into the final afternoon, the words will grow monstrously difficult. There are only a handful of people on the planet—of any age—who could spell these words, and about six of them are in this ballroom today.

One factor enables top competitors to handle even these ultra-hard words: the Consolidated Word List, or CWL as it's known to spellers. If a polysyllabic nightmare is listed on the CWL, it can be memorized ahead of time. Some 23,000 words long, the CWL is composed of words from past bees, among other sources, and is compiled by the Scripps organization. Any speller can download the CWL for free from the SpellingBee.com site.

According to Bee officials, 87 percent of the words used in the National Bee come from the CWL. In the same way that memorizing the 3,800-word *Paideia* gives a speller a good chance of winning regional, memorizing the entire 23,000-word CWL improves a speller's chances of winning the National Bee.

That is, if they're lucky. Because 87 percent is not 100 percent, so each speller is going to face a handful of off-list words. It's these non-CWL words that make a speller's etymology training necessary; armed with expertise in the lingual patterns of Greek, Latin, French, and other tongues, they can recognize word roots and decipher unknown spellings (or at least make an educated guess). But if the word is from the dark side, an odd confection with a Dutch double *jj* and a rare French ending—or worse, a proper name—etymology training isn't enough. Those words are impossible.

It's necessary for Bee organizers to sprinkle these impossible words in the list; otherwise, the Bee would never end. In this year's contest, perhaps six to ten kids of the remaining twenty-nine have the entire CWL memorized. If the Bee stayed within this list, we would be here for a week. Each of these top spellers could step up and rattle off any of the CWL's 23,000 words any time of the day or night. They have drilled and drilled for this moment, and for them a CWL word, no matter how hairy it seems to a civilian, offers no challenge.

So this afternoon, when each of the hypercompetitive spellers walks to the microphone, they know they're playing word roulette. Will they get an old friend they know from the CWL, or will they face a non-CWL word? It's a matter of luck.

And, if they do get a non-CWL word, will it be one that can be sounded out and deciphered, or will it be an impenetrable mass of vowels and consonants that no one alive can spell? Again, that's a matter of luck.

☉☉☉

On the way back from lunch, I'm talking with a bunch of ESPN cameramen. One of them, whom I'll call Joe, suggests a gentlemanly wager. "We could each throw in $10 and pick a kid, and the winner takes the pot. And if none of our picks wins, then the money stays in."

I tell him I'm in, but, I note, since I've been following these kids so long, I have the inside track. "Hell," he says, "I've been watching these kids for ten years." I concede that Joe has a point—he's been videotaping this event since ESPN began coverage in 1994, so he certainly knows how to recognize a winner. Okay, I say, so who are you putting your ten spot on?

"I'm betting on that little blonde girl."

"You mean Kerry Close?"

"Yeah."

The actual betting pool never happens (or, if it does, I'm not in on it). But I have to admit he has a point—Kerry has been looking unflappable. It's a pretty good bet.

Kerry, however, runs into a wall. Her word is *vorago*. But it doesn't sound like *vorago*; it sounds like *varago*, or perhaps *virago*, or possibly *verago*, or, maybe, *vurago*. Its second letter is not revealed by its pronunciation. Formed from a Latin root, the word means an engulfing chasm; an abyss. And that's what Kerry looks into as she considers the word. She doesn't know it, and she's going to have to guess.

Her hands are jammed in her pockets; for luck, in her balled-up hand she holds a small angel medallion. Given that she's unsure of the word, she doesn't take much time—Kerry's not one to monopolize the spotlight. She asks for alternate pronunciations (there are none) and language of origin, and, without much hemming and hawing, prepares to spell. She thinks for just a moment, pronounces the word, and begins to issue the letters: "V—"

"Wait," says head judge Mary Brooks. "Would you say it one more time

334

for the judges directly toward the microphone, please." Somehow, in the infinitesimally small difference between Kerry's pronunciation and Bailly's pronunciation, Brooks sensed Kerry was about to misspell based on a mispronunciation. (And indeed Kerry was about to misspell it as *varago*.) Kerry pronounces it again, after which Brooks directs Bailly to pronounce it again for guidance.

Bailly's pronunciation, of course, does nothing to clarify the mystery of *vorago*'s second letter; even correctly pronounced, the word sounds like it could be spelled with any of five letters. Such is the nature of the English language. But Kerry now knows she has to dig deeper. But where?

She again asks for the definition, then falls into silence; as she ponders, nothing is heard except the snapping of cameras. She confirms all the clues she already knows. She asks Bailly if the word is pronounced *VIRago*, emphasizing the *i* as she asks the question, but he can't help her out. He merely repeats the correct pronunciation, in all its mystery. As she ponders, with her eyes looking upward, the time clock beeps—her two minutes are up. "Can I have my bonus time, please?" She's down to her last thirty seconds.

She's staying cool, which is itself amazing. She has worked for this moment for hours per day, over years, and now, with the clock rapidly ticking, on live television, with a squad of photographers focusing on her, not to mention a row of judges, a full ballroom, her parents, and her grandmother, she has about twenty seconds to choose which letter it might be. And she's handling all this pressure at age twelve.

She takes a breath and spells quickly, voicing all the letters in one continuous rush: *v,o,r,a,g,o.*

She's right! The crowd erupts in applause, and Kerry raises her clenched fists in triumph as she walks back to her seat. Seatmates on either side of her give her a high five. Her smile radiates relief. After that one, the entire ballroom needs to catch its breath.

⊙⊙⊙

Now in mid early afternoon, the words travel ever further from the planet Earth, prompting the misspell bell to ring with unfortunate frequency. James Clark from Atlanta tries *keratinophilic* as *coratinophilic*, and Joe Shepard, from neighboring Augusta, attempts *tombolo* as *tambalo*; Joe has worked tirelessly for this, and there's something brave in how he manages to keep the dismay on his face to a minimum as the bell ends his four-year spelling career. Yiping Wang from Charleston, West Virginia, takes a run at *canzonettas*, but it comes out as *cansinettas*. Jonathan Horton, from Scottsdale, Arizona, guesses that *fustian* is spelled *fustion*, earning a trip to the Comfort Room for his efforts.

In contrast, Aliya Deri looks stronger with every passing round. Facing *devastavit*, the San Francisco girl confirms its Latin roots and moves through it confidently, alternately closing and opening her eyes on every syllable, walking back to her seat with a big smile of relief. When the roving cameraman walks over to get an in-her-face close-up, she merely turns away coolly. Also looking like a contender is Rajiv Tarigopula, from St. Louis, in his third year here, having tied for sixteenth last year. He steps through the peculiar *inion*—"the most prominent point in the occipital bone"—like he uses it every day; it might help that both his parents are physicians.

When Samir Patel gets *hooroosh*, he immediately asks, "Does it mean a great confusion?" which it does. He is an eleven-year-old whose vocabulary extends to the edges of the known world. Samir thinks for several seconds—is he stumped?—then sprints flawlessly through the letters in one continuous effusion. Impressive. His morning upset stomach looks like it's long gone.

Hannah Rae Smith appears unsure of *coelostat*, but, as she always does, the fresh-faced Minnesota girl seems to plant her feet for a do-or-die effort; somehow, she always pulls in the audience with her. After some thought, she issues each letter deliberately, cadencing on the last consonant with a modest smile—and she gets it. The crowd, leaning forward, cheers as she skips back to her seat with an oversize grin. Elicia Chamberlin, a New Hampshire girl who this fall will attend high school in France (she has studied the language for nine years), gets the French word *badigeon*. That's like asking a Frenchman to find a baguette in Paris. Grasping her number placard to her chest like a security blanket, she spells *badigeon* easily, if hesitantly.

The words, as they do every year at this time, are taking yet another steep turn up the mountain, forcing some good spellers to bid adieu. Arjun Modi is not familiar with Jean Le Rond d'Alembert, the eminent eighteenth-century

French philosopher-mathematician who helped define the laws of motion (and who, as an infant, was found on the steps of the St. Jean le Rond church). When Arjun attempts to spell *Alembert*, he misses the silent *t*, which means the laws of motion propel him to the Comfort Room.

The talented Jack Ausick draws the same challenge, a proper name—there's nothing worse for a speller. In Jack's case, it's *Meissen*, a city in eastern Germany after which a delicate style of porcelain is named. Jack has extricated himself from some tough spots, but he can't get out of *Meissen*. He ponders, looks up toward the ballroom ceiling, and then blinks in minor agony as the bell rings.

Anurag Kashyap gets *pompier*, a word of French origin. He doesn't know it, but, having studied four hours a day to get here, he's not giving up without a struggle. Glasses sliding down his nose, he goes to work. "Does it relate to the Italian *pompeii*, meaning fire?" Associate pronouncer Dr. Brian Sietsema, checking his etymology notes, says that this reference isn't listed, but he informs Anurag that the word did pass through Italy in its lingual journey, and that one of its definitions relates to firefighting. Equipped with this clue, Anurag makes an educated guess, drawing on his knowledge of Italian etymology and French lingual patterns. He inflects the last letter upward as a question: *P,o,m,p,i,e,r?*

He's right! The San Diego boy goes bounding back to his seat in delight, his orthodontia flashing.

Marshall Winchester can hardly believe his good fortune when he gets *rathskeller*—sometimes a real softie sneaks into the later rounds, and this is it. His eyes widen upon hearing it, and he begins to breathe heavily, as if a $500 bill just floated down from the sky. The sheer serendipity is almost too delicious. "Language of origin?" he asks, struggling to contain himself as he realizes he's getting a freebie round. After confirming that this is the Germanic word he knows so well, the North Carolina boy exclaims, "YES!" It is indeed blessed to receive, and for all the gifts we are given we must be thankful. Spelling without hesitation, he respirates deeply as he sings out the letters, each consonant and vowel building in intensity, climbing the melodic scale to a natural dramatic climax. Should spelling be this joyous? The crowd applauds and Marshall raises his fists in triumph on the way back to his seat.

John Minnich's fortune is just the opposite. He gets the hopelessly opaque *ulpan*, defined as "an Israeli study center for newcomers . . . " Upon hearing the word, his face blanks and he utters a complaint: "What?!" The audience chuckles affectionately at his predicament. There's no way to psych out this word, so John, after coming surprisingly close with *uhlpan*, begins the long walk.

Joining him in the Comfort Room is the last remaining Canadian speller, the resolutely upbeat Finola Hackett, who spells *nisse* as *nyssa* and gets a hearty cheer as she leaves the stage—North American unity is very much alive. Also headed that way is John Tamplin, the Kentucky four-timer who earned everyone's respect by navigating *flamborough*, and who is sunk by *levirate*, which he spells as *leverate*.

Hannah Rae Smith, the Minnesota fourteen-year-old who has charmed the audience with her pluck, is dealt *cancrizans*. She listens to the word's definition; it means "moving backwards; especially, of a musical canon, repeating the theme backwards," and it offers no toehold. After pondering it, she laughs, shakes her head, and says, "Whatever." She tries it as *cancrazanz* and earns a big cheer for her efforts.

The stage is draining. Ding, ding, ding goes the bell. The field, inexorably, narrows.

୦୭୦

We've reached a major line of demarcation. With just ten spellers left, the parents of those ten are called up onstage. The mothers and fathers walk up on stage hesitantly, many with camcorders in hand. Some stop to give their kids a hug before sitting, with great careful hopefulness, over on the stage's left side.

The words are now torturous. Aliya Deri gets *orfevrerie*, a conflagration of French and English history that resembles the Battle of Hastings, yet she greets it with an unabashed smile. Her French classes allow her to slay the word with comparative ease. She's looking like she could take the trophy.

The father of Theodore Yuan, twelve, from Chicago, shuts his eyes and moves his lips silently, as if in quiet prayer, when his son faces *retiary*. But Mr. Yuan's hopes are disappointed. Theodore spells it as *rheciary*. Next year, though, the Chicago boy could be a top contender.

So could Saryn Hooks, who, perhaps because she lives in North Carolina rather than Louisiana, spells *etouffee* as *etufe*. With one more year of eligibility, Saryn could well meet Theodore at this same point one year from today. But Alexis Ducote, a fourteen-year-old Louisiana boy who's been a cool competitor, is too old to come back. He retires from competitive orthography the moment he spells *Pepysian* as *Piepsian*.

Rajiv Tarigopula handles *zouave* suavely; Elicia Chamberlin tackles *paraselene*; Samir Patel has no problem with *cholecyst*, voicing a triumphant "Yes!" upon hearing it—he knows it backwards, it seems; Marshall Winchester spells *schnecke* as if it's his middle name; and Anurag Kashyap, after confirming the word's Greek roots and finger-scribbling on his placard, masters *tristachyous*.

Kerry Close gets *Laetrile*. The way she inflects the word as a question reveals that she's in the dark. The word is a proper name referring to a discredited cancer medication, and its spelling is an idiosyncratic combination of Latin and international scientific vocabulary. It can't be figured out with standard word roots. In fact, it can't be figured out at all; with a proper name, you either know it or you don't. Any guess is just a roll of the dice. Kerry asks the pronouncer all possible questions, but none of the answers provide real hints. Finally, she guesses *laotryl*.

Hearing the misspell bell, she tilts her head back with the disappointment of it, as the crowd's applause acknowledges the end of her fourth year here. In a moment of great graciousness, she thanks the pronouncer before walking to get a big hug from her parents. With one more year of eligibility, it's probable she'll be back with her parents onstage next year.

◎◉◎

Round Eleven begins with six spellers. The end is near.

Anurag Kashyap gets *schefflera*, a tropical plant often cultivated as a houseplant. "There's one right there," says pronouncer Bailly, pointing to a leafy plant right offstage. Anurag chuckles agreeably, then spells the word without doubt.

The word *domra* refers to a Russian musical instrument like a lute, and it's a complete stranger to Aliya Deri. She's going to have to walk the plank. Her father Bob and sister Joya look on from their seats on the stage's edge; her mother Chandan can't bear the tension and so waits in the family's hotel room. Aliya ponders the word, looks skyward, ruminates, and asks again for the definition. It offers no clues. She hasn't worked a lot with Russian, so her guess will be sheer intuition. She decides to spell the word exactly as it sounds to her. Her mind made up, she proceeds without delay, issuing the letters squarely and firmly. She's right! She clenches her fist and gives a big "Yes!" as her sister beams happily.

Rajiv Tarigopula dispatches *plumassier* as if he strolls daily down the boulevards of Paris, then walks back nonchalantly to his seat, stopping only to accept a high five from Aliya.

Upon hearing that her word is *rupicaprine*, Elicia Chamberlin turns it in to a question: *rupicaprine?* Her voice seems to say, Why? Why is this word in our world? The beginning and ending are straightforward, but the vowel in the second syllable is a schwa; there's no way to know the spelling by hearing it. The New Hampshire girl guesses that the *i* is an *a*, sending her to her mother's arms.

Marshall Winchester's mother, Grindl, aims her camcorder at her son, and his father, Eric, looks on with concern as Marshall gets *serang*. Marshall doesn't know this one. Some detective work is called for. The puzzle is that second letter; it sounds like *a*, but it could be any one of a few possibilities: perhaps *o*, maybe *e*, could be a *u*. Essentially, he's faced with a one in four chance. Marshall sighs deeply, pursing his lips in thought. This is going to be tough. He knows he's gambling. He begins: *s* . . . then pauses. Geez. One in four—what's it going to be? He lets fly: *s,a,r,a,n,g.*

The audience lets out a deep "oh" when the bell dings, knowing how close Marshall had come to taking the trophy. His mother gives him a big smile and his father gives his shoulder a warm rub, though Marshall appears deeply disconsolate. His shoulders heave as he talks with his mother, as if to say, darn! darn! darn! It's a hard moment—in his last year he had his heart set on winning. He'll need a while to think this one through.

Samir Patel ends the round by spelling *giusto* with an easy panache. He correctly identifies it as Italian, allowing him to jog through the letters surely.

For him, spelling *giusto* is so routine that it warrants no gesture of triumph as he walks back to his seat.

☉☉☉

As we begin Round Twelve with four spellers remaining, a recent trend in the Bee becomes evident: All the remaining finalists, Anurag Kashyap, Aliya Deri, Rajiv Tarigopula, and Samir Patel, are Indian-American. (Actually, Aliya's mother is from Bangladesh, which was once part of India and still shares a common culture, and her father is of German-Hungarian heritage.)

Of the six National Bees prior to this one, four were won by Indian Americans. At the conclusion of today's Bee, given the remaining spellers, that winning streak will be extended to five of seven champions. Of this year's 273 spellers, more than thirty are of Indian descent, though Indians compose less than 1 percent of the US population. The trend is inarguable: Indian Americans are dominating the Bee.

The reason why this is so could be debated by sociologists ad infinitum, but certain factors do appear clear.

First, in classic American fashion, the recent immigrant is often the hardest striver. And the parents of the four remaining spellers are definitely recent immigrants: Of the eight parents, seven were born in India.

In American history the word "immigrant" conjures images of a family who sails in steerage, carrying all their worldly belongings on their backs. But that's far from the case for many Indian immigrants. Rajiv Tarigopula's parents are both physicians. Samir Patel's father is an engineer, and his mother attended good schools in London. Aliya Deri's mother traveled to the United States to earn her master's degree in physics. When Anurag Kashyap's father applied to a doctoral chemistry program in India, he was one of 7 out of 2,000 applicants who were accepted. India is a country of more than one billion people, many of whom are desperately poor and illiterate, but the elite of the elite, the strivers who make it to America, often do so because of great intelligence and a determined work ethic.

And great education, too. I asked a few of the Indian parents at the Bee their opinion about why Indian-American children so dominate the contest, and their answers were all the same, independent of each other: the reverence for education in the Indian culture. "I am only here because of my education," says Sudhir Patel. Explains Chandra Tarigopula, in his soft Indian accent: "The Indian culture places great importance on education." (And, anecdotally, the Indian culture in America places less emphasis on sports, which devours so much of the time of so many American kids.)

And take another look at the list of professions of the parents who are still onstage: physician, engineer, chemist, physicist. Many of the Indians who immigrate to America come for professions that require long hours of study and that prize disciplined, linear thinking—which is exactly what the Bee is all about. Competitive spelling, like the engineering and medical fields, requires linear analytic skills and hours and hours of study, long past when it's fun. In today's Bee, if you don't have a focused mind and an unwavering work ethic, you're not going to win the trophy. (One of the few non-Indian spellers who has won recently, 2004 champion David Tidmarsh, studied the entire dictionary. Based on my informal survey of Indian families at the Bee, that's a step beyond even where they're willing to go.)

Immigrant pride plays a role as well. Indian Americans were deeply inspired by the 1985 Bee win of Balu Natarajan, a thirteen-year-old son of Indian immigrants. Imagine, a young Indian competitor winning this quintessentially American contest. For a group of arrivistes hoping to make a place for themselves in a new country, the Bee offered an ideal arena. Plenty of Indian-American families began to devote time to competitive spelling. By the early '90s, the North South Foundation, an Indian-American organization, began hosting nationwide bees that gave Indian children invaluable competitive experience. Samir Patel won the North South's national bee; 2003 Bee champion Sai Gunturi also competed in North South. In the Indian-American culture, top spellers are not weirdos; they're heroes. News of Indian spelling victories travels far and fast in the Indian culture, both in the United States and in India itself.

Trends at the Bee, of course, come and go. Over its seventy-nine years the contest has seen plenty of changes. Whether the Indian strength at the Bee will continue, or be usurped by some other group still hungrier for acclaim, remains unknown. But this afternoon, Indian newspapers are getting ready to print some very proud headlines.

☉☉☉

With Round Twelve, which begins at 3:30 in the afternoon, the tension ratchets up to the pins and needles level. The ballroom audience has swelled to capacity, cameramen and photographers are everywhere, and the audience is leaning forward. The television audience sits watching in living rooms across America. The Associated Press reporter in the front row types away on her laptop, sending updates as the contest progresses.

Anurag steps up to face *ornithorhynchous*. He's calm, which is in contrast to his long journey to this moment. Since his first unsuccessful bid to win his regional in 2003, he has grown ever more nervous with each successive contest. But now, he's feeling relaxed and, by his own description, "patient." *Ornithorhynchous* is a long word, but it can be taken apart root by root. Anurag uses his etymological expertise, querying the judge. "Does it come from the Greek *orthnitho*, meaning bird?" Yes. "Does it come from the Greek *rhynchos*, meaning beak?" Yes. He spells it confidently, then skips happily back to his seat.

Aliya lets loose with a wide smile when she hears her word is *gallipot*. It's so nice to meet an old friend when the going gets tough, and *gallipot* is a swell old chum. She shuts her eyes and spells easily.

The lengthy *mucedinaceous* is Rajiv's word. He has to work to confirm the pronunciation—he listens to the judge again to figure out whether it's a *d* or a *t* in the middle—yet he retains his cool. He's a handsome boy, always a bit better dressed than his competitors; today his khakis even seem pressed and tailored. With his hands stored nonchalantly in his pockets, and his voice steady, the twelve-year-old seems well into his teenage years. And he's a veteran. In 2003 he tied for forty-eighth place; in 2004 he tied for sixteenth. Without too much pause, he spells correctly.

When Samir hears that his word is the odd *lochetic*, he immediately exclaims, "Yes!" getting a big laugh from the audience. He asks only the definition—his mother, Jyoti, won't let him spell without asking at least one question, though in this case he doesn't need it. After he spells he goes bounding back to his seat, there to blow a big kiss over to his mother.

Round Thirteen. Anurag handles *agio* easily, and Aliya dispatches *brunizem* in about twenty seconds flat.

Rajiv struggles to pull out *tontiner*, falling into silence for a moment, only to hustle through the letters in a single burst—correctly. His eyes go upward in amazement at his success and his father and mother beam proud smiles. Rajiv shakes his head as he sits back down: *I really must stop tightrope walking over such high places.*

Samir gets *entrecote* and exclaims: "Yes—again, again, *yes*! Definition, please?" The ballroom chortles merrily. After Samir confirms the word's French roots, he quips, dryly, in mock complaint, "Yes, I do get all the French words." The audience keeps on chuckling. At age eleven, the kid is charming the crowd as much as any veteran stand-up comic. His father, Sudhir, looks on bemusedly as Samir sails through the spelling.

Round Fourteen starts with a big gasp from Anurag, as he learns his word is *agnolotti*. It's a gift, a CWL word, and he smiles over at his spelling buddies in the audience—this one's going to be a cinch, and it is. He grins largely as he sits back down.

Aliya tries to keep her smile undercover as she's issued *nopalry*. But she knows the uncommon word too well to keep her joy incognito. Her letters ring out clear and confident, and then she says, "Thank you, Mom," after spelling.

When Rajiv gets *odylic*, he repeats the word as a question, as in—gulp— *odylic?* He continues to voice uncertainty as he works through the clues. Clearly, he's going to have to leap and hope. Hands stuffed in his well-tailored khakis, he remains calm until he takes the plunge, letting his last few letters fly out in a flurry. He makes the best possible guess, spelling it as *odyllic*. After all, the similar-sounding *idyllic* has two *l*'s, so it's likely that *odylic* does too.

At the misspell bell the audience gives a long groan, yet Rajiv is his usual assured self. He listens to the judge's correct spelling, then smiles and walks casually over to sit with his parents. He's a cool customer.

Samir steps up to face *akaryote*. He knows the word in his sleep; it's a CWL word. He gives a clenched fist gesture of happiness, then quickly gets to work. A small detail of Samir's spelling method reveals what a professional he has become. When he asks for the definition, instead of asking, as most spellers do, "Can I have the definition, please?" he asks, "Definition, please?" He makes all his queries this way. With a two-minute time limit, the precious seconds he saves could become highly valuable. Samir spells *akaryote* deliberately, then takes his seat and gives his parents an emphatic thumbs-up signal.

With Round Fifteen, head judge Mary Brooks announces that the Bee will now go to the Championship Words. This is a list of twenty-five words, known for their difficulty. It's the Bee's endgame: If more than one speller is left standing after these twenty-five words, they are declared co-champions. It's rare that more than one speller would survive that long; although there have been three Bees with co-champions, the most recent was 1962.

Typically, when the Bee moves to the Championship Words, there are just two spellers remaining, and they are set for a final duel. But this year three spellers remain—Anurag, Aliya, and Samir—which means we could have a three-way tie. However unlikely, it's a delicious prospect, because the media would feast on the oddness of it, allowing the Bee winners to bask longer in the spotlight.

Anurag walks to the microphone to face *peccavi*. He knows it, and as Jacques Bailly gives the definition, Anurag, rushing in the heat of the moment, interrupts to get the language of origin. He apologizes to Bailly quickly, then just as quickly spells without doubt. But he walks back to his seat with apparent calmness. He is, it seems, determined to stay cool.

Aliya gets *canitist*, which offers her no challenge. It's a CWL word, so she and her father have covered it during their daily breakfast sessions. Those sessions are paying off this afternoon, as she smiles, shuts her eyes, and issues the letters in a confident voice.

Samir is well familiar with *onomasiologic*, but he is now too focused to bother with a gesture of happiness on hearing it. The eleven-year-old quickly confirms the word's Greek origin and checks for alternate pronunciations, then announces the letters at a prudent pace.

Round Sixteen begins with Anurag facing *ceraunograph*. He wants to race through it—it's a CWL word—and he again interrupts Bailly in mid-definition.

He again apologizes, then confirms the word's origins. "Does it come from the Greek *ceraunos*, meaning thunder?" Yes. Glasses sliding down his nose, he spells easily.

Aliya gets *eminentissimo*. She thinks she knows it, then confirms her hunch: "Does it come from the Latin, *eminent*, meaning prominent?" It does. Now it's simply a matter of adding the standard Italian suffix and she's home. After dispatching it, she jumps in the air with the sweet happiness of it. As she sits back down, Anurag gives her a cool high five, and Aliya puts her hands over her mouth at the largeness of this moment. She's doing it—the girl who was so gripped by anxiety at the start of regionals is now flying at cruising altitude at the end of Nationals. Her smile keeps beaming.

Samir gets *onychophagy*. "Does it mean the biting of fingernails?" he asks, getting a big audience laugh as the pronouncer confirms that yes, it does. Samir smiles surely as the audience chuckles along with him—when he's done with the Bee, he's ready for the college circuit as a linguist-humorist. He confirms the word's Greek origin, then spells posthaste.

Round Seventeen begins with an odd moment. Anurag gets *exsiccosis*, which he clearly knows. He repeats the word a couple of times, nervously, as if trying to slow himself down enough to avoid a simple slip of the tongue. As he does so, a minor technical mishap takes place. Behind him, hanging on the stage's rear wall, is a large Scripps logo in white plastic letters. Just as Anurag is grappling with *exsiccosis*, the letter S from the Scripps logo falls from the wall, tumbling down to the stage.

The audience begins to laugh and, as the odd appropriateness of it sinks in, keeps on laughing. Here we are in the final throes of a spelling bee, and *a letter* falls to the floor—and the letter is from the logo of the very company that hosts the Bee. It's as if all the words in the room, even the plastic ones on the back wall, are exhausted from the orthographic huffing and puffing taking place. The ESPN roving cameraman picks up the fallen S and shoots a close-up of it as the audience continues chuckling.

Anurag looks behind him to see what everyone is laughing about. He finds not the slightest humor in it—his goal is to stay focused, and that's what he does. He spells *exsiccosis* easily and steps back to his chair promptly.

Aliya gets *epideictic*, which she's unfamiliar with. Her voice cracks as she repeats it, and she works deliberately through her queries. When she confirms its Greek origin, she knows she has an even chance—Greek words are logical, unless they've been mixed with a mishmash of other languages through the millennia. She begins: *e, p, i, d*, then she stops. She stands on the precipice. The second syllable sounds like *die*, but her knowledge of Greek tells her it should be spelled *dei*. Should she go with the phonetic spelling or her knowledge of Greek roots? After letting the silence hang for several long seconds, she bets on the Greek spelling—and she's right.

She's a bundle of relief as she walks back to her seat, sitting down with a wan smile. That one took something out of her.

Samir needs to ask only one question about *sobornost*: "Is it Russian?" When that's confirmed, he wastes no time, marching through the letters without breaking a sweat. Incredibly, over the course of this Bee he has not been stumped by a single word. His mother gives him a little thumbs-up, then hangs her head to catch her breath.

Round Eighteen—there are now just sixteen words left in the Championship Word list—begins with Anurag getting *hodiernal*. He's moving at double time, speaking at double speed, wanting no delay. On hearing the word he's sure he knows it. He quickly gets the definition and language of origin then deftly moves through the spelling, striding purposefully back to his seat, sitting without much expression. His time at the microphone took exactly seventeen seconds.

Aliya voices her word, *trouvaille*, as a deep question: *trouvaille?* Her father knows it, as does her sister—they exchange knowing glances. Does Aliya? Apparently so. She asks: "It comes from the French verb, *trouver*, meaning 'to find,' right?" Yes. She whispers the word, thoughtfully, pondering, then begins her spelling: *t,r,o,u,v,a,i,l*—yes, so far, so good. But then she pauses. Instead of issuing more letters, she pronounces the word again, which signals that her spelling is over.

Upon hearing the bell, she leans her head back—ugh! The audience issues a deep groan of disappointment, then, as she walks to a huge hug from her father, the crowd stands to give her an ovation. As the applause rains on,

Aliya sits down and smiles happily, laying her head on her sister Joya's shoulder.

With the exit of Aliya, the last girl in this year's contest, an unusual trend continues: A girl has not won the Bee since Nupur Lala in 1999. The 2005 Bee will be won by a boy, which makes it the sixth Bee in a row without a girl winner. That's an anomaly in Bee history; over the years girls have won more than half the time. Since 1925 there have been forty-two girl winners and thirty-nine boy winners. And that tally includes the recent streak of boy winners. If you look at the numbers at the end of 1999, before this streak began, the ratio was forty-two girls to thirty-four boys. (See The Birth of the Modern Bee on page 68 for an additional discussion of gender at the national contest.)

It's unclear why boys have been winning so consistently recently. By one theory, because the Bee has been broadcast on sports channel ESPN since 1994, it has drawn more interest from boys. Yet I've heard a couple of girls at the Bee say they became interested in the competition after seeing it on ESPN. Amber Owens, a star of the 2003 competition, decided to compete after flipping channels and coming across the Bee. So the ESPN theory may be of limited value.

Regardless of who wins, up until this year there were usually a few more girls than boys earning a spot at Nationals. In 2003 there were 126 girls and 125 boys; in 2004 there were 135 girls and 130 boys. This year saw a jump in the number of boys, with 146 male spellers and 127 female spellers. Again, the reason for this is unclear.

Over the course of Bee history, there have been similar winning streaks by one gender or the other. Boys won eight times in a row starting in 1959 (with one of those years being a tie between a boy and a girl), yet overall girls have still won more. Looked at in the context of decades of competition, the current six-year winning streak by boys is simply a statistical blip, which will return to the mean in the coming years. To be sure, as you read this, there are hyperdedicated girls poring over their word lists, working tirelessly to make that true.

◎◎◎

As Samir steps to the microphone after Aliya's misspell, he knows that only one speller stands between him and the trophy that gleams to his left. Two years ago, at age nine, he placed third, so at the very least he has now bettered his best ranking. But he hasn't come to better his ranking; he has come to win.

On paper, it's hard to say which of these two competitors is a better speller, but on balance it appears that Anurag is the underdog. Both Samir and Anurag scored a perfect twenty-five on their written test, so both can claim to be virtuosic spellers. Yet Samir is in his third year at Nationals, while Anurag has been here just twice. In contrast to Samir's third-place finish, Anurag's highest ranking has been forty-seventh; that was in 2004, the year that Samir placed twenty-seventh. Then again, Anurag is two years older, which is like half a generation between an eleven-year-old and a thirteen-year-old. So perhaps it's a toss-up. Whatever the case, luck is likely the biggest factor at this point.

Samir's word is *Roscian*, meaning "of, relating to, or skilled in acting." "Roscian?" Samir asks, making the word a big question. He looks, for the first time in this competition, a bit uneasy. Instead of his usual panache, the uncertainty in his voice reveals that he's going to be gambling. Well, not completely. When Samir finds out that the word comes from Latin, he knows the famed Roman actor that the word is based on. "Was his name Roscious?" Samir asks. The associate pronouncer, Dr. Brian Sietsema, looks through his notes and replies, "I suppose that would be one possible pronunciation of the name."

The problem is that the word is a proper name, so knowledge of roots won't help—either you've memorized it or you haven't. Actually, the problem is still worse. *Roscian* is a proper name that has been turned into an adjective. The English language follows no set rules for what letters are dropped or added in this case. *Roscian*, then, requires a guess within a guess.

As Samir pronounces the word again, his voice quavers, then he stutters as he asks for the alternate pronunciations. He ponders, asking for clarification about the word's central vowel sound; Bailly repeats it again for him. Samir, clearly, is struggling. He takes his best guess, attempting it as *Rossian*. The bell dings, prompting a deep moan from the audience.

Samir remains cool, then goes to sit with his parents. But that's premature—he's not out yet. Anurag still needs to spell correctly; otherwise, Samir is back in.

Samir's walk to his parents is a measure of how much he has grown up in the last two years. When he was eliminated at age nine, he ran to his mother's arms and began to shed big tears. Now, he walks calmly over to his father's lap, and when the cameraman zooms in for a close-up, Samir manages to smile and wave—which at this moment requires serious intestinal fortitude. His lips are smiling, but his eyes aren't. The audience stands to give him a rousing, cheer-filled ovation. But again, this Bee isn't over. It's up to Anurag now.

Mary Brooks makes it clear: "Anurag Kashyap, since you are the only speller at the end of Round Eighteen, you will be given the next word on the pronouncer's list, and if you spell this word correctly, you will be the champion." Anurag accepts this with an apparent level head, waiting patiently.

Jacques Bailly pronounces Anurag's word: *appoggiatura*. The moment Bailly says it, Anurag looks up in recognition—and his spelling buddies in the audience begin to screech. It's an amazing gift for this late in the competition: a straight Italian word, a well-known musical term with no hidden tricks—it could well have been a Round Six word. He starts to scribble with his finger on his placard, but that's more of a nervous tic than spelling effort; he's not looking at his own finger scribble—he doesn't need to with a word this accessible.

This moment for Anurag is all about presence of mind. While the spelling will present no challenge, keeping one's cool at this point is somewhere between difficult and impossible. Yet he remains assured, remarkably so. He asks for the definition and language of origin—it's Latin to Italian—then, quickly gathering himself, he begins issuing the letters. As much as he tries to stay calm, toward the end of the word the letters start to run away from him, to rush out pell-mell. He inflects the last few letters as a question, not because he's unsure but because it's so hard to believe he's this close to something this incredible. At the very end the letters surge out as a powerful and all-consuming question, the vowels and consonants inflected wildly upward, they're on the verge of escaping, taking flight without him, he has to hang on, to keep his grip for just a few more letters: "a,p,p,o,g,g,i,a,T,U,R,A?"

He's right! Anurag Kashyap has won the 2005 Scripps National Spelling Bee! OMIGOD! As the ballroom erupts into screams and cheers, Anurag takes his placard and covers his face, staggering back from the microphone as if struck by a mighty blow. *I've won the Bee!*

He jogs into his father's open arms, crying, tears streaming down his face, his father giving him an all-encompassing bear hug, his face buried in his father's shoulder. He tries to wipe away the tears as a Scripps executive walks over to put the big gold trophy in his hands. Crying freely, Anurag hoists the trophy aloft, and it gleams in the bright lights as the crowd stands and cheers uproariously, snapping photos, yelling and clapping. The applause rolls onward as Anurag walks center stage, attempting to dry his tears. Parents stand on tiptoes with cameras to try to catch a snapshot of the champion's big moment.

Anurag has well earned the trophy he holds. There were many great spellers on this stage, but few spelled with the sureness that he did. By all appearances, in those rare moments when he was stumped, he was using his analytic skills and etymological expertise, not guesswork, to come up with the word. He kept a level head in a high-pressure situation, and he was polite and sportsmanlike throughout, always giving a high five to other kids who spelled correctly.

An ESPN interviewer approaches Anurag and notes that he seemed to cruise through his words. He's gracious in victory. Fighting tears, he says, "Um . . . it was very hard. I went up against 272 great competitors . . ." His words trail off as he's overcome with emotion; he puts his placard up to cover his face. He tries to continue but can't. "I'm speechless."

The ESPN interviewer asks him what's going through his mind right now. "Ah, ecstaticness"—this gets a few random chuckles, because this most literate person has just used a word that doesn't exist; he quickly apologizes, unnecessarily, for his verbal gaffe. "Just pure happiness . . . and, like . . . it's just amazing . . ."

With prompting from the interviewer, he talks about the importance of having a past Bee under his belt going into this year. "It helped me to know what I should study, because knowing the type of words they would ask could help me . . . and guide what I should study to win this thing."

Interviewer: "You can't compete in the Bee anymore. What's next?"

Anurag: "Next is to do well in school, get into a good college, and get a good job that makes me happy."

Reporters shout out questions as the event turns into an impromptu press conference. Anurag, starting to catch his breath, fields queries from a chair in center stage, with the trophy next to him.

Did he think he would win?

"I knew I had the capability, but I didn't think it was a real possibility. But it was, and here I am now."

What role did your mom and dad play?

"They encouraged me to keep going."

What advice would you give to other spellers?

"Keep trying. This competition is a game of perseverance. Also, have fun." He goes on to talk about a subject that touches him deeply, his online study group, the eight or so spellers of Speller Nation who conduct constant real-time bees over the Internet. Tearfully, he says, "I wouldn't be anything without their friendship and camaraderie."

What do you do to relax?

"Talk—just talk. It gets out your fear."

Are you glad it's over?

"Yes and no. I'll miss it so much."

The questions conclude and Anurag is whisked off, soon to be flown to New York for interviews with national TV networks. As he leaves, the ballroom turns into a media feeding frenzy, with reporters from the regional newspapers that sponsored spellers—there are dozens of them here—circulating among the kids for quickie interviews. ("What word did you misspell? Would you please spell that for me?")

Aliya Deri, onstage, is surrounded by a gaggle of reporters with microphones and notepads, and she's happily answering questions, looking very much like a young rock star as she smiles for the camera and holds forth. Her mother, Chandan, has emerged from the family hotel room wearing a festive red top, and Chandan's usual smile has also returned.

Kerry Close, who surely had her eye on the trophy, appears no worse for wear as she walks through the crowd. I say hello and she chats easily. If she's not jubilant at having placed so highly, she's not distraught at not having won. In just a few weeks she'll likely begin studying for next year.

The Winchesters are glum. They had their heart set on the trophy for Marshall, and this was his last year. He did exceptionally well, tying for fifth place, but not getting first place feels like a loss to them. His mother, Grindl, is doing a good job of keeping up a happy face, his father, Eric, less so. Marshall himself, surrounded by reporters, is talking earnestly. He'll have some long sighs in the days ahead.

Samir presents a professional demeanor to reporters in the ballroom, cool and levelheaded, but back in his hotel room he's frustrated and upset. He wanted to win, and in his third year here, having worked unstintingly, he expected to win.

Whatever his frustrations, he'll have another chance next year. Actually two more—he's only eleven years old. The number of years remaining in Samir's eligibility is a small joke in the Patel family. Spellers are eligible up until the eighth grade, but because he skipped a grade, eighth grade will come a year early for him. Samir, who's homeschooled, could get that extra year back if he "flunked" a grade. But the Patels can only chuckle at what the reaction would be if they announced that Samir had been "held back a year" in school due to poor performance. So he has just two more years.

⊙⊙⊙

The following evening, Friday night, is the awards banquet, held in the same Grand Hyatt ballroom that hosted the Bee the day before. Everyone has had a chance to get a night's sleep, and to put their perceived victory-defeat in perspective, so the contest's ups and downs are beginning to turn into a memory. The evening has a warm glow of togetherness; there's no more competition, just a sense that it's an achievement to have made it here. All the spellers and their families are present, dressed formally.

This dinner is surely the most quintessentially American event held across the land tonight. Before we get started, everyone mingles, *e pluribus unum*: the doctors and the plumbers, the Hindus and the Christians, the Midwesterners and the Californians, while the Marine Band Brass Quintet toots out jaunty patriotic tunes. The ballroom doors open, and in marches the US Joint Armed Forces Color Guard, eight tall soldiers in full military regalia, immaculately tailored and polished down to the last button. Two soldiers carry carbines, with the remaining holding flags representing the various branches of the service. They march with august slowness, in formation, to the head of the room. Then we all stand, hands over our hearts, as the Marine Band renders "The Star-Spangled Banner."

As the Color Guard stands at attention with flags and carbines held upright, a Bee staffer reads the Traditional Ecumenical Invocation for the National Spelling Bee. It's a call-and-response invocation, with the staffer reading most of the text and the families voicing the capitalized sections. Its text includes:

"IT WAS GOOD when so many could say 'Aha, I got it right.'

"IT WAS GOOD when, even in tears, all but one had to say, 'Oh well, I gave it my best' . . .

"Most of all IT WAS GOOD to discover some of the deeper meaning of words we long ago learned to spell . . .

"Words to live by like friendship, care, patience, gentleness, faith, generosity, trust, comfort, courage, and especially love . . .

"So we pray together, AMEN."

The invocation finished, the Color Guard lowers their flags and marches stiffly from the room, accompanied by brass music performed by the Marine Band.

On large-screen projectors, we watch video clips of recent media coverage of the Bee, including the national TV interviews of Anurag in the last twenty-four hours. He's with Katie Couric and Matt Lauer on NBC's *The Today Show*; both Couric and Lauer make comic attempts to spell difficult words, with limited success. During Anurag's CNN segment, the interviewer asks him, "Do you ever get tired of seeing that clip of you winning?"

"No," he says.

All of the top finalists sit at a dais up onstage, and each is honored with a short speech, after which they give their own speech. Giving a speech to a full ballroom is a major feat for a twelve- or thirteen-year-old, yet each of the finalists does so with reasonable aplomb. Looking at the row of top spellers, it's remarkable how many of them were part of the online study group: Anurag

Kashyap, Kerry Close, Elicia Chamberlin, and Saryn Hooks. Of the top nine spellers, four of them worked together closely for most of the year. Peer interaction makes a big difference.

In a festive moment, Bee organizers, realizing that today is Aliya Deri's fourteenth birthday, bring out a surprise birthday cake, and the entire ballroom sings happy birthday to her. She smiles hugely as she blows out all her candles.

Bee director Paige Kimble bids the spellers and their families farewell, as she does every year, by pointing out the plight of the bumblebee. According to the experts, she tells us, the creature shouldn't be able to fly; its body is too heavy for its wing structure. Yet, undaunted by naysayers, the humble bee takes flight daily.

And with this reminder of the value of belief in self, the event comes to a close. The seventy-eighth annual National Spelling Bee is entered in the record books.

☙☙☙

On Saturday morning the members of the Bee tribe are starting to leave the hotel en masse. Kerry Close's parents, Paula and Jim, are getting ready to check out, and both are feeling the wear and tear of the week. They and several other parents were up until 2:30 a.m. last night, because many of the spellers, including their daughter, engaged in a marathon talkfest in the lobby, and the parents wanted to keep an eye on them. For the tweens, though, it hadn't been enough: The first thing this morning, Kerry noticed her friends in the lobby and rushed out of the Closes' hotel room to join them.

Now, as her parents prepare to check out, she's in the thick of a busy power chat, with ten to twelve spellers all crammed together in a group. They stand so close that it would be impossible to walk between them, and several conversations percolate at once. As usual, it's like molecular action, as energized cells circulate around one solid nucleolus of intense peer interaction.

It's been like that all week, Paula notes, with Kerry leaving her parents to socialize every available minute with her friends. Kerry will miss her spelling friends dearly, Paula notes. "She'll cry on the way home."

And then Paula herself, for a moment, seems close to tears. "Look at her," she says, noting her daughter, some forty feet away, chatting with friends. "She's having a *great* time." Despite her happy words, in Paula's voice is a small wellspring of emotion—some combination, it seems, of fatigue, sheer maternal love, and perhaps a wee bit of loss. The catch in her voice prompts a small look of concern on her husband Jim's face. But Paula's not sad. Rather, she's feeling, it appears, that complicated mix of parental emotions: a great joy at seeing one's child grow and do well, mixed with the knowledge that this will result in an inevitable leave-taking.

Indeed, Kerry, by the looks of her, *is* having a great time. She's with her friends, talking, laughing, clearly enjoying herself. She'll miss her Bee friends, but she'll stay in touch, and she'll almost certainly be back next year. She's on her way.

Epilogue

The weeks of summer fly by with surprising swiftness. The 2005 Bee, as long anticipated as it was, soon becomes a distant reflection in the rearview mirror. The spellers are off to the swimming pool, to soccer camp, to family vacations. Their long lists of spelling words are, in most cases, blissfully forgotten.

In August, before the Bee fades too far into memory, I check in with the five spellers I've profiled. Now that the shouting is over, what do they make of it all—and where are they headed?

☙❧

The memory of the 2005 Bee will always be a slightly surreal one for Aliya Deri. Her third-place finish brought a surge of media attention. That afternoon it took her about ninety minutes to get out of the ballroom, as reporters and cameramen kept her surrounded; that evening at 10:00 p.m. she did a television interview with a California NBC affiliate. "Once we got home there were a lot of people who wanted to get pictures," she recalls.

"It doesn't really seem to be real anymore," she says. "Because, I don't know, after that kind of thing, having all the media coverage and everything, and then you come back here, it's kind of distant now."

Not that she has any regrets. "It was pretty cool, I'm still a local

357

celebrity," Aliya says. "I still have people recognize me in the library and other places."

While onstage at the Bee, she definitely felt the anxiety of competition. "I mean, I was so terrified in the moments when I really didn't know the word . . . There were a lot of times when I had to guess." (Although, she notes "probably not that many considering the entire list of words I got.") The event brings "a lot of pressure from everybody—it's not the most comfortable setting to do a bee in."

She feels she could have spelled her last word, *trouvaille*, had she been in a more relaxed setting with more time. "I think at the time I was thinking, 'you know, I've come far enough'—it doesn't seem very rational, but I was really *tired* . . . I think pretty much everyone was glad it was over."

She'll soon enter the ninth grade, so her spelling bee days are behind her. As she prepares for her freshman year in high school, Aliya has carved out a big challenge for herself. She's enrolled in as many honors classes as possible and she's also taking an oversize course load. Her school allows a maximum of six courses, unless a student is willing to get to school an hour early, which she is, so she'll be handling seven courses. "I just want to get a 4.0 [grade point average], if possible," she says.

Her study sessions with her father, which played such a critical role in her Bee success, are on hiatus—but only temporarily. Notes her father: "We'll probably end up doing similar things as we get closer to SAT time."

❦❦❦

Marshall Winchester has been spending a lot of time at the pool this summer, and has caught plenty of Frisbees, too. He's also been singing in a local youth choir.

During this year's Bee—his last, since he'll be a ninth-grader—he noticed that his years of hard study had paid off. Before he met *serang*, he sailed through round after round with utter confidence. "I knew all my words," he says. "It was different from the other years . . . I knew them cold."

His fifth-place finish (along with his fourth-place finish in 2004) has earned him a delicious bit of celebrity. The producers of the Hollywood film *Akeelah and the Bee*, due for 2006 release, asked the Winchesters if they could use footage of Marshall at the Bee. So Marshall will soon be trooping down to the multiplex to watch himself on the silver screen.

Yet the Bee, which so consumed him before the competition, is no longer something he spends much time thinking about. "I just think it's basically in the past now. I'm working on other things," he says.

Among those other things are a Latin class he has recently begun. He already knows many Latin roots from his spelling study, yet he sees a purpose to higher fluency. "We saw there's another competition"—the National Latin Competition—"which naturally got me interested," he says. "We researched it and Mom and Dad thought it would be good." A high score in this national contest can lead to scholarship funds, which he has his eye on.

Marshall has found a new passion, on which he focuses all the energy he once directed toward spelling: chess. He spends innumerable hours studying the techniques of the masters. "I got involved with the chess club a month ago, and I've been reading everything I can get my hands on," he says. He had played casually for a long time, "but in the last few months I've had extra time, so I've been hyping up my commitment."

He's planning on participating in a tournament so he can get ranked against other players. "I want to go very high," he says. "With a late start, I don't know where I'll be in a couple years' time. At this point I'm just trying to dedicate all my spare time to it." He notes that some people start in the second or third grade, so he's playing catch-up.

To polish his chess skills, he often plays against his father. "I usually beat him pretty good," Marshall says.

◎◎◎

Kerry Close achieved an unlikely feat at this year's Bee. In her four years of competition, she has now improved her ranking every year. She has placed ninety-first, sixteenth, eighth, and seventh. Moving up in such an orderly trajectory is far from guaranteed. Due to the quirky winds of orthographic fate, spellers' rankings tend to bounce around, both up and down, and many kids end up lower ranked than where they started. Her high finish (and years of experience) sets her up as a top contender in 2006.

The word that finally tripped her up this year, *Laetrile*, is one she had never come across, she says. And in the absence of recognizable root words, guessing was a low-percentage gamble. Yet hearing the misspell bell didn't color her experience too much. "It was a really fun week," she says. "I met a lot of people, I saw old friends again, the competition was good, and I just had a great time."

This summer has been full of sun and water. Kerry goes to the beach nearly every day—easy since she lives four blocks away from the Atlantic. She's also taking a class to learn the software program Flash, which is used in Web design.

Sailing, which she has become so adept at in the last few years, is being put on hold. "I'm taking a summer off from sailing. I'm in the in-between stage where I'm too big for the boat that I have," she says. "The next boat you move up to you need a partner." But athletics will certainly continue; this year she'll once again go out for the basketball and soccer teams.

And she may get involved in her student council. She's considering running for office, though she's still mulling over which office to seek. "Probably vice president or something like that—I haven't decided yet," she says.

Undoubtedly, this year will be a big one in her spelling career. Not only will it be Kerry's fifth time at Nationals, but since she'll be an eighth-grader, it will also be her last.

Her prep work has begun. "I'm trying to learn words off the regular list, to learn more obscure words that have a chance of coming up." She's using the search tool in her dictionary software to plumb the depths of the language, and she's consuming as much of the *Unabridged* as she possibly can. She'll resume studying with the online group that has helped her so much, Speller Nation. The Internet group has worked only a little this summer, she says, but it's not yet in full swing.

Over the next year her effort will be intense, with one goal in mind: the champion's trophy. "I'm studying as hard as I can for my last year—to go for it."

◎◎◎

Of all the kids I talk to about their recent Bee experience, none is as enthusiastic as Jamie Ding. He enjoyed his time in Washington immensely, he

360

says, "because you meet so many other nice people, and you get to learn lots of nice things." In fact, Jamie says, "The Bee week was probably the best week of my life."

But, I remind him, at the time his mother said he was deeply disappointed. The prior year he had placed twenty-seventh, and this year, after working with his English teacher, he was out after the second round, disqualified by a low score on his written test.

"Well, I felt a little disappointment," he concedes, "I felt I might be able to go farther." Yet he found a way to talk himself through it, with his mother's help. After being eliminated, he said to himself: "There's only going to be one winner all the time. So if everybody got really upset, we'd have about 272 really very upset kids in Washington."

Providing the most consolation (if any consolation is needed—after all, he made it to Washington) was the fullness of his academic load. That spring he competed in a plethora of intellectual contests, from the Science Olympiad to the Geography Bee. And the eighth-grader's enrollment in a twelfth-grade math class meant he was immersed in the intricacies of pre-calculus. "Near the end of the year we were doing limits and derivatives, which are pretty tricky," he explains.

He knows he was spread thin, yet he wouldn't have changed that. "I'm glad I did them all because that's an experience that's hard to get," he says. "I think I'd actually rather have done them all, rather than won one of them."

His spelling days over, he now heads into the ninth grade with his usual omnivorous academic appetite. He plans on joining the math club and the quiz bowl team, which tests social studies and geography knowledge, competing against other area schools. He'll also participate again in the Science Olympiad. Looking further ahead, he's considering a career in medicine, but, he notes in a clear understatement, "I really like a lot of other things."

Actually, his spelling career isn't completely over. His younger sister, Jessie, is dreaming of making it to the Bee, and he's been coaching her. "She really likes spelling. She's been studying this summer, every day," he says. They use the audio *Paideia*, and he's telling her what words to study. "I can teach her word roots, because they're helpful. And she's already a very good memorizer."

His advice for novice spellers? If you start in an early grade, he cautions, "prepare yourself for probable disappointment at some time, because there aren't many very young champions"—most are eighth-graders. Also, "never give up studying, unless you realize that, and I'm not sure why, spelling is not what you should be doing." He makes one last recommendation, which he considers key: "Try to enjoy yourself."

❀❀❀

Few spellers have turned spelling into as full a career as Samir Patel. His orthographic skills have caught the eye of television producers far and wide: This summer he's been invited to tape his third spelling-related TV show.

His first show was *Lingo*, for which he flew to Los Angeles in 2003, then in the spring of 2005 he went to London to be a "lifeline" in a televised celebrity spelling match. Now, his parents have been asked to bring him to Australia at the end of September to tape *The Great Australian Celebrity Spelling Bee*. Rounding out his schedule, the Fort Worth Library has invited him to give a motivational speech to students in October. The kid gets around, no doubt about it.

Part of why he gets so many invitations is his charming stage presence. When Samir is at the microphone, the audience often chuckles at his astute observations or unrestrained expressions of enthusiasm. Yet he makes no deliberate attempt to entertain the crowd. "I don't try to be funny," he says. "And actually, the spelling bee puts an enormous amount of stress on me, so all I want to do is spell the word." As for his natural affinity for an audience: "I guess it's just my natural self."

This summer has allowed him a chance to relax, doing things like "playing with my friends, and all sorts of stuff." The "all sorts of stuff" includes attending a summer camp called College for Kids, where he played "crime scene detective," polished his Ping-Pong skills, and took part in mock debates—he particularly enjoys debate. One day he went to work with his father and met some top executives at Motorola. The management "had a blast" meeting Samir, Sudhir says, and awarded him the company's newest cell phone.

He enjoyed the 2005 Bee, but the one thing he didn't like was what he refers to as "the fairness of the words, the difficulty level." Specifically, he feels it was unfair in the final round that he got *Roscian* and Anurag got *appoggiatura*. *Roscian* is "definitely harder than *appoggiatura*," Samir says.

As his mother, Jyoti, notes, "Samir was upset this year, upset because, the first thing in our minds was 'oh no, we're going to have to do it again.' I was looking forward to focusing on other stuff. He did a tremendous job, but still we have to put in another solid year."

She counsels her son to put his experience in perspective. She says to Samir, "Be very grateful, grateful that the word *Roscian* was not asked to you in the fifth round—you would not have gotten second place."

As he heads into the seventh grade, Samir has begun preparing for the 2006 Bee. After competing in Washington, he took the rest of June off and then resumed intense spelling work in July.

With this year's high finish, he'll clearly be seen as a top contender next year, yet his years of competition have taught him that fate is fickle. He points to the example of Erik Zyman Carrasco, the top contender in 2004 who was eliminated in an early round by the surprisingly hard *Gomorrah*.

"Erik, who was probably better than I was last year, probably better than a lot of the spellers who went on to the next round—he was a really good speller—I just think if he would have gotten any other word in that round besides *Gomorrah*, he would have advanced," Samir says. "In the same way, if I would have gotten any word besides *corposant*, I would have advanced. I came in third in 2003, and the next year, obviously I knew more, but I came in twenty-seventh."

His mother sums it up: "Ultimately we can't get away from one thing, an element of luck. You can work very, very, very hard, but toward the end [of the Bee], it's still going to be a matter of luck, who gets the word they know, and who gets one of the balls that are thrown designed to knock somebody out."

Luck at the Bee, she notes, "is something that you can't plan for."

Notes

CHAPTER 2

[1] "Another Cause which hath contributed . . ." Robert McCrum, et al. *The Story of English* (New York: Viking, 1986).

CHAPTER 4

[1] "The spelling went on for forty . . ." *The New York Times,* June 14, 1906.

[2] "Overcome by the strain of almost five hours . . ." *The New York Times,* May 28, 1949.

[3] "to recuperate from severe mental strain." *The New York Times,* June 2, 1908.

[4] "The expression aroused Nellie's wrath . . ." *The New York Times,* October 19, 1877.

[5] "Twenty-one embarrassed men . . ." *The New York Times,* April 6, 1930.

[6] "such modern conveniences . . ." *The New York Times,* March 30, 1930.

[7] "The small children did not come . . ." An unnamed historian, *The Life and Public Career of the Hon. Horace Greely* (Boston: William Mason Cornell, 1872), 34.

[8] "As soon as the stars began to glisten . . ." Dean Dudley, *Pictures of Life in New England and America* (Boston: 1851). Quoted in Allen Walker Read, "The Spelling Bee: A Linguistic Institution of the American Folk," *PMLA* 56, no. 2 (June 1941).

[9] "It occurs once in a fortnight or so . . ." *Western Clearings* (New York: 1845). Quoted in Read.

[10] "You wants to know the rest, my dears? . . ." Bret Harte, *The Spelling Bee at Angels* (1878).

[11] "There was laughing, and talking, and giggling . . ." Edward Eggleston, *The Hoosier Schoolmaster* (1871).

[12] "the 'spelling matches,' which, last winter, became epidemic." *Proceedings,* American Philological Association (July 13, 1875). Quoted in Read.

[13] "the prevailing infatuation..." London *Times*, April 16, 1875. Quoted in Read.

[14] "One man insisted on knowing the authority for putting two *L's* in *labeled* . . ." *The New York Times*, April 4, 1875.

[15] "Finally there remained only one bright boy and one bright girl . . . ." *The New York Times*, April 28, 1875.

[16] "What could cause the present outbreak of spelling matches . . ." *The New York Times*, April 9, 1875.

[17] "there was usually some jollification . . ." H. L. Mencken, *The American Language: An Inquiry into the Development of English in the United States* (New York: Alfred A. Knopf, 1960), 203.

[18] "slaughtered both divisions and stood alone with the medal . . ." Mark Twain, *Mark Twain's Autobiography* (1924), 257. Quoted in Read.

[19] "Some people have an idea . . . " Mark Twain, as recorded by the *St. Louis Republican*, May 23, 1875. Quoted in Read.

[20] "an old-fashioned spelling bee . . ." *The New York Times*, December 11, 1892.

[21] "the beauty of this entertainment . . ." *The New York Times*, January 27, 1910.

[22] "Miss Whitcomb, who gave out the words . . ." *The New York Times*, December 13, 1895.

[23] "thousands of electric lights . . . " *The New York Times*, June 7, 1908.

[24] "But of all the many interesting features . . . " *The New York Times*, June 28, 1908.

[25] "Colored Girl Wins Big Spelling Bee," *The New York Times*, June 30, 1908.

[26] "A little negro girl . . . " Ibid.

[27] "I did not enter the spelling contest . . . " Ibid.

[28] "The Arizona Senator . . . " *The New York Times*, June 6, 1913.

[29] "justify his reputation . . . " *The New York Times*, July 17, 1913.

CHAPTER 5

[1] "Certainly the indoor sport of spelling bees . . ." *The New York Times*, February 12, 1922.

[2] "As the three-hour contest wore on . . . " *The New York Times*, May 26, 1929.

[3] "Accompanied by her mother . . . " Ibid.

[4] "And the climax was when the girls were having a spelling bee . . . " *The New York Times*, July 24, 1930.

[5] "You remember, Daddy . . ." *The New York Times*, May 30, 1934.

[6] "a shy Indiana farm lass with long blond curls . . ." *The New York Times*, June 1, 1938.

[7] "I sort of remember how words look . . ." Ibid.

[8] "a League of Nations conference," *The New York Times*, May 20, 1929.

[9] "in State contests . . . many of the county winners . . ." *The New York Times*, August 20, 1922.

[10] "pale and exhausted" *The New York Times*, January 31, 1938.

[11] "perfectly simple word to spell . . ." *The New York Times*, May 23, 1953. Quote is a reporter's approximation based on Elizabeth's telling of the story.

[12] "most certainly would not change . . ." *The New York Times*, June 25, 1962.

[13] "The loser shook hands . . ." *The New York Times*, June 5, 1964.

[14] "all at once she started . . ." *The New York Times*, June 9, 1967.

[15] "There was no way I thought . . ." *The New York Times*, June 11, 1976.

[16] "I suggest going back to the old rules." *The New York Times*, June 20, 1983.

[17] "I didn't want to . . ." *The New York Times*, June 9, 1983.

[18] "The first rule of scouting . . ." Ibid.

[19] "There's too much Federal Government . . ." *The New York Times*, June 7, 1983.

[20] "that's compliment with 'i' . . ." Ibid.

CHAPTER 6

[1] "Can I buy a vowel?" *The New York Times*, June 7, 1989.

[2] "didn't feel like getting up on the stage at all" *The New York Times*, June 7, 1989.

[3] "I started recognizing a lot more words . . ." Ibid.

[4] "The president always tells the vice president . . ." All quotes from Quayle incident, *The New York Times*, June 17, 1992.

[5] "must not have eschewed normal school activity . . ." *Bee Week Guide*, published by Scripps Howard, 2004.

[6] "After about twenty minutes . . ." *The New York Times*, May 29, 1998.

[7] "I hope you grow up . . ." *The New York Times*, May 30, 1998.

Sources

Reporting for this book began at the 2003 National Bee in Washington, DC, and extended through the 2004 and 2005 Bee seasons. Over that time I talked with dozens and dozens of spellers and their families about their experiences. Additionally, I attended regional bees in Texas, North Carolina, and New Jersey and viewed tapes of bees in Detroit and San Francisco. I visited each of the homes of the five families whose speller I profiled for the 2005 Bee, with the exception of the Deri family (who felt they couldn't spare time from Aliya's study schedule); my profile of the Deris is from interviews of the family prior to and during the 2005 Bee.

Helping to fill out the story were interviews with Bee officials and staff members, including director Paige Kimble, head judge Mary Brooks, word panel manager Carolyn Andrews, and pronouncer Jacques Bailly. I also interviewed John Morse, president and publisher, Merriam-Webster; Jim Lowe, senior editor, Merriam-Webster; John Wells, president of the Simplified Spelling Society; Dennis Baron, professor of linguistics at the University of Illinois at Champaign-Urbana; and Geoffrey Nunberg, a researcher at Stanford University's Center for the Study of Language and Information. Providing important background about the national contest were my interviews with the nine Bee champions listed in the champions' profiles section.

My descriptions of the spelling bees of earlier eras are based on contemporaneous press accounts originally published in the *Associated Press* and *The New York Times*, in editions dating back to the 1870s. Also particularly helpful was Allen Walker Read's "The Spelling Bee: A Linguistic Institution of the American Folk," published in the June 1941 *PMLA*.

Bibliography

Barnhart, Robert K., editor. *The Barnhart Dictionary of Etymology*. New York: The
H. W. Wilson Company, 1988.

Baron, Naomi S. *Alphabet to Email: How Written English Evolved and Where It's Heading*.
London: Routledge, 2000.

Bryson, Bill. *The Mother Tongue: English and How It Got That Way*. New York: William
Morrow and Company, 1990.

———. *Made in America: An Informal History of the English Language in the United
States*. New York: Harper Collins, 1994.

Chantrell, Glynnis. *The Oxford Dictionary of Word Histories: The Life Stories of Over
12,000 Words*. Oxford: Oxford University Press, 2002.

Green, Jonathon. *Chasing the Sun: Dictionary Makers and the Dictionaries They Made*.
New York: Henry Holt and Company, 1996.

Hendrickson, Robert. *The Facts on File Encyclopedia of Word and Phrase Origins*. New
York: Checkmark Books, 2004.

McCrum, Robert, et al. *The Story of English*. New York: Viking, 2002.

McKean, Erin. *Weird and Wonderful Words*. Oxford: Oxford University Press, 2003.

Mencken, H. L. *The American Language: An Inquiry into the Development of English in
the United States*. New York: Alfred A. Knopf, 1960.

———. *Supplement One, The American Language: An Inquiry into the Development of
English in the United States*. New York: Alfred A. Knopf, 1961.

Moore, Bob, and Maxine Moore. *NTC's Dictionary of Latin and Greek Origins: A
Comprehensive Guide to the Classical Origins of English Words*. Chicago: NTC
Publishing Group, 1997.

Nunberg, Geoffrey. *The Way We Talk Now*. Boston: Houghton Mifflin Company, 2001.

Pinker, Steven. *The Language Instinct: How the Mind Creates Language*. New York:
William Morrow and Company, 1994.

Read, Allen Walker. "The Spelling Bee: A Linguistic Institution of the American Folk." *PMLA*, 56, no. 2 (June, 1941).

Schur, Norman W. *British English A to Zed*. New York: Checkmark Books, 2001.

Webster, Noah. *The American Spelling Book; Containing the Rudiments of the English Language for the Use of Schools in the United States*. Bedford, Massachusetts: Applewood Books, 1824.

Winchsters, Simon. *The Professor and the Madman: A Tale of Murder, Insanity, and the Making of the Oxford English Dictionary*. New York: Harper Collins, 1998.

Acknowledgments

My deepest heartfelt thanks go to each of the families who allowed me into their lives to report the story of the Bee: Sudhir and Jyoti Patel; Ning Yan and Yuchuan Ding; Paula and Jim Close; Eric and Grindl Winchester; and Bob and Chandan Deri. And, of course, their talented orthographers: Samir, Jamie, Kerry, Marshall, and Aliya. It was a joy getting to know them all.

This book would hardly have been possible without the help of the staff and officials of the Scripps National Spelling Bee—an interesting and talented bunch if ever there was one. Many, many thanks to Carolyn Andrews, Jacques Bailly, Mary Brooks, Cybelle Weeks, and, especially, Paige Kimble.

Very special thanks to my editor at Rodale, Leigh Haber—the publishing gods created very few editors like her. Also at Rodale, I'm grateful to Nancy Bailey for her deft copyediting, and to Caroline Dube for her always helpful assistance. And a big-time thank-you to my agent, Agnes Birnbaum, for providing oodles of invaluable support.

Much gratitude goes to Ms. Sydney Jones and Mr. John Frain for their always apt feedback in all matters pertaining to my manuscripts. Thank you to Geoff Nunberg, who gave me far more assistance with the history of spelling section than his brief quotes in that section would suggest. My dear father, Bruce Maguire, helped hugely by taping all the National Bees so I could review them when I returned from Washington, DC.

The biggest thanks of all, of course, go to my wife, Corinne, who spells her name with a silent *e*, but whose cheering is always clearly audible.